The Literature of Reconstruction

The Literature of Reconstruction

Authentic Fiction in the New Millennium

Wolfgang Funk

Bloomsbury Academic
An imprint of Bloomsbury Publishing Inc

B L O O M S B U R Y
LONDON • OXFORD • NEW YORK • NEW DELHI • SYDNEY

Bloomsbury Academic
An imprint of Bloomsbury Publishing Inc

50 Bedford Square	1385 Broadway
London	New York
WC1B 3DP	NY 10018
UK	USA

www.bloomsbury.com

BLOOMSBURY and the Diana logo are trademarks of Bloomsbury Publishing Plc

First published 2015
Paperback edition first published 2017

© Wolfgang Funk, 2015

All rights reserved. No part of this publication may be reproduced or transmitted in any form or by any means, electronic or mechanical, including photocopying, recording, or any information storage or retrieval system, without prior permission in writing from the publishers.

No responsibility for loss caused to any individual or organization acting on or refraining from action as a result of the material in this publication can be accepted by Bloomsbury or the author.

Library of Congress Cataloging-in-Publication Data
Funk, Wolfgang.
The literature of reconstruction : authentic fiction in the new millennium / Wolfgang Funk.
pages cm
Summary: "Shows through an analysis of the form and content of significant contemporary British and American novels that the notion of reconstruction figures as a major aesthetic factor in recent works of narrative fiction"-- Provided by publisher.
Includes bibliographical references and index.
ISBN 978-1-5013-0616-7 (hardback)
1. American fiction–21st century–History and criticism. 2. English fiction–21st century--History and criticism. 3. Post-postmodernism (Literature) 4. Literature–Aesthetics. 5. Narration (Rhetoric) I. Title.
PS380.F86 2015
813'.609--dc23
2015004382

ISBN: HB: 978-1-5013-0616-7
PB: 978-1-5013-3072-8
ePub: 978-1-5013-0617-4
ePDF: 978-1-5013-0618-1

Typeset by Fakenham Prepress Solutions, Fakenham, Norfolk NR21 8NN

Contents

Acknowledgements		vi
Abbreviations		viii
1	Postmodernism's Wake: From Deconstruction to Reconstruction	1
2	'To Thine Own Self be True': Eight Theses on Authenticity	13
3	Holding the Mirror up to Fiction: Metareference in Art	67
4	From Innocence to Ignorance: Julian Barnes's *England, England*	107
5	Reconstructing the Author: Dave Eggers's *A Heartbreaking Work of Staggering Genius*	123
6	Reconstructing Literary Influence: Jasper Fforde's Thursday-Next Series	139
7	Reconstructing Narration: Jennifer Egan's *A Visit from the Goon Squad* and Julian Barnes's *The Sense of an Ending*	169
8	*Remainder*	189
Bibliography		193
Index		213

Acknowledgements

The author's name and the category 'monograph' may suggest that this book is the work of a single human being. While this may be true from a purely materialistic and copyright perspective, it is also the case that the lives and opinions of a great number of people have shaped and influenced the final result you now hold in your hand. Without them, book and author would not have become what they are. The first and foremost to thank in this regard is Rainer Emig, my mentor since my earliest days at university. He trusted and believed in me long before I even thought about starting a project such as this. I hope that he reads the following pages as a tribute to his genuine combination of valuable guidance and advice (if needed) and unconditional trust and freedom (if desired).

During the long years it took for this project to develop from a series of fuzzy ideas into the material object of a book, I had the great fortune to meet a number of human beings whose ideas and personalities have significantly shaped this project and its author. My fellow explorer of reconstruction, Irmtraud Huber, has been an inspiration in more ways that she will ever know. I am indebted to Adam Kelly, Antonius Weixler and Tim Baker for valuable and enjoyable discussions of central ideas behind this book. I am proud to thank Katharina Bähne, Julia Boll, Claudia Georgi, Florian Groß, Maria Marczek-Fuchs and Sven Schmalfuss, whose superior knowledge and scholarship and quick wit, but above all loyal friendship, have made the journey exciting and delightful in equal measure. I thank my colleagues in Regensburg and Hannover for providing an atmosphere in which working has always been a great pleasure. I am particularly grateful to Lucia Krämer, whose affability, open ear and dialect have made our office a real home from home for me.

In preparing a manuscript for publication, there are always people who get involved without quite actually meaning to. I am immensely grateful to Ruth Mayer and Werner Wolf for reading earlier drafts of this book and very much hope they can recognize their ideas in the finished product. The same goes for the unnamed reader at Bloomsbury, who – judging from the suggestions proffered – understood the project better than I did myself. Haaris Naqvi has been a superbly supportive commissioning editor, and Mary Al-Sayed has shown extraordinary patience in answering any question I threw at her. Any remaining mistakes or misjudgements in the texts are my own.

Although a project like this takes up a rather substantial portion of one's waking (and occasional sleeping) hours, there is luckily also a big chunk of life where authenticity is lived rather than written about and where any notion of metareference tends to meet with a rather bemused shrug of the shoulders. Without the unconditional love, trust and support of my dear parents, Werner and Marieli Funk, I would be a lesser human being, and their life has been a living proof that authenticity is much more than merely an academic issue. My sister Moni has been my trusted confidante for as long as I can think, and her warmth, honesty and caring protection have put me back on track on more occasions than I care to remember. My two sons, Ferdinand and Florian, are too young – bless them – to remember their dad being mired in metareference, but their arrival has introduced a sparkle, devotion and purposefulness into my life which has so far stubbornly refused to go away.

And finally, the one on whom everything depends. Susie has been my be-all and end-all for so many wonderful years. Her love and affection, companionship and criticism, tolerance and kind-heartedness are certainly more than I deserve, and I know that a book is nowhere nearly adequate to requite this. Nevertheless, this is for you.

Abbreviations

EA	Jasper Fforde, *The Eyre Affair*
EE	Julian Barnes, *England, England*
FS	Jasper Fforde, *First Among Sequels*
HW	Dave Eggers, *A Heartbreaking Work of Staggering Genius*
LGB	Jasper Fforde, *Lost in a Good Book*
MKM	Dave Eggers, *Mistakes we Knew we were Making*
OTM	Jasper Fforde, *One of our Thursdays is Missing*
SE	Julian Barnes, *The Sense of an Ending*
SR	Jasper Fforde, *Something Rotten*
VGS	Jennifer Egan, *A Visit from the Goon Squad*
WLP	Jasper Fforde, *The Well of Lost Plots*
WDL	Jasper Fforde, *The Woman who Died a Lot*

1

Postmodernism's Wake: From Deconstruction to Reconstruction

In part X of his *Marginalia*, Edgar Allan Poe muses on the impossibility of writing truthfully about one's inner self:

> If any ambitious man have a fancy to revolutionize, at one effort, the universal world of human thought, human opinion, and human sentiment, the opportunity is his own – the road to immortal renown lies straight, open, and unencumbered before him. All that he has to do is to write and publish a very little book. Its title should be simple – a few plain words – 'My Heart Laid Bare.' But – this little book must be *true to its title* … But to write it – *there* is the rub. No man dare write it. No man ever will dare write it. No man *could* write it, even if he dared. The paper would shrivel and blaze at every touch of his fiery pen. (Poe 1981: 150; emphases in the original)

This book can be seen as an attempt to challenge Poe's dictum. It investigates how contemporary works of literature renegotiate the relationship between experience and its representation in an attempt to truthfully re-enact experience through representation. I will argue that the notion of authenticity provides the formal and theoretical parameters for this renegotiation. The present relevance of authenticity is thereby not restricted to the field of academic criticism, where it is 'making a comeback, in the guises of memory, ethics, religion, the new sincerity, and the renewed interest in "real things"' (Haselstein, Gross and Snyder-Körber 2010: 19). Authenticity also pervades many aspects of everyday life, as Charles Lindholm's wide-ranging inventory demonstrates:

> The quest for authenticity touches and transforms a vast range of human experience today – we speak of authentic art, authentic music, authentic food, authentic dance, authentic people, authentic roots, authentic meanings, authentic nations, authentic products. A desire for authenticity can lead people to extremes of self-sacrifice and risk; the loss of authenticity can be the source of grief and despair. Authenticity gathers people together in collectives that are felt to be real, essential, and vital, providing participants with meaning, unity, and a surpassing sense of belonging. Authenticity can be sought internally, through transformative ecstatic experiences, or externally, in the consumption of goods that symbolize the really real. If a Rembrandt can be called authentic, so can Coca-Cola. Authenticity

can describe tourist sites, the scent of floor polish, and the president of the United States. (2008: 1)

In this book I will make a case for the aesthetic category of metareference as the most fitting model for re-enacting the effect of authenticity on a formal level. I will argue that the effect of authenticity enacted in and through metareferential literature is the result of processes of reconstruction, which are triggered by the epistemological and ontological paradoxes inherent in metareference. I will therefore introduce the pragmatic and procedural category of 'reconstructive literature' to describe this new development.[1]

There seems to be general agreement nowadays that postmodernism, the cultural and philosophical paradigm which has so significantly shaped and inspired the second half of the twentieth century, has fallen out of fashion. Its decline had been a long time coming. Uneasiness about the efficacy and topicality of the term can be observed at least since the 1990s. In 1995 the subtitle of Hans Bertens's monumental study on *The Idea of the Postmodern: A History* indicates that its theoretical panache may have spent itself. To become history means after all to be put into perspective and to be disconnected from the dynamic immediacy of the here and now. Historical concepts may still prove useful and accurate, but they can no longer be considered the default mode for explaining the world. By the end of the twentieth century, it is safe to say, the patient postmodernism lay etherized upon the table. The turning point of the new millennium and the attacks of 9/11 in particular presented a disruption in the collective imaginary, the ultimate impetus, as it were, to force the postmodern moment to its crisis and relegate it to history once and for all. Roger Rosenblatt's essay 'The Age of Irony Comes to an End', published in the wake of the terrorist attacks, claims that the one positive upshot of the collapse of the Twin Towers is that they will take with them the postmodern mode of scepticism and detached aloofness.

The demise of somebody considered dear or important typically involves two forms of reaction: a, usually positive, review of the achievements and activities of the deceased, followed by an outlook – emotionally ranging from utter hopelessness to cautious self-confidence – on how the future might be tackled without them. In the case of postmodernism, the former duty has been carried out to the fullest. The overriding significance of its predominant ways of thinking need not even be demonstrated in eulogistic acclamations but is confirmed most articulately by the fact that notions such as simulation, *différance*, deconstruction, the death of the author or the end of grand narratives have become indispensable elements of our theoretical vocabulary and imaginary.

The second aspect of this process of grieving for postmodernism, that is, the outlook as to what will come afterwards, presents a much more difficult task. As is often the case with people who had been hanging around for quite a while, acute devastation

---

[1] My use and understanding of the term 'reconstruction' in this context is influenced by Niklas Luhmann's analysis of 'Deconstruction as Second-Order Observing'. Here, Luhmann highlights the structural importance of paradox for a non-dialectical economy of knowledge and describes his approach as 'a reconstruction of deconstruction' (1993: 770).

and inconsolable grief about the departure keep within limits. Nevertheless, there is the palpable sense of a terminological rug having been pulled from under the congregation's feet. Since an end of postmodernism also entails the nullification of many habitually used instruments and conceptual approaches, there is a resounding loss for words to delineate a potential way ahead. This speechlessness and general lack of direction, as well as first painful attempts to overcome it, have characterized and shaped the cultural discourse of the past decade.[2]

Yet, so far there has not emerged a generally recognized terminological successor for 'postmodernism' as a cultural marker. This is not due to a shortage of proposals, however. Among the many who have come forward with suggestions are Gilles Lipovetsky with his idea of the 'hypermodern', Nicholas Bourriaud with his notion of the 'altermodern', Alan Kirby, who first suggested 'pseudo-modernism' before finally opting for the term 'digimodernism', and Timotheus Vermeulen and Robin van den Akker with their concept of 'metamodernism'. If there is anything which unites these concepts, apart from their unwillingness to abandon modernism as their terminological basis, it is a focus on the media-related transformations of recent years and the effects these are having on the representation of the human self. Kirby, for instance, stresses the structural empowerment granted to the recipient in new forms of media communication, as 'the digimodernist text permits the reader or viewer to intervene textually, physically to make text, to add visible content or tangibly shape narrative development' (2009: 1). Bourriaud imagines 'a positive vision of chaos and complexity [and] a positive experience of disorientation' as a result of current developments in the media, a chaos which will eventually form the basis for a new aesthetic approach to make sense of what he calls our 'heterochronic' existence (see 2009: 13). Adam Kelly likewise diagnoses a formal and structural indecisiveness as the salient feature of what he simply labels 'post-postmodernism': 'Whereas postmodernism emphasizes the singular and "readily visible" event, the identifiable moment "when-it-all-changed", for post-postmodernism, in contrast, an event will always have an undecidable and indeed paradoxical status: never certain, wholly visible or consignable to a past that is fully behind us' (2010c: 327–8).

Likewise using the idea of indeterminacy as a theoretical basis, Vermeulen and van den Akker centre their concept of 'metamodernism' on the formal characteristic of *metaxis*, a Platonic term which refers to a perennial state of uncertainty and oscillation generated by epistemological and ontological ambiguity. Unlike postmodern *différance*, which emphasizes the ultimate emptiness of any act of signification, however, this metamodern metaxis opens up new aesthetic spaces where a meaningful correspondence of signifier and signified might again be possible (see 2010). Synthesizing the most significant ideas from these different approaches, I want to establish an aesthetics of reconstruction as the principal literary development in recent years. This new form of literary communication draws on structural and

---

[2] For attempts to gauge the theoretical implications of the end of postmodernism in more detail and from a variety of theoretical perspectives, see among many others Hassan (2003), Stiersdorfer (2003), Kirby (2006), Brooks and Toth (2007), Hutcheon (2007), Burn (2008) and Lethem (2011).

formal paradox in order to create effects of authenticity in the reception of literary texts. My choice of 'reconstruction' as the term to describe this development is founded on two pragmatic propositions. In keeping with the customary protocols of mourning, one is a retrospective observation, while the other looks tentatively ahead. Considering the suppositions described above, it becomes evident that any attempt to bury postmodernism apparently implies the establishment of a new version of '-modernism'. This, however, represents a contradiction. If postmodernism, as its etymology determines, indeed refers to a period after modernism, then the insistence on retaining the determiner '-modern' in all attempts to denominate a successor would indicate a nostalgic retrogression rather than a radically new imaginary; adapting Bruno Latour's famous adage, one might even be tempted to ask if we have actually never really been postmodern at all. Having said that, I am in no doubt that the term 'postmodernism' will prevail to denote the dominant cultural and philosophical discourses of the second half of the twentieth century. What I do doubt, however, is that the break between modernism and postmodernism is quite as significant and comprehensive as is often assumed, most influentially perhaps by Brian McHale, who claims that 'postmodernist fiction differs from modernist fiction just as a poetics dominated by ontological issues differs from one dominated by epistemological issues' (1987: xii).

Perhaps the unquestionable political and, in many cases, personal discontinuity caused by World War II has come to overshadow the conceptual continuities between modernism and postmodernism. In my understanding, modernism refers to a cultural and critical condition which can be deduced from, but certainly not restricted to, several key events round the turn of the twentieth century, such as the full implementation of industrial capitalism, Freud's psychoanalysis, the *Stahlgewitter* of World War I or the onset of structuralism. These (and indeed many others) combined to uncover the essential incongruity of human experience and its representation. This, in turn, instigated a compulsion to analyse, depict and enact, in short to reflect upon, this incongruity in and through art, a process of aesthetic reflection which reiterates rather than overcomes the initial rift it seeks to represent. Nevertheless, this defensive and defective reflectivity comes to figure as the default mode, or at least the inescapable foil, of cultural representation throughout the century. Postmodernism then must not be understood as a reaction to but rather as the consistent and radical continuation of modernism's aesthetic premise of dissociation and a crisis of representation.[3] Paradoxically it might even turn out to be postmodernism's most lasting achievement to have shown that eventually even an endless free play of signifiers will *not* be able to deliver us – as individuals and as a society – from an inherent pining for closure and congruence.

My book pursues a pragmatic approach when it comes to acquiring the one definite signifier which may eventually replace (post)modernism as a marker for a

---

[3] In the field of sociology this continuity between modernist and postmodernist thinking is evidenced in terms like 'second modernity' (Beck and Grande 2010), 'reflexive modernization' (Beck, Giddens and Lash 1994) or 'liquid modernity' (Bauman 2000).

contemporary cultural perspective on the interplay of experience and representation. It concentrates on clearly observable aesthetic phenomena by retracing predominant formal patterns which can be detected in contemporary literature and for which I suggest the term 'reconstruction'.[4] Evidently, the bridge to postmodernism is provided by Derrida's notion of 'deconstruction', a process of reception which privileges the indeterminacy, performativity and aporia inherent in any form of representation, its ultimate and irremediable *différance* from experience and reality. This technique of deconstructive analysis, of inscribing into any representation a fundamental undecidability and its own aporetic insignificance, is an irrevocable cultural and philosophical achievement. In a sense it is impossible to undo this logic of deconstruction and *différance*, as Derridean deconstruction represents a theory to end all theory, in so far as it can – in a potentially endless game of deferral – always insert another layer of apparent constructedness and relationality to protect (the absence of) its essential core.

In a nutshell, the objective of deconstruction – in so far as deconstruction can ever have a clear objective – is to demonstrate and enact the autonomy and solipsism of each of the constituent factors which have a share in the act of cultural and literary communication. Deconstructive analysis eviscerates this communicative process by revealing and parodying its unspoken hierarchical and relational structures. It is literally reduced to the *différances* and apertures between its elements (author, reader, text, context), to the extent even that significance itself can be lost in a 'movement without origin or end' (Miller 1985: 264). Reconstructive texts, on the other hand, attempt to close these very gaps, to rekindle the connections between the constituents of the act of communication by renegotiating the relations and hierarchies between the individual elements. These texts can be said to enact Ihab Hassan's appeal 'to discover new relations between selves and others, margins and centers, fragments and wholes – indeed, new relations between selves and selves, margins and margins, centers and centers' (2003: 6). In this regard, reconstruction can be seen as an attempt to open up new depths in artistic representation in a reaction against the 'kind of flatness or depthlessness, [the] new kind of superficiality in the most literal sense' which Fredric Jameson sees as emblematic of postmodernism (1991: 9). It proposes to erect a new common ground for signification, thereby contesting Baudrillard's verdict that in the postmodern imaginary 'nothing remains for us to base anything on' (1993: 5). While deconstruction is driven mainly by epistemological scepticism and suspicion, reconstruction is founded on an attitude of confidence in the power of sign systems to actually convey experience rather than reflect the workings of the sign systems themselves. Hassan describes this change in attitude as an investment in what he calls an 'aesthetic of trust' (2003: 9), while I propose that the notion of 'authenticity' is the most appropriate theoretic concept to account for this development.

In the following, I will combine a diachronic and synchronic investigation of various discourses of authenticity, understood as an interface between experience and

---

[4] I refrain, on purpose, from using the term 'reconstructivism', since it implies a definite and clearly demarcated movement and would thus only replace one historical and crystallized concept with another. For similar uses of the term 'reconstruction' in cultural criticism, cf. Klepper (1996), Vermeulen and van den Akker (2010) and in particular Huber (2014).

representation, with the analysis of textual metareference, which acts as authenticity's formal correlative. Unduly condensing the argument of this book, I suggest that reconstructive texts use the formal technique of metareference, which can be imagined as tangling and invalidating traditional hierarchies within a given text, to generate ontological and epistemological paradoxes that are irresolvable within the logic of the text itself. These paradoxes challenge and require the reader's response and responsibility to recreate a coherent act of literary communication. As a consequence, both the text and the process of its reception become imbued with a reconstructive effort which I suggest to identify as the authenticity effect of the text.

The first part of this book presents a comprehensive examination of a range of **discourses on authenticity**. Based on the assumption that this concept derives its contemporary appeal from its essential terminological undecidability and ambiguity, I will not offer a retrospective historiography and archaeology of the term, which would then lead to a straightforward and ready-to-use present-day definition. Instead, I will highlight significant developments and mark out key aspects which have shaped the current understanding of the term by proposing eight theses on authenticity. These touch on a wide range of historical, philosophical and epistemological issues but also take in aspects of aesthetics, mediation and communication.

Thesis one starts by presenting evidence for authenticity's fundamental elusiveness concerning any effort to distinctly and clearly define it in positivist terms. This strategic resistance to unambiguity functions as the conceptual basis for all subsequent considerations. I shine a light on the epistemological causes, semiotic roots and aesthetic implications of this fundamental ambiguity. Also in thesis one I present a selection of critical attempts to classify and categorize the term in spite of this opacity.

Thesis two looks back at crucial steps in the development of authenticity as a philosophical and critical concept by claiming four decisive turns in its historical understanding. These turns coincide, very roughly, with the conventional demarcations of Antiquity, the Renaissance, Romanticism, Modernism and Postmodernism. The recurrent theme in all these turns is that whenever authenticity moves into the discursive limelight there is a noticeable sentiment of loss accompanying it. I highlight the implications of each turn by concentrating on one key proponent of the new way of imagining authenticity. Hamlet's uncompromising insistence on 'that within which passes show' signals an understanding of human selfhood and authenticity which is based on radical self-determinacy rather than on positioning oneself in a larger transindividual frame of reference, as classical notions of self-knowledge had demanded. Jean-Jacques Rousseau then promotes this internal centre of self-reference as the only possible reliable benchmark and therefore the only valid arbiter of truthfulness and authenticity. With Modernism the irreducibility of individual selfhood is finally being superseded by industrial mass (re)production and the mass slaughter in the trenches of World War I. As a consequence, the focus of authenticity shifts again. It is not the human self anymore that is described in terms of its authenticity, but the category shifts to evaluate cultural objects. Walter Benjamin's swansong to the aura of artworks in an age of technical reproduction finally lays to rest an understanding of authenticity as rooted in notions of originality, inimitability and genuineness. With postmodernism finally, critics like Charles Guignon try to reinvest the term with new meaning by dissociating it completely from the idea of a unified self and promoting a fragmented experience of selfhood as the true human condition and therefore the standard by which to assess authenticity.

Thesis three elaborates on the tumultuous relationship of authenticity and selfhood. It first investigates this connection on a practical level by examining how authenticity is seen as both the ultimate goal and a major impediment to contemporary configurations of identity. After that I will analyse how the correlation of selfhood and authenticity has pervaded critical concepts and theories throughout the twentieth century, from Foucault's notion of *parrhesia* to Heidegger's 'being-towards-death', and from Adorno's denigration of Heidegger's 'jargon of authenticity' to Levinas's fundamental alterity. It will become evident that the notions of selfhood and authenticity are caught in a paradoxical loop of mutual interdependence, and I will argue that it is precisely this structural circularity which accounts for authenticity's appeal both to describe the postmodern condition *and* to hold the prospect of a potential new paradigm.

In **thesis four** I take a closer look at some of the areas where authenticity converges or collides with key concepts of the postmodern imaginary. First I will examine how Baudrillard's ideas on hyperreality and the simulacrum influence the possibility of authentic representation and if the paradigm of authenticity might even offer a device to penetrate the screen of simulation. Further developing ideas by Baudrillard and Heidegger, I will then turn towards the paradox of death as the only remaining begetter of authentic experience. Based on Jameson's understanding of postmodernism as rooted in the logic of late capitalism, I will finally address the question in how far authenticity itself has been incorporated into consumerist ideologies by being marketed as an indispensable commodity.

Thesis five concentrates on one particular example of how the notion of authenticity can and must be renegotiated in the broader context of a post-postmodern paradigm. I will argue that recent transformations in media and communication pose the most significant contemporary challenge to rethink the individual self and therefore the idea of authenticity. With identity displayed and performed more and more in virtual and digital cyberspace, a revaluation of what it means to possess and to exhibit an individual self becomes inevitable. I claim that current forms of communication provide a framework for reconceptualizing authenticity as an essentially communal and interactional model of self-expression which is based on an aesthetics of participation and mutuality.

While the first five theses provide a diachronic and synchronic overview of crucial debates on the topic, the remaining three present my own contribution towards this contemporary renegotiation of authenticity. In **thesis six** I propose to understand authenticity as an *emergent phenomenon* which can never be fully accounted for by being broken down into its constitutive elements. Instead, it necessarily includes an aspect of paradoxical self-transcendence which can only appear as the result of unplanned and spontaneous rather than focused and teleological creative endeavour.

Thesis seven takes up this idea of authenticity as a self-transcending construction in so far as it describes authenticity in terms of a black box, a process which evades direct observation and resists positive definition. Instead, it can only be analysed obliquely by the effects it has on ideas and concepts that come in touch with it. The key effect of authenticity in this regard is its potential to sublate the antagonism of binary dichotomies. I will argue that by dint of its own ontological and epistemological ambiguity, authenticity invalidates oppositions such as original and fake, essence and construction, reality and fiction, authorship and reception or even ethics and aesthetics.

Thesis eight summarizes the previous reflections specifically in terms of their aesthetic implications. I will argue that the category of metareference offers the most promising analytical approach towards an aesthetics of authenticity because it re-enacts the essential undecidability and paradoxicality at the heart of authenticity on a formal level.

The obvious link between authenticity and metareference is that both are centrally concerned with the dialectic of real experience and its aesthetic representation. Additionally, both imply a transcendence of traditional boundaries of reference and signification. Authenticity lays claim to a direct and immediate link to a realm beyond symbolic representation, while metareference can disrupt clear-cut ascriptions and hierarchies of reference within a work of art. Accordingly, the use of metareference can be seen as authenticity's objective correlative in art. Both are rooted in a deliberate embrace of paradox and ambiguity. Both originate in and thrive on ontological oscillation and epistemological confusion. As a consequence, both entail a challenge to confront this confusion, to reconstruct the paradox as it were. I claim therefore that the transcendental meditations on authenticity and the formal analysis of metareference can be united within the framework of an aesthetics of reconstruction.

Before offering a systematic account of the aesthetic and narratological dimensions of metareference, I will introduce the notion of **realism** in literature as a notional counterpoint to the deliberate confusion of levels of mediation induced by metareference. Yet, the term 'realism' can only be meaningfully used when there is broad consensus as to the nature of the reality which is to be depicted. Just as the notion of the individual self is subjected to a thorough re-examination in the light of recent transformations in communication and identification, reality as well becomes an object of scrutiny. Despite fervent and ingenious efforts to reinvigorate the term 'realism', I think that the capacity of the concept to describe the relationship of experience and representation has exhausted itself. After postmodernism, the notion of reality has become too refracted and differentiated to provide a useful basis for any aesthetic paradigm. In its stead, I argue, authenticity now constitutes a more appropriate theoretical framework for negotiating how to relate experience in and as art.

The investigation of metareference starts by distinguishing it from related concepts such as metafiction and self-reference. Following Werner Wolf's observation of a 'metareferential turn' in contemporary arts and media, I will first examine the conditions in which this development occurs. I use Douglas Hofstadter's model of the tangled hierarchy as a dominant metaphor to describe and explain the aesthetic and epistemological processes involved in metareferential representation. In a further step I will then submit my own typology and classification of metareference in literature. This typology consists of four dimensions – display, location/direction, focus and effect – which establish a coordinate system in which every metareferential element can be positioned and classified according to its formal features and affective impact on the reader. Keeping with Hofstadter's metaphor of the tangled hierarchy, I will then propose a systematic framework for the various forms of entanglement which can occur in a literary text. This framework first examines the literary work as a communicative act and shows how reconstructive devices are used to blur the boundaries between the constituents of this act. In a second step, I will investigate how, through metareference, different levels of fictionality are introduced into literary texts, which again demands reconstructive efforts from the reader. I will finally examine specific literary strategies – metalepsis, irony, ergodic reading and intertextuality – to demonstrate the actual shape and form metareference can assume in a literary text.

The final section of this book uses a sequence of **case studies** to show in what ways and to what effects metareference is actually employed in contemporary English-speaking literature. The analysis of Julian Barnes's *England, England* functions as a transition between the two parts. While the novel does not itself explicitly employ metareference, it can be seen as a profound abstract meditation on the possibility of authentic experience in a world governed by simulation and rampant consumer capitalism. It sets the tone for the subsequent readings by interpreting the discourse on authenticity in terms of a dialectics of form and materiality. Schiller's triadic model of cultural development is used as a philosophical backdrop for this negotiation. The life of Martha Cochrane, the novel's protagonist, is described as a journey which begins with an implicitly formalistic and naively authentic rapport with the world of her childhood. After taking part in the avowedly inauthentic simulation of the novel's eponymous theme park 'England, England', where form and significance are actively superimposed on the materiality of the real, Martha ends up in a state of reflective authenticity which is based on the eventual acceptance of the sheer materiality of human experience.

Starting with Dave Eggers's autobiographical novel *A Heartbreaking Work of Staggering Genius*, I then apply the theoretical framework of metareference to the analysis of individual narrative texts. I show how Eggers employs a great variety of metareferential strategies on different textual levels in order to collapse the conventional configuration of literary communication. This pertains primarily to his authority as an author, which he incessantly undermines by making explicit the narrative devices and ploys used in the aesthetic rendition of the events depicted. Through his use of metareference, Eggers ultimately enacts an amalgamation of the roles of author, reader and text, thereby *performatively* pulling the formal and distancing blanket of representation from the pure materiality of the experience he tries to communicate.[5]

---

[5] I will repeatedly emphasize the performative nature of this aesthetic mode of reconstruction, in order to reflect the fact that the gap between material reality and its formal/aesthetic representation can never *actually* be bridged, and that therefore any such reciprocity can only ever be enacted or performed rather than accomplished. In other words, I claim at no point to be referring directly to

The excessive employment of formal structures of metareference paradoxically stimulates and simulates an overcoming of form and a convergence with pure materiality.

Jasper Fforde's Thursday-Next series, to which I turn in the following chapter, uses metareference in a fundamentally different and ostensibly much more playful way. Beneath the impish and genial surface, however, lurks a profound challenge to conventional certainties about cause and effect. The first part of my analysis is concerned with *The Eyre Affair*, the first book of the series. It demonstrates how Fforde employs intertextual references in order to upend traditional conceptions of originality and influence in literature. I will use Jameson's notion of pastiche as a descriptive tool to illustrate how Fforde entangles the hierarchies between his own novel and its intertext, *Jane Eyre*, to a degree which forces the reader to re-enact this epistemological confusion in the very act of reading itself. In a second step I will show how, as the series progresses, Fforde extends his metareferential scope to include his own earlier work. In an ever more complex and multilayered literary universe, he constantly rewrites and reimagines the series itself, thereby depriving the reader of any dependable basis from which to assess the fictionality of the narrated events and the reliability of the first-person narrator.

The final analytical chapter explores in more detail this question of narrative perspective in the context of reconstructive literature. In *A Visit from the Goon Squad*, Jennifer Egan formally fragments the narrative perspective into a loose assembly of viewpoints and apparently incidental episodes. The novel performs a thorough withdrawal of narrative authority, leaving the reader literally with the task and responsibility of picking up and reconstructing the pieces into a coherent narrative. In a marked contrast to Egan, Julian Barnes's *The Sense of an Ending* features a very definite and self-evident narrator. Barnes uses a device which I will call 'implicit narrative' to implicate the reader into reconstructing the authority and reliability of his narrator, Tony Webster, outside the textual boundaries presented by the novel. In doing so, Barnes initiates a reconceptualization of narrative reliability as such.

My choice of texts for these case studies might at first appear somewhat incidental, as it features writers from the US and the UK and embraces such different genres as autobiography (Eggers) and utopia (Fforde). The broad scope of authors and genres, however, underlines the fact that the reconstructive tendencies and strategies I diagnose in my book are of universal significance for the intellectual and cultural self-image of the global North. Moreover, the novels have all been very much in the public as well as the academic focus. All have featured prominently on the bestseller lists and some of them have received prestigious literary prizes (Pulitzer 2011 for *A Visit from the Goon Squad*; The Man Booker 2011 for *The Sense of an Ending*; *A Heartbreaking*

---

an experiential reality or a truth external to the texts I investigate. Any such reality or truth can only ever be aesthetically invoked, and my analysis can only concern the formal means of this invocation. Having said that, one could also have recourse to speech-act theory and argue that by aesthetically enacting this reconstructive approach, this reciprocity and authenticity is performatively brought into existence. Lubomír Doležel points the way in this respect when he claims that 'authentication is a special illocutionary force analogous to the force of performative speech acts described by Austin' (1980: 11).

Work of Staggering Genius was *TIME* magazine's 'Book of the Year' in 2000). All of them are taught regularly in university courses in Europe and the United States and feature on many reading lists of contemporary literature in English. There is also a structural foundation for my choice of texts, since each case study illustrates how reconstructive metareference affects one particular aspect of literary communication. *England, England* symbolizes the socio-cultural context for re-evaluating the concept of authenticity. *A Heartbreaking Work of Staggering Genius* brings metareference to bear on the author function of the text, while the Thursday-Next series scrutinizes its own intertextual background. Finally, *A Visit from the Goon Squad* and *The Sense of an Ending* offer insights into text-intrinsic narrative strategies of reconstructive metareference.

In a short concluding chapter I will summarize the preceding argument by demonstrating how Tom McCarthy's novel *Remainder* uses authenticity as an aesthetic ideal which can only be approximated, albeit never truly be attained, by formally prescribed means. In the book, the quest for authentic experience is only fulfilled in an utterly solipsistic and eventually fatal self-reflectivity. I will argue that the sceptic attitude displayed in *Remainder* is the result of a profound misunderstanding of the central paradox inherent in any intentional display of authenticity, the sheer materiality of which necessarily exceeds the boundaries of any formal display. Only through the deliberate use and acceptance of paradoxical metareference can this excess of materiality be aesthetically enacted in the process of reconstruction.

2

'To Thine Own Self be True': Eight Theses on Authenticity

If there is one definite statement about authenticity, it is that there is no definite statement about authenticity. Its essential paradoxicality lies in the fact that by definition authenticity eludes definition, because it signifies or at least hints at a sphere located outside or beyond the defining powers of language. This extra-discursive position is deducible from but not reducible to authenticity's roots in a realm of emotion and radical subjectivity. Authenticity envisions human experience as a state of pure presence, unmediated by symbolic abstractions. Even though it is precisely this ephemeral and elusive quality which makes authenticity a valuable concept for describing a post-postmodern aesthetics of reconstruction, it is still necessary to present a precise outline of its terminological background and historical development. I refrain from attempting any straightforward definition and will rather delineate the indefinable by way of eight thesis statements. They take in historical as well as contemporary perspectives and touch on ontological, ethical, aesthetic as well as epistemological issues.

The theses I propose and investigate look back as well as ahead. They retrace the development of the concept, its changing implications and take into account a variety of historical, philosophical and aesthetic positions. They also introduce concepts and terminology of my own which will help me to develop the idea of authenticity in a post-postmodern context.

Thesis one: It is impossible to clearly define authenticity

As suggested in my introductory words, any study of authenticity first has to negotiate a very fundamental contradiction, its gate-keeper paradox as it were: authenticity cannot be perceived in or for itself but can only be externally ascribed or observed as an effect of mediation. Jonathan Culler calls this dialectic of simultaneous absence and presence 'the dilemma of authenticity':

> The paradox, the dilemma of authenticity, is that to be experienced as authentic it must be marked as authentic, but when it is marked as authentic it is mediated, a sign of itself, and hence lacks the authenticity of what is truly unspoiled, untouched by mediating cultural codes. ... The authentic sight requires markers, but our notion of the authentic is the unmarked. (1988: 164)

It is André Gide who is generally credited with first putting this paradox into words when he writes in *The Immoralist* that 'one can't simultaneously be sincere and be seen to be sincere' (2000: 72). Jean Améry argues along similar lines by asking which 'one of us could step forward with the reckless assurance of having lived, not a lie, but one's own innate authenticity? None of us. Because the latter, which constantly constructs itself just to be itself, destroys itself permanently' (1999: 147), while Marshall Berman embraces this indissoluble ambiguity by declaring that 'those who seek authenticity insist that this paradox is built into the structure of the world they live in' (2009: xxiv). My first thesis considers this (con)founding paradox of simultaneous assertion and denial, presence and absence, at the heart of authenticity from different perspectives, aesthetic as well as semiotic and epistemological. After that I will survey several attempts which have been made to introduce an idea of order into the discourse on authenticity by presenting a variety of existing typologies and terminologies.

Whenever authenticity is called upon, a notion of truth is also invoked. This notion of truth can take very different shapes depending on whether it is applied to human beings or inanimate entities like works of art or linguistic utterances. There is a truth based on individual sentiment ('a true friend'), on historical fact ('it is true that Dickens was born in 1812') or on aesthetic judgement ('*Jane Eyre* is a true masterpiece'). The boundaries between these forms are, needless to say, very permeable. What unites these disparate truth claims is that they represent, almost in the manner of performative speech acts, absolute and apparently incontestable statements about the genuineness and/or facticity of the person, object or value judgement thus ennobled. It can count among postmodernism's more significant legacies to have shown that such absolute truth claims and universal ascriptions do not relate directly to the 'reality' they designate but are reducible to the self-contained system of symbolic language or, in Derrida's famous words, '*il n'y a pas de hors-texte*' (1976: 158–9). In contrast to this, so Jacob Golomb claims, 'the notion of authenticity ... signifies something beyond the domain of objective language' (1995: 7). Thus, authenticity poses a challenge to any enclosed and hermetic system of reference, since it proposes a direct access to a realm beyond symbolic structures. Although frequently used in a similar sense, authenticity's relationship to truth is in fact dialectical. Truth can only be positively stated inside the symbolic frames of reference which human imagination has imposed on reality, such as language, symbols or binary oppositions. It can never transcend these systems to signify reality in any meaningful way. Authenticity, on the other hand, claims to surpass these confines of human-made reference and to hint at a reality beyond representation. In consequence, it can by definition never be fully subsumed and incorporated within established structures of meaning. It infers a surplus of signification that exceeds conventional frames of reference at the cost of terminological accuracy. A failure to recognize this antagonistic correlation of truth and authenticity means that the latter is falsely imbued with a claim to absoluteness; it becomes in Michael Pickering's words a 'relative concept ... used in absolutist terms' (1986: 213). Ursula Amrein likewise observes how the equation of authenticity with a yearning for positive truth infuses it with a problematic pretence to absolute authority (see 2009: 9).[1]

In so far as it exceeds conventional frames of reference, authenticity comes with an inbuilt promise of transcendence. Therefore, it is no surprise that it is often approached in terms of the spiritual and mystical. Frequently its investigation is expressed in terms of a 'quest' (see Handler and Saxton 1988; Mayer 2010; Potter 2010; Schulze 2011; Funk 2011a; Huber 2012). This term seems appropriate, as it combines the motif of investigation – its etymological root is the Latin *quaerere* meaning 'to seek, inquire' – with notions of moral obligation, ventures into unknown territory and more than just a creeping suspicion that the endeavour may eventually be futile, its reward being the journey itself rather than its fulfilment. This ethereal and transcendent subtext of authenticity is grist to the mills of both its apologists and its critics. The former tend to see it as the high road to overcoming outmoded and meaningless routines of representation and thus as a way out of the current postmodern fatigue. Its detractors put authenticity on a par with other presumably relativistic and essentially meaningless postmodern whims which suffer from an acute denial of the materiality of the real world and the written word. Geoffrey Hartman can be cited as an example in this regard, as he dismisses notions of the spiritual and the authentic alike, claiming that 'except for "spiritual" itself, "authentic" may be the most inauthentic word around' (2002: 5). Antagonistic as these two assessments may be, they still point to the fact that authenticity seems to follow from postmodernism. It marks either its logical extension or its eventual overcoming. I will try to prove that it can be both at the same time and that the quest for significance in a post-postmodern framework can be genuinely conducted only in an epistemological mode which aligns itself with paradoxical and oscillatory authenticity rather than with absolute positive truth.

The etymological origin of the word is rather unequivocal. It relates back to a Greek family of words which includes the adjective αὐθεντικός ('of first-hand authority, original') as well as the nouns αὐθεντία ('original authority') and αὐθέντης ('one who does a thing himself, a principal, a master, an autocrat'). The latter combines the prefix αὐτ(ο), meaning 'self', with an agent noun ἕντης, which derives from the verb 'ἀνύειν, meaning 'to accomplish, to bring about'.[2] From an etymological perspective, there are two key aspects to the notion of authenticity. First, it involves an act of creative endeavour or accomplishment. And, this accomplishment must be attributable to 'that which in a person is really and intrinsically *he*', as the *Oxford English Dictionary*'s rather gender-insensitive definition of 'self' suggests ('self, *pron., adj.*, and *n.*' 2014; emphasis in the original). It could be argued that the ambiguity inherent in the concept of authenticity already has its origins in this initial blending of essence ('self') and construction ('bring about'). On a more pragmatic level this dichotomy engenders

---

[1] In spite of the connection, etymological as well as conceptual, between authenticity and authority, this study deliberately avoids an explicitly political reading of authenticity, as proposed, for instance, by Berman (2009). An emphasis on the applicability of notions of authenticity to actual political issues would distract unnecessarily from my focus on the aesthetic implications of the concept.

[2] For a more detailed account of the word's development in the English language, see Schulze (2011: 27–8).

one principal differentiation in the use of the term: its applicability both to persons and to objects, a differentiation to which I will return in more detail presently.

Before that, however, there is another significant observation to make about the semiotics of authenticity. A cursory survey of various attempts to define the concept shows that authenticity is often approached or explained *ex negativo*. Rather than asserting what the word actually refers to, it is circumscribed by what it does not refer to. To give one representative case in point, Hartman provides a list of potential conceptual counterpoints to authenticity, which in his view 'contrasts with imitation, simulation, dissimulation, impersonation, imposture, fakery, forgery, inauthenticity, the counterfeit, lack of character or integrity' (2002: 25). Irmtraud Huber offers a plausible explanation for this indirect approach to authenticity by linking it to trauma. Both discourses, she claims, are grounded in the impossibility of direct representation. Both are literally indescribable. In her analysis of Jonathan Safran Foer's (non)representation of the Holocaust in *Everything is Illuminated*, Huber paraphrases Cathy Caruth who maintains that 'in its immediacy of experience a traumatic flashback is literal or, if you will, authentic, precisely *because* it is not verbal. Every verbalization, every assimilation of the event into a narrative would therefore imply a loss of authenticity' (2012: 122; emphasis in the original). The anthropologist Mattijs van de Port argues along similar lines. He claims that 'traumas may take on the "positive" quality of being *incontestably real* exactly because they are positioned beyond the confines of the (corrupting) symbolic order' (2004: 14; emphasis in the original). It is this essential resistance to signification, this position beyond words, which connects trauma with authenticity, which makes traumatic experience both sublime and authentic. In van de Port's words, it is 'this quality of incontestability that helps to bring about a felt ground of authenticity' (11).

All of the above suggests that any notion of authenticity apparently entails what I would describe as a *resistance to unambiguity*, an inbuilt defiance to definite classification. In view of this intrinsic tendency towards ambiguity and uncertainty, the question arises whether authenticity can actually signify in any meaningful way at all. Lindholm's list of contemporary applications of the term, which I have quoted in my introduction, demonstrates how the label 'authenticity' can nowadays be attached to a Rembrandt as well as to Coca-Cola, to ecstatic experiences and to the scent of floor polish. Some critics argue that this proliferation of discursive uses renders the underlying concept to all intents and purposes empty and meaningless. This view is held among others by Vannini and Williams who see authenticity as 'a hook either employed to sell products and services, or a hegemonic discourse through which various ideologies are being articulated' (2009: 10). This is undoubtedly a substantial objection and I will return to it in more detail in the context of the commercial exploitation of authenticity. For the moment I merely want to confirm the ambiguity and structural instability integral to any notion of authenticity, which is, in Charles Larmore's words, an essentially 'protean concept' (2004: 8).

Reality cannot be accessed directly but must first be transposed into symbolic code. Consequently, there can be no such thing as unmediated experience, no conscious existence before or beyond representation. Accordingly, authenticity cannot be understood as an essential, unalienable quality which mysteriously inheres in certain persons, things or utterances but only ever as an articulation which must first be aesthetically established. Similar claims have been put forward by Jonathan Lethem, who emphasizes that the establishment of authenticity is primarily an effect of a subjective mode of reception rather than the result of distinct forms and techniques of production (2011: 91), and by Jochen Mecke, who describes authenticity as a secondary phenomenon which no artist can depict directly and by itself and who establishes what he sees as the fundamental double bind of authenticity: it has generated countless attempts to aesthetically unravel its mystery, while at the same time structurally foreclosing the success of any such strategy (see 2006: 93, 108).

Conversely, it could also be argued that precisely because it is impossible to address and explain authenticity directly, the only way to approach it is to investigate the formal procedures and methods by which effects of authenticity are created. In other words, authenticity can *only* be appreciated as an aesthetic phenomenon. Art that aspires to authenticity, it seems, would always have to embrace paradox and must essentially forego any claim to essence. In order to signify at all, it must first renounce its own authority of signification. Ruth Mayer describes this aesthetic paradox as a 'quest for pure hybridity' (2010: 163). Or, to put it differently, authentic art can only ever be insignificant and beside the point. It is, in Adorno's words, 'the expression of the expressionless, a kind of weeping without tears' (2013: 161). Art cannot directly depict authenticity, just as language cannot distinctly and positively define it. The aesthetic criteria by which art can be analysed as authentic, however, do not claim distinctness. On the contrary, they embrace and incorporate the epistemological undecidability which I have just shown to be crucial for authenticity. Bruce Baugh highlights the paradoxical and circular logic behind this claim when he writes that 'the authentic work creates the conditions for its own proper reception in establishing the criteria by which it is to be understood' (1988: 482). Authenticity, in this regard, could be considered a performative concept, a simulation even in so far as it postulates essence while eluding definition (cf. Nunius 2012). In view of this fundamental ambiguity, it is all the more crucial to challenge the mystical 'pathos of authenticity' (Haselstein, Gross and Snyder-Körber 2010) and to investigate methodically the aesthetic strategies employed to invoke intimations of authenticity.

In order to draw up an interim balance of this thesis, I want to introduce Christoph Zeller's formula of authenticity as 'mediated immediacy' (*vermittelte Unmittelbarkeit*), which strikes me as an elegant attempt to capture the aesthetic, epistemological and semiotic paradoxes inherent in a concept which claims immediacy but can only display the effect of immediacy through artistic mediation (see Zeller 2010: 8). Authentic experience can only come to be perceived in and through precisely this paradox of mediated immediacy (see 285). To put it another way, experience (life) and representation (art) touch in the infinitude of paradox. My central claim in this book is that the ontological and epistemological ambiguity generated by metareference provides an appropriate formal instrument to investigate this infinitude.

Above, I have illustrated how the ascription of authenticity to animate beings as well as inanimate things can be deduced from the word's etymology. This distinction between authentic subjects and authentic objects is fundamental for any theoretical examination of the concept. It generates two ostensibly very different kinds of authenticity which Susanne Knaller initially called 'subject authenticity' and 'object authenticity' (see 2006: 22).[3] As I will deal with both types in more detail in the subsequent chapters, I will confine myself to only a very cursory overview at this point. Prima facie, the criteria by which authenticity is ascribed to sentient human beings and inorganic artefacts appear scarcely compatible. For a person to be perceived as authentic, it is essential that there is no perceivable gap between the appearance and the assumed essence of the person in question. The outward performance of the self needs to be in utmost congruence with the inner self, or, in Erving Goffman's seminal terminology, front stage and back stage must coincide (1959). The quest for this concurrence of inner self and its outer representation is a recurring theme which unites philosophers like Rousseau and Søren Kierkegaard with contemporary self-help guidebooks such as *Self Matters: Creating Your Life from the Inside Out*, where author Philip McGraw makes clear that 'the authentic self is the *you* that can be found at your absolute core' (2001: 30; emphasis in the original). Authentic existence in this perspective is defined as 'a project of becoming the person you are' (Guignon 2004: 3). It entails a challenge to the individual, the successful mastery of which is said to ensure both external approbation and internal self-fulfilment. The obvious logical hitch in all this is that the only authority that can ascertain the success of matching self and representation is this very person itself. This, in turn, renders this one individual both observer and object of observation, a constellation which pre-empts any valid results right from the start. One could therefore conclude that, in purely formal terms, the authenticity of subjects is always the effect of a circular argument. It can by definition only ever be self-ascribed and is thus prone to be either self-delusional or pretentious. I will return to this ambiguous relationship between authenticity and selfhood with my third thesis.

The authenticity of a manuscript or a work of art, on the other hand, seems to be properly confirmable. Used in this context, the term 'authenticity' exhibits its close etymological association with the notion of authority. A work of art, for example, is classified as authentic if it can be proven and certified to originate with a certain artist or from a certain period. This attribution is usually provided by an acknowledged authority and based on supposedly verifiable criteria such as the age of material used or the genuineness of the signature. Instances where this authority is revealed to be mistaken or misled can cause severe disturbances, because they expose the ultimate fragility of the whole concept of originality on which these attributions are based. The recent example of the German 'art forger' Wolfgang Beltracchi, who painted pictures in the style of Heinrich Campendonk or Kees van Dongen, sold them as 'originals' and was sentenced to six years in prison, is a

---

[3] In her defining study of authenticity, *Ein Wort aus der Fremde*, Knaller presents a revised typology which retains the notion and category 'subject authenticity', replaces 'object authenticity' with the more specific 'referential authenticity' and installs a third form, 'aesthetic or artistic authenticity' (*Kunstauthentizität*), which unites the former two on a higher ontological level (see 2007: 21–34; the English terms for these categories are used in Knaller 2012: 29).

very recent illustration of this.[4] Cases like his raise the question on what grounds artworks are authenticated as original: the style, the signature, the market value? Following a similar logic of originality, everyday objects can have authenticity assigned to them when they are perceived to be genuinely characteristic for a certain group of people, like 'authentic' Chinese cuisine, or a distinctive period of time, like 'authentic' Victorian furniture.

It is the idea of genuineness, confirmed through the incontestability and truthfulness of origins, which connects both forms of authenticity, and it is in and through art that this connection can manifest itself most obviously. The arts figure in this regard as a medium and an intermediary between an incommensurable reality and the human being's finite powers of apprehension. They occupy an ideal position to integrate and illustrate authenticity in all its paradoxicality because they are 'always dealing with two kinds of authenticity. They are authentic to the extent that they do justice to the facts of reality, and they are authentic in quite another sense by expressing the qualities of human experience by any means suitable to that purpose' (Arnheim 1993: 537). Knaller's categories have proven to be the most influential and widely used endeavour to systematize different forms of authenticity. There is no shortage, however, of other attempts at typology and classification. They give evidence of the broad range of applications for the notion of authenticity, which is variously employed to provide the analytical framework for profound ethical questions as well as serial murders, for studies on tourism and musical performances alike.

Both in his study on Rousseau (1993) and in his pivotal work on *Reflective Authenticity* (1998), Alessandro Ferrara focuses on the subjective dimension of authenticity, which he defines as the 'courage to stand by one's ethical intuitions even in the face of one's contingent inability to work them out in the language of abstract reflection' (1993: 136).[5] Taking this definition as a starting point, he provides an intricate model of authentic subjectivity. It consists of four separate dimensions which open up a complex coordinate system allowing every individual to locate the position of their very own subjective authenticity. Ferrara identifies the four dimensions as follows (see 1998: 54–8):

– substantialist/existentialist ⇔ intersubjective
– antagonistic ⇔ integrative
– centred ⇔ decentred
– immediate ⇔ reflective

I will come back to Ferrara later in more detail in theses two and seven. Suffice to say at this point that Ferrara's model envisages two fundamentally dissimilar configurations

---

[4] The Dutch painter Han van Meegeren, who painted pictures in the style of Dutch masters such as Pieter de Hooch or Johannes Vermeer, also presents a relevant case in point here. For a detailed account of van Meegeren's case, see Dutton (2003).
[5] Ferrara deduces his understanding of authenticity from the Aristotelian notion of *phronesis*, which he defines as the 'ability to choose between conceptual schemes embedding incompatible or differently ranked values in contexts where no a priori or external standard can be involved' (1998: 70). He states Luther's famous, if apocryphal, phrase 'Here I stand. I can do no other' as a relevant case in point (5).

of authenticity which mark the extreme poles between which the concept can be located. One prioritizes, even against the rules of society if need be, an uncompromising, existentialist and radical self-determination; this could be called *solipsistic authenticity*. As its counterpoint Ferrara imagines another form, which emerges from the selfless, respectful and honest exchange between individuals, a 'capacity to express a *uniqueness* [which] has been socially constituted through the interplay of the singularity of the formative contexts and the singularity of our responses to them' (1998: 54; emphasis in the original). Elsewhere, I have introduced the term *interauthenticity* for this interactive configuration of authenticity (see Funk 2012: 132).

In his article on 'Authenticity as Authentification' in the context of popular music, Allan Moore proposes a different typology. In spite of its evident genre-specificity, Moore's terminology is illuminating and will prove helpful even when applied to other contexts, such as the analysis of literary texts. His model is based on the grammatical category of person. Accordingly, he distinguishes three types of authenticity: 'first-person authenticity', which he describes as the authenticity of *expression* and which 'arises when an originator succeeds in conveying the impression that his/her utterance is one of integrity, that it represents an attempt to communicate in an unmediated form with an audience'; 'third-person authenticity', or authenticity of *execution*, which ensues 'when a performer succeeds in conveying the impression of accurately representing the ideas of another, embedded within the tradition of performance'; and 'second-person authenticity', or authenticity of *experience*. It is the last type that is particularly relevant for my analysis because it situates authenticity in an emergent and interstitial space opened up but not clearly delineated by the factors performer, listener and work. Moore explains that this second-person authenticity 'occurs when a performance succeeds in conveying the impression to the listener that the listener's experience of life is being validated, that the music is "telling it like it is" for them' (Moore 2002: 214, 218, 220). This means that the criteria by which authenticity is assigned are no intrinsic property of either performer or work but that authenticity emerges from an alignment of the listener's experience of life with the aesthetic performance on offer. In his analysis of Dub Poetry and in particular the phenomenon of sound systems, David Bousquet describes a similar occurrence when he emphasizes the 'relational nature of authenticity, which is seen primarily as a process by which an audience accepts, or does not accept, to relate to one or several performers and thus form a community'. In consequence, authenticity is not a static and clearly definable quality but 'is produced in the contingency of a unique performance and celebrates its very transience and specificity' (2012: 189–90). In thesis seven, I use the image of the black box to account for this oscillatory and interstitial character of authenticity in more detail.

The typologies introduced so far have more or less taken for granted without really spelling out that authenticity is something that can be both known *and* felt, that appeals to the cognitive as well as to the sensory faculties. In the introduction to his collection *The Tourist Image*, Tom Selwyn proposes the terms 'cool authenticity' and 'hot authenticity' to explicitly distinguish these two types (see 1996: 21–8). The first hardly requires further explanation. It is the authenticity of a Vermeer painting or a handwritten manuscript of *Beowulf*. It is conventionally attributed and confirmed through expert knowledge and authority. The hot variety of authenticity, in contrast, cannot be validated by knowledge or expertise. It can only be corroborated through individual sentiment.

I have already indicated that, due to its ambiguity and broad scope, the category 'authenticity' is susceptible to manipulations and exploitations. Ascriptions of authenticity are used to sell everything from clothing and food to self-empowerment and lifestyle recommendations.[6] With a view to separating the profound wheat from the hollow chaff, Joshua Glenn sets up a dichotomy of 'existential authenticity' and 'fake authenticity'. While the latter is denounced as a cynical, calculating and ultimately heteronomous pose, 'an overly subjective, anti-bourgeois rebelliousness in which the cause of social and political revolution is furthered by wearing pre-frayed Dockers, driving a luxury version of a rancher's utility vehicle, and maintaining a sarcastically vague and noncommittal suspicion of bourgeois society', existential authenticity is characterized as 'that mode of existence in which one becomes ironically and radically suspicious of all received forms and norms, and in which one strives to lucidly affirm and creatively live the tension of human reality in all its contingency, ambiguity, and absurdity' (2010). Drawing on Glenn's understanding of authenticity as based on ironic self-reflection, Florian Groß formulates the category of *sincere authenticity* in his analysis of the TV series *30 Rock*. The constant ironic self-reflections and interruptions in the show's aesthetics, he argues, result in 'a heavily constructed form of authenticity that highlights this construction as a conscious aesthetic strategy' (2012: 240).

I want to conclude this thesis by introducing Stefan Höltgen's taxonomy of aesthetic approaches to authenticity, which he proposes in the context of his analysis of serial murders in the medium of film. A similar caveat as in the case of Allan Moore applies here, as the media specificity of film analysis is not entirely transferable to other art forms without friction. Still, Höltgen's approach offers a very useful and comprehensive summary of the aesthetics of authenticity. He bases his classification on the different objectives pursued by different aesthetic procedures of authentication. These, he claims, can be subsumed under three major strategies:

– Historicizing aesthetics (*historisierende Authentizitätsästhetiken*), where the claim to authenticity is grounded in a particularly faithful evocation or recreation of a historical setting (see 2010: 30–1). This tends in the direction of object authenticity, because the confirmation of such faithfulness needs to be ascribed by confirmed expert authority.
– Ontologizing aesthetics (*ontologisierende Authentizitätsästhetiken*), which claim authenticity on the basis of a disclosure of the fictional status of the artwork in question. One strategy in this regard is the metaleptic referencing of real-world events or characters in the artwork, which results in a confusion of ontological hierarchies (see 39). This type shows similar features to Knaller's

---

[6] For in-depth analyses of the commercial exploitation of authenticity, see Gilmore and Pine (2007), Outka (2009) and Potter (2010).

'artistic authenticity' in that it is founded on the revelation and display of the illusory status of art. Its implicit ontological uncertainty makes it metareferential and therefore particularly relevant for my argument.

– Somaticizing aesthetics (*somatisierende Authentizitätsästhetiken*), which derive their authenticity from a direct impact on the physical constitution of the recipient (see 41). Höltgen's examples for this type include evocations of horror, revulsion, shock or acute surprise. Even though this last category seems to be the most genre-specific of the three, my analyses of literary case studies will show that an aesthetics of reconstruction frequently draws on such visceral and physical effects.

Although my selection of taxonomies and explanations is by no means exhaustive, it makes evident that all attempts to squeeze the notion of authenticity into one classificatory system is doomed to fail. Too divergent and often enough downright contradictory are its potential applications. All typologies and terms used to see through authenticity's game remain at a loss as to any conceivable essence to the concept. Even apparently clear-cut divisions, such as the distinction between authentic subjects and objects, tend to raise more complex issues upon closer inspection. Where, for example, should one classify the authenticity of statements that entail subjective assessments of objects? There seems to be a certain consensus, however, that the sphere of the aesthetic is the preferential area for approaching the ambiguity of authenticity. It may be tempting to dismiss this resistance to unambiguity as a mere consequence of an all-pervasive postmodern scepticism about signification in general. My next thesis will demonstrate, however, that such an argument would be too simplistic and narrow. Systematic ambiguity has in fact a very long tradition in the history of authenticity and can be traced back at least to the very epitome of classical ambiguity, the Delphic oracle.

Thesis two: The history of authenticity is a history of loss

In his *Guide to Greece*, the ancient travel writer Pausanias tells that the words γνῶθι σεαυτόν were engraved on the Temple of Apollo in Delphi (see 1979: 466). The phrase, usually rendered as 'know yourself' in English, can be read as a warning to those seeking advice from the priestess of the temple, known as the Pythia. The inscription implies that in order to understand the divine revelations, it is essential that you know and understand yourself first. The instructions given by the oracle were habitually ambiguous and open to many, often contradictory, interpretations, so that arguably the only unmistakeable recommendation coming out of Delphi was just that admonition to self-knowledge and self-assessment itself. Even though the myth of Narcissus stands as a stark warning against the potential solipsism and complete abandonment inherent in this activity, and despite the fact that the voice of the Pythia eventually fell silent in the fourth century CE, the phrase 'know yourself' has endured and reappears in countless forms throughout Western history, from the dialogues of

Socrates via Shakespeare's Polonius and Alexander Pope's *Essay on Man* to contemporary manuals on how to live the good life.[7]

While the phrase itself has undergone little variation, its meaning and implications have changed considerably over the centuries. This chapter is an attempt to retrace some of these transformations. It examines the social, philosophical and media-related parameters according to which self-knowledge has been established, and the performances and different criteria in which this self-knowledge has found expression. Still, it by no means aspires to represent a complete history of the authenticity of the subject. It rather seeks to highlight paradigmatic changes in the development of the concept and to relate these changes to their respective cultural context.

I have chosen four paradigmatic 'turns' in the development of authenticity, which roughly coincide with the onset of the cultural periods customarily designated as the Renaissance, Romanticism, Modernism and Postmodernism. My aim is first to illustrate the diachronic variance and adaptability of the concept. The analysis also paves the way for an exploration of the contemporary aesthetic and epistemological potential of authenticity by highlighting the contextual parameters that have an impact on post-postmodern conceptions of authenticity.

Fashioning the self: Hamlet and the humanistic turn

An understanding of the self as implied in the inscription at Delphi or by Socrates is fundamentally different from our own. The idea of a split between inner and outer personality, on which the whole idea of authentic subjectivity is premised, would arguably have made little sense to ancient Greeks. In antiquity the quest for self-knowledge was not meant as an exploration of whatever mysterious core might be found at the heart or bottom of one's existence but rather as an awareness of one's position *sub specie aeternitatis*. The individual was not supposed to seek emancipation from the bonds of heteronomy but rather admonished to recognize its position in a greater social and cosmic interrelation. The sentence γνῶθι σεαυτόν should probably be translated as 'know thy place' rather than 'know thy self'. Similar limitations affect St Augustine's *Confessions*, an ur-text of autobiographical self-scrutiny, where the painful process of externalizing inner feelings and developments does not aim at elevating the self for its own sake but, quite the contrary, retraces the strenuous renunciation of self-determination solely for the greater glory of God.[8] Contemporary conceptions of authenticity evidently do not apply under these circumstances, as classical models of selfhood were essentially rooted in trans-individual systems of identification, be they religious, political or mythical. Despite an increasing significance of individuality in the Western world, this state of affairs remains more or less unchanged until the Renaissance.

---

[7] For a comprehensive historical account of the Delphic oracle, see Broad (2006). For a detailed description of the origin and development of the phrase 'know yourself', see Tränkle (1985).
[8] For an in-depth analysis of Augustine's understanding of self-knowledge, see Hölscher (1986: 126–81).

It is only with the transformations brought about by the disintegration of structures such as the feudal system, the monopoly of the *una sancta catholica* or the geocentric model of the universe that new modes of conceiving the self become available. It is here, at a point where supposedly eternal truths and configurations collapse, that a modern version of authenticity is first intimated. This intrinsic connection with feelings of loss turns out to be a recurring theme throughout all discourses on authenticity. Shakespeare's Hamlet guards the threshold of this new paradigm of self-reflection. His entire character can be read as a profound meditation on what it means to be or not to be authentic. His calamitous deferment of action can be attributed to the fact that he has to perform a part which is out of joint with his inner self. He refuses to conform to any of the possible role ascriptions on offer for him – prince, avenger of his father, loving son to his mother, loyal nephew, lover, friend, fool – because despite many a soliloquy he is unable to align any of these patterns in its totality with his own inner feelings. In this context, Aleida Assmann describes Hamlet as 'the paradigmatic modern hero in search of his own self in a kaleidoscope of attributed and self-chosen roles' (2012: 40). In his character he exhibits a primeval split between inner and outer personality, and it is the uncompromising assertion of the former which forces him into feigning madness and eventually triggers the play's cataclysmic finale. The time seems not yet ripe for radical self-determination. Hamlet's insistence on 'that within which passes show' (1.2.85) stands in stark contrast to Polonius's counsel for his son Laertes 'to thine own self be true' (1.3.78). Polonius's notion of selfhood is still very much one of pre-subjective adherence to the rules and expectations of society, its principal objective is not to 'be false to any man' (1.3.80) rather than to himself. In the play the consequences of this particular understanding of self-realization are no less tragic than Hamlet's, as Laertes loses any ability to think and judge objectively and is turned into a compliant tool in the hands of Claudius, who himself in many ways presents a case of self-determination gone spectacularly awry.

Lionel Trilling famously uses a comparison between Hamlet's and Polonius's conceptions of self to introduce and illustrate his distinction between the concepts of authenticity and sincerity, a distinction which still reverberates today. The basic difference, Trilling suggests, is one of direction. Sincerity is always aimed at an external point of reference. We are sincere when 'we actually are what we want *our community* to know we are' (1971: 11; emphasis added). Kenneth J. Gergen similarly describes sincerity as a version of 'self-knowledge [that] did not require a tortuous journey into an exotic interior region, but simply meant that one gained clarity about values, beliefs, or intentions' (1991: 217). Authenticity, in contrast, is described by Trilling as 'the downward movement through all the cultural superstructures to some place where all movement ends, and begins' (1971: 13). Thus it necessarily faces towards the within and lacks any reliable and consistent external point of reference. As a consequence, sincerity is comparable, relative, relational, heteronomous and describable in terms of social and intersubjective norms, while authenticity is incommensurable, absolute and self-contained: 'sincerity is discovered *within* social roles, authenticity *behind and beneath* them', as Peter L. Berger succinctly summarizes (1973: 82; emphasis in the original). Golomb even considers this shift to be 'at the heart of the existentialist revolution: the eclipse of "truth" by "truthfulness", the transition from objective sincerity to personal authenticity' (1995: 8). While Trilling sees the development of authenticity and the decline of sincerity as a sign of progress, recent critics are taking a more equivocal view.

In the introduction to their collection of essays on *The Rhetoric of Sincerity*, Ernst van Alphen and Mieke Bal relate the decline of sincerity in early modern Europe to a transformation of public culture, which is propelled among other things by the invention of printing and the rise of theatre. This transformed media environment, in turn, caused sincerity to become 'entangled in medial forms that complicated ... the integrated semiotic field where body and mind were believed to be one' (2009: 3). Van Alphen and Bal update the relationship between sincerity and authenticity and herald a renaissance of the former. Since sincerity in their view is always concerned with how the individual relates to others, it necessarily implies an aspect of performance; it is 'considered fundamentally corporeal rather than textual'. They reinforce the dialectical relationship between authenticity as internal and sincerity as external when they describe sincerity as 'a natural enactment of authenticity' (1). In her contribution to the same collection, Jane Taylor states that 'sincerity can be called upon to stage itself in relation to an external authority' (2009: 27), and Kerry Sinanan and Tim Milnes propose a similar view when they claim that 'authenticity is a state, sincerity a practice' (2010: 4). It is by dint of precisely this ostentatious theatricality and interactivity that sincerity is considered by some to be more suitable as an aesthetic paradigm than the elusive inwardness of authenticity. Adam Kelly's study on a 'New Sincerity' in American fiction (2010a) is only one pertinent example of this tendency, as is Groß's attempt to reconcile both concepts in what he calls 'sincere authenticity'. In view of this terminological imbroglio, one might be tempted to conclude that in an early modern framework sincerity and authenticity are themselves no more than merely 'words, words, words' and that it is after all not the one specific linguistic marker that is essential but rather the insight that the decline of medieval bondage and constraints and the rise of Humanism are attended by a new quality to the notion of the self. One could say that for the first time there actually is a self to be true to.

Je sens mon coeur: Rousseau and the romantic turn

Even though Renaissance Humanism may have generated a new model of the self, this self is not yet a space in which the individual can be fully absorbed, to which it can relate and retreat in its entirety. Any notion of the self must still be seen within the context and as part of an all-encompassing, abstract system of rationalism, which seeks to shine the bright light of reason into the remotest nooks and crannies of the micro- and macrocosm. The rational human being might have liberated itself from Kant's famous 'self-imposed immaturity' but only to serve the new master of reason. It is only with the onset of Romanticism that a space of withdrawal is being accorded to the self, and it is this act of withdrawal which still resonates in our contemporary perception of authenticity. Guignon identifies three main features at the heart of this

Romantic reappraisal of authenticity, which, again, is invoked against a backdrop of lost certainties:

> The attempt to recover a sense of oneness and wholeness ... the conviction that real 'truth' is discovered not by rational reflection and scientific method, but by total immersion in one's own deepest and most intense feelings [and] the discovery, at the limits of all experience, that the self is the highest and most all-encompassing of all that is found in reality. (2004: 51)

The central figure in this ontological and, for the first time, explicitly aesthetic, revaluation of the self is Rousseau, who marks a turning point in the history of the concept in so far as he specifically equates modern individuality with the representation of this individuality.[9] Rousseau's relentless quest for self-knowledge, for his inward manner of being (*sentiment propre de mon existence*), can be seen as an internalized version of his pursuit of an original and natural state of man (*homme naturel*), unspoilt by reason, education, industry and progress. Rousseau seeks 'a direct presence of self to self' (Guignon 2004: 66) and inaugurates along the way a new economy of truth. If the self is the only valid arbiter of itself, if, in other words, abstract rationality and reason do *not* offer direct access to the self, it follows that truth itself can be neither objective nor objectified. Truth, for Rousseau, is personal, individual and incomplete. A true self presupposes one's very own subjective truth.

Although this self-aware self can never be fully realized, it must still be continually explored and reassessed, and this continual self-searching can only be pursued in aesthetic terms. This is Rousseau's second important contribution to the development of authenticity. He understands and uses art, and in particular autobiography, to reflect the fragmented condition and the interminable exploration of the self; for him 'the self-portrait presents not a faithful copy of the subject but a representation of the subject's ongoing search for the truth of the self. The image is authentic because *the self just is this search*' (Guignon 2004: 69; emphasis in the original). Rousseau instigates a poetics of self, both in aesthetic terms and in the etymological sense of ποιεῖν as 'to create, produce'. Art describes the self *and* art creates the self, an apparent paradox which has influenced the aesthetics of authenticity ever since.

Even though Rousseau is on all accounts the key figure in the Romantic reconfiguration of selfhood and authenticity, he is certainly not the only one. Johann Gottlieb Fichte's *Ich-Setzung*, that is, the assertion that in order to interact with the world, the self must first become conscious of itself, is an important step in the advancement of self-identity, as is Hegel's rather sensible reformulation of authenticity as the end instead of the source of selfhood, a twist which almost manages to collapse dialectically the chasm between rational and Romantic notions of the self. With this conception of the individual self as essentially autonomous and irreducible, however,

---

[9] The scope of this book precludes a more systematic account of Rousseau's role in the development of authenticity. I must refer at this point to more exhaustive and knowledgeable studies, in particular Ferrara (1993), Guignon (2004), Russett (2006), Mecke (2006) and Nübel (2011). For more comprehensive studies on Rousseau and his significance for the genre of autobiography, see Williams (1983) and Kuhn (2009).

the notion of authenticity has reached a profound crisis of representation. Originating in individual subjectivity alone, it can no more claim universal validity. It comes as no surprise therefore when the next significant development centres on the authenticity of objects rather than the human subject.

The end of an aura: Benjamin and the modernist turn

So far I have presented the history of authenticity exclusively in terms of notions of selfhood and subjectivity. The authenticity of objects has been neglected, despite the fact that media-related changes, such as the invention of movable letters and the subsequent revaluation of the authenticity of scripture, have arguably played an important role in the refashioning of the Renaissance self. Rousseau even grants material objects, in the form of works of art, a privileged access to the impenetrable self. Nevertheless, the principal debates in the two previous turns were still conducted in the field of subjectivity. The next major benchmark in the evolution of authenticity, however, results primarily from transformations in the media environment and an ensuing change in perspective on the materiality of objects in general and works of art in particular. It is again a perception of loss which triggers this transformation. When Walter Benjamin sets out to examine *The Work of Art in the Age of Mechanical Reproduction*, what he finds is vacuity: 'Even with the most perfect reproduction, one thing [is lost]: the here and now of the work of art – its unique existence in the place where it is at this moment' (2008: 5). Photographic reproduction robs an object of its aura, its intrinsic and inalienable location in space and time, its genuineness, which Benjamin defines as 'the quintessence of everything about it since its creation that can be handed down, from its material duration to the historical witness that it bears' (7). Reproduction literally disinvests objects of their context and turns them into free-floating signifiers. Although Benjamin's claim is very much rooted in its own time and space, it enjoys renewed interest today, when new forms of media and interaction create a potential for reproduction and simulation on a scale Benjamin could hardly have imagined. I will therefore return to Benjamin's notion of the aura when I discuss the effect of new media constellations on the idea of authenticity in thesis five.

Benjamin's influence on the development of authenticity is significant for two principal reasons. First, he grants to objects and artworks a form of authenticity which is structurally similar to the one already accorded to human beings, namely one that is not primarily dependent on external ascription but which resides in the object as such. This authenticity is grounded in the artwork's incorporation in ritualistic habits of religion, magic or secularized alternatives like the cult of beauty. Although the ritual which invests the artwork with such authenticity could itself be considered a form of external attribution, it is in the very nature of the ritual to conceal this agency by invoking the sacred status of the object in question. As a result, it is impossible from then on to deal with the authenticity of the subject, the object and of art separately. The invocation of one will now always necessarily call forth the others. In a further step, Benjamin links the destruction of the auratic object with a general change in perspective which he observes in society as a whole: 'Stripping the object of its sheath, shattering the aura, bear witness to a kind of perception where "a sense of similarity in the world" is so highly developed that, through reproduction, it even mines similarity from what only happens once' (19). For Benjamin, the artwork's loss of aura symbolizes the alienation of mankind from itself, which has often been cited as symptomatic of the modernist condition and which can be traced back to the theories of Darwin and Freud as well as to the cataclysm of World War I.

Where next to turn? Postmodern authenticities

I have tried so far to demonstrate how transformations in the discourse on authenticity can be used as a yardstick for wide-ranging cultural and social reorientations. These can be triggered both by media transformations and by changes to the paradigms of human self-perception. Both can be summarized as breakdowns of the dichotomy of inside and outside, essence and appearance. Before the Renaissance, no such split was imaginable, which made the notion of authenticity literally pointless. In the Renaissance then the division into inner and outer personality was first proposed and tentatively tested. In Romanticism the inner personality gained absolute pre-eminence. Modernism swung back the pendulum and focused on appearances rather than essence. As Baudrillard's simulacrum, Derrida's *différance* and Jameson's critique of postmodern superficiality attest, art and theory in postmodernism have effectively put an end to any meaningful distinction between inner and outer personality, surface and deep structure, essence and representation. Does this now mean the end of authenticity? Ferrara reports evidence which seems to point in this direction. He observes how 'spokesmen of poststructuralism ... avoid using the term authenticity because to their sensibilities it conveys the illusory myth of a totalizing, harmonious, unitary self, which they seek to replace with the image of a fragmented, plural, centerless and irreconcilably split subjectivity' (1993: 24–5).

Nevertheless, there have been a number of attempts to formulate a specifically postmodern version of the concept. Virginia Richter neatly encapsulates the motivation behind these endeavours when she maintains that 'we need authenticity *because* it doesn't exist' (2009: 68; emphasis in the original), claiming further that 'our collective investment in it is so high that even after decades of deconstructivism and anti-essentialism it is impossible to get rid of' (73). It can be argued that postmodern invocations of the concept again originate in a profound perception of loss. This time, however, it is the idea of the self itself which is lost. What unites most postmodern notions of authenticity is an aesthetics of an essentially anti-Rousseauian absence of self to self. Guignon attests how 'our attempt to find the true self beneath all social masks seems to have ended up in a maelstrom of centerlessness, dispersal and multiplicity' (2004: 126), and he goes on to provide a very concise delineation of the contemporary state of affairs when he maintains that the

> postmodern version of authenticity ... is the ideal of clear-sightedly and courageously embracing the fact that there is no 'true self' to be, of recognizing that where we formerly had sought a true self, there is only an empty space, a gap or

a lack. The postmodern ideal, then, is to *be* that lack of self with playfulness and ironic amusement. (119; emphasis in the original)

If we align Guignon's claim that 'we are really true to ourselves ... when we unflinchingly face the fact that there is nothing to be true to' (120) with the assumption that the integrity of the self has up to now been the *conditio sine qua non* for being (perceived as) authentic, then such ideas are indeed emblematic of a pervasive postmodern *inauthenticity* and thus for the end of authenticity as we know it. A similar argument pervades the 'Tate Declaration of Inauthenticity' by the International Necronautical Society, which counts among its members Tom McCarthy and Simon Critchley. Based on the assumption that every 'attempt at authenticity slips back into an inauthenticity from which it cannot escape, but which it would like to evade', they put forward the idea of an *original inauthenticity* which accounts for the fact that 'inauthenticity is the core to the self, to what it means to be human, which means that the self has no core, but is an experience of division, of splitting' (International Necronautical Society 2009: 5).[10]

Yet, there is still hope for those who believe in authenticity. For Guignon, the postmodern context, with its apparent absence of originality and correspondence, presents the culture medium for a new version of authenticity, one which offers the opportunity to unite freewheeling relativity with ethical responsibility: 'To be authentic, on this account, is to take a wholehearted stand on what is of crucial importance for you, to understand yourself as defined by the unconditional commitments you undertake, and, as much as possible, to steadfastly express those commitments in your actions throughout the course of your life' (2004: 139). This approach, however, entirely discards the aesthetic dimension. It replaces an aesthetics of authenticity with an ethics of authenticity, or in other words, it rejects the examination of the self for an unreflecting self-realization, the 'knowing yourself' for the 'being yourself'. I believe that such sedimentation of the aesthetic from the ethical is not helpful, if not downright impossible, and in the following I will try to make a case for the aesthetic dimension of authenticity. In order to do so, the next thesis addresses in more detail the relationship of selfhood and authenticity in a contemporary context.

Thesis three: Authenticity both presupposes and generates a notion of self

The third thesis unites the previous two. It takes the paradoxical ambiguity and circularity that I have defined as essential to any notion of authenticity in thesis one and applies it to contemporary conceptions of the individual self. The context in which this selfhood can manifest itself is shaped by the larger cultural and philosophical

---

[10] The presentation of the declaration, which was first (supposedly) performed in New York in 2007, itself is a shrewd play with and applied commentary on the insoluble interplay between authenticity and inauthenticity, between original and copy, because the declaration is read out by two actors impersonating McCarthy and Critchley (see McGirk 2010).

framework as well as the individual's experience of everyday life, so both have to be taken into account. My argument will proceed in three steps. In order to prepare the ground for my subsequent analysis, I will first give an account of a number of attempts that have been made to clarify the link between authenticity and the self in general. In a second step I will then examine in more detail two different assessments of the possibility of authentic self-expression: Foucault's notion of *parrhesia* and Adorno's stern denunciation of Heidegger's 'jargon of authenticity'. Poststructuralist thinking has made it all but impossible to conceive of the Self in lower case and without its significant Other. In a third step I will therefore investigate the implications of this inextricable association of selfhood with otherness, as embodied most forcefully in the thinking of Emmanuel Levinas. Ultimately, the notions of a true self and of authenticity are tied up in a circular argument. They presuppose one another and can only function on the assumption of the validity of the respective other. In logical terms, they act as both the premise and the conclusion of their own syllogistic proposition.

The path towards an authentic self has been described as both the high road and a major impediment on the way to success in our contemporary society. It is either seen as restricting the individual's opportunities to act and develop, as unprofessional, an irksome encumbrance on the path towards a self-realization which is predicated on subordinating any semblance of individuality to the ultimate 'common good' of materialistic aggrandisement (see, for example, Niermeyer 2008: 18–25). A successful personality in this regard is patently inauthentic, because the criteria by which it judges its success – wealth, social consensus, appearance – are all relational and comparative. It might be tempting to loftily dismiss such rhetoric as the inconsiderate and wholly unscholarly ideology of capitalism unleashed, were it not for the fact that some of these allegations are based on some of the prevailing social and economic conventions of the day.

On the other end of the spectrum, there are those who take up the cudgels on behalf of the authentic self as a path to personal accomplishment. Only by embracing and implementing that which is inalienably individual about human being, so the argument goes, can humankind redeem itself from the duplicity and deceitfulness of a world governed by dissimulation and play-acting. As I will elaborate on this idea in more detail in the following thesis, I will merely return at this point to Philip McGraw's guidelines for *Creating your Life from the Inside Out*, as the subtitle of his book *Self Matters* (2001) proposes. According to McGraw, the essential key towards personal success in life is the recognition, acceptance and willing display of one's authentic self, which he defines as

> the *you* that can be found at your absolute core. It is the part of you that is not defined by your job, or your function, or your role. It is the composite of all your unique gifts, skills, abilities, interests, talents, insights, and wisdom. It is all your strengths and values that are uniquely yours and need expression, versus what you have been programmed to believe that you are 'supposed to be and do'. (2001: 30; emphasis in the original)

Ning Wang sings a similar tune. He describes 'a special state of Being in which one is true to oneself, and [which] acts as a counterdose to the loss of "true self" in public roles and public spheres in modern society' (1999: 358) and designates this state 'existential authenticity'. In this shape and form, as 'a project of becoming the person you are' (Guignon 2004: 3), authenticity achieves the status of an ideal. In a contemporary appropriation of Rousseau's central tenet, it locates the ultimate point of reference for truth exclusively within the individual. It represents both a surplus and a residue in relation to the expectations of society. Eventually, both Niermeyer and McGraw seem to concur with Berger's opinion that, if perpetrated in earnest, 'authenticity is a lonesome business' (1973: 88). It inexorably throws the individual back onto itself, with only the possibility of aesthetic expression to fall back upon.

Leaving behind the supposedly hands-on approach of the self-help manuals, I will now turn to the more abstract question of why authenticity is still regarded as a quality the individual should measure itself against. Again, one is faced with a paradox. Authenticity is used as an argument to liberate the self from its social role and responsibility at the same time as it supposedly commits it to responsible behaviour; it is in Corey Anton's words 'a dutiful autonomy, one liberated by indebtedness' (2001: 160). On the one hand, it harks back to medieval perceptions of knowing oneself through reflecting one's place in the greater scheme of things, or, as Guignon asserts, 'to make sense of the social role of authenticity, we need to see that becoming authentic involves becoming more clear-sighted and reflective about the issues that face us in our current situation' (2004: 161). On the other hand, it can be construed as the basis of an ethics and aesthetics of radical subjectivity. To be authentic means, in Golomb's words,

> to invent one's *own* way and pattern of life. Here the concept of originality does not refer so much to the idea of *origin* as to undogmatic openness – or, to use Nietzsche's terminology, a 'horizon of infinite perspectives' from which the individual can survey his or her own life and mould it accordingly. (1995: 19; emphases in the original)

Authenticity apparently has the potential to integrate the communal and the individual, the private and the political. Through reflecting (on) the self, it achieves the status of a trans-individual categorical imperative, a self-fulfilling prophecy in every sense of the word. Guignon captures the circuitousness of this projection when he writes that 'one crucial reason why we value authenticity is because we believe that being authentic plays a fundamental role in nurturing and sustaining the kind of society in which something like authenticity as an ideal can be possible' (2004: 161).

In view of the underlying argument of this book, I would like to accentuate one particular aspect of this authentic act of self-searching: it is necessarily self-reflective, not only in a contemplative way but also in an epistemological sense of being seen through the distorting lens of formal self-reference and (Romantic) irony. Authentic selves, it would seem, can only ever appear in fragmented and refracted form. In yet another paradox in which the notion of authenticity is shrouded, it could even be argued that a desire for authenticity is not an effect of individual self-reflection but, quite the contrary, that it is the very idea of the human self that is an effect of a precognitive desire for authenticity. The quest for authenticity, in this light, would amount to a *primum movens*, an explanation perhaps for what Hofstadter describes as a 'special type of abstract pattern or structure ... that gives rise to what *feels* like a self' (2007: 95; emphasis in the original). I would not go quite as far at this point. Instead, I would argue that authenticity as a fundamentally interstitial concept arises from the endlessly reflecting and refracting interplay between the self and the demands made on it – by itself as well as by its environment. Human experience can only be authentic to the extent to which it is self-reflective. How and by which aesthetic means this self-referentiality is expressed can thus be the only formal criterion by which to determine authenticity. Still, Hofstadter's concept of the self as an effect of metaleptic and interminable self-reference and self-perception – he calls human beings 'little miracles of self-reference' (363) – presents a neat metaphor for the seemingly contradictory connections between self and authenticity in our day and age. Ferrara conceptualizes this interplay in terms of an 'authenticity *against* or *despite* the self or, in other words, a theme of authenticity played on the register of the *sublime*' (1993: 25; emphases in the original). Ferrara uses the term *reflective authenticity* to describe this decentred and self-referential version of authenticity, which he explicitly sets up against 'a view of the self and of subjectivity as coalescing around a center of gravity ... which sorts out what is crucial and what is peripheral for the self, understanding authenticity as the quality of a life whose plurality of experiences, detours, and side-narratives can be meaningfully seen as variations on a unique and recognizable theme' (2009: 25). The notion of reflective authenticity, in contrast, acknowledges the essentially ambiguous ontological status of the authentic self and offers 'ways of thinking of limits to the self-shaping power of the self without either locating these limits outside the self or invoking the dubious notion of an essential self to be true to' (35).

The pluralistic connection between self and authenticity which Ferrara points out adds to the latter's resistance to unambiguity. There is not only no unequivocal cause-and-effect relationship to be established between the two. The gate-keeper paradox introduced in thesis one also makes it impossible for the 'authentic self' to express itself directly and definitely. Nevertheless, I will now introduce a conception of authentic self-expression which is based on an attempt to externalize without too much frictional loss the deliberations and processes inside the self: Michel Foucault's notion of *parrhesia*.

Foucault takes recourse to this ancient Greek model to describe a form of discourse which moves beyond the obligation to evidential truth, an obligation he sees as characteristic for the modern Western episteme. Foucault translates the term as 'free speech' but etymologically it derives from πᾶν (= 'all') and ῥῆμα (= 'utterance, speech') and thus means 'to say/speak/utter everything'. Foucault argues that it is only because truth is traditionally regarded as something that can be 'obtained in a certain (mental) evidential experience' that an irreconcilable gap exists between human utterances and truth. For the Greeks, 'the coincidence between belief and truth does not take place in a (mental) experience, but in a *verbal activity*' (2001: 14; emphasis in the original), and this verbal activity he calls *parrhesia*. In parrhematic discourse the truth of an utterance does not have to be established by evidential observation or experience but emanates from the utterance itself, which – almost in the manner of an Austinian performative speech act – makes real/true the thing it declares. In anticipation of the argument in thesis six, one could say that, provided certain criteria are met, truth *emerges* in and through the statement itself. In the literary analyses, I will later investigate the formal circumstances in which contemporary aesthetic representation can emerge as authentic. According to Foucault, the presuppositions for *parrhesia* are first that the speaker is someone 'who has the moral qualities which are required, first, to know the truth, and secondly, to convey such truth to others' and second that the telling of the truth puts the teller in danger (15–16). This implies that the telling of truth is only possible from an exposed and potentially vulnerable position. The Greek conception of truth which reverberates in the notion of *parrhesia* is not based on evidence but on personal morality and courage. The assertion that truth can only be told to power and from an unprivileged position opens up an interesting angle on the relationship between power and truth. Pace Gayatri Spivak, it could be argued that it is *only* the subaltern that can speak … the truth.

There can hardly be any doubt that Theodor Adorno believed in the authenticity of works of art. Harro Müller identifies the authentic work of art and the unconditional truth claim it implies as one of Adorno's key weapons against any kind of a capitalist context of delusion (*Verblendungszusammenhang*) (see 2006: 63). A case in point can be found in the *Aesthetic Theory*, where Adorno claims that the 'seal of authentic artworks is that what they appear to be appears as if it could not be prevaricated, even though discursive judgment is unable to define it' (2013: 180). Knaller notes in this context that Adorno 'was the first to describe consistently how the notion of authenticity, as an aesthetic concept of validity and value, mediates between the empirical, form, and transcendence' (2012: 27). It is, however, equally unquestionable that the idea of subjective authenticity did cut no ice with Adorno. In his *Jargon of Authenticity* (2003), he casts aspersions on any notion of individual genuineness (*Echtheit*) in general and Heidegger's elevation of it in particular. In this elegant polemic, Adorno systematically picks to pieces the idea of a retreat into the genuineness of the self which is implied in the term *Echtheit* and which for him is itself the grossest of dissimulations. For Adorno, such *Echtheit* can never be more than a simulation, posing as the genuine and unique, while in fact following and resulting from the logic of capitalist mass production (see 2013: 76). Adorno's fierce opposition to subjective authenticity is based first and foremost on his conviction that the individual self can never be perceived outside or beyond the framework imposed on it by its symbolic representations and social interactions. The self, in other words, must necessarily interrelate in order to relate at all. Adorno's main objective in this context is to show how capitalism and the culture industry misappropriate and undermine any conception of individuality. The underlying assumption, that thinking about the self is impossible without also taking into account the non-self, however, has had massive reverberations and has, under the heading of alterity, become one of the central pillars of postmodern identity politics. I would argue that this change of perspective, that is, the recognition that there is 'no such thing as an authentic identity which does not presuppose a moment of recognition on the part of the other' (Duvenage 2004: 130), can be seen as postmodernism's pivotal contribution in the development of authenticity. Arguably the most influential theoretician of this paradigm change is Emmanuel Levinas.

In a nutshell, Levinas's basic assumption is that the notion of the self is the result of an original encounter with an other, which he understands as 'that which escapes the cognitive powers of the knowing subject' (Critchley 1992: 5).[11] The self, in other words, can only become self-aware in the face of its significant other. The other interpellates the self into significance and signification. The connection established between self and other which ensues from this primordial confrontation is one of responsibility; Levinas even assumes that 'the identity of the subject comes from the impossibility of escaping responsibility' (1981: 14). He reduces the process of symbolic representation to this elemental ethical encounter with the other: 'Signification, the one-for-the-other, the relationship with alterity, has been analysed ... as proximity, proximity as responsibility for the other, and responsibility for the other as substitution' (184). It follows logically that, from the moment it conceives of itself, the self is inevitably integrated in a profoundly dialogical mode; it cannot but relate to the other. Since Levinas believes that all abstract reasoning becomes meaningless when actually facing the other, he feels no need to provide definite statements as to the initial cause of this encounter, the big bang of signification as it were: 'The order that orders me to the other does not show itself to me, save through the trace of its reclusion, as a face of a neighbour' (140).[12]

Levinas's thinking in this regard is substantially influenced by Martin Buber's conception of the 'I-Thou' (*Ich-Du*). Like Levinas, Buber believes the dichotomy of self and other to be primary to any formation of subjective identity: 'by its nature it precedes *I*' (2008: 24). Any human capacity for spirituality and ethical behaviour emerges from the dialogue of I and Thou: 'in each *Thou* we address the eternal *Thou*' (14). Buber also highlights the interstitial and oscillatory character of this pre-symbolic capacity which he calls 'spirit' (*Geist*): 'Spirit is not in the *I* but between I and *Thou*' (36).

One of the foremost qualities of the Levinasian other is its essential unknowability. Consequently, it could be argued that signification itself is an emergent phenomenon which results from the interaction of parameters that in and for themselves elude direct observation and definition. When the self answers to the appeal of the other in the form of symbolic representation, of itself and the world, this is always a response to an ultimately unanswerable and unresolvable question. Alphonso Lingis, one the most perceptive exegetes of Levinas, explains that 'in his alterity the other is faced, that is, not recognized, cognized, but answered, by a speaking that is a response. To face another is to answer to him. Or, we may say, speech structured as response is the modality of recognition that recognizes irreducible alterity' (1987: xiv). Just as sentiments of loss and a consequent yearning for compensation have shaped the history

---

[11] I have decided to keep the Levinasian 'other' in lower case, as he conceives of it not primarily as an abstract entity but rather, in Critchley's words, as 'a singular other who does not lose him or her self in a crowd of others' (1992: 17).

[12] For an elegant summary of this idea, cf. Judith Butler's statement that for Levinas 'the pre-emergent "I" that I am is nothing more at this point than a radical susceptibility subject to impingement by the Other. If I become responsible only through being acted on by an Other, that is because the "I" first comes into being as a "me" through being acted upon by an Other, and this primary impingement is already and from the start an ethical interpellation' (2005: 89).

of authenticity, signification itself is a compensation for the other's radical otherness. Lingis emphasizes this structural similarity between authenticity and alterity when he writes that the 'alterity of the other is not determined, not grasped nor comprehended, by the I; alterity weighs on the I with the force, the disturbance, of its passing, its infinite and unrepresentable withdrawal' (xix). The material *primum movens* of symbolic interaction can itself never be expressed in symbolic form.

Accordingly, Levinas perceives two distinct forms of self-expression, which he calls 'the said' (*le dit*) and 'the saying' (*le dire*). The former is a symbolic mode of asserting positive truth and falsehood, '"ascriptions of meaning", which are inscribed as tales' (Levinas 1981: 48). The saying, in contrast, is non-assertive and refers directly to the primeval, pre-symbolic encounter with the other. Saying cannot appear in and by itself because it originates with the unknowable other. In order to become meaningful, it must adopt the idiom of the said. Levinas explains that the 'correlation of the saying and the said, the subordination of the saying to the said, to the linguistic system and to ontology, is the price that manifestation demands' (6). The saying therefore represents an excess of signification, an incommensurability that cannot be conceived of in symbolic terms; 'the saying overflows the very being it thematizes in stating it to the other' (18). It is in Critchley's sensitive interpretation 'the non-thematized ethical residue of language that escapes comprehension, interrupts philosophy, and is the very enactment of the ethical movement from the Same to the Other' (1992: 7). In opposition to the ascribed meaning of the said, the saying is 'a "signifyingness dealt the other", prior to all objectification; it does not consist in giving signs' (Levinas 1981: 48). It is this resistance to definition and unambiguity and the oscillatory state between stable configurations of identity which connects the saying to authenticity. Levinas himself highlights this connection when he declares that in the 'sincerity [of the saying] as a sign given to another, it absolves me of all identity' (50), and Lingis maintains that for Levinas 'authenticity is not formed simply in the relationship with the clearing of the world; this state of being capable of answering for what it is and says and does, of being possessed with a passion for justification, arises in a relationship not with nothingness which attracts and threatens, but with alterity which appeals and contests' (1987: xv).

In *Entre Nous* (1998) and *Alterity and Transcendence* (1999), Levinas sets up his version of authenticity in opposition to that of Heidegger. Both originate from a confrontation of the self with its own insignificance. In both cases this insignificance, which is also an inability to signify, is in consequence of an encounter with death. For Heidegger, this death is necessarily the death of the self, an event which signifies both this self's ultimate negation and the only definite objective of its very existence. Individual existence (*Dasein*) is always a 'being-towards-death' (*Sein zum Tode*), a '"situatedness" in a temporal framework delineated by a certainty of *our death*' (Hanlon 2004: 515–16; emphasis added). This gives rise to a monolithic and absolute notion of authenticity, which Heidegger refers to as *Eigentlichkeit* and which is 'altered by nothing – neither support nor help nor influence – conquering, but distaining the exchange in which a will awaits the consent of the stranger' (Levinas 1998: 207). According to Lingis, the 'anticipation of the end subtends the constitution of an authentic time, a time of one's own' (1987: xxiv). For Levinas on the other hand, it is 'the powerless confrontation with the *death of the other*' (1999: 30; emphasis added) and the ensuing obligation to responsibility which creates a reciprocal form of authenticity, an authenticity of 'being-for-the-other' rather than for oneself (1998: 213). Signifying not for or as itself but for another, the authentic self for Levinas establishes a form '"otherwise than being" ... consuming the bases of any position for oneself and any substantialization which would take form in this consummation' (1981: 50). The self, like the notion of authenticity proposed in this study, can only meaningfully and ethically exist outside the realm of definite meaning, in a position beyond essence, in a state of essential paradox.

Dissimilar as these different approaches to selfhood might be, they agree that the relationship between self and authenticity, the internal tension that makes up a supposedly authentic self, is circular and contradictory. Logical rules of cause and effect do not apply, as the notion of an autonomous self and subjective authenticity presuppose one another and bring each other into being. They are functions of one another. Following Levinas, I would therefore propose to describe authenticity as emerging in the interplay of self and other. It is due to this transitional and ambiguous position that authenticity has attained such a central place in attempts to describe the (post)postmodern condition. In its ontological undecidability and epistemological ambiguity, it mirrors many of the positions traditionally bestowed on postmodern discourse. At the same time, however, it is frequently invoked as a solution or answer to postmodern discontents such as simulation, casualness or lack of conviction. In the following thesis I will take a closer look at some of the epistemological and aesthetic constructions behind such invocations.

Thesis four: Authenticity is both the antithesis to postmodern simulation and the ultimate simulacrum itself

After the previous thesis has retraced various symbolic representations of and quests for the authentic self, this thesis now attempts to explore the relationship of authenticity and postmodernism in more detail. Following on from my argument that authenticity can be construed to both embody central tenets of postmodern discourse *and* to eventually overcome them, I will first present a summary of the postmodern discontents and anxieties which authenticity is habitually invoked against. Crucial here is the lament that it has become impossible to penetrate the ubiquitous layers of symbolic representations and simulations which nowadays apparently occlude reality and overwhelm the human cognitive facilities. Due to its connotations of originality and irreducibility, authenticity lends itself as a notional counterpoint in this regard. One of the key features of the postmodern period is the inescapability of theories and practices of consumption which affect virtually every aspect of personal and cultural experience. I will focus on this particular aspect of postmodern authenticity by juxtaposing its claims to genuineness with the subtle

– and sometimes not quite so subtle – ways in which authenticity itself is advertised and marketed as a commodity in the postmodern cultural logic of late capitalism as described by Jameson.

It is a commonplace of postmodern wisdom to assert that the wood of reality has been obscured for good by the trees of representation. The project of structuralism, starting with de Saussure's observations on the inherent and essential arbitrariness of the linguistic sign, later extended to and utilized in other contexts by Lacan (psychoanalysis), Lévi-Strauss (anthropology) or Barthes (semiotics in general and myth in particular), is brought to its logical conclusion by Derrida and Baudrillard. The former stipulates the structural impossibility of transcendent signification in an indeterminate process of reference called *différance* (see Derrida 1973, 1978, 1982), thereby creating, quite against his own conviction one would assume, one of the most pervasive *grands récits* of postmodern theory. Baudrillard goes even further by overturning the hierarchy of reality and representation, of original and copy, in his claim that the real itself has been reduced to an aesthetic effect. He assumes, in fact, that 'we are now living entirely within the "aesthetic" hallucination of reality' (1993: 74). He refutes the logic of representation as such, as it 'stems from the principle of the equivalence of the sign and the real' (1994: 6), an equivalence which no longer applies. Quite the contrary, the idea of representation has been aberrantly used to 'conceal ... the fact that the real is no longer real' (13). In its stead, Baudrillard establishes a regime and an aesthetics of simulation, that is, 'of substituting the signs of the real for the real' (2). The resultant hyperreality is characterized by its detachedness from first causes and clear references; it is free-floating and radically self-referential. It consists merely in 'the generation by models of a real without origin or reality' (1). In view of Dave Eggers's use of metareference, it is important to note that one of the main distinctions between the real and the hyperreal for Baudrillard is the existence and absence, respectively, of an imaginary interspace, a distance between the real and its representation, which shrouds the real in mystery. The hyperreal, in contrast, collapses this distance, as it is 'produced from a radiating synthesis of combinatory models in a hyperspace without atmosphere' (2). Employing Lacanian terminology, one could summarize that the real can only manifest itself in the contingencies of the imaginary rather than in the abstractions of the symbolic.

Baudrillard's ideas have become a staple feature in descriptions of *la condition postmoderne* and have been taken up, reformulated and developed further by numerous theorists. Often they are merely cited as the knock-out argument to corroborate postmodernism's alleged superficiality and relativism, its infamous dictum of 'anything goes', which can be employed to reduce any symbolic system to a Humpty-Dumptian regime of epistemological solipsism. If this were indeed the case, two contradictory deductions could be drawn: either symbolic representation has ceased to play any significant part at all in the field of human experience or, conversely, symbolic representation is indeed all we will ever get to know about this experience. Either way, any external truth value of symbolic representation has forever been relegated beyond our ken. Timothy Bewes highlights the paradox that the devaluation of representation as proclaimed by Baudrillard ultimately results from the ever increasing accuracy of our technological means of reproduction. He argues that 'as our *representations* attain an ever higher degree of definition, so the signifier is increasingly taken to be the thing itself' and infers that 'society has reached a point beyond which nothing is true' (1997: 55; emphasis in the original). In his excellent study on virtuality and identity, Scott Bukatman provides a succinct summary of the semiotic implications of Baudrillard's insights, which lead to 'the simultaneous over- and undervaluation of sign systems at a time when the sign *is* everything but *stands for* nothing' (1993: 106; emphases in the original). According to Daniel Boorstin, this state of affairs is in direct consequence of the economic and cultural conditions that have shaped the Western world: 'The world of our making, how we have used our wealth, our literacy, our technology, and our progress,' he argues, 'create a thicket of unreality which stands between us and the facts of life' (1985: 3). Simulation, in other words, is intrinsic to our increasingly technological rapport with our environment. It is a symptom of decadence and dissolution with the potential to support and at the same time disrupt postmodern delusions of (hyper)reality. Hillel Schwartz puts this rather pithily when he states that 'the more adroit we are at carbon copies, the more confused we are about the unique, the original, the Real McCoy' (1996: 11).

There are, of course, too many illustrations of this tenuous relationship of reality and representation than could be reasonably analysed in the space of this study. Cases in point cover the range from multilayered films like Spike Jonze's *Adaptation* (2002) or Charlie Kaufman's *Synecdoche, New York* (2008) to the inanities of 'reality television', a self-evident terminological contradiction which has, nevertheless, ceased to confound nowadays. The virtualization of reality, which resonates in the concept of simulation, affects how we perceive the world and ourselves, as the diversification of identities and profiles facilitated by online media environments such as Facebook, World of Warcraft or Second Life attests. In thesis five I will investigate in more detail the question of how this transformed environment forces a revaluation of the relationship of reality and representation and consequently a renegotiation of the notion of authenticity. At this point, I will merely introduce two concepts to illustrate and pinpoint some of the questions and issues raised by this renegotiation of what exactly the word 'reality' refers to.

Originally written in 1961, Boorstin's book *The Image: A Guide to Pseudo-Events in America* very much anticipates Baudrillard's simulations of hyperreality. It foreshadows not only many aspects of Baudrillard's radical critique of the reliability of images but also prefigures the fusion of information and entertainment which facilitated the rise of political spin. Boorstin claims that the American citizen 'lives in a world where fantasy is more real than reality, where the image has more dignity than its original' (1985: 37). American life, he argues, is shaped and inspired to such an extent by media representations that only those events can attain realness which are staged and performed for media consumption. These so-called 'pseudo-events' are chiefly characterized by their lack of spontaneity, as they are 'planted primarily for the immediate purpose of being reported or reproduced' (11). The images that make up such a pseudo-event pose as real but are set up to conform to the standards of media representation and consumption – a dramatic setting and story arc, easy dissemination or repeatability at any times, with the consequence that their 'relation to the underlying reality of the situation is ambiguous' (ibid.). In fact, they annul the distinction of real and fictional, of true and false, as the easy availability and high recognition value of such pseudo-events ensures the precedence of the image over reality: 'The very same advances which have made them possible have also made the images – however planned, contrived, or distorted – more vivid, more attractive, more impressive, and more persuasive than reality itself' (36). As in the case of Baudrillard, the question about what is real and what is not has been made insignificant by the all-encompassing hyperreality of the image: 'Fact or fantasy, the image becomes the thing. Its very purpose is to overshadow reality. American life becomes a showcase for images. For frozen pseudo-events' (197).[13]

The relevance of Boorstin's ideas for an analysis of authenticity is self-evident. If one accepts the rough and ready understanding of an authentic image as one anchored in and referring to an indisputable aspect of external reality, then one must concede that the American way of life and representation as portrayed by Boorstin is profoundly and irretrievably inauthentic. One of the main objectives of the novels I will analyse later on is to provide an aesthetic procedure with which to reclaim or reconstruct the contingency and spontaneity of experience from and against the heteronomy of the staged (pseudo-)event.

Around the year 1980 the innocent English word 'spin' acquired a new connotation, which the *OED* has listed since its 1993 edition as 'a bias or slant on information, intended to create a favourable impression when it is presented to the public; an interpretation or viewpoint' ('spin, *n.*1' 2014). This new meaning entails a practical application of Boorstin's and Baudrillard's theories to the area of politics and information management. Reality, in this interpretation, no longer consists of factual events and situations to which politicians react accordingly. What is considered as real, rather, is a particular set of images and information which can be created, assembled and fabricated from the vast reservoir of actions, images, opinions and statistics on offer. The most infamous acknowledgement of this new spin on reality is found in an article for the *New York Times Magazine* where journalist Ron Suskind recounts an interview with an aide to President George W. Bush – identified later as Karl Rove by Mark Danner (see 2007: 17) – who utters the memorable words that

> guys like me were 'in what we call the reality-based community' which he defined as people who 'believe that solutions emerge from your judicious study of discernible reality' ... 'That's not the way the world really works anymore. We are an empire now, and when we act, *we create our own reality*. And while you're studying this reality – judiciously, as you will – we'll act again, creating other new realities, which you can study too and that's how things will sort out.

---

[13] It is not only Boorstin's analysis of the pseudo-event that makes for eerily topical reading today. In one fell swoop, he also dismisses the concept of 'celebrity', on which so much of today's culture industry seems to rely. He unmasks the celebrity person as a 'human pseudo-event ... fabricated on purpose to satisfy our exaggerated expectations of human greatness' and very elegantly exposes the logic underlying this concept as circular, since a celebrity is 'a person who is known for his well-knownness' (1985: 57–8).

We're history's actors ... and you, all of you, will be left to just study what we do.'
(Suskind 2004; emphasis added)

In this view, political discourse is no longer based on a 'judicious study of discernible reality' but on the absoluteness of personal convictions and the capacity to present these convictions as incontrovertible and general truth.

In the pilot episode of his satirical news show *The Colbert Report*, comedian Stephen Colbert uses the term 'truthiness' to describe this faith-based approach to truth and reality. For Steven Poole, the practice of linguistic spin doctoring, which he calls 'Unspeak', comes close to the worst of Orwell's dystopian predictions. He infers its success from the media's 'inbuilt structural bias towards the snappy phrase, the soundbite' (2006: 8). In his book on *The Decline and Fall of Truth from 9/11 to Katrina*, Frank Rich investigates the causes of this public revaluation of truth. He finds them primarily in a transformed media environment, which he blames for obscuring the categories of information and entertainment, paving the way for, indeed even necessitating, an amalgamation of fiction and reality. He claims that 'only an overheated 24/7 infotainment culture that had trivialized the very idea of reality (and with it, what once was known as "news") could be so successfully manipulated by those in power' (2006: 2–3), arguing further that 'in this new mediathon environment ... definable distinctions between truth and fiction were blurred more than ever before, as "reality" was redefined in news and prime-time entertainment alike' (225). It could be regarded as a particularly piquant case of historical irony that it took the Republican President Bush and his administration to demonstrate the practical applicability of postmodern theories.[14]

In view of the apparent inadequacy of signs to refer to reality, I will argue that one primary function of art nowadays must be the thorough disclosure of such strategies and mechanisms of 'second-order reasoning' as exemplified by the pseudo-event and political spin (cf. Baecker 1994; Luhmann 1993, 1999). This can be achieved through an excessive employment of self-referentiality, which reveals, by way of ironic re-enactment, these undercurrents. A similar point is made by Adorno in the *Aesthetic Theory*, where he claims that in 'the authentic artwork what is dominated – which finds expression by way of the dominating principle – is the counterpoint to the domination of what is natural or material. This dialectical relationship results in the truth content of artworks' (2013: 381). It is, in other words, only by infiltrating – and perhaps dispersing – the layers of simulation through aesthetic and epistemological self-awareness that one can address the question of whether notions like reality or first-order reasoning are (still) tenable, or if there is indeed nothing left to base anything on and *il n'y a pas dehors-simulation*.

I have already pointed out that authenticity has often been construed to be located outside or beyond conventional systems of representation. The mode in which authenticity has to be pursued is therefore necessarily one of penetration, of invasion, maybe even a quest for Adorno's notorious true life within a false system. Authenticity, in

---

[14] For more in-depth analysis on the shaky relationship of truth and power in early twenty-first-century American politics, see also Bennett, Lawrence and Livingston (2007) and Danner (2007).

short, is that which 'lures us on' (Schwartz 1996: 373). In this configuration, the authentic self as a constructed aspiration and ideal is pitted against the forces of dissimulation. In the words of Schwartz, 'we must reconstruct, not abandon, an ideal of authenticity in our lives' (117). Zygmunt Bauman is one of the key proponents of this view. In *The Art of Life* he demands with remarkable directness that 'fraudulent or botched selves need to be discarded on the grounds of their "non-authenticity", while the search for the real one should go on' (2008: 15). Mirroring Ferrara and Guignon, he claims elsewhere that it is exactly the loss of real reference through ubiquitous postmodern simulation which facilitates a resurrection of an authenticity founded on 'individuals ... thrown back on their own subjectivity as the ultimate ethic authority' (1992: xxii). It would be, after all, 'quixotic to debunk the distortion in the representation of reality once no reality claims to be more real than its representation' (viii). Bauman concludes that the uncertainty and radical scepticism that the postmodern condition induces is 'the natural habitat of human life' (2008: 20). Taking up Max Weber's influential terminology, he reimagines 'postmodernity ... as restoring to the world what modernity, presumptuously, had taken away; as a *re-enchantment* of the world that modernity tried hard to *dis-enchant*' (1992: x; emphases in the original). He argues that we must learn to think of reality in a new way, and it is ultimately only in and as art – authentic art in Adorno's sense – that this novel conception of reality can be traced. When Bauman declares that 'our lives ... are works of art' (2008: 20), he in effect proposes an amalgamation of the three distinct forms of authenticity as described by Knaller. Authenticity can only emerge when the self is imagined in and as an aesthetic object.

It is quite in keeping with postmodern logic that there is always one more turn of the screw possible. It is, therefore, equally imaginable to conceive of authenticity not as a corrective to simulation but as an effect of it and to dismiss it as an altogether hopelessly naïve illusion. In a development of Baudrillard's conception of the simulacrum as a copy without an original, Norbert Bolz argues that it is only the always already reflective nature of contemporary mediascapes that calls up a yearning for an authentic reality (see 2004: 101). Bewes adds another intriguing twist by imagining the layers of simulation that engulf postmodern subjects and objects as part of a specific postmodern aura, and thus of a specifically postmodern authenticity in the sense of Benjamin: 'This perceptible urge towards nakedness and clarity, towards the purity of the thing itself rather than its symbolic representation or its corrupt imitation, constitutes a progressive and systematic mass cultural stripping-away of the aura from the object' (1997: 51). Any attempt to locate or construct a genuine self behind the simulation would in this understanding result in the loss of authenticity. Only the simulated is really authentic. It seems that again the only aspect of authenticity which eludes the indeterminate play of signification and simulation is its essential paradoxicality.

There is, of course, one eventuality which can finally and ultimately sublate any possibility of simulation and paradox: death. In Jean Améry's opinion, death represents 'the only truth that, like the God of the faithful, encompasses all contradiction in itself and cancels them in its embrace' (1999: 109). As I have shown in the preceding thesis, both Heidegger's and Levinas's conception of authenticity derive from the incommensurability of death, from the impossibility to integrate death – one's own and the other's, respectively – into any system of representation. Baudrillard likewise bemoans that death has been banished beyond the realm of any symbolic exchange, that it has been 'thrown out of [the] symbolic circulation' (1993: 126). It is after all the sure fact of death which infuses human experience with its ontological, epistemological and aesthetic dimension. Because of the ultimate otherness and unrepresentability of death, however, this meaning of life is always defective, an endless process, a quest – or as Critchley puts it: 'If there can be no phenomenology or representation of death because it is a state of affairs about which I can find neither an adequate intention nor intuitive fulfilment, then *the ultimate meaning of human finitude is that we cannot find meaningful fulfilment for the finite*' (1997: 31; emphasis in the original).

The singularity of death and its paradoxical status as both essentially mine (Heidegger's *Jemeinigkeit*; see also Hanlon 2004: 514–20) and radically other forces transcendence on the human imagination and creates 'an opening onto a metaphenomenological alterity, irreducible to the power of the Subject, the will or *Dasein*' (Critchley 1997: 87). Huber and Seita point out the reciprocal and indeed circular nature of this relationship when they describe the 'desperate desire for authenticity [as] a deep longing for death', while at the same time establishing death as 'the ultimate Other that guarantees authentic experience' (2012: 274). It is in this projection of transcendence that the idea of authenticity connects with death. Paradoxically, both can only signify in and through their incomprehensibility. In a postmodern framework, it is therefore only in the ultimate singularity of death that experience and representation connect.

Postmodern theory has variously been regarded, most famously by Jameson, as the cultural and theoretical underpinning for the neoliberal regime of consumer capitalism which has reigned supreme in the Western world since at least the 1990s. The renunciation of genuine images and stable identifications for superficial simulations and virtual identities undoubtedly plays into the hands of a system which is reliant on an economy of literally consumptive self-realization, where the value of a person or an object appears to be coextensive with its price. Bauman drily observes that 'being an individual in the society of individuals costs money – a lot of money' (2000: 25), and Baudrillard emphasizes how the iterative logic of production and reproduction facilitates the advancement of hyperreality:

> The very definition of the real is *that of which it is possible to provide an equivalent reproduction*. It is a contemporary of science, which postulates that a process can be reproduced exactly within given conditions, with an industrial rationality which postulates a universal system of equivalences ... At the end of this process of reproducibility, the real is not only that which can be reproduced, but *that which is always already reproduced*: the hyperreal. (1993: 73; emphases in the original)

If this logic of production, reproduction and consumption really is that pervasive, then it should come as no surprise that it can also easily appropriate and exploit the notion of authenticity itself by construing it as a commodity, by marketing the irreducibility of the self as a desirable and indispensable lifestyle accessory. It is once again Bauman who pointedly illuminates the logic underlying this process:

> In a society of individuals desperately seeking their individuality there is no shortage of certified and/or self-proclaimed helpers who (at the right price, of course) will be all too willing to guide us into the dark dungeons of our souls where our authentic selves are supposed to stay imprisoned and from where they are struggling to escape into the light. (2000: 17)

Its protean character and its essential resistance to unambiguity make authenticity prone to such (mis)appropriation and ensure that imaginaries of authenticity can be integrated into the structural desires of consumer capitalism without too much friction. In her excellent study on *Consuming Traditions*, Elizabeth Outka locates the origins of what she calls the 'commodified authentic' at the turn of the twentieth century, when 'marketers began to focus less on a particular object for sale at a particular price, and more on aura and setting, promising consumers not single products but new identities and new ways to live' (2009: 7–8). Jörn Lamla emphasizes how authenticity as a commodity is an effect of the specific symbolic frame of reference of market economies (see 2009: 323), and Zeller insists that constructions of authenticity have themselves become a very lucrative commodity (see 2010: 287, 324). Bewes even refers to a 'fetishization of authenticity', citing the popularity of 'real life' drama on TV as a case in point (see 1997: 50), while Andrew Potter sees the contemporary quest for authenticity as no more than 'a disguised form of status-seeking, the principal effect of which is to generate resentment among others' (2010: 15). It is symptomatic of the inseparable association of authenticity with notions of selfhood that the commodification of authenticity also necessarily implies a conception of the self as essentially tradable and profit-oriented. Lindholm explains in this context how the 'consumption of various forms of commodified authenticity has provided these anxious buyers with feelings of autonomy, control, community, as well as feelings of distinction, status, and self-actualization in a risky and anonymous society' (2008: 64).

In summary, the relationship of authenticity and postmodern theories is one of mutual and concurrent appropriation and evasion. Constructions and imaginations of authenticity can at one and the same time be set up as the negation *and* the epitome of simulation and consumer capitalism. The authentic self is at once the transcendent inaccessible other of postmodern superficiality and its *raison d'être*. In the following thesis I will now expand on the relationship between authenticity and cultural discourses in the wake of postmodernism by focusing on the specific changes to the media environment of the recent past and present that have forced a renegotiation of what it means for a human subject or a work of art to be perceived as authentic.

Thesis five: Recent media transformations necessitate a rethinking of authenticity

The dissociation of reality and (its) representation which characterizes much of postmodern theory is mirrored in the development of the communicative patterns which have accompanied it. Just as the rise of printing had inaugurated a period of logocentrism and the virtually automatic authority of the written or printed word, the spread of computation-based forms of knowledge acquisition and interaction around the turn of the twenty-first century, from email to social networks and from Google to copy-and-paste, is having fundamental reverberations on many aspects of human self-perception. Key among these is a universal acceptance of the constructedness of reality, as reality in the digital age increasingly becomes accessible only in the form of mediated information and can thus ultimately be reduced to a sequence of binary code. Bukatman claims that digital technology necessarily entails 'a loss of representation, a loss of the object, and finally, a lost relationship to the real. What we regard as "reality" stands revealed as a construction – a provisional and malleable alignment of data' (1993: 30). One consequence of this 'lost relationship to the real' is the inauguration of a new space of signification, one that 'exists parallel to, but outside of, the geographic topography of experiential reality' (105). This new realm of signification and interaction has no central point of gravity anymore because it fragments 'the world into a billion personalized truths, each seemingly equally valid and worthwhile' (Keen 2007: 17). It represents, in Jameson's words, 'a subjectivity which is objective' (2005: 21). While Jameson refers to this 'enclave of a new sort' as 'cyberspace', I will use the term 'virtual reality' for this technologically created sphere of interaction, in order to emphasize its ambiguous status with regard to reality and simulation.

In his programmatically titled book *Holding on to Reality*, Albert Borgmann shows persuasively how the specific framework of the medium in which information is communicated has direct consequences for the image of reality generated by means of this information. Borgmann asserts that once 'the paradigmatic carrier of information is neither a natural thing or a cultural text, but a technological device, a stream of electrons conveying bits of information' (1999: 2), this kind of digital information opens up a new perspective on traditional concepts of reality. He reminds the reader of the etymological origin of the word 'information', that is, 'to impose form on something' and claims that 'to information *about* and *for* reality [digital information] adds *information as reality*' (2; emphases in the original). It might seem all too obvious to cite the enormous influence of social networks like Facebook or Twitter as relevant cases in point here. There is, however, no denying that the reality as communicated through the images, texts and connections of one's online personality is the effect of digital mediation and is therefore in Borgmann's terms 'both more transparent and less heavy' than the reality of immediate experience and direct interaction (216). Borgmann's personal evaluation of this state of affairs is evident. Although he acknowledges the obvious appeal and charm of this 'preternaturally bright and controllable quality of cyberspace [which] makes real things look poor and recalcitrant in comparison', he very much takes up the cudgels for the indubitable existence of non-digitalized reality, which for him 'remains inescapable and unfathomable'. He assumes an almost prophetic tone and augurs that 'we are stunting and ignoring this ancestral attunement to reality at our peril' (220). He warns that this version of reality *lite* as generated by digital information is sincerely defective when it comes to moral convictions and truths, which are too complex to be represented simply in terms of binary code. Seen in this light, the penetration of the superficial layers of virtual reality becomes imbued with an ethical imperative, as 'the material vigour and splendour of reality will rest on … our ability to respond to it' (221).

The prospect of penetrating this virtual reality has arguably become much bleaker since the publication of Borgmann's book in 1999. The introduction of Facebook's Timeline feature enables a virtual synchronization of life and its online representation, thus in fact matching the contingent reality of direct experience with its digital image. In an article for German weekly *Die Zeit*, Thomas Assheuer even envisions the dawn of a new episteme he calls 'platonism 2.0', in which existence itself is defined exclusively by its representability in terms of digitalized information, where the world is reduced to that which Google reveals about it (14 October 2010: 41). Sherry Turkle paints a similarly gloomy picture in her book *Alone Together*, where she outlines the consequences of a society addicted to technologically enhanced experience. One is that there will be a point where 'performances of identity may feel like identity itself' (2011: 12). In an adaptation of Ludwig Wittgenstein's famous dictum, one could conclude that in the digital age the world is no longer that which is the case but that which is online.

Against these predictions of doom, Frank J. Tipler puts a positive, or at least redemptive, spin on the potential impact of digitalized information. With his considerations about the 'Omega Point', he massively extends the focus of the topic to take in an eschatological dimension. In a nutshell, Tipler envisages a point in time where the technological capacities to store information will be infinite. This, in turn, means that it will be possible to simulate the entirety of the known world, since its inception in the Big Bang and encompassing every organism ever to dwell on earth, in the form of digitalized information. In Tipler's more refined explanation, this point will be reached when 'the amount of processed information between now and [a] future c-boundary is infinite in the region of spacetime with which the worldline γ can communicate; that is, the region inside the past light cone of γ' (1995: 133). At this particular point, which Tipler following Teilhard de Chardin calls the Omega Point, the physical universe will disintegrate into a gravitational singularity in which laws of space-time no longer apply. The Omega Point eliminates the difference of reality and representation as it is 'the completion of finite reality, and hence includes all finite reality' (188). Experience will only survive in the abstract form of representation, that is, as information computed on the infinitesimal particles left in the singularity. Only in this digitalized shape and form will reality and representations be infinite, a state Tipler describes as 'social immortality' (217). In a rather bold move he therefore equates the Omega Point with notions of 'the afterlife hoped for by the great world religions' (269), since both comprise features such as eternal duration, immortality and the resurrection of the dead.

Kirby paints an altogether different picture of the interconnected and virtual world in which we live and signify today. Like Bukatman, he senses the inception of a new era of signification, which he calls 'digimodernism'. This new paradigm, he explains, 'owes its emergence and pre-eminence to the computerization of text, which yields a new form of textuality characterized in its purest instances by onwardness, haphazardness, evanescence, and anonymous, social and multiple authorship' (2009: 1) and results in a radical reconfiguration of textual authority, with the recipient of any cultural text being endowed with their own creative authority. This revaluation of textual authority and the concurrent shift in interpretative responsibility is of crucial importance for the narratological analyses that follow. It should also be noted that it is precisely the apparent dissociation of a digitally mediated, 'virtual' reality from the analogous experience of 'real' life which makes metareference a valid aesthetic strategy to illustrate the authenticity of the self in art. Digitalization, as Winfried Nöth convincingly argues, 'contributed to the increase of self-reference. No longer originating in a world which leaves its documentary traces on the negatives of a film, the pictures of the new media have become the result of digital imaging and art work, whose origin is the software of the semiotic machines by means of which they are produced' (2007: 3).

The new possibilities of self-expression promised by virtual reality have been considered both a threat and a chance for its users, as they potentially take away from and add to conceptions of the self. Both positive and negative views result from the insight that the shift of much of human interaction into a virtual space causes a blurring of boundaries between the self and the other as prescribed by traditional parameters such as corporality and an exact location in time and space. Jeffrey Sconce asserts in this context that 'electronic telecommunications have compelled citizens of the media age to reconsider increasingly disassociative relationships among body, mind, space, and time' (2000: 7), and Bukatman underlines the close connections of virtual reality with postmodern notions about simulation:

> Such ontological and epistemological issues as the nature of the human, the real, experience, sensation, cognition, identity, and gender are all placed, if not under erasure, then certainly in question around the discursive object of virtual reality and the postulated existence of perfect, simulated environments. Virtual reality has become the very embodiment of postmodern *disembodiment*. (1993: 188; emphasis in the original)

In his study *Becoming Besides Ourselves*, Brian Rotman introduces the term 'para-self' for this ambiguous state of disembodied embodiment, which he defines as 'an embodied agent increasingly defined by the networks threading through it, and experiencing itself (notwithstanding the ubiquitous computer screen interface) as much through touch as vision, through tactile, gestural, and haptic means as it navigates itself through informational space'. One of the essential features of this para-self is that it cannot be reduced to an unalienable, singular and monolithic core, since 'it is internally heterogeneous and multiple, and, like the computational and imaging technologies mediating it, its behavior is governed by parallel protocols and rhythms – performing and forming itself through many actions and perceptions at once – as against doing or being one thing at a time on a sequential, predominantly endogenous, itinerary' (2008: 8). Kenneth J. Gergen provides another label for this decentred and fractioned conception of the self. In his book *The Saturated Self*, he criticizes how any configuration of selfhood in postmodernism is never accepted as an end in itself but only ever serves as a means to an end. This results in a state he calls 'multiphrenia', a 'splitting of the individual into a multiplicity of self-investments' (1991: 73–4). The plural, porous, immersive and multiphrenic para-self envisioned by Rotman and Gergen can only come into existence in the very act of mediation and communication, and thus can be said to stand in direct logical opposition to traditional notions of the authentic self as precisely that which eludes and resists systems of representation.

In keeping with his Cassandra calls about the moral insufficiency of virtual reality, Borgmann deduces from this alleged loss of authenticity disastrous consequences for the individual's ability to know itself. Technological information, so he ruminates,

> has infected our sense of identity with doubt and despair. Are my tangible traits just so much noise that distorts the true message of my self? Is my ethereal Internet self the genuine me, freed from the accidents of my place, class and looks? Or is it a flimsy and truant version of what, for better or worse, I am actually and substantially? (1999: 4–5)

Bauman expresses similar anxieties when he claims that 'it is the widespread characteristic of contemporary men and women in our type of society that they live perpetually with the "identity problem" unsolved. They suffer, one might say, from a chronic absence of resources with which they can build a truly solid and lasting identity, anchor it and stop it from drifting' (1997: 26). If one accepts Doležel's assumption that 'to exist actually is to exist independently of semiotic representation; to exist fictionally means to exist as a possible constructed by semiotic means' (1998: 145), there is the clear and present danger that human experience might soon be regarded as entirely fictional and not grounded in a relationship with external reality any more.[15] One upshot of this could be that humankind becomes relegated to a zombie-like state of disintegrating self-awareness, or as Sconce puts it, that 'where there was once stable human consciousness, there are now only the ghosts of fragmented, decentered, and increasingly schizophrenic subjectivities' (2000: 170–1).

While Sconce explicitly links these new subjectivities with ideas of the uncanny – the title of his book talks of *Haunted Media* and *Electronic Presence* – Bukatman chooses the metaphor of the cyborg, an organism which consists of organic as well as

---

[15] That this claim carries with it not only aesthetic but also potentially existential implications becomes evident in Jorge Luis Borges's famous musing about the doubling of ontological layers in literature in his essay 'Partial Magic in the *Quixote*': 'Why does it disturb us that Don Quixote be a reader of the *Quixote* and Hamlet a spectator of *Hamlet*? I believe I have found the reason: these inversions suggest that if the characters of a fictional work can be readers or spectators, we, its readers or spectators, can be fictitious' (1964: 196).

artificial parts, to describe the human subject(ivitie)s interpellated by virtual reality: 'The body must become a cyborg to retain its presence in the world, resituated in technological space and refigured in technological terms. Whether this represents a continuation, a sacrifice, a transcendence, or a surrender of "the subject" is not certain' (1993: 247). He stresses the paradigm shift inherent in this 'terminal identity' (a term he appropriates from William Burroughs), which can denote both 'the end of the subject and a new subjectivity constructed at the computer station or television screen' (9). When Sconce summarizes his exploration of the eerie side of electronic identity, he offers a similarly undecided outlook. He claims that 'whether electronic media and spectatorship represent the "death" of human subjectivity (in the annihilating simulations of television) or its magical "rebirth" (in the ever expanding architecture of cyberspace), both accounts draw vividly on the uncanny animating presence so long perceived in electronic media' (2000: 172).

In the same book, however, Sconce also puts forward an argument for the liberating potential inherent in virtual reality. Also influenced by Donna Haraway's seminal feminist appropriation of the cyborg metaphor, he celebrates the redemptive promises of virtuality, as 'technology allows one to escape traditional (and now increasingly boring) social markers of gender, sexuality, race, age, and class to fashion entirely new identities' (Sconce 2000: 203). He waxes lyrical about the liberating potential of this brave new cyborg world, claiming that 'electronic postmodernity is no longer a lamentable "condition", but is instead a hip and exciting lifestyle in which those who are willing to shed the illusion of the "human" will be rewarded in the emancipating splendor of techno-bodies and the enlightened consciousness of "virtual subjectivity"' (202).

On which side of this argument one eventually comes down seems to be a direct consequence of one's understanding of what an authentic human self actually is. If one shares Borgmann's neo-Romantic conviction that the self is the unalienable and ultimately unrepresentable core of human consciousness, then it follows almost inevitably that the de-essentialized and insubstantial subjectivities floating through cyberspace attest to the cataclysmic threat presented by virtual reality and to a complete displacement of the analogous by the digital. If, on the other hand, one adheres to Bewes's view that the self is always already a symbolic representation, a construction which is necessarily unstable with regard to time, space and bodily manifestation, then one must welcome the unlimited possibilities for ever-new identity configurations facilitated by virtual reality. It is beyond the ken of any literary and cultural analysis to justify the privilege of one response over the other, as this ultimately falls under the authority of philosophy, sociology or theology. What I can and will do, however, is explore how this antagonism is recreated and re-enacted in aesthetic terms.

One major consequence of the technological innovations outlined above is the blurring, if not elimination, of the boundaries of certain areas of demarcation and definition, for example between human being and machine (cyborg) or between information *about* reality and information *as* reality (simulation). I will now focus my attention on one concept in particular which is massively scrutinized in the prevalent media environment: the notion of authorship and textual/narrative authority. If, as Sconce maintains, the digital self can indeed only be represented or narrated as fragmented and decentred, then the idea of an author as an absolute entity overseeing and ordering this representation makes little sense. The claim about the end of authorship has long figured as a staple feature of postmodern thinking, phrased most influentially by Foucault (1977) and Barthes (1978), and does not need to be further elaborated at this point. I will focus instead on a logical supplement to this statement, that is, the rise of what Timothy Jacobs calls a 'participatory aesthetics' (2001: 226) and what Henry Jenkins refers to as a 'participatory culture' (2006). Jacobs adopts the idea about the infinite malleability of the human self in virtual reality and applies it to the description and analysis of works of art. Both can only signify, Jacobs argues, if they are constructed from a radically subjective perspective. He claims that 'an artifact lives when it is adopted by active readers who transform it into their own *mythos*' (2001: 226; emphasis in the original). This aesthetics of participation can be incorporated into a wider framework of an escalating ethos of sharing and involvement that made possible such defining manifestations of contemporary culture as Wikipedia, YouTube or the ubiquitous blogosphere. Already back in the 1970s, biologist Francisco J. Varela foresaw the potential of participation for the area of knowledge acquisition. He declared 'knowledge and reality [to be] participatory' and relative, implying that 'a useful perspective does not require an objective, solid ground to which everything can be finally pinned down' (1979: xvi, xvii). Varela explains further that this regime is founded on the essential subjectivity of reality and discerns an 'immense potential for systems to carve their own reality and be rendered viable, without being unique and without representing a stable given world' (277).

The issue of a postmodern decline of any notion of definite interpretative authority cannot be reduced to the deterioration of the author function alone. Another concept challenged by the rise of an aesthetics of participation is that of the authority of knowledge and truth as such, or more precisely the authentication of truth and knowledge. If everybody can contribute to the cultural output without being checked or edited, how is it then possible to assess the relevance and validity of the individual statement? In his book *The Cult of the Amateur*, Andrew Keen decries both the loss of reliable expertise and a form of 'digital narcissism' (2007: ix), which he sees abetted by a so-called 'democratization [of] media, information, knowledge, content, audience, author' through the participatory epistemology of the Web 2.0 (14). Keen reveals 'the noble abstraction behind the digital revolution [as] that of the *noble amateur*' (35; emphasis in the original) in an environment where 'the crowd has become the authority on what is true and what is not' (92).

Keen's argument is directed at theorists such as Kevin Kelly, who celebrates the egalitarianism and ready availability of knowledge in this 'single liquid fabric of interconnected words and ideas' that is the Web 2.0. Discussing Google's plan to assemble a universal library from all books available in print, Kelly ventures an optimistic outlook as to the economic consequences of this system of reproduced cultural content. 'In a regime of superabundant free copies, copies lose value,' he argues. Information and knowledge can thus no longer be regarded as commodities or as the currency of Bourdieu's famous *capital culturel*. Instead, he foresees a cultural environment which is essentially based on partaking and contribution, where 'relationships, links, connections and sharing' will be 'the basis of wealth' and where with the 'deep structuring of knowledge comes a new culture of interaction and participation' (2006). For Keen, this is utopian wishful thinking. He sees the reality of Web 2.0 interaction as characterized predominantly by the triumph of superficiality over essence and an increasing solipsism. In terms reminiscent of Borgmann's lament over the loss of a genuine self in virtual reality, he declares that 'one chilling reality in this brave new digital epoch is the blurring, obfuscation, and even disappearance of truth' (Keen 2007: 16), as 'our knowledge – about everything from politics, to current affairs, to literature, to science – is being shaped by nothing but the aggregation of responses' (93). Moreover, he denounces the dialogical nature of this participatory endeavour as a mere illusion, because the possibility for everyone to express themselves about anything all the time will only lead to a digitally enhanced form of solipsism and navel-gazing which forecloses any real dialogue with dissenting voices, because 'the only conversations we want to hear are those with ourselves and those like us' (55). Keen's dim view of contemporary cultures of participation is shared by Nicholas G. Carr, who argues that the structure of the Web 2.0 has adverse effects on our cognitive abilities in terms of memory capacity and attention span. In tune with those who are sceptical about the ways the new media influence our potential for self-awareness, he argues that 'in Google's world, the world we enter when we go online, there's little place for the fuzziness of contemplation. Ambiguity is not an opening for insight but a bug to be fixed. The human brain is just an outdated computer that needs a faster processor and a bigger hard drive' (2008). Jaron Lanier, an erstwhile pioneer of virtual reality, makes a similar case when he warns of an 'ideal of the intellectual mob rule' disguised as wisdom of the crowd and exposes the circular logic of what he calls 'digital Maoism [which] overwhelmingly rewards the one preferred hierarchy of digital metaness, in which a mashup is more important than the sources that are mashed up' (2010: 144, 79).

If one accepts Jameson's argument about postmodernism as the cultural logic of (late) capitalism, then it is hardly surprising that a paradigm of cultural participation can very efficiently be described in economical terminology. In 1980, Alvin Toffler coined the term 'prosumerism' to designate what he predicted to be the economic future of Western society. Toffler initially uses the term to describe a pre-industrial society, which he calls the First Wave, where 'most people consumed what they themselves produced [and] were neither producers nor consumers in the usual sense' (1980: 277). It is only with the dissociation of production and consumption brought about through industrialism (the Second Wave) that the division into producers and consumers becomes significant. Toffler is convinced, however, that this division will collapse once again as prosumerism is 'brought back into the centre of economic action – but on a Third Wave, high-technology basis' (286).[16] With hindsight, one

---

[16] Toffler and others have variously updated and adapted the concept of prosumerism, so in Toffler and Toffler (2006) or Don Tapscott and Anthony D. Williams, who use an analysis of *Second Life* as an instance of online 'prosumption' in the general framework of what they designate as *Wikinomics* (2006). See also Bruns (2008), who uses the phrase 'produsage' to describe a user-based form of

could argue that it has been precisely the inbuilt (etymo)logical paradox of individualized and 'personalized' *con*sumption that helps to bring about this collapse.

The implications of participation, prosumerism and digital narcissism also necessitate an aesthetic revaluation of works of art in general. Kirby suggests that the rise of new technologies around the turn of the century 're-structured, violently and forever, the nature of the author, the reader and the text, and the relationships between them' (2006). I will use the concept of metareference to describe this tangling of ontological and epistemological hierarchies and role ascriptions in the act of literary communication, which leads to a recalibration of notions of authority and responsibility.

Thesis six: Authenticity is an emergent phenomenon

Two anecdotes from ancient Greece are often quoted to illustrate the paradoxical, even magical, circumstances required for the creation of a truly authentic work of art. Both are centrally concerned with the question of mimesis, the faithful reproduction of real-life phenomena by means of art. The first anecdote, related by Pliny the Elder in Book XXXV of his *Natural History*, gives an account of a competition staged between two famous painters of the fifth century BCE, Zeuxis and Parrhasius, to find out who was the better craftsman. Zeuxis paints a bunch of grapes that look so real and natural that they attract a flock of hungry birds. Quite pleased with himself one imagines, Zeuxis invites Parrhasius to pull away the screen veiling his painting. The screen itself, however, is Parrhasius's painting, whereupon Zeuxis 'ceded the prize to his rival with frankness and modesty, saying that he had only fooled the birds while Parrhasius had fooled him, an artist' (quoted in Dubus 2008: 67). By suggesting and creating by artistic means an additional layer of representation, Parrhasius's painted veil proves that under certain circumstances playful self-reference can be perceived as more truthful and realistic than conventional mimetic depiction.

The second anecdote, recounted originally in Sextus Empiricus's *Outlines of Scepticism*, tells of the celebrated artist Apelles, who, while working on the painting of a horse, is unable to get right the froth and saliva coming from the horse's mouth. Exasperated by his evident ineptitude, he throws a sponge at the canvas and – lo and behold – the mark of the sponge creates a perfect likeness of the froth. If one shares Sextus's opinion that the froth represents an example of authentic representation, then one must ask where exactly this authenticity originates. It is arguably not a direct product of the artist's craftsmanship, because it is brought about entirely without artistic intention. It cannot be ascribed to Apelles's superior mimetic abilities but

---

collective content production. An attempt to apply the idea of prosumerism to the analysis of cultural artefacts has been made by Pamela C. Scorzin, who observes an increase in audience participation in contemporary performance art and explains that '"prosumer"-oriented works are defined by addressing all our senses and thus slowly transforming "passive" spectators into immersed but highly activated participants. They thus become performers of their own roles in this holistic play, while becoming increasingly physically as well as psychologically involved as a consequence of a tricky play of illusions, sensations and emotions which unfold in space and time' (2011: 266).

rather to his frustration resulting from an experience of his mimetic inadequacy.[17] The authenticity of the representation does not reside in the depicted object either, as saliva and froth can hardly be considered as auratic or authenticating features in themselves. Third, an attribution of authenticity is also not primarily an effect of the medium. The sponge does serve as the artistic medium through which the mimetic effect is generated, but this can hardly be regarded as its intended purpose, which is presumably to clean the artist's tools once the creative endeavour has been accomplished. The effect of authentic representation cannot be unequivocally attributed to either the representing subject, the represented object or the means of representation. Where, it seems fair to ask, does the authenticity of the depiction then derive from?

A first provisional answer appears obvious. After almost a century of structuralist and poststructuralist thinking, the instinctive response would probably be to point out that any attribution of authenticity can never be more than just that, an attribution by an observer who is not part of the artistic process as such. The effect of authenticity is an effect *on the observer* rather than an effect *of the artwork*. In Apelles's case, this observation is even further removed, as the painting in question is not extant any longer and its effect is conveyed merely via the verbal descriptions of Sextus Empiricus. While this logic of ex-post attribution is perfectly in keeping with a contemporary postmodern perspective, it does not serve, however, as a model of explanation in the context of Apelles or Sextus Empiricus.

What this anecdote shows is that authenticity cannot be attributed solely to the contribution of artist, object, medium or audience, but is dependent on a unique and incidental interplay of these factors. The role played by all of these constituent factors in the formation of the effect of authenticity is clearly discernible and describable. Yet, under the given circumstances these individual contributions generate in their combination an additional value of signification which cannot be unambiguously defined or attributed. In a very dissimilar context, Thomas Susanka identifies a similar phenomenon in his investigation of contemporary war photography; he argues that often 'the authenticity of deception supersedes the intentionality of the creator, the image being regarded as a truthful reflection of reality that is not entirely subject to the will of the photographer' (2012: 96). It is this excess of signification which generates an effect of authenticity in the artwork in question and I propose to describe the authenticity that results from this interplay as *a phenomenon of emergence*.

The basic idea underlying the concept of emergence can be traced back all the way to Aristotle's famous assertion in the *Metaphysics* that the whole can be more than the sum of its parts. The term 'emergence' itself was first used by G. H. Lewes in 1875 in the context of psychology. Lewes says that 'the emergent is unlike its components in so far as these are incommensurable, and it cannot be reduced to their sum or their difference'. He contrasts emergent processes with 'resultant' processes, where any product can be explained and defined as the logically conclusive and unambiguous

---

[17] Sextus presents this story in order to illustrate the Sceptic ideal of *ataraxia*, usually translated as 'tranquillity', which can only result from a complete suspension of critical judgement. For a more detailed account of *ataraxia*, see Striker (1990).

product of observable interaction of its constitutive parts (2005: 412–13). In what has come to be regarded as the standard definition, Jeffrey Goldstein describes emergence as referring to 'the arising of novel and coherent structures, patterns, and properties during the process of self-organization in complex systems' (1999: 49). The concept has been employed for various complex systems in fields as diverse as philosophy (Hartmann 1964), linguistics (Keller 1994), urban architecture (Johnson 2002) and even particle physics (Laughlin 2005).[18] One field where emergence has had a particularly strong impact is the history of science, and I will use the notion of 'emergent evolution' as proposed among others by David Blitz (1992), Peter Corning (2002) and Michael Weinstock (2010) to illustrate the internal logic and structural characteristics of the concept. Evolution, Blitz argues, must be understood as 'a process of change which is productive of qualitative novelty in all domains of reality'. The appearance of this qualitative novelty is described as emergence, because it features 'the possession by a whole of emergent properties not possessed by any of its parts' (1992: 175). Blitz claims further that the emergence of these new properties, in turn, leads to a diversification of observable reality, the analysis of which can be broken down to four separate levels: matter as the 'physical-chemical level', life as the 'cellular-organismic level', society as the 'population-ecological level', and mind as the 'mental or perceptual-conceptual level' (181–2). I claim that the paradigm of metareference represents an additional evolutionary level in this sequence; it facilitates a new understanding of reality as it were, which is premised on paradox and ambiguity and the central analytical operation of which is the process of reconstruction.

Two structural aspects of emergence in particular connect it closely to both metareference and authenticity. One is its classification as a 'self-transcending construction' (Goldstein 2005: 64). Slightly modifying his initial definition of 1999, Goldstein emphasizes that 'the emergence of new order is more appropriately conceived as *constructed* and not self-organized *per se*, albeit according to a special type of construction which I have termed *self-transcending construction* (STC)' (ibid.; emphases in the original). In other words, although emergence is a phenomenon which can and must be analysed in theoretical and structural terms, it always implies an aspect of transcendence and it is precisely this transcendental aspect which links emergence with authenticity on a semiotic level and with metareference on a formal level. Furthermore, it is important to note that although the development described in terms of emergence is apparently one of progress and increasing complexity, the structure of the interplay of the constituting parts and the resulting emergent effect should not be imagined as unidirectional. On the contrary, the relationship of the constitutive part and the emergent effect is one of reciprocity and mutual interference. It is not only the *outcome* of the interaction which is predicated on the interaction

---

[18] While not actually using the term 'emergence', Derek Attridge ascribes much of literature's continual influence and relevance to this property. He points out how 'literature always seems to present itself in the final analysis as something *more* than the category or entity it is claimed to be … This "something more" or "something other" remains obscure, however, although many different attempts have been made to specify it' (2004: 5; emphasis in the original). For a rare example where the term is used in literary criticism, see Domínguez (2006).

of the constitutive parts. A process can only be designated as truly emergent when the components themselves are subjected to unaccountable changes in the process. Corning states that 'emergent effects would be associated specifically with contexts in which constituent parts with different properties are modified, re-shaped or transformed by their participation in the whole' (2002: 10–11). Consequently, one of the side-effects of emergent processes is an irrecoverable tangling of the epistemological hierarchy of cause and effect.

The pattern of emergence can be regarded as a quintessentially postmodern concept, because it uses the insufficiency of positivist observation and the negation of clear-cut relations of cause and effect as a structural predisposition. It is only by retracing the tangled hierarchies of their paradoxical self-transcendence that emergent phenomena can be perceived and appreciated. Emergence, however, may also point beyond postmodern structures of deconstruction and radical scepticism. In his article 'Beyond Postmodernism', Hassan claims that 'only through nihilism is nihilism overcome' (2003: 10), and it might be tempting to adapt this slogan to mean that it is only through postmodern paradox that postmodern paradox can be overcome. By using metareference as the formal yardstick for an aesthetic revaluation of authenticity, this book explores whether beyond deconstruction there is really only ever more deconstruction or if there is another mode of aesthetic experience and representation to be reconstructed from the paradoxes of postmodernism.

I am aware of one other serious attempt so far to describe authenticity in terms of emergence. In his article on the commodification of authenticity in the context of tourism, anthropologist Eric Cohen notes how 'tourist-oriented products frequently acquire new meanings for the locals, as they become a diacritical mark of their ethnic or cultural identity' (1988: 383). He uses the term 'emergent authenticity' to designate the process in which 'crafted products initially produced merely for sale to visitors and tourists, may eventually become authentic products' (379–80). Instances of this emergent authenticity are not restricted to manufactured goods, however, as Cohen convincingly argues that Disneyland, a tourist-oriented simulation if ever there was one, is nowadays considered as part of an authentic American culture.[19] Cohen's example is indeed very significant in the context of the present study, because it results from the interplay between an author/artist/craftsman, an object, a recipient and a context, all of which are significantly transformed in the apparent emergence of authenticity. This instance of emerging authenticity can also be seen as decidedly postmodern on account of the fact that the manufactured products are commodified simulations of originals, which paradoxically achieve authentic status in spite of their intended purpose. They also represent a fitting example of a self-transcending construction in Goldstein's sense.

Goldstein sees emergence as 'just a temporary mark for something about which we don't *yet* know enough' (1999: 59; emphasis in the original). Understood as an emergent quality, authenticity likewise remains a provisional term, a substitute for something not yet identified, a hazy symbol for an unspecified inkling of

---

[19] For further investigations of authenticity in tourism, see MacCannell (1973) and Schindler (2003).

transcendence. The impenetrable process of emergence always produces excess value which oscillates between its constituent parts and the emergent effect. It is this paradoxical residue, transcendental to observable reality and in excess of conventional systems of reference, which can be aesthetically described in terms of authenticity and which metareference formally re-enacts. Goldstein explains the process of emergence by employing the metaphor of a black box, that is, a mechanism in which 'one could discern both the lower-level inputs and the higher-level outputs but not how the lower was transformed to the higher during emergence' (54). In my next thesis I will now apply this metaphor of the black box to the concept of authenticity in order to illustrate some of the effects authenticity can have on various discourses with which it comes into contact.

Thesis seven: Authenticity functions as a black box which sublates discursive dichotomies

The previous theses have shown that if anything is to be said conclusively about authenticity then there is nothing to be said conclusively about it. The concept is born of and thrives on essential structural, epistemological, ontological and aesthetic paradoxes which resist and evade any affirmative descriptions. In order to find an abstract framework for this structural and systemic opacity and ambiguity, I use the concept of the black box.[20] The *OED* attests that the term 'black box' is of rather recent origin. Its first recorded use dates from 1949 and denotes a 'device which performs intricate functions but whose internal mechanism may not readily be inspected or understood; [hence] any component of a system specified only in terms of the relationship between inputs and outputs' ('black box, *n*.' 2011). It has been used in this sense most notably in the domains of cybernetics (e.g. Wiener 1965) and in the behaviourist school of cognitive psychology (e.g. Friedenberg and Silverman 2012). René Thom defines a black box as a 'box with opaque walls' and explains that 'we can only know the system through its explicit interaction with the external world realized by the inputs and outputs of the system' (1983: 297). He also emphasizes the potential of this type of system for playful analysis as well as radical innovation when he says that 'the only conceivable way of unveiling a black box is to play with it. All the major technical and scientific achievements of humanity consist of unveiled black boxes' (298).

This ludic potential of the black box is highly significant for an analysis of the discursive significance of authenticity today. Instead of forever chasing illusive representations of authenticity, I will reverse the perspective and examine what happens to cultural and literary terms and notions once they are subjected to the black-box mechanism of authenticity. Authenticity, as it were, shall be known by its fruits, that

---

[20] I first developed the idea of authenticity as a black-box phenomenon together with Lucia Krämer in the introduction to our collection of essays *Fiktionen von Wirklichkeit: Authentizität zwischen Materialität und Konstruktion* (see Funk and Krämer 2011: 9–17).

is, by investigating how it impinges on concepts with which it comes into contact. I contend that it can be described as a catalyst which collapses what are traditionally considered to be binary oppositions or at least complementary ideas. My understanding of this essentially opaque but productive capacity of authenticity shares significant features with Derrida's conception of 'undecidability', a term he defines in *Limited Inc.* as 'a determinate oscillation between possibilities (for example, of meaning, but also of acts)' (1988: 148). While his earlier texts focus on undecidability as an offshoot of the unbridgeable *différance* between signifiers and signifieds, in 'Force of Law' Derrida first charges this state of epistemological vacillation with an 'obligation' to the individual. In a direct reference to his long-time friend and foil Levinas, Derrida claims that, due to its very opacity and impossibility, the condition of undecidability poses a challenge of responsibility for the *tout autre*:

> The undecidable, a theme often associated with deconstruction, is not merely the oscillation between two significations or two contradictory and very determinate rules, each equally imperative ... The undecidable is not merely the oscillation or the tension between two decisions; it is the experience of that which, though heterogeneous, foreign to the order of the calculable and the rule, is still obliged – it is of obligation that we must speak – to give itself up to the impossible decision while taking account of law and rules. A decision that didn't go through the ordeal of the undecidable would not be a free decision, it would only be the programmable application or unfolding of a calculable process. (1992: 24)

Derrida further develops this link between undecidability and responsibility in *The Gift of Death*, where he imagines Abraham's decision to sacrifice his son Isaac as an ultimately undecidable conflict between human regulations and God as the wholly other. According to Derrida, Abraham in this situation assumes 'the responsibility that consists in always being alone, entrenched in one's own singularity at the moment of decision' (1995: 60). Like other instances of the undecidable put forward by Derrida, such as the spectre, the gift or the trace, the authentic likewise is literally neither here nor there. It evades and resists binary and exclusionary structures of absence and presence, of essence and constructedness, of possibility and impossibility, and thus foregrounds the paradoxical simultaneity of the absence of compulsory regulations and the consequent call for and obligation to individual responsibility.

In the following I will now illustrate this black-box effect of authenticity by briefly summarizing how particular sets of discursive binaries disintegrate under its influence of authenticity, before finally narrowing my focus to the implications this mechanism has for the analysis of literary texts.

Beyond fake and original

I have already shown in thesis two that authenticity, when applied to material objects, is usually used almost synonymously with originality. An authentic Rembrandt is only accepted as such if it can be unquestionably ascribed to the famous artist's hand. Authentic Elizabethan wallpaper must be certified to have been produced in the eponymous era. Benjamin's lament for the loss of the aura of art in the face of its mechanical reproduction makes a convincing case for the end of this particular understanding of material authenticity grounded in an undisputed localization in time and space. Combine this with postmodernism's detrimental effect on any clear-cut boundary between the real and the virtual, the genuine and the simulated, then there are two potential consequences for the notion of material authenticity. It has either become an unsustainable supposition per se, an impossible dream, at best, or a nostalgic retrojection. Richter argues in this direction when she claims that authenticity 'has been thoroughly deconstructed and discarded as the product of an impossible nostalgia for "pure origins"' (2009: 60) and Potter even identifies 'a dopey nostalgia for a non-existent past, a one-sided suspicion of the modern world, and stagnant and reactionary politics masquerading as something personally meaningful and socially progressive' as the enabling conditions for what he flatly dismisses as 'the authenticity hoax' (2010: 270). Alternatively, one could conclude that for material authenticity to still signify in a meaningful way it must be renegotiated along radically new theoretical lines, and I will attempt to outline such a new understanding by introducing the concept of fake as the apparent antithesis to the notion of originality. I will then submit the dialectics of origin and fake to the black box of authenticity and show that in fact both terms have lost their significance for describing creative processes in a contemporary cultural context.

The etymology of the word 'fake' is doubtful. What is beyond doubt is that the term and the underlying concept have become a widespread device for labelling a variety of contemporary aspects in different forms of cultural discourse. Both a smile and a Persian rug can be faked nowadays. The word can denote persons as well as objects, feelings as well as actions. Someone who succeeds in suppressing any original trait or emotion might even be roundly portrayed as 'a fake'. What unites all these diverse meanings is the ostensible refutation of genuineness and originality, a refutation which at the same time evokes this originality. A fake version of van Gogh's *Les Souliers* might fool only the most gullible of collectors but still takes its meaning solely from its connection to the Dutch master. One might almost be tempted to consider fake, in its versatility and ubiquity, to be authenticity's postmodern complement, and there are indeed critics who hail the fake as the quintessential postmodern paradigm. Stefan Römer, for one, notes a paradigm change from a modern aesthetics of originality to a postmodern aesthetics of fake (see 2001: 13), and Judith Mair and Silke Becker propose to think of fake as a Mephistophelian force of incessant negation, which is keen to interrupt any idea of order (see 2005: 238).[21] I would argue that this view does not do justice to the positive regulative power that the idea of the fake assumes nowadays. The logic of postmodernism privileges an ethics and aesthetics of fake and hyperreality over a belief in genuineness and origins. If, as Wendy Doniger declares,

---

[21] The scope of my investigation prohibits a more detailed account of the history and many diverse implications of the notion of fake. For in-depth analyses of the relation of fake to the postmodern, see Römer (2001), Mair and Becker (2005), Chidester (2005) and Glenn (2010). For more specific accounts of the idea of the fake in the history of art, see Radnóti (1999), Dutton (2003), Reulecke (2006) and Knaller (2007: 113–30).

in postmodern thinking 'nature is itself already an imitation of the imitation of nature by art' (2005: 15–16), then it follows almost naturally that a condition of fakeness becomes the only possible template left to frame descriptions of experience and aesthetic expression: 'to be a copy is to be more, not less, authentic that the original. At the very least, only when you see the fake do you see what is authentic: for A not to be B, you have to know what B is' (214).

I think, however, that this somewhat simplistic inversion of the hierarchy of original and fake is not sufficient as an explanation for why the logic of the fake has come to figure so prominently in postmodernism. Lindholm argues convincingly that the success of fake is not due to the total rejection of profundity in postmodernism's logic of impervious surfaces and superficiality but paradoxically rather to the longing for something beyond this very surface. Taking his cue from Boorstin and Umberto Eco's perceptive assessment that 'the American imagination demands the real thing and, to attain it, must fabricate the absolute fake' (1995: 8), Lindholm presents the absolute fake as the inevitable and indeed quintessential manifestation of postmodernism's trademark combination of simulation and commodification. He claims that 'the media fabricates "absolute fakes" that appear more brightly colored, vivacious, and compelling than the factual world itself' in response to popular demands for authentic forms of self-expression (2008: 53). These simulations provide 'anxious buyers with feelings of autonomy, control, community, as well as feelings of distinction, status, and self-actualization in a risky and anonymous society' (64). The stylization of Coca-Cola as 'the real thing', which is apparently supposed to infuse its consumers with a sensation of being genuinely American/cool/true to themselves, is only the most obvious example in this context. Glenn puts a slightly more negative perspective on this contemporary blurring of authenticity and fake in his notion of 'fake authenticity'. In a scathing condemnation of the 'misdirected quest for authenticity' today, he asks:

> Will there never be an end to the spectacle of (usually white, middle-class) people draping themselves in exotic tribal fabrics, bribing sherpas to haul them up mountains, spending $15 for turkey-burgers in urban hunting lodges, throwing out perfectly good kitchen tables for expensive new tables made out of old barn doors, and fetishizing people darker and/or poorer than themselves?

Glenn decries the misapplication of the term 'authenticity' for such precipitated and premeditated, second-hand experiences and concludes that faked authenticity 'is so little removed from life that it makes reality itself inauthentic' (ibid.). In a more positive estimation of the interplay between fake and authenticity, David Chidester analyses the role of 'authentic fakes' in the religious imagination of contemporary America, where, he claims, 'discourses and practices of life, death, and ultimate values are all authentic fakes, simultaneously simulations and the real thing' (2005: xiii). His examples of such authentic fakes range from the actor-turned-President Ronald Reagan to even more abstruse outfits such as the Holy Order of the Cheeseburger. Van de Port also strikes a tentative blow for authenticity when he maintains how, despite the alleged constructedness of contemporary reality and experience, 'most people do not seem to experience their life worlds as fake', and he argues that by allowing for the incontestability of ideas such as authenticity, theorists might be better able to understand 'how the people we study manage to *transcend* the constructedness of their life worlds' (2004: 9–10; emphasis in the original).

In conclusion I would argue that it is the black-box quality of authenticity which is responsible for this new reimagination of fakes as originals and originality as fake. In a context where fakes can be authentic and authenticity can be, or indeed has to be regarded as, fake, there appears to be no good reason any more to uphold the traditional distinction between original and fake.

Beyond essence and construction

In thesis three I have shown how issues of authenticity are both essential to and at the same time invalidate the conception of a genuine self. Subjective authenticity is not conceivable without the assumption of an inner core to everyone's personality, a pre-discursive and inalienable source of one's being-in-the-world.[22] The gate-keeper paradox of authenticity, however, ensures that this true self, characterized as it is by its own hermetic singularity, can never be faithfully represented in conventional systems of reference based on difference. Authentic expression entails a promise to genuineness, to an aesthetic ideal of unaffectedness. Yet, the expression in itself is always already an aesthetic effect, a performance, a *mise-en-scène*. Considered in the traditional framework of an indispensable difference between *Sein* and *Schein*, between essence and performance, authenticity has no signifying power; it is an empty and pointless referent. Turning this argument on its head, however, one could propose that, seen from the perspective of authenticity, it is the very distinction between self and representation, between essence and performance, which no longer carries any meaningful significance. The authentic self and its authentic representation, both in everyday life and in art, vacillate inconclusively between essence and performance. The black box of authenticity apparently abrogates the division of inside and outside which is presupposed by the logic of difference. If at all, this dialectic can only be sublated in paradoxical conceptions such as Zeller's mediated immediacy. Due to its structural undecidability, authenticity can paradoxically figure as both the performative effect of the black box and its fundamental enabling condition. It can move the discourse beyond conventional semiotics by collapsing the difference of signifier and signified.

Beyond reality and fiction

It is not only the concept of a genuine self that becomes structurally untenable under the influence of authenticity. The black box of authenticity also collapses the

---

[22] The ontological quality of this true self is quite aptly captured in the German word *unveräußerlich*, which alleges both that it cannot be adequately transported or displayed to the outside world and that it is immune to any (commercial) attempt of appropriation.

distinction between reality, as something out there independent of perception, and simulation or fiction in the etymological sense of something created by artificial means. Baudrillard's definition of the real as 'that of which it is possible to provide an equivalent reproduction' encapsulates one essential postmodern conjecture, according to which reality is always already virtual, a simulation and a hyperreality (1993: 73). The entirety of human existence is framed by signifiers of the real rather than the real itself, so that 'we are now living entirely within the "aesthetic" hallucination of reality' (74). In view of this, it might well be assumed that an authentic understanding of experience is no longer attainable, as there is no distinct point of reference any more which might ground and thus authenticate such a rapport. If, however, one acknowledges that authenticity is generated precisely through an oscillation between experience and representation, between essence and construction, then postmodern life and art can only be perceived as being authentic when and because they are liberated from the shackles of being either real or virtual. To be perceived as being authentic means to be real and virtual at the same time – or neither, for that matter.

One example of this peculiar state of vacillation between reality and simulation is the contradictory entity of an online identity, which is created entirely in a virtual space but most definitely shapes the perception of experienced reality. At least since the time of Aristotle, literary criticism has used the term 'mimesis' to negotiate the gap between the material experience of the world, traditionally called reality, and its transfer into the particular systems of representation, called the arts. The tension created by the, apparently unbridgeable, mismatch between the two has been channelled into debates on the literary category of 'realism', a concept I will investigate in much more detail in the second part of this book. Suffice to say at this point that it should come as no surprise if the term proves to be invalidated in view of the apparent collapse between reality and fiction which characterizes both postmodern discourse and the notion of authenticity, in which any original differentiation between the real and the virtual is being sublated.

Beyond authorship and reception

I have already shown earlier how a contemporary culture of sharing and involvement, which is based on the virtualization of information and human interaction, brings about an aesthetics and epistemology of participation. One key structural element in this new configuration of knowledge and communication is the suspension of the difference between authors and recipients. The ready access of everyone – everyone who has the chance to be online that is – to the means of creative production means that everybody can receive and partake of all sorts of information at the touch of a screen. It also potentially makes authors of us all and enables users to create and disseminate art, opinions, identities and communities as we go along. This brave new interactive world forces its inhabitants to oscillate constantly between the roles of author and recipient. Taking Bewes's description of cyberspace as 'a zone of anonymity and therefore of authenticity, where people can set free pure "selves" unencumbered by their physical, worldly baggage' as a logical basis (1997: 62), the virtualization of information and interaction seems to permit a novel type of authentic identification and communication. This new type is quite in keeping with authenticity's etymological origins, as it readily facilitates the generation and expression of the self by the self, even though the self that is expressed is largely construed at the keyboard or touchscreen. I have presented Toffler's notion of the 'prosumer' as a persuasive description of this hybrid, virtual form of interaction and in my literary analyses I will later examine how descriptive models of literary communication have to be reconsidered in the wake of this paradigm change.

Beyond aesthetics and ethics

The last pair of terms I want to examine, ethics and aesthetics, is not really dichotomous. Even though different stages in cultural development might have privileged one aspect over the other, any thorough analysis of a work of art will always have to deal with aesthetic perspectives *and* ethical criteria. Still, the significance of a specifically ethical perspective has made a spectacular comeback in recent years, even to the extent that critics have diagnosed an 'ethical turn' in contemporary arts (e.g. Davis and Womack 2001). Doris Feldmann, for instance, diagnoses how 'ethics has gained new resonance in literary studies during the past fifteen years, and it may become the paradigm-defining concept for post-poststructuralist criticism' (2007: 123). Its revival can be read as a sign for the exhaustion of the sort of radical postmodern aestheticism which is based purely on issues of form and structure and not on 'showing moral character', as the etymological origin of the word 'ethic' implies ('ethic, *adj.* and *n.*' 2014). There are also critics who stress that the very project of postmodernist deconstruction has been inherently ethical from the outset. In his seminal study on Derrida, Geoffrey Bennington tries to unravel the complex relationship between postmodernism and ethics as follows: 'Deconstruction deconstructs ethics, or shows up ethics deconstructing (itself), in deconstruction, but *some* sense of ethics or the ethical, something archi-ethical, perhaps, survives the deconstruction or emerges as its origin or resource' (2000: 34; emphasis in the original). Critchley, on the other hand, displays greater confidence in the underlying ethical impetus of postmodern thinking by asserting that 'an ethical moment is essential to deconstructive reading and that ethics is the goal, or horizon, towards which Derrida's work tends' (1992: 2). Shifting his focus to Levinas, Critchley explains further that 'ethics occurs as the putting into question of the ego, the knowing subject, self-consciousness' (4). Adam Z. Newton, too, highlights the fundamentally unsettling and deferring character of ethics with reference to Levinas and Stanley Cavell by locating 'ethical action and language [on] a plane which is not primarily epistemological or ontological'. This ethical level, he goes on to explain, 'lies traverse to or, as Levinas puts it, "otherwise than" the dimensions of being and knowing whose common projection of adequation – the grasp after persons – it cuts across and interrupts' (1995: 28). David Haddorff, likewise, refers to Levinas in his attempt to synthesize the ethics of postmodernism. He claims that 'an adequate postmodern ethic must be both critical and hopeful, deconstructive and constructive, decentering and centering. The latter polarities of this dialectic cannot be grounded in the anthropocentric theory of the autonomous self, but in the moral claims of the other' (2004: 286).

I want to synthesize these different opinions by arguing that a contemporary renegotiation of authenticity can eventually render the distinction between ethics and aesthetics as such redundant, because any form of literary communication that aspires to authenticity must invariably conjoin aesthetic and ethical considerations. To illustrate this, I will demonstrate how theorists like Ferrara and Charles Taylor use the notion of authenticity specifically to highlight the ethical dimension of human existence. Both Taylor and Ferrara start out from a rather traditional understanding of authenticity as an ability to know and judge oneself, to live and express one's inalienable values without yielding to fickle fashions and transient trends. Taylor's deliberations in *The Ethics of Authenticity* clearly show the influence of Levinas, but Taylor reverses the hierarchy between self and other. While Levinas takes the existence and recognition of the other as the fundamental prerequisite for any kind of subjective identification, Taylor argues that 'recognising difference, like self-choosing, requires a horizon of significance' (1993: 52). Echoing Rousseau, he locates this horizon of significance in a truthful relationship between selfhood and self-expression, as for him 'moral salvation comes from recovering authentic moral contact with ourselves' (27). If such authentic self-realization were indeed taken as the lodestar for individual identification, he suggests, this would open up an 'age of responsibilization' (77), and in *A Secular Age*, published 14 years after *The Ethics of Authenticity*, Taylor acknowledges that some headway in this direction has already been made. 'Let's call this the Age of Authenticity', he exclaims and proceeds to correlate what he sees as a budding 'culture of authenticity' with a quest for individual spirituality, for finding one's 'own way of realizing our humanity' (2007: 473–5). For Taylor, authenticity amounts to an autonomy of identification, to the assumption that every individual is inherently invested with the parameters for such identification and self-fulfilment and can therefore only be led astray when blindly pursuing the dictates of society. He is well aware of the criticism potentially put forward against this assessment. He knows that his creed, 'let each person do their own thing, and we shouldn't criticise each other's "values"', might easily be construed as 'simple egoism and the pursuit of pleasure' and 'soft relativism' (480, 484), the postmodern wine of 'anything goes' in new bottles as it were. Taylor does not attempt to refute such allegations. He tries rather to reintroduce a sense of purpose into the solipsistic logic of ceaseless differentiation. For him, the demand to know oneself and one's self is paramount to accepting the other as an autonomous self and thus a necessary consequence of a strong ethical perspective on the world.

For Ferrara, the idea of authenticity is likewise charged with ethical challenges. While Taylor envisages authenticity as a firm refusal of heteronomy in the shape of the fads and whims of commodified and superficial models of identification, Ferrara build his theory on another, again essentially Rousseauian, feature of authenticity, that is, its refusal to be distinctly categorized. In his book *The Force of the Example*, he develops the notion of an indeterminate position for authenticity, in between the positivist discourse of empirical facts and the abstractions of philosophical value. He designates this interstitial and unattached location of judgement, to which he also assigns concepts such as integrity, beauty, aura and charisma, as 'exemplarity' and explains why he sees authenticity as a paradigmatic case in point:

> For something to possess exemplarity, rather, means to be a law unto itself, to possess that exceptional self-congruency for which the term *authenticity* – born within a specific moral tradition but not confined to it – seems particularly apposite. But this quality should not be understood, in turn, along merely coherentistic lines. If we conceive our exemplarity as the ability to set the imagination in motion and all our mental powers into a self-maintaining motion, thereby producing an aesthetic experience linked with the feeling of the promotion, affirmation, or furtherance of life, we need not confine the relevance of this nonfoundationalist kind of normativity to the realms of aesthetics. (78; emphasis in the original)

Authenticity, in other words, can figure as a quintessential example of this new paradigm precisely because it annihilates the distinctions between ethics and aesthetics. Seen through the focus of authenticity, aesthetic representation is in the very process of representation already thrown back on its ethical dimension.

This indissoluble connection of ethics and aesthetics is, of course, not entirely original. When Plato and Aristotle debated the relative value of art in society, they used its moral effect as a benchmark, and Wittgenstein unequivocally claims that indeed 'ethics and aesthetics are one' (1999: 183). Why then is it necessary to go over this apparently self-evident conjuncture between ethics and aesthetics again? One reason is that recent critics have selected the realm of literature as a particularly appropriate area in which this amalgamation of ethics and aesthetics can manifest itself. Geoffrey Galt Harpham updates Wittgenstein's proposition by declaring that 'if ethics and aesthetics are one, they conjoin in narrative', explicating further that 'narrative is the "aesthetic" countenance, and ethics the "philosophical" countenance of a discursive ensemble including theoretical rationality and aesthetic form' (1992: 159–60). Newton argues along similar lines when he ordains the process of narrative to be an inherently ethical procedure. He proposes to imagine 'narrative *as* ethics: the ethical consequences of narrating story and fictionalizing person, and the reciprocal claims binding teller, listener, witness, and reader in that process' (1995: 11; emphasis in the original). Bearing all this in mind and encouraged by J. Hillis Miller's postulation that 'an understanding of ethics as a region of philosophical or conceptual investigation depends, perhaps surprisingly, on mastery of the ability to interpret written stories' (1987: 3), I will now in my final thesis attempt to justify my endeavour to employ the tools of narratology and literary analysis, and in particular metareference, in order to investigate the paradoxical constructions and effects of authenticity.

Thesis eight: Metareference constitutes an appropriate formal approach to authenticity

In my analysis of literary case studies in the third part of this book, I will put the focus on fiction's *formal* character as expression generated through aesthetic means rather than on the *referential* value of fiction in relation to a reality that lies outside it. In other words, I will be interested in how fiction is made rather than to what extent it is made up. After (post)structuralism, a foregrounding of formal aspects is an indispensable procedure for any cultural and literary analysis, even when they concern an apparently transcendental and paradoxical concept such as authenticity. Dennis Dutton emphasizes this formal aspect of authenticity when he distinguishes between *nominal authenticity*, which is defined simply as 'the correct identification of the origins, authorship, or provenance of an object', and *expressive authenticity*, which 'refers less to cut-and-dried fact and more to an emergent value possessed by works of art' (2003: 259, 267). His use of the term 'emergent' to designate the aesthetic significance of this form of authenticity insinuates a quality which eludes straightforward ascriptions of mimetic consistency and referential truth. In the following I will attempt to trace this indefinable quality in the tangled hierarchies of metareference.

Before that, however, I want to summarize my theses on authenticity and thereby prepare the field for my claim that metareference constitutes the most appropriate aesthetic device for evoking, enacting or at least investigating authenticity. In a nutshell, my argument concerning the connection between authenticity and metareference could be summarized like this: an inquiry into various historical and contemporary configurations of authenticity shows that the term is structurally ambiguous, paradoxical and oscillating. In consequence, it is impossible to define it directly and positively. It is emergent in the sense that it cannot be broken down into the sum of its constitutive factors. As it evades direct terminological access, it can only be detected in the impact it has on other discourses and concepts. This black-box character of authenticity, in turn, is a prime cause for its construction as both postmodernism's ultimate symptom and its most significant other. In terms of epistemology, ontology and aesthetics, authenticity's inherent and fundamental resistance to unambiguity finds its structural and objective correlative in the formal aspect of metareference, which is based on similar premises of essential paradoxicality, ambiguity and oscillation.

I am not the first to make this connection between authenticity and self-reference. In the introduction to their study on *Performance and Authenticity in the Arts*, Salim Kemal and Ivan Gaskell provide a succinct synopsis of the paradigm shift that characterizes contemporary epistemological and aesthetic approaches to authenticity in art: 'Previously art sought authenticity by the reference to the divine origin of all things. Now authenticity retains a parallel with the traditional structure by still referring works of art to origins; but the reference is not external: art is authentic the more clearly it is autonomous, when its value is distinctive to its aesthetic character' (1999: 4). In a similar vein, Johan Fornäs refers to what he calls 'cultural authenticity' or 'meta-authenticity' as a form of authenticity which 'moves within (and derives legitimacy from) the level of the symbolic expressions (texts) themselves: the well-formedness of cultural works related to historically determined aesthetic genre rules'. Like Kemal and Gaskell, he argues for a formally more complex, self-reflective conception of authenticity, due to the fact that 'an increased demand for reflexivity has forced older and more naïve conceptions of authenticity to develop meta-authentic traits' (1995: 276). Kemal and Gaskell as well as Fornäs assume that the point of reference from which a work of art can be authenticated can only be found in the formal parameters offered by the artwork itself. Authenticity, accordingly, is transformed from being a factual attribute or a self-contained structure of feeling to being a purely aesthetic phenomenon.

This is not to say that there is no need for an external arbitrator of this aesthetic manifestation anymore. Authenticity always entails a degree of attribution. Contrary to traditional forms of subject and object authenticity, however, the arbitrator, which in the case of literature means the reader, is not invested with absolute powers of ascription. Both the expert who authenticates a Rembrandt and the subject that authenticates the Rousseauian self can only do so from a superior position of unquestioned authority. They can confer authenticity because they are once removed from its object of expression. If, however, the point of reference for attributions of authenticity is located in the aesthetic object itself, this means that the reception/attribution is construed as structurally inherent to the aesthetic act of communication in question. The reader becomes a quintessential constituent of the authenticity of the work in question and not merely its detached adjudicator. Literature in a sense represents an aesthetic *mise-en-scène* of the fundamental human impulse to imagine the self and the world in the form of narrative. It can treat this relationship of self and world both explicitly, by presenting it as story, and implicitly, by mirroring it in its formal set-up. This dual approach arguably accounts for the fact that literature, and in particular narrative fiction, is increasingly seen as the foremost genre of art in which this new form of authenticity can be negotiated. Since literature always necessarily has to stage/frame its communicative situation and perspective, it could be considered inherently self-referential. On the other hand, literature's unbridgeable detachment from actual reality can generate a spontaneous and visceral form of cognition which is not comprehensible in positivist terms and which Dorothy Hale describes as 'ethical knowledge … that is beyond reason, that is of the emotions, and that is so intuitive as to seem a bodily knowing' (2009: 903). Timothy C. Baker strikes a similar tone when he claims that 'instead of trusting immediate perception, then, knowledge about the world can only be revealed through the movement between art and reality' (2009: 508). This transcendental quality renders narrative fiction 'an aesthetic means of investigating lived experience through imagined models, and addressing those grand themes – morality, the ethical life – previously mediated through religion' (Head 2008: 12).

I will try to show in the following how the authentic work of art challenges traditional roles and hierarchies in literary communication. In my case studies, author, reader and text are becoming formally enmeshed, making straightforward, transparent designations both structurally impossible and aesthetically unwelcome. It is worth remembering, however, that in a sense literature remains no more than merely a game of representation and mediation. But if this game is outlined by a new set of aesthetic rules, it might be transformed into a genuine challenge for all involved. David Foster Wallace once compared fiction to 'a knife unprecedentedly vulnerable to its own blade' (1988: 51) and it is not least the status and function of fiction itself which is challenged in the framework of an aesthetics of authenticity and reconstruction.

3

Holding the Mirror up to Fiction: Metareference in Art

The key link between authenticity and metareference is that both represent essentially ambiguous concepts which thrive on paradox and undecidability. According to its etymological roots, the word 'paradox' denotes a form of knowledge or representation directed 'against received opinion' (παρά δοξα). In his treatise *On Nature*, which explores the metaphysical dimension of reality, the Greek philosopher Parmenides sets up the dichotomy of δόξα ('opinion/appearance') and ἀλήθεια ('truth'). The underlying assumption, that behind the screen of appearances there is a pristine, fundamental truth, anticipates Plato's famous distinction between εἶδος ('ideas') and φαινόμενα ('appearances'), and one can assume from the notable circumstance that Parmenides's inquiry is composed in the form of a poem that he considered art to be the high road towards this fundamental aletheia.[1] One of the most passionate recent advocates of this idea is Martin Heidegger, who takes up the term 'aletheia' and defines it as 'the unconcealment of beings', adding that in the 'artwork, the truth of beings has set itself to work. Art is truth setting itself to work' (1998: 161, 165). He cites van Gogh's painting *Les Souliers* as an example of such aesthetically generated truth and claims that aletheia in art only emerges when traditional parameters of signification are displaced. This displacement can occur either in consequence of a state of ecstasy, literally 'being beside oneself', on the part of the recipient or through an enigmatic and logically irresolvable paradox inherent in the artwork itself. In my analysis of *A Heartbreaking Work of Staggering Genius*, I will illustrate this redemptive employment of formal paradox in detail.

The truth and nothing but: Does realism still matter?

Before exploring how metareference can be employed to re-enact this Heideggerian aletheia in works of fiction, I must first address an issue which has shaped literary

---

[1] It should not go unmentioned that any exegesis of Parmenides's work must remain sketchy, as only about 150 lines of *On Nature* are still extant. For the most comprehensive interpretation of these fragments, see Sandywell (1996: 300–12). For further analysis, see Schrödinger (1996: 26–30) and Kirk, Raven and Scofield (2002: 239–62). For a short outline of Parmenides's ideas for the notion of authenticity, see Assmann (2012: 37).

discourse ever since its inception: realism.[2] The longevity of this debate can be attributed to the fact that it tends to manifest itself in three rather contradictory, not to say mutually exclusive, views, all of which can be traced back to the unbridgeable gap between ideas and appearances as described by Parmenides and Plato. In book X of *The Republic*, Plato himself takes this incommensurability of reality and representation as proof of art's structural insignificance and falsity (see 2003: 335–53). Aristotle, in contrast, turns the argument on its head by assigning to art an access to a higher, abstract kind of truth. Precisely due to its disconnection from reality, so he argues in the *Poetics*, art need not concern itself with petty assumptions about what is right or wrong in a particular situation but can aim at more fundamental issues that transcend the mundaneness of everyday life (see 1987: 1–43). Structuralist and analytical approaches to literature and language around the turn of the twentieth century add to this dichotomy a third position, to wit that from a strictly semiotic perspective, speaking of the truth value of artworks is quite literally beside the point, as a distinction between true and false does not apply in the realm of fictional discourse in the first place (cf. Doležel 1980; Rorty 1982).

If one accepts Plato's dictum about the irremediable fracture between reality and its representation, then the notion of literary realism as such acquires a slightly paradoxical complexion; it becomes, in Robert Alter's words, 'a tantalizing contradiction in terms' (1975: x). In his recent stocktaking of realism and its antinomies, Fredric Jameson also highlights this inherent ambiguity, when he describes realism as 'a hybrid concept, in which an epistemological claim (for knowledge or truth) masquerades as an aesthetic ideal with fatal consequences for both of these incommensurable dimensions' (2013: 5–6). Françoise Gaillard's claim that 'nothing puts up so much resistance to representation as the real' not only reiterates this apparent contradiction but alludes to a fundamental structural imbalance in the way we traditionally conceive of this binary opposition. When she goes on to argue that '"knowable" is perhaps not a predicate of the real but a quality *added* by its representation' (1984: 753, 756; emphasis added), she implies that any supposedly realistic form of representation, literary or otherwise, emphatically does *not* aim to truthfully recreate or adequately stand in for reality. On the contrary, representation as such imposes on this reality a semiotic framework of its own authority and disinvests it of its essential contingency so as to make it fit the finite criteria which necessarily define, and therefore delimit, any system of knowledge and representation. Consequently, it stands to reason that the same reality can inspire a variety of different representations, corresponding to different ontological and epistemological configurations and systems of knowledge and belief. Accordingly, there is no such thing as a fixed and unalterable definition of realism, and every attempt to explain the concept is inherently circular and self-fulfilling, as it is always already

---

[2] I will use the capitalized form 'Realism' to refer to specific, presumably well-defined genres or periods of literary history, such as nineteenth-century Realism, Social Realism or Magical Realism. The lower-case variant, in contrast, describes a general attitude which is founded on the conviction that art has the inherent capacity to provide a truthful image of the external world. Hilary Putnam remarks in this context that 'Realism, with a capital "R", is, sad to say, the foe, not the defender, of realism with a small "r"' (1987: 17).

pervaded by the prevalent perceptions of what constitutes and distinguishes reality and fiction.

In its traditional understanding as representing 'things as they really are, in the sense of portraying objectively and concretely details of actual life' (Kaminsky 1974: 217), literary realism has often been dismissed as either hopelessly naïve or remarkably presumptuous. Meticulous adherence to its principles can make authors prone to what Michael Boyd calls 'realism's epistemological complacency' (1983: 19), as it restricts them to 'the tyrannical constraints of ... aesthetic verisimilitude' (Barthes 1989: 144). In this interpretation, the doctrine of realism would be an example of what Nassim Nicholas Taleb maliciously calls 'platonicity', that is, 'the desire to cut reality into crisp shapes', which itself is symptomatic of the human urge to avoid or imaginatively override the contingency of experience by 'focus[ing] on those pure, well-defined, and easily discernible objects like triangles, or more social notions like friendship and love, at the cost of ignoring those objects of seemingly messier and less tractable structures' (2008: 15, 309). A too firm belief in the imitative powers of art can, on the other hand, betray an elitist 'notion that art is a means to truth because the artist has a privileged insight into a common sense of what constitutes "reality"' (Lee 1990: 4). Lynn Wells involuntarily confirms this preconception when she deduces a moral obligation from the artist's apparently superior insight into how the world really works: 'Owing to this unimpeded intercourse between world and text, the novelist, who is conventionally *a person of uncommon sensibility*, should be able to convey a picture of reality which is not only mimetically faithful and "true", but also morally edifying' (2003: 11; emphasis added). Either way, realism is often portrayed as a quintessential articulation of a self-satisfied, conformist, in a word middle-class, perspective on life and art and their interrelation. In this view, realism is imagined as a two-way, self-sustaining system of illusion, concerning both the orderliness of life and the imitative capacity of art. Robert Stam succinctly summarizes this attitude when he flatly announces that 'rather than give the public a cold invigorating shower of demystification, realism gives it a bath in the tepid water of its own ideology' (1985: 13). This disparaging view is, predictably, quite in vogue in postmodernism. In *The Postmodern Condition* Jean-François Lyotard opines that it was the 'task which academicism had assigned to realism ... to preserve various consciousnesses from doubt'. In an exemplary deconstruction of the concept, he claims that the only valid description for realism is that 'it intends to avoid the question of reality implicated in that of art' (2004: 74–5).

In spite of these rather deafening swansongs, there are still those who believe in the current relevance of realism. There is first and foremost Zadie Smith, who has repeatedly advocated the continuing importance of realism. Her confidence in the possibility of truthful representation derives from her belief in language as a means, indeed as the only means, to convey reality. The novel, she writes, 'is made out of language, the smallest units of which still convey meaning, and so they will always carry the trace of the real'. Her conception of realism appears to be somewhat prelapsarian, in so far as it largely neglects the qualifications of the linguistic turn, for example when she invokes 'the transcendent importance of form, the incantatory power of language to reveal truth, the essential fullness and continuity of the self'

(2008). While the kind of realism which Smith so ardently defends is infused by a firm trust in the representational capacities of language, it still pays respect to the increasing individualism and subjectivity of our time. She denies language the power to provide a true likeness of the objective world. Instead, her realism focuses on the representation of the writer's self. The proper study of realism, she claims, is 'one person's truth as far as it can be rendered through language'. In contrast to the moral imperative inferred by Wells, this representation does not aim outward to the real world but inward; 'writers have only one duty, as I see it: the duty to express accurately their way of being in the world' (2007). This combination of responsibility and form, of ethics and aesthetics, as well as the insistence on the self as the sole acceptable object and subject of representation, raises the question if an aesthetics of authenticity could possibly replace or reanimate realism after all.

Before confronting this question directly, I will look back on central ideas and developments which have shaped the idea of realism. Since its theoretical inception in the thinking of Plato and Aristotle, the notion of *mimesis* has been central to any discussion of realism, and contributions by the likes of Erich Auerbach (1946), Michael Riffaterre (1984), Christopher Prendergast (1986), Paul Ricœur (1991), David Lodge (1996) and Heinz Ickstadt (1998) have kept the discourse alive to this very day. The term 'mimesis' traditionally refers to the imitation of an external reality by artistic means. The etymology of the word, however, hints at a more complex and constructivist rather than straightforward, essentialist relationship between imitation and imitated. The word derives from the Greek μῖμος, which can denote either a performer or a performance, and is therefore closely connected to the modern English word 'mime'. Traditionally the mimetic impulse had been directed from the artist's (re)creative imagination towards the reality to be imitated. Prendergast's definition of mimesis as 'a capacity, or a potentiality, rooted in nature (*physis*) and realized by human nature (*physikai*)' clearly shows the direction of this impulse (1986: 19). That the mimetic imagination can never fully catch up with reality and that the sheer materiality of reality needs to be moulded into symbolic form has been widely acknowledged. Ernst Gombrich's remark that 'nature cannot be imitated or "transcribed" without first taken apart and put together again' serves as evidence in this regard (2002: 141). In spite of this structural irreconcilability of reality and effigy, the quest for mimetic representation had been considered a worthwhile and meaningful artistic endeavour for the best part of Western cultural history.

The question of the possibility of truthful mimetic depiction is brought to a head in the wake of postmodernism's theoretical abolition of objective reality. In *The Death of the Novel*, Ronald Sukenick poignantly describes this zero hour of mimesis by declaring that 'the contemporary writer is forced to start from scratch: Reality doesn't exist, time doesn't exist, personality doesn't exist. God was the omniscient author, but he died; now no one knows the plot, and since our reality lacks the sanction of a creator, there's no guarantee as to the authenticity of the received series of discontinuous moments' (2003: 41). What happens to the idea of mimesis, and thus to realism, in postmodernism can be understood as a reorientation of the direction of the mimetic impulse. If one accepts that with ideas like *différance* and simulation objective reality becomes an untenable theoretical assumption, then of course the unidirectional structure of a creative formalization of reality no longer pertains. In consequence, the mimetic impetus is being redirected. It either focuses towards the within, to the individuality of the creative artist, which, in Zadie Smith's neo-Romantic view, constitutes the last vestige of authority and objectivity. Or, alternatively, the mimetic impulse can target its own symbolic system and enquire into the possibilities and conditions of formal representation as such. This shift in the understanding of mimesis is convincingly captured by Foucault in his differentiation between 'resemblance' and 'similarity'. While the former is predicated on the unidirectionality of original and copy, in that it still 'has a "model", an original element that orders and hierarchizes the increasingly less faithful copies that can be struck from it', the latter 'develops in series that have neither beginning nor end, that can be followed in one direction as easily as in another' (1983: 44). Roland Barthes and Alain Badiou also highlight the hermetic nature of any system of representation. Barthes relates postmodern *différance* back to Plato's essential difference between ideas and appearances when he notes that 'to depict is to … refer not from a language to a referent, but from one code to another'. Realism, he concludes, therefore 'consists not in copying the real but in copying a (depicted) copy … Through secondary mimesis, [realism] copies what is already a copy' (1974: 55). Badiou likewise emphasizes the constructedness of reality and suggests that 'nothing can attest that the real is the real, nothing but the system of fictions wherein it plays the role of the real'. This elimination of reality from its representation generates a fundamental dialectic constellation by positioning 'the univocity of the real against the equivocity of semblance' (2007: 52, 164).

In his essay 'Mimesis and Representation', Ricœur devises a typology of different levels of mimesis which traces the trajectory of the concept from antiquity to postmodernism. He starts out with Aristotle, who, after the damning verdict of his teacher Plato, extols the virtues of mimetic representation, which in the form of a dramatic reproduction of human action not only represents the purest form of *poiesis* but which also 'brings about an augmentation of meaning in the field of action, which is its privileged field' (Ricœur 1991: 138). Accordingly, Ricœur sees the *primum movens* of mimesis in a universal human disposition to make abstract sense of one's contingent being-in-the-word. He labels this primeval instinct to formal recreation *mimesis*1 and defines it as a 'pre-understanding of what human action is, of its semantics, its symbolism, its temporality' (142). It is only from this common instinct to create a symbolic resemblance of the contingency of reality and experience that any textual or fictional form of mimesis originates, as 'fiction would never be understandable if it did not configurate what is already figured in human action' (143). The result of this desire for formal abstraction generates a level which Ricœur calls *mimesis*2, where the term 'signifies the production of a quasi world of action through the activity of emplotment' (ibid.), on which, in other words, mimesis generates a *mythos* in the sense of Aristotle, 'a "fable", which reaches the profoundest essence of reality' (142). This stage corresponds most closely to the notion underlying traditional theories of literary realism, that is, as a 'configuration of action … governed by a schematization that is historically structured in a tradition or traditions, and it is expressed in individual works which stand in varying relations to the constraints generated by this schematism' (148). The essentially textual nature of the cosmos in and through which this *mimesis*2 manifests itself, however, already contains the seeds for its eventual overcoming, as it ultimately establishes a closed system of reference. Ricœur envisions 'a new type of relation between texts, an intertextuality which serves to cut fiction off from the world of actual action, in such a way that texts, in completing, correcting, quoting, and crossing out one another, form a closed chain, a library in the precise sense of the term' (144). While the development of *mimesis*2 from *mimesis*1 is predicated on a change in focus from the reality of human experience to a reality of textual representation, on the level of *mimesis*3 the emphasis shifts to the reality of the one realizing these textual representations, or as Ricœur puts it, 'it is the reader – or rather the act of reading – that, in the final analysis, is the unique operator of the unceasing passage from *mimesis*1 to *mimesis*2 to *mimesis*3. That is, from a prefigured world to a transfigured world through the mediation of a configured world' (151).

I would argue that this three-step development of mimesis cannot only be understood as a chronological sequence but also as an epistemological progression from a prefigured reality of pure experience through formal configurations of this reality towards a reconstructive re-enactment of experience in and through literature. Later, I will introduce Schiller's triadic model of cultural progress as a foil against which this development can be read. Ricœur finally encourages us that 'we must dare to form the paradoxical idea of a productive form of reference' (152), thereby providing a link between his endorsement of a self-reflective form of mimesis and the notion of authenticity proposed in this book, which could be understood as a 'productive form of reference' based on paradox. As my subsequent analysis will demonstrate, the reconstructive effort demanded in the reading process of novels such as *A Visit from the Goon Squad*, *The Sense of an Ending* or the later books in the Thursday-Next series need to be understood in this context.

This necessary paradox of productive mimetic representation has also influenced some of the most prominent recent attempts of reimagining realism. James Wood uses the phrase 'hysterical realism' for his observation that an 'excess of storytelling has become the contemporary way of shrouding, in majesty, a lack … That lack is the human' (2001a). Resulting from this excess of storytelling are 'novels of immense self-consciousness with no selves in them at all, curiously arrested and very "brilliant" books that know a thousand things but do not know a single human being' (Wood 2001b). By exposing and parading the formal features of their own mimetic endeavours, such literary works in fact overstrain the principles of realism to the extent that 'this style of writing is not to be faulted because it lacks reality – the usual charge against botched realism – but because it seems evasive of reality while borrowing from realism itself' (Wood 2001a). Works of hysterical realism collapse under the weight of their formal enactment of reality.

While Wood denounces this contemporary form of realism for its lack of human beings, Hal Foster attaches his conception of realism to a lack *inside* the human being. Based on the assumption that the autonomous subject could not have survived the postmodern onslaught unscathed, Foster develops the idea of 'traumatic realism'.

Taking up Lacan's reading of trauma as a failed confrontation with the pre-symbolic real, Foster locates the real in 'a rupture ... in the subject – between the perception and the consciousness of a subject *touched* by an image' (1996: 132; emphasis in the original). In consequence, he contends that 'in contemporary culture truth resides in the traumatic or abject subject, in the diseased or damaged body' (166). The abject subject can convey truth precisely because it resists being entirely absorbed in representation but signifies through the excess of the sheer actuality of its trauma, its overwhelming absence, as it were, in terms of representation.[3] Here again conceptions of the real and the authentic seem to merge, as both are only possible beyond frameworks of definite positivist signification. Foster considers this shift 'from reality as an effect of representation to the real as a thing of trauma' as paradigmatic for contemporary art (146), not without emphasizing the paradoxical effects of this shift for traditional configuration of authority and authorship: 'This strange rebirth of the author, this paradoxical condition of absentee authority, is a significant turn in contemporary art, criticism, and cultural politics' (168).

Already back in 1988, David Foster Wallace emphasized the essential significance of paradox in any contemporary reconfiguration of realism. He uses the phrase 'catatonic realism' to describe a new generation of writers characterized by 'a comparative indifference to the imperative of mimesis, combined with an absolute passion for narrative choices that conduce to what might be called "mood"'. Wallace sees the potential of this new literary approach in its

> unblinking recognition of the fact that the relations between literary artist, literary language, and literary artifact are vastly more complex, and powerful than has been realized hitherto. And the insight that is courage's reward – that it is *precisely* in those tangled relations that a forward-looking, fertile literary value may well reside. (1988: 41; emphasis in the original)

I follow, in essence, Wallace's argument but suggest a new terminology, one that does not rely on realism, however catatonic, traumatic or hysterical but rather employs the notion of authenticity as a gauge for recalibrating the relationship of reality and representation.

That realism is, and always has been, so difficult to grasp is due to the questionable status of its supposed target of representation: reality. Reality is not only as such 'too enormously large and multifaceted' to be known or represented (Barth 1995: 139), but the word is also used to denote a number of different concepts. First, there is the question if reality is objective or subjective or both. This basically boils down to the philosophical inquiry into the possibility of unperceived existence, originating with Bishop Berkeley and most memorably formulated by Mann and Twiss in the question: 'When a tree falls in a lonely forest, and no animal is nearby to hear it, does it make a sound?' (1910: 235). For argument's sake, I will assume for the moment that indeed there is a sound in the forest, that there is an all-encompassing, trans-personal

---

[3] For more detailed discussions of authentic representations of traumatic subjectivities, see Huber (2012) and Schönfelder (2012).

cosmic reality, which includes all the Higgs bosons and parallel universes that may eventually turn out to be the case, and which John Barth subtly refers to as 'God's text, his significant fiction' (1981: 47). The slice of reality which contains the sensual impressions within the reach of the individual's perception forms a subset of this cosmic reality, which is then filtered through the individual's consciousness in a process which subjects the contingent stream of sense impressions to relational processes of causality, signification, differentiation and spatial and temporal organization; Jerome Bruner describes this process as the 'narrative construction of reality' (1991). This means that what we commonly experience as reality is always already a construction, something, as Hayden White reminds us, 'the completeness and fullness of which we can only *imagine*, never experience' (1980: 24; emphasis in the original). Everybody's individual experience of reality can be described as an aesthetic formalization, as an emplotment of the informal and potentially boundless wealth of all that is the case. Any attempt at artistic realism would then just re-enact this primary representational act – the making present of one's experiencing self – or, in Mark Currie's words, 'we do not really believe something to be real until it is archived as narration' (1998: 100).

At least since the linguistic turn, there appears to be wide consensus that reality has lost its epistemological precedence to language, that, as John Gibson puts it, 'there is a divide between language and reality, and that bridging the gap requires the semantic tools the sceptic has taken from the humanist'. Language and reality are treated as two exclusionary entities, and 'our opting for language intimates the absence of any participation of reality in determining the linguistic specification of "what kind of object anything is"' (2003: 52, 56).[4] Language interposes itself between reality and reception to the point that 'the relation between words and the world is to be understood by seeing how words are *used*, rather than by starting with the point at which they attach to reality' (Rorty 1982: 114; emphasis in the original). If one understands the word 'fiction' in its etymological sense as something that is man-made and -formed, then it follows that everyday reality is always a fiction. Rather than constituting an incommensurate antagonism, reality and fiction appear as two counter-directional configurations to understand the same representational process of given form to the contingent materiality of the world.

This conflation of reality and fiction has given rise to a number of theoretical assumptions on the status of literary fictional discourse. The idea that reality is an internal effect of language rather than its external point of reference renders any theory of literary realism which aims at truthful representation of an outward reality not only inadequate but structurally misleading. Art can only ever simulate rather than imitate reality. On the other hand, however, fiction is simultaneously freed from the obligation to attempt any objective representation of reality in the first place. The

---

[4] In order to assess one's own attitude towards this issue, it might be helpful to consider the relative truth value one concedes to Jeffrey Williams's snippy line that 'a dog is a dog, not a word' (1998: 6). Note also Richard Rorty's statement that the 'question whether to view truth as "correspondence to reality" or as "warranted assertability" is the question whether to treat language as a picture or as a game' (1982: 110).

authority of post-structuralist conceptions of literary realism strongly depends on how fiction uses this new freedom, and I would argue that the developments generally subsumed under the heading of modernism are to a large extent shaped by this very revaluation. These range from an uncompromising disavowal of the representational capability of symbolic systems, as in Hugo Ball's and Ernst Schwitters's Dadaist sound poetry or in Kazimir Malevich's famous *Black Square*, to the radical subjectivization of perspective manifested in a stream-of-consciousness in Joyce, Woolf or Faulkner.

The advent of postmodernism marks another significant step in the development of reality's relationship to fiction. With Derrida's famous verdict that there is indeed nothing outside of text, the possibility of any reality external to systems of representation is abolished for good. Moreover and more to the point, postmodern theories point out the incapability of any such system to provide a coherent, comprehensive and unambiguous image or artifice in and through itself, as it is always shot through by the traces of its own absences. Reality, as constructed through language, is essentially based on difference, iteration and the inconsistencies of reference. Berger and Luckmann's assertion about the 'capacity of language to crystallize and stabilize for me my own subjectivity' (1966: 38) no longer applies. Seen in the light of narratology, reality itself has become an unreliable narration. The primary aesthetic reflex to this epistemological challenge consists in a profound and thorough evisceration of the representational systems of art in general. This is brought about by subjecting the creative process to an interminable and inescapable play of self-reference, which serves only to illustrate its inherent epistemological lacunae. Obvious cases in point here would be the hermetic abyss of reference created in the works of Rene Magritte or Andy Warhol. In literature this obsessive self-examination has resulted in the predominance of metafiction in the 1960s and 1970s.

There are critics who see the space left after and by postmodernism as a chance to re-enliven the concept of literary realism. This optimism is fed either by a general belief in an inherent tendency to realism of the particular genre of narrative fiction, as evidenced by Malcolm Bradbury's assertion that 'the practice of realism has in some fashion never been far away from the main business of the novel' (1992: 15) or by the conviction that the theoretical whirlwind of postmodernism has indeed prepared the ground for a fruitful revaluation of what realism means. Winfried Fluck, one of the most persuasive proponents of the latter idea, claims that the 'realistic mode offers especially effective ways for continuously recharging the linguistic surface which is the basis for postmodern aesthetics'. This new kind of realism, however, cannot fall back on well-established postmodern certitudes; it must be 'not just a naïve backlash to postmodern daring and innovation, but a new type of writing with its own potential for contributing to our contemporary cultural situation' (1992: 83, 67).

The realist aesthetics, as envisioned by Fluck, Ickstadt and others, has its theoretical basis in two key tenets of postmodern thinking: radical subjectivity on the one hand and the essential hermetic closure and ineluctability of any system of representation on the other. This results in a foregrounding of self-reference, both in terms of inquiring into the roles of the creative and receptive subjects involved in any act of literary communication and with regard to the ontological status of the work of fiction itself. Vincent Colapietro, for instance, maintains that 'a fragile, fissured, and fallible self, as much (if not more) illusory as real, might have adequate resources (if only barely adequate resources) to know reality' (2007: 33). Even though none of its advocates explicitly spells it out, the aesthetics which results from a synthesis of these presuppositions must be grounded in formal paradox, as it combines a claim for the immediacy and immanence of representation with an assumption of the fundamental plurality and decentredness of experience:

> It is a realism that does not claim to know the real, but wants to come to terms with the fact that it is nevertheless there in an amorphous, ever changing shape. In the final analysis, this realism refers us to a cultural situation whose complexity and variety can no longer be represented by a single text or mode of writing, only by a set of relations within a growing plurality of cultural styles and modes of writing. (Fluck 1992: 85)

In view of the notion of authenticity described in the first part of this book, it seems an obvious conclusion to approach this new conception of realism by way of this very paradigm, since both centre on issues such as the representation of irreducible selfhood and the circularity and paradoxicality of its own formal properties and modes of expression. Indeed, Haselstein, Gross and Snyder-Körber draw this connection in the introduction to their volume on *The Pathos of Authenticity*: 'If authenticity is understood, for instance, as the perceived convergence of representation with its referent, theories of literary realism could open a path to analysing how the social production of reality is linked to the introjection of the "authentic" inner-self' (2010: 19).

By and large, however, it is another terminological framework which is currently invoked to explain such new configurations of literary realism, that of authenticity's longstanding counterpart sincerity. As the term 'sincerity' is often employed to foreground the performative character of the practice it refers to, it lends itself more evidently to illustrating the constructedness of contemporary subjectivities, the intersubjective nature of norms and truths and their manifestations in art. Adam Kelly therefore adamantly promotes a model he calls 'New Sincerity' and identifies David Foster Wallace as the pre-eminent theorist and practitioner of this novel conception of how literature should function and what it should set out to accomplish.[5] In an approach which evokes Ricœur's notion of *mimesis*3, Kelly attributes this aesthetics of sincerity to the pivotal new position and responsibility assigned to the reader. He develops an understanding of an aesthetic configuration 'structured and informed by this dialogic appeal to the reader's attestation and judgment' (Kelly 2010a: 148). Kelly also indicates that this radical dialogism must entail structural ambiguity and epistemological uncertainty. The elevation of the singularity of the reader's experience, he suggests, 'depends upon a kind of ethical undecidability in his [Wallace's] work, which opens up a space for the reader to inhabit and challenges

---

[5] Wallace's fiction is, of course, a conspicuous absence from this study, as he is often hailed as not only a theorist but also the most significant practitioner of this quest for literary sincerity. The only excuse I can offer for this is that the concern of my book is to widen the net from Wallace to other, less immediately obvious, authors who shape and participate in this kind of literary development.

the investment in writerly mastery that characterizes most modern and postmodern literature' (2010b). Furthermore, in a very intriguing comparison of the structural characteristics of sincerity to that of the gift (in a Derridean sense), he underlines the vague position of his concept by declaring that 'true sincerity, if there is ever such a thing, must take place in the aporia between the conditional and the unconditional' (2010a: 142).

Whether one prefers the term 'authenticity' or 'sincerity' respectively to describe this contemporary aesthetics of participation is ultimately down to a conviction whether one needs to be true to one('s)self in order to be able to be true to others, or vice versa, and in view of postmodernism's irrevocable legacy of the structural impossibility of separating self and other, identity and alterity, this question is impossible to answer in any conclusive and meaningful way. The difference thus is one of aesthetic emphasis rather than terminological principle. I would argue that while 'sincerity' accentuates the performative and procedural aspect of any ascription of genuineness, 'authenticity' highlights the structural paradoxes which these ascriptions necessarily entail. I therefore base my decision to conceive of a new aesthetics in terms of authenticity rather than sincerity on the rather pragmatic assumption that it is through the formal analyses of these paradoxes that a new aesthetics can be most appropriately investigated and formulated.

A framework for reconstruction: The metareferential turn

Self-reference has always been both an anthropological invariable and an important creative impetus. The self-conscious reflection of one's 'being-in-the-world' and the ability to create a mental image of oneself are defining characteristics of the human being as a rational animal (ζῷον λόγον ἔχον = 'animal possessing reason/words'). It arguably makes the human in Hamlet's admittedly rather sceptical words 'the paragon of animals' (2.2.307). The ambiguity implied in the Greek word λόγος, which, through its prominent position at the onset of creation according to the Gospel of John, has structured Western thinking from its very beginnings, fundamentally conjoins reason and language. Any human self-conception therefore is a symbolic representation, a verbal construction, a fiction even. That language has become humankind's key tool for making sense of itself and the world might, in turn, be due to its inherent self-reflectivity. As a system of representation which in every instance of expression always inevitably combines content and form, εἶδος and φαινόμενα, language cannot but point towards its own conditionality in every manifestation it assumes. An individual utterance might be used to refer to things that are external to itself. Its implicit primary reference, however, is always to itself and to its role within the system of representation.

While this inherent self-referentiality is a property common to all symbolic acts, it is notably so in the case of poetic language, and twentieth-century structuralist theories concerned with the system of language supply the terminological and notional framework best suited to account for this. A paradigmatic example is Jan Mukařovský's examination of the aesthetic function of language. Drawing on the works of Roman Jakobson and Ferdinand de Saussure, Mukařovský sees the poetic use of language as substantially at variance with all other uses that language can be put to.[6] This special mode of operation, for Mukařovský, is due to the fact that

> in all 'practical' functions, the telos lies outside of the object which is the vehicle of the function, either in the subject whose particular need is to be satisfied or in the surrounding context which is to be changed. In contrast to this, the telos of an object dominated by the aesthetic function lies in the object itself ... the difference between the practical and aesthetic functions is that the former is allotelic whereas the latter is autotelic. (Steiner 1978: xxii–xxiii)

In other words, aesthetic creations are 'not oriented toward a specific external goal but are themselves the goal'. From a semiotic point of view, the work of art is thus per definition not externally motivated or referenced but constitutes its meaning in and through itself alone. It is an 'autonomous sign lacking an unequivocal relation to reality' and therefore inherently self-referential (Mukařovský 1978b: 94).

Lest it be consigned to utter insignificance, however, this self-referential, aesthetic language must retain some sort of extrinsic point of reference. This point of reference, Mukařovský claims, is constituted by 'the total context of social phenomena of the given milieu' (1978a: 88). This means that – while everyday, practical language can only signify in a particular set of circumstances – the aesthetic language of art always necessarily references the totality of the discursive framework which enables and structures this very economy of reference in the first place. If one accepts Foucault's assumption that this frame of reference, which he calls 'episteme', is constantly being reshaped in and through discourse and symbolic interaction, it follows that the idea of unchanging aesthetic norms cannot be maintained. Rather, Mukařovský argues, if there is any regulatory principle which governs artistic creation, it must consist precisely in the ceaseless violation of the apparently normative structures which govern it; aesthetic discourse 'makes felt its activity and hence its existence precisely at the moment when its violation occurs' (Mukařovský 1978c: 54). Attridge argues along very similar lines. Literature, for him, 'rests on a certain inaccessibility to rules, as the aesthetic tradition recognizes, there is no way it can serve as an instrument without at the same time challenging the basis of instrumentality itself' (2004: 13). Art then is not only inherently self-referential; it is also necessarily transgressive and subversive with regard to the norms by which it is ostensibly regulated. In summary, aesthetic discourse has to be regarded as inherently self-referential on three crucial counts:

1. Since it manifests itself necessarily as both form and content, aesthetic discourse reflects (on) its own status as symbolic configuration and means of representation. I call this its *generic self-referentiality*.
2. Freed from the bounds of direct correspondence to specific external

---

[6] In Jakobson's influential model, which is itself derived from Karl Bühler's so-called 'Organon-Modell' (see 1999: 24–33), language can be differentiated in accordance with its relative communicative intention and effect. Apart from the aesthetic/poetic function, Jakobson famously identifies the referential, conative, emotive, phatic and metalingual function of language (see 1960: 353–8).

phenomena, aesthetic discourse inevitably reflects the entirety of the systems of symbolic representation which structure the cultural discourse of the time of both its creation and reception. Following Foucault, this could be called its *epistemic self-referentiality*.
3. Since the discursive frameworks which it references are in constant flux, aesthetic discourse can only signify by transgressing its hypothetical normative structures, which it must continually challenge and disrupt. This could be called its *subversive self-referentiality*.

In the following, I will now present various attempts to define and differentiate this self-reflective propensity of the aesthetic discourse, which has traditionally been regarded as a somewhat secondary phenomenon; Stam, for instance, calls it '"the other tradition" in literature and cinema' (1985: xi). Not subscribing to this belief and following Wolf's diagnosis of a 'metareferential turn' in contemporary arts and media (see 2011), I will rather argue that the inherent self-referential capacity of aesthetic discourse plays the central role in contemporary renegotiations of experience and representation.

It is not unusual for studies on self-reference in literature to start, as this section does, with the avowal that art in general, and literature in particular, has always been self-referential. Seminal works such as *Don Quixote* or *Tristram Shandy* are habitually cited in order to corroborate the claim that notably the genre of the novel has flaunted and made use of a full range of self-reflective strategies from its very inception. Still, there also seems to be agreement that some works are in a way more self-referential than others and indeed even merit to be grouped together and classified as a particular subgenre. In the case of literature, this subgenre has conventionally been labelled 'metafiction' and is commonly believed to have had its heyday in the 1960s to 1980s. I will return to this claim presently; first, however, I want to introduce a very basic distinction. Literature is, by dint of relating (to) reality in the referential system of language, inherently self-referential in so far as it always involves premeditated aesthetic decisions as to how this relation of reality and representation can be occasioned on the level of the representational code. I would propose to define this inherent generic form of self-referentiality, which is common to all literature, as the *weak form of self-reference*. In order to qualify as *metareferential*, which I understand as the *strong form of self-reference*, works of art must not only display self-referentiality, but their reception must also pose an irresolvable epistemological or ontological challenge to the reader, a challenge which cannot be resolved on the textual level and which therefore necessitates the imaginative reconstruction of the act of literary communication. This differentiation of self-reference and metareference by and large mirrors Werner Wolf's classification of metareference as 'not co-extensive with self-reference ... but a special, *cognitive* kind of self-reference' (2011a: 8; emphasis added).

Another qualification is required at this point. Any form of self-reference is not a quality that is immanent to a particular work of art. It rather constitutes a descriptive and interpretative stipulation imposed on this work from the outside. Consequently, one and the same novel, painting, poem or installation might be classified as realist, self-referential or metareferential, depending on the point of reference emphasized by the respective individual and/or critical approach. These may with equal entitlement foreground the external point of reference of a novel (the biography of the writer, say, or the historical context), the formal and structural techniques of referencing (as in formalist and New Critical approaches) or the paradoxes and fissures that inhere in the codes of reference used (as in deconstructivist approaches). Kant in his *Critique of Judgement* may have famously declared that proper art is characterized by its profound lack of purpose and interest; its analysis, however, tends to be motivated by purposes external to itself, from profane academic one-upmanship to a noble thirst for knowledge or a desire to share one's own beliefs. Attridge labels this attitude 'literary instrumentalism' and defines it as 'coming to the object with the hope or the assumption that it can be instrumental in furthering an existing project, and responding to it in such a way as to test, or even produce, that usefulness' (2004: 7). So, to a degree, both the realism and the metareferentiality which critics may detect in their objects of investigation are direct effects of the strategies they employ and the objectives they pursue.

Definitions of the phenomenon of self-reference in literature and art are as numerous as the names given to this phenomenon and often there is not much they agree on.[7] In general, however, there appears to be at least one unifying feature: the conviction that the objective of such art should not primarily be to entertain and divert but to analyse and interrogate. By exposing the premises and conditions of its own discourse, critical self-reflective art not only problematizes its own aesthetic and ontological status but also opens up a new perspective on the conditions, limitations and possibilities of the basic human need of representation. In one of the first major studies on metafiction, Robert Alter traces the development of what he calls the 'self-conscious novel' from Cervantes to Barth and Borges. For him, the main feature of this particular subset of narrative fiction is its investigative self-positioning between reality and fiction. Alter rejects the purely mimetic attitude of realism as 'a task of Sisyphus' (1975: 55). In opposition to this, he sets up the self-conscious novel as one 'that systematically flaunts its own condition of artifice and ... probes into the problematic relationship between real-seeming artifice and reality' (x). For Alter, the rise of the novel, just like that of authenticity one might add, is in consequence of a breakdown of hitherto uncontested certitudes; the novel, he claims, 'begins out of an erosion of belief in the authority of the written word and it begins with Cervantes'; its main objective is from the start to 'see in the mere fictionality of fictions the key to the predicament of a whole culture' (3). Although Alter is aware of the potential accusation levelled against this understanding of narrative fiction that it amounts to hardly more than self-obsessed navel-gazing, he defends the fundamental gravity and

---

[7] Since the focus of this book is on narrative fiction, I will restrict the short overview of the development of self-reference to this field, without disregarding the fact that similar developments occur in other artistic and media discourses. For comprehensive studies that foreground an intermedial perspective on self-reference, see Sperber (2000), Nöth and Bishara (2007), Hauthal et al. (2007) and Wolf (2009). For studies on self-reference in poetry, see Müller-Zettelmann (2000). For accounts of self-reference in drama, see Lehmann (1999) and Fischer and Greiner (2007).

significance implied in the laying open of fiction's own possibility: 'It is the tension between artifice and that which annihilates artifice that gives the finest self-conscious novels their sense of urgency in the midst of play' (235).

Raymond Federman proposes a similar view on the conditions and purposes of narrative fiction, albeit under a different name and in slightly more prophetic tones. Like Alter, he is convinced that the actual mission of fictional discourse should not be merely mimetic but rather 'to abolish the notion that reality is truth [and] to unmask its own fictionality, to expose the metaphor of its own fraudulence, and not pretend any longer to pass for reality, for truth, or for beauty' (1975: 8). Accordingly, he introduces the term 'surfiction' to describe 'the kind of fiction that constantly renews our faith in man's imagination and not in man's distorted vision of reality – that reveals man's irrationality rather than man's rationality' (7). He envisions an aesthetic shift in paradigm towards an understanding of the novel as 'an endless denunciation of its fraudulence'; the main function of narrative fiction will not be to provide metaphors to make sense of reality but to reflect the narrative properties and condition of that reality: 'fiction will become the metaphor of its own narrative progress' (11). In a similar vein, Inger Christensen describes metafiction as a variety of fiction 'whose primary concern is to express the novelist's vision of experience by exploring the process of its own making' (1981: 151), while Wenche Ommundsen argues that reflexivity in literature is generally 'a function which by analysing literary processes enables us to understand the processes by which we read the world as text' (1993: 4).

Even though some of Alter's and Federman's theoretical pronouncements on self-reference may have stood the test of time, their respective designations for it have not. They join a lengthy list of labels which have eventually fallen into disuse. These include John Barth's 'literature of exhaustion' (1972), Fletcher and Bradbury's 'introverted novel' (1978), Steven Kellman's 'self-begetting novel' (1980), Michael Boyd's 'reflexive novel' (1983) alongside later attempts such as Mark Currie's term 'theoretical fiction' (1998: 52). The label that would eventually stick is 'metafiction', a term originating with William H. Gass, who in *Fiction and the Figures of Life* describes as such a variety of novel 'in which the forms of fiction serve as the material upon which further forms can be imposed' (1970: 25). Two formative studies, Patricia Waugh's *Metafiction: The Theory and Practice of Self-Conscious Fiction* and Linda Hutcheon's *Narcissistic Narrative: The Metafictional Paradox* (both 1984), have contributed in no small measure to the fact that discussions of literary self-reference in the second half of the twentieth century are usually conducted under the heading of metafiction.

Waugh distils previous notions into what can be taken as the standard definition for this particular form of fictional discourse: metafiction is, she suggests, 'a term given to fictional writing which self-consciously and systematically draws attention to its status as an artefact in order to pose questions about the relationship between fiction and reality' (1984: 2). Waugh emphasizes the twofold thrust of such writing. First, it constitutes in and through itself an aesthetic and critical evaluation of the theoretical and practical conditions and limitations of its own literariness. By doing so, it also urges readers to gauge their own position with regard to reality as an experience and their own self-narrativization of this experienced reality. Metafictional texts therefore 'also explore the possible fictionality of the world outside the literary text' (2) and offer 'extremely accurate models for understanding the contemporary experience of the world as a construction, an artifice, a web of interdependent semiotic systems' (9). Like Alter and Federman before, Waugh maintains that metafiction has its origins in a profound experience of ontological insecurity; it 'rests on a version of the Heisenbergian uncertainty principle' (3). On the basis of the assumption that 'everything is framed, whether in life or in novels' (28), Waugh sees the 'laying bare' of traditional, realist constructions of fictional illusion as the foremost structural principal of metafiction (6).

This laying bare, the suspension of the suspension of disbelief as it were, can be driven by two, fundamentally different conceptions of the relationship between literature and reality. These two contrastive positions mirror the two attitudes towards literary realism which I have delineated above. Between them they draw up the conceptual continuum in which metafiction can be situated. On the one hand, the objective of the shattering of literary illusion could be to adumbrate a reality 'whose significance is not entirely composed of relationships within language'. On the other hand, it can just as well be used to emphasize the hermetic closure of the representational system, the impossibility altogether to 'escape from the prisonhouse of language' (53). The self-referential reiteration of this hermetic closure can signify either satisfaction or despondency about this state of affairs. Either way, metafiction for Waugh comes with an inbuilt promise to fathom and creatively exploit a potential in literature which can only be realized when traditions and conventions are laid bare and structurally disassembled.

By contrast, Hutcheon specifically emphasizes the liberating outlook offered by literature's aesthetic autonomy. For her, this autonomy finds its most evident expression in the avowed self-centredness of what she calls 'narcissistic narrative', for which she claims an 'aesthetic purity usually only associated with poetry' (1984: 96). In an argument that recalls Mukařovský, she asserts that it is precisely because fiction 'does not partake of the contingencies of life' that it can create 'a reality in its own right' (90, 91). This liberation from mimetic obligations accentuates and vitalizes in particular the role of the reader in the act of literary communication. In a metafictional text the novelist grants to the reader a perspective not merely on the product of the creative activities involved but rather on the process of creation as such, thereby offering 'a relationship based on a mirroring of the actual process in which he is engaged at that moment as he puts pen to paper' (138). The reader, in turn, is elevated from a passive recipient to an active critic of this process (see 144).

To sum up these ideas, let me highlight the relationship between metafiction and realism. The answer to the question of whether the anti-illusionist impetus of metafiction must also necessarily make it anti-realist depends largely on one's very own conception of what the word 'reality' actually refers to. For those who firmly believe in a reality outside of the 'relationships within language', metafiction constitutes the apotheosis of anti-realism, its hermetic self-referentiality symbolizing both the ultimate acknowledgement and an applied enactment of literature's inadequacy to represent reality. At best, it might be construed to be a 'rebellion against reality – or what commonly passes for reality' (Nordhjem 1987: 181). Alternatively, for those who believe that reality is radically constituted in and through the very symbolic systems employed to bring it into comprehensible form, metafiction's laying bare of the formal relationships that make up this representational code can legitimately claim to form a plausible account of reality. Metafictionality would thus be the 'real' realism, in so far as it calls the bluff of any external mimetic impulse which traditional forms of realism so deceptively strive to simulate. McHale summarizes this view concisely when he writes that 'postmodernist fiction turns out to be mimetic after all, but the imitation of reality is accomplished not so much at the level of its content, which is often manifestly un- or anti-realistic, as at the level of form … Postmodernist fiction achieves its aesthetic effects and sustains interest, in the process modelling the complex ontological landscape of our experience' (1987: 38–9). Fluck expands on this idea and points to the intricate semiotic gestures behind metafiction's realist appeal. In postmodern metafiction, he argues,

> aesthetic experience is neither provided by a mere play of words aimed at radical defamiliarization in the construction of meaning, nor by a deliberate textual disorder providing a quasi-mimetic representation of the chaos of our present-day world. Instead it is generated by a calculated and carefully constructed interplay between radical dehierarchization in the formation of meaning and brief moments of reauthorization, between desemanticization and the brief, but continuous semantic recharging of the sign, between a loss of emotional depth and the evocation of an emotional state that results from exactly this loss. (1992: 68)

It seems tempting to ask if metafiction actually does no more than put the old wine of mimesis into new postmodern bottles. It is again David Foster Wallace who puts these reservations into appropriate words: 'Metafiction, for its time, was nothing more than a poignant hybrid of its theoretical foe, realism; if realism called it like it saw it, metafiction simply called it as it saw itself seeing it' (1993: 161).

It is partly due to precisely such objections and misgivings that I claim a qualitative difference between the works commonly subsumed under the title 'metafiction' and a change in aesthetic paradigm in the texts I discuss in this book. As set out earlier, I understand postmodernism as the latest, aesthetically withdrawn and ultimately self-de(con)structive incarnation of modernism rather than as a radically new episteme. Consequently, the disillusionment perpetrated and displayed in metafiction can be seen as a seamless continuation and logical conclusion to the modernist project of revealing the structures underlying any system of reference and representation. If postmodern theory has taught us one thing, it is that such profound changes in perspective, which Thomas S. Kuhn famously described as 'paradigm shifts', are never spontaneous and incidental events, but rather result from determined and often protracted reorientations and renegotiations of the very parameters that define human knowledge. The categories and classifications with which such transformations are designated are ex-post attempts at ordering these often divergent struggles. The demarcations of such categories are therefore not so much an effect of actual transformations in philosophical or scientific discourse, but more to the point, they mark the incidental point in time when a new term or metaphor for these transformations catches on and establishes itself in the collective imaginary.

One of the more convincing metaphors for the recent paradigm change in the relationship of reality and representation is provided by Wolf's description of a 'metareferential turn' in contemporary arts and media (see 2009; 2011). Extending the focus of his investigation from metafiction towards a transmedial perspective, Wolf defines the phenomenon of 'metareference' as

> a special, transmedial form of usually non-accidental self-reference produced by signs or sign configurations which are (felt to be) located on a logically higher level, a 'metalevel', within an artefact or performance; this self-reference, which can extend from this artefact to the entire system of the media, forms or implies a statement about an object-level, namely on (aspects of) the medium/system referred to. (2009: 31)

In essence, Wolf argues that the use of metareference has become so ubiquitous today that it must be regarded as the default mode of representation.

Wolf and others who share this conviction integrate an assumed anthropological predisposition to reflect on oneself and one's self-representation with current transformations in the possibility and conditions of reference and representation. These include Aleida Assmann, who diagnoses 'an abyss of self-reflexivity in secular modernity' (2012: 43), Luigi Cazzato, who describes how a pervasive 'metaculture' developed in the wake of postmodernism (2000: 18), Dan Sperber, who draws attention to the inherent capacity of human beings to reflect upon their own status vis-à-vis the incomprehensibility of reality and claims that 'humans are unique in their ability to use metarepresentations' and are endowed with 'two dedicated mental mechanisms, one for language, the other for metarepresentations' (2000: 117, 121), Hans Lenk, who describes 'man as the ever-interpreting and meta-interpreting being' (2003: 214), and Douglas Hofstadter, who considers human consciousness itself as 'a mirage that perceives itself' (2007: xii). When Hofstadter tries to define the human self, he uses a terminology not unlike Wolf's definition of metareference: 'In any strange loop that gives rise to human selfhood,' Hofstadter claims, 'the level-shifting acts of perception, abstraction, and categorization are central, indispensable elements' (187). As I have shown in the first section of this book, the virtualization of contemporary means of self-identification and self-representation – through social-networking, sharing, liking, linking and the self-stylization as an avatar – is axiomatic for this inescapable and a priori obligation to reflect upon one's own representation. By positing a metareferential turn, Wolf tries to align this inherently self-referential human disposition with current developments in patterns of representation in the arts and media. Wolf describes the metareferential turn as 'an effect, and thus symptomatic of, this growing distrust and a concomitant conviction that all representations are actually constructions pretending to render reality or facets thereof and are thus at least shot through with fiction' (2011: 30).

It is only a thorough, deliberate and comprehensive 'metaization' of contemporary life and letters that can create the necessary preconditions for a new paradigm of conceiving the relationship between reality and reference.[8] This process of metaization is defined by Wolf as 'the movement from a first cognitive or communicative level to a higher one on which the first-level thoughts and utterances, and above all the means and media used for such utterances self-reflexively become objects of reflection and communication in their own right' (2009: 3). Wolf understands this increase in metaization as an evolutionary inevitability responding to an increasing internal differentiation of traditional systems of reference, which, he argues, 'increases the need for metareferential negotiations of these differentiations' (27). He is aware, however, that the metareferential turn must not automatically represent a turn for the better. Since it fundamentally and exclusively revolves around itself, metareference might just as well be regarded as a symptom and celebration of creative depravity and narcissistic self-indulgence, 'not only as a symptom of cultural weakness, but also as a problematic reinforcement of this weakness' (68–9). On the other hand, the metareferential turn indicates and bespeaks a profound feeling of inadequacy as concerns traditional forms of reference, a feature it shares with the discourse on authenticity. 'High art', Wolf asserts, 'may be regarded as having reached a stage of such overcomplication and experimental innovation that it has lost anchorage in familiar frames of reference' (2011: 31). In so far as it combines 'epistemological disorientation with amusement, perhaps even links the undermining of ontological certainties concerning the opposition "reality vs. fiction" with the metareferential awareness that a "trick" has been played on the recipient' (23), the playful and interactive aspect of metareference would 'permit the recipients, as it were, glimpses behind the scenes' and can thus signify 'a consequence and an index of more democratic attitudes underlying contemporary art' (32). The democratization of art through metareference also pertains to another level; as a proliferation of various forms of metareferential display across the cultural board may have the additional effect of lowering the inhibition to engage with it in the first place. By accepting metareference as the normative rather than the exceptional mode of reference, its recipients, so the argument goes, will gradually grow inured to this self-reflective perspective and attitude, which would thus help to disinvest metareference of its overtones of intellectual sophistication, theoretical detachment and formal impenetrability. Wolf, for one, is convinced that 'a frequent effect of metaization, namely defamiliarization, diminishes as an obstacle to wide-spread reception, which in turn facilitates the continuation of, and even a gradual increase in, metaization, since this has come to be experienced as something "normal"' (28–9).

Libraries full of books written on literary self-reference attest to the difficulty involved in differentiating and categorizing this heterogeneous mode of representation. As with every attempt to establish an idea of order into a blatantly disorderly field, any such classification reflects and enacts the presuppositions according to which it is carried out. In other words, no typology can lay claim to universal validity

---

[8] As Wolf points out, the term 'metaization' was first introduced in its German form *Metaisierung* by Klaus Hempfer (see 1982: 130). For a detailed analysis of the term and its various implications, see Hauthal et al. (2007) and in particular Wolf (2007).

but is always a function of the tactical criteria and prospective results of the individual typologist. Nevertheless, there are certain criteria which recur in most classifications of creative self-reference. I will therefore not try to reinvent the wheel by presenting a spanking new and original typology of metareference; instead, I will build on the extensive work already done in this respect and modify and amend it where necessary for my argument. Again, Wolf's work provides the main point of departure. In the introduction to his collection of essays on *Metareference across Media*, Wolf establishes four oppositional pairs which set up a theoretical framework within which any instance of metareference can be formally situated:

- intracompositional vs. extracompositional metareference
- explicit vs. implicit metareference
- *fictio* vs. *fictum* metareference
- critical vs. non-critical metareference (2009: 37–43; also Wolf 2007: 40)

Wolf's typology is influenced and in many way unites earlier classifications by Hutcheon (1984: 17–35), Nünning (2004), Müller-Zettelmann (2000: 170–239) and indeed Wolf himself (1993: 220–59). Hutcheon suggests two principal oppositions for classifying what she calls narcissistic narratives, overt vs. covert and linguistic vs. diegetic, the combination of which results in four distinct modes. The overt diegetic style, as manifested for example in John Barth's *The Floating Opera* or John Fowles's *The French Lieutenant's Woman*, makes the reader 'aware that he too, in reading, is actively creating a fictional universe' (1984: 28). The overt linguistic style, exemplified by Norman Mailer's *Armies of the Night*, foregrounds 'its building blocks – the very language whose referents serve to construct the imaginative world' (29). The covert styles do not explicitly address their own metareferentiality but rather implicitly mirror the conventions of generic (diegetic) and verbal (linguistic) models (31–2). Nünning, in stark contrast, comes up with no fewer than 18 different modes of what his typology labels 'metanarration'; these are grouped into formal, structural, content-related and functional criteria. Wolf's typology can be seen as an attempt to find an operable balance between the rather loose and imprecise system devised by Hutcheon and Nünning's somewhat overdetermined and therefore impracticable classification. Before I offer my own shot at a typology, I first have to introduce two formal aspects which are necessary to clearly differentiate and precisely analyse how the tangling of epistemological and ontological hierarchies in an act of artistic communication is brought about in each individual instance.

Monika Fludernik points out that in its conventional usage in English, the term 'metafiction' does not distinguish between the formal techniques used to suspend the mimetic illusion and the texts in which these techniques appear (see 2003: 11). In order to tackle this problem, I will revert to Sarah Lauzen's term 'metafictional device/element', which she uses to refer to any feature within a literary text that 'foregrounds some aspect of the writing, reading, or structure of a work that the applicable canons of standard (realistic) practice would expect to be backgrounded' (1986: 94). Following Lauzen, I suggest the term *metareferential element* to account for the difference between the generic term for the tangling of ontological and epistemological hierarchies on the one hand and the particular mechanism or device which facilitates this tangling on the other. Subsequently, I will use the term 'metareference' to refer to the underlying concept, while 'metareferential element' will designate a specific event, or set of events, in a text. Depending on the media form in question, these elements can manifest themselves in a variety of forms, from single words to sentences, allusions, references or quotations in literature to signatures, frame-breaking, reflections or *mises-en-abyme* in the pictorial arts. I propose this working definition of a metareferential element: *a metareferential element is any media display which reveals its status as a media display by inserting an additional level, which is called a metalevel, into the self-same display on which the basic level of the text is reflected. The relationship between these two levels must involve a fundamental epistemological ambiguity or ontological paradox which cannot be resolved on the level of the source text.*

In addition to this, I would like to introduce the term *metareferential moment* to describe how the deployment of a metareferential element affects the constituents of the act of communication in question. I will try to show that the insertion via metareferential element of a metalevel into any art or media display necessarily results in a moment of epistemological confusion which can be understood as an effect of a tangling of conventionally stable role attributions in the communicative situation. I therefore define the metareferential moment as *the imagined location within the framework of a communicative situation where the effect of metareference makes itself felt.*[9] In formal terms, the metareferential element refers to the material aspect of metareference, its concrete manifestation in any given medium, while the metareferential moment describes its operative and receptive effect. In view of the essentially oscillatory and undecidable quality of metareference, it will come as no surprise that practical applications show that metareferential element and moment necessarily interact and impinge on one another, which often complicates any clear-cut definition or ascription.

On the basis of Wolf's typology, I now propose my own classification of metareferential elements (see Table 1). The main modification I have applied to Wolf's system is that I have transformed his oppositional pairs into four basic dimensions, which I will describe in more detail below. This not only breaks up the restrictive binarism of his approach but also enables me to include more than two categories under one aspect. Since I understand the term 'text' in its widest sense so as to cover any meaningful expression which can be said to constitute an act of communication, my typology – like Wolf's – is in theory applicable to a wide range of artistic and media discourses, even though its use in this study is restricted to literary texts. As with every typology, this one comes with the caveat not to use it in absolute terms. It is meant as an instrument rather than a doctrine. It provides suggestions rather than principles.

---

[9] The term 'metareferential moment' is appropriated from J. Hillis Miller, who uses the term 'linguistic moment' to designate that particular moment in poetry which signifies 'a breaking of the illusion that language is a transparent medium of meaning' (1985: xiv). For Miller, this moment indicates a point of rupture, the precise instance when the all-pervasiveness and therefore the ultimate arbitrariness of the linguistic sign annihilates the mimetic pretension of the literary signifier. Jeffrey Williams also takes up Miller's idea by proposing the term 'narrative moments' to describe 'moments in which the act of narrative itself is depicted and thus thematized or called into question' (1998: 1).

Table 1 Typology of metareferential elements/moments

1 Display
    1.1 Explicit
    1.2 Implicit
2 Location/Direction
    2.1 Endo-Reflective
        2.1.1 Level of the Enounced
        2.1.2 Level of the Enunciation
        2.1.3 Paratextual Level
    2.2 Exo-Reflective
        2.2.1 Allo-Reflective
        2.2.2 Pan-Reflective
    2.3 Interactional
3 Focus
    3.1 Textuality
    3.2 Alethiology
4 Effect
[4.1 Affirmative/Illustrating]
4.2 Deconstructive/Cynical
4.3 Reconstructive/Authenticating

Display

This represents the most clear-cut category, since it pertains to the phenomenological expression of the metareferential element, to the question whether it appears in form of a direct reference or rather as an indirect – structural, linguistic, media-based or aesthetic – allusion. It distinguishes, in other words, between literal and metaphorical manifestations of metareference. This dichotomy appears in one form or another in almost any existing typology. While Hutcheon puts it into the binary 'overt vs. covert', I will follow Wolf's terminology and distinguish between *explicit* and *implicit* displays of metareference.

Location/Direction

This dimension draws on Wolf's distinction between 'intracompositional vs. extracompositional' forms of metareference and concerns the position of the metareferential moment relative to the text in question. The primary distinction here is between *endo-reflective* and *exo-reflective* forms. In the first case, the metareferential element which opens up the metalevel inside a source text reflects back on the text itself, which means that the metareferential moment occurs within one and the same text. In the second instance, the metareferential element refers to or invokes another text or body of texts, which means that the metareferential moment occurs in an imagined space in between the texts in question. In addition, I want to propose a third subcategory which I call *interactional*. This category accounts for cases where the metareferential moment results from a direct interpellation of the reader's participation, where, in other words, the metareferential moment can be said to occur in the act of participation as such.

The endo-reflective category is further subdivided depending on whether the metareferential element refers to the level of the *enounced* (= the content of that which is expressed) or the *enunciation* (= the act of expressing) of the source text.[10] Drawing on Genette, I want to propose an additional level here, which in effect sits on the fence between the endo-reflective, exo-reflective and interactional domains and which, due to this oscillating position, will be particularly important in the subsequent analyses. This is the expansive area of *paratexts*, which Genette defines as 'the means by which a text makes a book of itself and proposes itself as such to its readers, and more generally to the public' (1991: 261). These include but are not limited to the author's names, prologues, epilogues, notes, mottoes but also blurbs, reviews or criticism, with which a specific text is supplemented.

The exo-reflective category also comprises two very distinct forms: I will call *allo-reflective*, derived from the Greek ἄλλος = 'other', these metareferential elements which specifically and explicitly refer to or invoke a *particular* text or body of texts. In such cases, the metareferential moment occurs in a space in between the two specific texts; it oscillates between the allo-text and source text. The category *pan-reflective*, from the Greek πᾶν = 'all-encompassing', in contrast, covers instances where the metareferential element alludes to *general* conventions, such as canonicity, genre traditions or media-specific code systems.

Focus

This category reformulates Wolf's distinction between *fictio*-metareference, where the metareferential moment foregrounds the condition and constructedness of the configuration of a text as a text, and *fictum*-metareference, which focuses on and examines the text according to its rapport with reality and/or truth. I think this is a very useful and perceptive distinction but take issue with the specific vocabulary Wolf puts forward, which, in particular when applied to works of literature, can cause unnecessary terminological complexity and confusion. I therefore suggest a distinction between a metareferential focus on the *textuality* of its source text and a focus on what I propose to call *alethiology*, that is, an investigation into the status of the source text as a product of the imagination, as an abstract model of reality.[11] The

---

[10] I am using Émile Benveniste's terminology here because it can be applied to a variety of media forms. In the field of literature, this distinction is usually expressed in Genette's terminology as the difference between the level of *histoire* as 'the totality of the narrated events' and that of *narration* as 'the real or fictive act that produces that discourse – in other words, the very fact of recounting' (Genette 1988: 13).

[11] I use this somewhat unwieldy and archaic name rather than apparently more or at least equally pertinent ones such as authenticity, sincerity, genuineness or veracity, because, pace Heidegger, it lacks the ideological and philosophical charge of such terms and is therefore, I hope, reasonably devoid of conceptual in(ter)ferences.

former, in other words, highlights on a metalevel the creation and constructedness of the source text, while the latter deals with its recreation and simulation of reality.

Effect

This category is in fact situated on a different logical register than the other three. The display, location and focus of metareferential elements generally occur on the textual level and can thus be clearly defined with regard to their phenomenological appearance. Contrarily, this last category of *effect* is not primarily a phenomenological but rather a performative dimension. It is supplementary to the other three aspects in so far as it constitutes an interpretation of the formal qualities established by the first three aspects. As the interpretative component necessarily involves a certain degree of intuition, individual judgement and even sentiment, the terminological terrain here is even more slippery than elsewhere. When I now propose to break up this category further into subdivisions, this must therefore be taken with a particularly generous pinch of salt. The principal differentiation is again based on Wolf, who distinguishes between critical and non-critical uses of metareference. Among the latter he counts instances where the intrusion of an omnipresent narrator does not first and foremost destroy the narrative illusion but in fact helps to sustain it by suggesting to the reader that 'the story one is reading is authentic' (2009: 44). Again I agree with Wolf's basic observation that self-reference can indeed be deployed strategically to reveal media conventions and therefore artistic illusion but also to support and maintain it. I think, however, that the dichotomy of critical vs. uncritical is not precise enough to do justice to the complexity of this category and needs further differentiation and explanation. In a first step, I adopt Wolf's initial distinction but rename it as a dichotomy of *affirmative* vs. *disruptive* effects of the metareferential elements employed. The criterion for this assessment is the relative reconcilability of the metalevel with the source text: if the metalevel can be plausibly integrated with the illusionary logic generated in and through the source text, the effect is affirmative; if it results in an epistemological impossibility or an ontological paradox which cannot be logically resolved within the framework of the source text, the effect is disruptive. Only instances of the latter actually qualify as metareferential; therefore the category of affirmative effect does not apply for metareference and only appears in my typology in brackets.

Supplementary to Wolf's distinction, I suggest a further subdivision of the disruptive effects of metareference. My contention is that even in cases where the use of metareference irresolvably tangles the hierarchies and disrupts the logical premises of the artistic illusion in the source text, it can nevertheless result in an increase of this text's believability. The literary analyses in the next section will attempt to retrace the formal features of this elusive believability, which I consider to be an effect of a process of reconstruction. I therefore propose to label this effect as *reconstructive* or *authenticating*. It is vital to note that this authenticity does not concern the text in and by itself but more exactly the communicative act established in and through this very text.

Not every tangled hierarchy, however, automatically engenders authentic encounters, and I suggest the category of *cynical* or *deconstructive* effect to account for this circumstance. This discrepancy between authenticating and cynical metareference mirrors Glenn's distinction of 'existential authenticity' and 'fake authenticity' introduced earlier. Both effects are generated by similar formal and structural deployments of metareference and ultimately depend largely on the individual assessment of the recipient. It is therefore all but impossible to establish any authoritative, definitive and durable criteria for this distinction, and one and the same text might be allocated to different categories by different recipients. As every individual perception of a text can thus be said to be performative, so are the criteria by which the believability/authenticity of this act of communication can be judged. Making a virtue of this terminological undecidability and vagueness, I claim that this interpellation of the individual recipient's judgement and responsibility, this performative and interactional interpretation which the texts in question demand, is the constitutive force behind the paradigm of reconstruction.

Essentially strange loops: Metareference as tangled hierarchy

As already indicated at various points, I see the notion of the tangled hierarchy, as proposed by Douglas Hofstadter, as the most appropriate analogy to illustrate the operational properties of metareference and to highlight its structural parallels to the notion of authenticity. Hofstadter first develops this idea in his ground-breaking study on *Gödel, Escher, Bach*, where he diagnoses a comprehensive breakdown of the hierarchy of ontological and epistemological structures which hitherto induced meaning into and deduced meaning from the contingent disorder of reality. He observes that the 'distinction between games, rules, metarules, metametarules, has been lost. What was once a nice clean hierarchical setup has become a Strange Loop, or Tangled Hierarchy' (1979: 688). Hofstadter does not mourn this loss of structural certitude. Instead, he sees in precisely this tangled and undecidable state the fundamental und ineluctable formula which underpins and enables any form of knowledge in any complex system of representation. Representation, he argues, must not be understood as a straightforward, logical and hierarchically ordered process but rather as an endlessly deferred and ultimately incongruous and paradox procedure, which feeds on the simultaneity of apparently exclusionary positions and the confusion of hierarchical structures of reference. Luhmann proposes a similar argument when he asserts that 'all knowledge and all action has to be founded on paradoxes and not on principles; on the self-referential unity of the positive and the negative – that is, on an ontologically unqualifiable world' (1993: 770). Hofstadter goes on to elaborate on the formal characteristics of this tangled hierarchy, which arises, so he claims, 'when what you presume are clean hierarchical levels take you by surprise and fold back in a hierarchy-violating way. The surprise element is important; it is the reason I call Strange Loops "strange"' (1979: 691).

It is important to note that this tangling of hierarchies does not abolish the concept of hierarchy as such. On the contrary, it is dependent on the validity of a conventional understanding of hierarchy in order to signify at all. Any epistemological challenge to an existing order necessarily presupposes a fundamental *idea* of order, or as Hofstadter puts it:

> There is an Inviolate level – let's call it the I-level – on which the interpretation conventions reside; there is also a Tangled level – the T-level – on which the Tangled Hierarchy resides. So these two levels are still hierarchical: the I-level governs what happens on the T-level, but the T-level does not and cannot affect the I-level. No matter that the T-level itself is a Tangled Hierarchy – it is still governed by a set of conventions outside of itself. (688)

Hofstadter's primary example of this paradoxical epistemology on the T-level is the human perception of and as an autonomous self. This rests on imaginary concepts such as consciousness, imagination or free will, all of which are, according to Hofstadter, 'based on a kind of Strange Loop, an interaction between levels in which the top level reaches back down towards the bottom level and influences it, while at the same time being itself determined by the bottom level' (709).[12] The entangled structures that enable this self-conception in the first place eventually become impenetrable: 'Just as we cannot see our faces with our own eyes, is it not reasonable to expect that we cannot mirror our complete mental structures in the symbols which carry them out?' (697). This endless feedback loop of self-deception, which gives rise to the first-person singular of human consciousness, eventually becomes so hard-wired through habitual use that 'causality gets turned around and "I" seems to be in the driver's seat' (Hofstadter 2007: 205). As a consequence, human beings can only behold the paradoxical and circular structure of their own epistemological condition by proxy, that is, by tracing and uncovering similar epistemological structures in other fields.

Hofstadter provides many such cases from fields as diverse as mathematics, music, literature, linguistics and the pictorial arts. The most famous and most frequently quoted of these examples is his interpretation of M. C. Escher's famous *Drawing Hands*, which displays a logically self-cancelling interplay of creator and creation, which 'sucks us so effectively into its paradoxical world, it fools us, at least briefly, into believing in its reality' (103). This short quote highlights two aspects central to the tangled hierarchy, which will continually reoccur in my own analyses: first, the *epistemological paradox* that is represented on the level of the source text, and second the moment of *ontological perplexity and bewilderment* which the reception of this paradox generates.[13] This almost somatic experience of astonishment and perplexity,

---

[12] In one of the few systematic applications of Hofstadter's theory to the area of cultural development and art, Jean-Pierre Dupuy propounds a similar notion when he states that the 'tangled hierarchy characterizes the autonomy of a self that is "always already" constituted' (1990: 107).

[13] One could, of course, argue that the belief in more than one level or hierarchy of representation within one media display is hopelessly naïve and that there is always only the one level of representation which Hofstadter calls the I-level. For, when all is said and done, the hands in Escher's drawing exist purely on the level of the drawing itself, and any construction of a metalevel is mere esoteric conjecture without any phenomenological proof. This constitutes a phenomenological

which David Foster Wallace calls 'the click' (see McCaffery 1993: 139), forms the activation energy which propels the recipient to become an active participant in the communicative act constituted by the metareferential element in question. It also presents a link to Höltgen's somaticizing dimension of his aesthetics of authenticity.

I will now try to make a case for the practical benefit of a metareferential approach to literary analysis by delineating some of its specific aesthetic and structural characteristics. In literature there are two fundamental aspects which lend themselves particularly well to a tangling of hierarchically organized levels: the *communicative act* constituted by the work in question and the ontological status of the text, that is, the attitude towards reality the text conveys through its *mode of mediation*. Both of these textual dimensions can be understood in terms of interplay between distinct and supposedly fixed epistemological quantities. In the case of the former, these are best described with Jakobson as the constituent factors of the communicative act, while the latter refers to the levels of narrative mediation in the text. I will first outline these two dimensions in more detail, before introducing four key stylistic devices which operate on and in between these categories and which facilitate the metareferential tangling of these hierarchies.[14]

I suggest the following adaptation of Jakobson's model of communication (1960: 353–4) so as to conform more precisely to the specific parameters of literary communication which I investigate. In my view any act of literary communication can be understood as an interface of the factors *context, content, author, reader, parabasis* and *self-reference*. The first four are well established and do not require further elaboration. I substitute the Jakobson factor 'channel' with the term 'parabasis', which in Greek theatre describes instances where the plot of a play is temporarily interrupted and the chorus addresses the audience directly, usually in order to connect the contents of the play to the extra-textual world. Parabasis, in Thomas K. Hubbard's words, 'stands between the mimetic discourse of drama and the external world of the signifieds (political and social reality) and thus helps the audience to connect the worlds of drama and reality' (1991: 28). In keeping with Jakobson's understanding of the phatic function of the factor 'channel', parabasis in my model denotes those structural

---

truism and is therefore not contestable in terms of pure positivist logic. So, any serious involvement with Hofstadter's tangled hierarchies is premised on a certain amount of uncertainty tolerance, a playful and willing suspension of disbelief or, as Michael Saler calls it, a 'willing activation of pretence' (2012: 28). In his analysis of René Magritte's famous painting *Les Deux Mystères (Ceci n'est pas une pipe)*, however, Hofstadter himself makes an elegant attempt to justify his approach in formal terms. He argues that however positivist the approach to the painting may be, it nevertheless presents a structural aporia, as the 'only way not to be sucked in is to see both pipes merely as coloured smudges on a surface a few inches in front of your nose. Then, and only then, do you appreciate the full meaning of the written message "Ceci n'est pas une pipe" – but ironically, at the very instant everything turns to smudges, the writing too turns to smudges, thereby losing its meaning' (1979: 701).

[14] I am aware that by sticking to the term 'hierarchy' to describe the workings of metareference I run the risk of suggesting that the constituent factors can be organized according to principles of precedence or pre-eminence. This, however, is not the case. Hierarchy in this case does not imply an order of relational dominance between the constituents but rather refers to their respective autonomy, their allocation of a predetermined position with regard to one another in the framework of literary communication. It is the fixity of these positions which metareference challenges.

elements in literary communication which ascertain the connection between author and reader. In addition to that, I will use the term to refer to the specific stylistic device when a character on the level of the enounced assumes to speak with the voice of the extra-textual author.[15] The second modification I suggest to Jakobson's model is the substitution of the factor 'code' with the term 'self-reference'. The specific use of this term in this context reflects the inherent self-reflective propensity of aesthetic discourse which I have delineated above with reference to Mukařovský.

The dimension of mediation can, of course, not be perceived independently from the communicative dimension of a fictional text. They are inextricably intertwined and interact constantly, so that any sharp separation can only ever be hypothetical abstraction. What aggravates the situation in this particular case is the confused and often contradictory state of affairs as regards the extant terminology, where the terms 'story', 'discourse', 'narration' and 'diegesis' are often used in apparently random fashion.[16] The organization of levels of mediation which I am proposing here makes generous use of many terms already in use. It cannot claim to overcome the complexities with which the use of these terms is fraught. It should rather be understood as a pragmatic and strategic attempt to pare down the intricacies of existing classifications. While the hierarchy that governs the communicative aspect of literature is rhizomatic rather than tiered, the sequence of levels I suggest here does adhere to a logical gradation, one that can be described as the *degree of fictionality* in a text. An extra-textual, epistemic correspondence with 'the real world' constitutes, as Mukařovský has shown, the basic point of reference of all aesthetic mediation. It can incorporate the political, social or philosophical background of the text, the material actuality of the author's biography as well as the history of a text's reception, or, in the specific case of intertextuality, the allo-textual reference of the source text. The next stratum concerns the factual configuration of the text in question. It includes both possible paratexts and what Genette calls the *récit*, the material manifestation of the imaginary events, its arrangement in the time and space allowed for by its medium (see 1988: 13). This level concerns what amounts to the *Gestalt* of the text and will therefore be designated as its '*Gestalt* level'. In particular Eggers's text, but also to a lesser extent Fforde and Egan exploit this level of textuality for their enactments of readerly reconstructions.

---

[15] This function is covered by the traditional usage of the term, for example in Aristophanes's *The Clouds*, where the chorus in lieu of the poet addresses the audience thus: 'As much as I wish to emerge victorious and be recognized as brilliant, so I believed that you were smart theatergoers and that this was the most brilliant of my comedies' (quoted in Major 2006: 139). Brian Stonehill is one of the few critics to deploy parabasis as a tool for describing instances of metareference. Contrary to the way I use the term, however, he sees its function primarily in uncovering the fictional illusion of a text, as a 'marked disruption of style which reminds the reader of the performing artificer' (1988: 41). I would argue that such a narrow and indeed interpretative focus does not do justice to the broad range of usages to which parabasis was apparently put in Greek drama (see Bowie 1982) nor to its potential usefulness for investigating contemporary forms of self-reference in the arts.

[16] Much of the confusion is no doubt due to problems of translation, as Russian Formalist notions (like the distinction of *syuzhet* vs. *fabula*) are adopted by French theorists such as Todorov (*discours* vs. *histoire*), Benveniste (*discours* vs. *histoire*; *énoncé* vs. *énonciation*) or Genette (*récit* vs. *histoire* vs. *narration*) and then rendered into English. For laudable but ultimately insufficient attempts to induce order into this terminological disarray, see Genette (1988: 13–20) and Martinez and Scheffel (2000: 22–6).

The subsequent levels leave the tangible realm of materiality and cross the threshold to the realm of the imaginary. Genette's distinction of *histoire* as 'the totality of the narrated events' vs. *narration* as the act that conveys these events (1988: 13) is indeed very discerning but marred by the terminological inferences I have already cited. Therefore, and in order to keep the terminology instrumental for the analysis of forms of discourse apart from literature, I will use Benveniste's terms 'enounced' and 'enunciation'. The *level of the enounced* corresponds to the narrative *content* of the source text; it refers to what Genette calls the intradiegetic dimension of the text. The *level of the enunciation* concerns the narrative *form* or perspective in which this content is conveyed, or, in Genette's terminology, its diegetic dimension.[17]

The next level already crosses the threshold of metareference. In non-metareferential texts, the *Gestalt* of the text, its enunciation and its enounced, usually add up without much epistemological inconsistency or ontological friction to form a rationally consistent reading experience. It is only through the introduction of another level of mediation that the metareferential paradox can be brought to bear. This metalevel arises when an epistemological or ontological mismatch occurs between any of these three levels, a mismatch which disrupts the logical consistency and aesthetic sovereignty of the source text. It is important to reiterate here that the mere existence of a metalevel alone does not inescapably result in metareference. If the paradox can be resolved on the next higher level, this constitutes a form of weak self-referentiality which leaves the general hierarchy of levels unaffected. It is only when, as in the case studies on *A Visit from the Goon Squad* and *The Sense of an Ending*, the introduction of metalevel involves the tangling of this hierarchy and thus an irresolvable logical contradiction or paradox that the term metareference should be applied.

Metalepsis

Following on from these general structural remarks, I will now examine four specific stylistic devices and forms in which metareferential elements can occur in a literary text. These are metalepsis, irony, ergodic reading and intertextuality. As I said, the effect of metareference can be imagined as an intertwining of the supposedly autonomous and logically detached roles and levels which make up the act of literary communication. Consequently, one of the key stylistic devices for bringing about metareferential moments is the metalepsis. Introduced into narratological discourse by Genette, who defines it as 'a deliberate transgression of the threshold of embedding' (1991: 88), this device denotes any instance within a work of art where the focus of representation shifts from one ontological level onto another, an instance which Wolf refers to as a narrative shortcut (see 1993: 357). It is also Wolf who delivers the most comprehensive definition of the term. He describes metalepsis as 'a salient phenomenon occurring

---

[17] The terms 'diegetic' and 'intradiegetic' have also been used in many, often confusing and sometimes contradictory ways. Genette originally came up with this typology, which also includes the categories 'extradiegetic', 'autodiegetic', 'homodiegetic' and 'heterodiegetic', to describe what he calls 'voice', that is, the perspective of the narrator relative to the narrated events, and only later, and in my view not entirely convincingly, applied them to the different levels within a text (see 1991: 79–96).

exclusively in representations, namely as a usually non-accidental and paradoxical transgression of the border between levels or (sub)worlds that are ontologically (in particular concerning the opposition reality vs. fiction) or logically differentiated' (2009: 50). In literature this transgression most frequently affects the levels of the enounced and the enunciation, for example when hitherto intradiegetic narrators suddenly shift their focus onto aspects concerning the enunciation, such as their status as a constituent in an act of literary communication; Jane Eyre's famous 'Reader, I married him' is a pertinent case in point. Fanfan Chen highlights the subversive potential inherent in this device by proposing that metalepsis 'can be employed to effect transgression on three different levels: that of the author and his product, that of the diegetic story and the hypodiegetic story and, finally, that of the reader and the work' (2008: 409). Seen from a purely formal perspective, metalepsis is susceptible to similar objections as those I have delineated earlier for the parabasis, namely that the shift between different levels of textual representation is indeed no such thing at all but only a mischievous deception which can never actually transcend the boundaries of its text. Sonja Klimek summarizes this attitude by stating that 'apart from such special cases of metalepses in the performative arts [the direct interplay between actor and character], metalepses can only appear within artefacts, creating the *impression* of a transgression between a fictitious and a real world and hiding the fact that also the level of what seems to be "real" is merely part of the artefact, not of the reality outside the artefact' (2009: 172; emphasis added). Although this is a logically unassailable position, my subsequent analysis of Dave Eggers's *A Heartbreaking Work of Staggering Genius* will offer a striking illustration of how metalepsis can indeed be employed to severely disrupt the stability and autonomy of the constituent factors of literary communication.

While every metalepsis is inherently self-referential, it need not always be metareferential. The example of *Jane Eyre* clearly shows that it does not necessarily result in a paradoxical and therefore metareferential moment. Wolf suggests a differentiation between three types of metalepsis: a *rhetorical* form, which consists merely in a 'narratorial transgression of the border between extra- and intradiegetic levels'; an *epistemological* form, which concerns a case of '"impossible" knowledge fictional characters appear to have of their being mere characters'; and an *ontological* form, which is constituted by the 'physical transgression of a logical or ontological border between two levels/worlds by a character or object' (2009: 52–3). While this terminology is no doubt useful for the description of individual cases, its categories still tend to overlap and interact in a way which renders it inadequate for a more general formal analysis. For the purpose of this investigation, I will only differentiate between those instances of metalepsis which are merely self-referential and can be integrated into the logic of the communicative act and those which constitute proper metareferential elements because they generate a logical aporia or paradox which induces an active renegotiation and reconstruction of this particular act of communication.

One variety of metalepsis in particular has recently enjoyed great critical popularity: the *mise-en-abyme*. The term itself originates from heraldry, where the *abyme* (= 'chasm, abyss') denotes the centre-part of a coat of arms, which often consists of another, smaller coat of arms. The French term actually allows for two interpretations: it can either denote that which is 'put into the chasm', that is, an object of representation, or the act of 'putting into the chasm', that is, a performative process; it can refer to a process as well as to its result. It is André Gide who reassigns the term to the domain of art criticism. He uses it to denote any work of art which includes 'transposed, at the level of the characters, the subject of the work itself' (Gide quoted in Dällenbach 1989: 7). In his authoritative study on the *mise-en-abyme*, Lucien Dällenbach defines it first very broadly as 'any aspect enclosed within a work that shows a similarity with the work that contains it' (8) and then more specifically in the context of narrative as 'any internal mirror that reflects the whole of the narrative by simple, repeated or "specious" (or paradoxical) duplication' (36). Drawing on the origins of the terms, he characterizes the *mise-en-abyme* as a stylistic device which 'installs the problematic of the work at the heart of the work itself' (25). It can do so by revealing, that is, making present, on the level of the enounced, the ontological strata of mediation of the source text and the constituents of its communicative act. This disclosure can thus either concern 'the producer or receiver of the narrative', the 'production or reception *per se*' or 'the context that determines (or has determined) this production/reception' (75). Following Gide, Dällenbach distinguishes three formal variants of the *mise-en-abyme*: *simple* duplication, as in the coat-of-arms mentioned above; *infinite* duplication, as in the famous *Droste* cocoa container, which gave its name to the so-called 'Droste effect' or songs like 'There's a Hole in my Bucket'; and *aporetic* duplication, which, like Julio Cortázar's famous story 'The Continuity of Parks' (1978), consists of 'a sequence that is supposed to enclose the work that encloses it' (Dällenbach 1989: 35).

Again, all instances of *mise-en-abyme* are inherently self-referential, but it is only the aporetic, paradoxical form that is also metareferential in the sense used in this book. Escher's *Drawing Hands* is a case in point for the latter, as is Michael Mandiberg's project aftersherrielevine.com/afterwalkerevans.com (2001), which – in its puckish embrace of fake and appropriation – might even suggest a way out of the crisis which Dällenbach diagnoses for the *mise-en-abyme*: as an 'index of the break with representational thought, which has dominated the Western literary tradition', it is surplus to requirements in an environment which no longer subscribes to the mimetic understanding of representation (1989: 165).[18] Perhaps, one might assume, it is not primarily the mirroring effect of the *mise-en-abyme*, described by Dällenbach as a 'lacuna within the identity' of a text (111), which accounts for its transgressive metareferential potential. As Mandiberg's work shows, metareference can also occur in cases where there appears to be complete congruence between the source text and the metalevel. In such cases, the lacuna becomes transposed. It is no longer an explicit effect of representation and thus formally restricted to the intratextual domain but rather an implicit effect of the reflection on representation and thus transferred to a space essentially outside of the materiality of the text. Jorge Luis Borges frequently plays with this notion

---

[18] See Funk (2011b: 225–6) and Bantleon (2011: 329–32) for in-depth analyses of this project, which uses reproductions of photos taken by Walker Evans in 1936 and appropriated by Sherrie Levine in 1979 to cleverly tangle notions of adaptation, authorship and authenticity.

of complete congruence. In 'Pierre Menard, Author of the *Quixote*', for example, the eponymous writer's chief oeuvre consists of a word-by-word reproduction of 'the ninth and thirty-eighth chapters of the first part of *Don Quixote* and a fragment of chapter twenty-two' (1964: 39). Although 'Cervantes's text and Menard's are verbally identical', the story claims that 'the second is almost infinitely richer', because it implicitly incorporates every event since the novel's original publication and therefore altogether 'points to a new conception of the historical novel' (42).[19]

Irony

In the conclusion to *The Mirror in the Text*, Dällenbach imbues the *mise-en-abyme* with a philosophical dimension. Drawing on Fichte, he assumes that 'the absolute subject can only asymptotically catch up with itself at the end of an infinite series of duplications, through which self-consciousness continually takes itself as its own object' (1989: 175). He sees the *mise-en-abyme*, both in its infinite and in its aporetic variety, as a symbolic manifestation of this paradoxical self-realization. Friedrich Schlegel calls this productive form of unending self-reflection 'Romantic irony' (see 1986: 82), and Oliver Kohns explains that it is only when the reflection of the self is transformed into contemplation (*Anschauung*) that this process can come to an end (see 2007: 198). David Roberts is more interested in the formal aspects of Romantic irony, which he considers to be a prime example of his conception of self-reference in literature as the 'paradoxical achievement of the re-entry of form into the form'. The introduction of one or more metalevels into a work of art, so he argues, both provides evidence for the inherent inadequacy of any formal system of representation and simultaneously elevates the same system 'to a higher power, the power of potentially infinite self-reflection' and can therefore be considered to be 'the objective self-reflection of the work' (1999: 37). Combining these two approaches, one might conclude that it is the purpose of Romantic irony to symbolically enact the aporia of representation in order to facilitate a form of contemplation which is at the same time selfless and objectless and which thereby imitates the structural paradox of authenticity.

Prima facie, irony looks like the very opposite of authenticity, as etymologically it is intrinsically tied to notions of dissimulation and pretence. It derives from the Greek word εἴρων, which describes someone who feigns to be naïve or ignorant in order to throw into relief the boastfulness, arrogance or inanity of others. Socrates is often credited with employing irony in this sense as 'feigned ignorance and disingenuousness ... during philosophical discussions' ('irony, n.' 2014). In Aristotle's fragmentary theory of comedy, the εἴρων appears as a stock character, who 'masks his cleverness under a show of clownish dullness' (Cornford 2011: 138).[20] In its original

---

[19] In the 152-word short story 'On Exactitude in Science', Borges presents another version of this complete congruence. The text features a 'map of the Empire whose size was that of the Empire, and which coincided point for point with it', which ultimately renders it useless (Borges 1999: 325). For further analysis of Borges's use of metalepsis, see Gracia (2001) and Lie (2009).

[20] To be more precise, the εἴρων as a character is mentioned in the *Tractatus Coislinianus*, where he is opposed to the ἀλαζών. In his translation, Richard Janko renders this pair as the 'buffoonish' and

sense, then, irony indicates a form of dedicated and truth-seeking deception, which is employed in order to reveal other, one would assume even more destructive, forms of deception. Over the course of time, this benign aspect has been relegated to the background. With generations of students scouring texts for an 'expression of one's meaning by using language that normally signifies the opposite' ('irony, *n.*' 2014), irony has become virtually synonymous with an inauthentic – *uneigentlich* in Adorno's sense – use of language. On a formal level, this ironic use of language could be defined as a latent rift between the signifier and the signified. Considering that the same definition could also be applied to Derrida's notion of *différance*, it can hardly surprise that irony is frequently cited as one of the key structural components of postmodern aesthetics (see, e.g. Wilde 1981: 127–65); Hutcheon even ascribes to it a 'governing role ... in postmodernism' (1988: 4).

In view of this, it is plausible to assume that the demise of postmodern theories would also portend the end of irony in its present form and practice. In a much-debated article for *TIME* magazine entitled 'The Age of Irony Comes to an End', Roger Rosenblatt espouses this very opinion. For him it is the collapse of the Twin Towers in the attacks of 9/11 which symbolically and actually marks the end of postmodern thinking, a period 'roughly as long as the Twin Towers were upright [when] the good folks in charge of America's intellectual life have insisted that nothing was to be believed in or taken seriously. Nothing was real.' If, so Rosenblatt's pernicious argument goes, the excess of the reality of pain and suffering induced by the terrorist attacks generate 'one good thing', it is the elimination of these postmodern *eirônes*, the 'ironists [who by] seeing through everything, made it difficult for anyone to see anything' (2001).[21] In *Flaubert's Parrot*, Julian Barnes muses how irony can be 'either the devil's mark or the snorkel of sanity' (1984: 155). It would seem as though with the decline of postmodernism the pendulum has swung decidedly towards the former. In one of the most influential detractions of postmodern irony before 9/11, David Foster Wallace criticizes that 'irony and ridicule are entertaining and effective, and that at the same time they are agents of a great despair and stasis in U.S. culture' (1993: 171). Drawing on Wallace, Adam Kelly lists irony, among solipsism, narcissism and insincerity, as one of the benchmarks of postmodernism which the practice of New Sincerity aims to overcome (see 2010a: 148).

Not everybody, however, is convinced that irony has actually breathed its last. Interestingly, many attempts to re-establish and reimagine irony for a post-postmodern age trace it back to its conceptual and etymological roots. Zoe Williams rightly emphasizes irony's corrective and didactic function by declaring that the 'end of irony would be a disaster for the world – bad things will always occur, and those at fault will always attempt to cover them up with emotional and overblown language' (2003: 28). Even

the 'ironical' character (Aristotle 1987: 45). The same opposition also occurs in the *Nicomachean Ethics*, where it describes the two contrary approaches to truth-telling any orator can subscribe to. Terence Irwin's translation uses the terms 'boastful' and 'self-deprecating' in this context (2000: 27).

[21] I will not even grace Rosenblatt's contemptible reasoning with the contention that this 'excess of reality' on 9/11 was, for the vast majority of people, in actual fact itself the result of incessant media representation rather than any brush with the unmediated real.

before 9/11 there are theorists keen to highlight the redeeming, sanitizing candour of irony rather than its diabolical dishonesty. Golomb identifies irony as 'a royal path to authenticity' and goes on to explain that irony 'facilitates the emergence of authenticity by helping the individual to become detached from her self' (1995: 26, 29). Lawrence Grossberg playfully stresses the intricate but potentially fertile interplay between irony and authenticity by suggesting that *ironic inauthenticity* constitutes the most productive form of what he calls 'authentic inauthenticities'. This ironic approach to inauthenticity, he argues, 'seems to celebrate the absence of any center or identity, [while] it actually locates that absence as a new center' (1994: 227). In mathematical terms, one could express this in the, admittedly very simplistic, form of a double negative from which quite logically a positive result ensues: irony + inauthenticity = authenticity. Alexei Yurchak even explicitly links irony with the aesthetics of what he calls 'new sincerity', which, 'as a post-postmodern phenomenon, is acutely self-aware and self-ironic. However, it is a particular brand of irony which is sympathetic and warm, and allows its authors to remain committed to the ideals that they discuss, while also being somewhat ironic about this commitment' (2008: 258). One of the most elaborate and substantial pleas for a renegotiation of irony as a constructive rather than a caustic force in contemporary culture comes courtesy of Florian Groß. He shows how current meta-televisional formats like NBC's *30 Rock* bring about an innovative fusion of irony and authenticity by displaying 'these two concepts in a dialectical relationship that alternates between paradox, contradiction, and mutual dependency' (2012: 256). Groß's claim about the possible merger of irony and authenticity chimes in with Jerry Saltz's assessment that contemporary 'artists not only see the distinction between earnestness and detachment as artificial; they grasp that they can be ironic and sincere at the same time, and they are making art from this compound-complex state of mind' (2010).

It is in a similar fashion that I understand the notion of irony. I propose to understand it not so much as a textual effect or literary style but as an attitude towards art itself, more precisely as a capability to simultaneously entertain different levels of consciousness, which must be adopted by author and reader alike in order for an act of literary communication to be authentic and reconstructive. This stance is characterized by a feigned humility which, true to the original sense of the word, seeks revelation in dissimulation and veracity in deception. Vermeulen and van den Akker similarly describe their concept of metamodernism as 'a kind of informed naivety' (2010). In the context of literature, this paradoxical epistemology of the ironic can assume the formal guise of metareference as an aesthetic procedure which enables the ironic sublation of an hierarchical level of mediation and fixed roles of communication.

Ergodic reading

Much of what I have outlined so far remains safely in the sphere of the theoretical. It is now time to look into the material effects which the tangling of hierarchical structures has on the actual act of reading, in other words, how metareference can in fact alter the reception process. Espen J. Aarseth's notion of 'ergodic literature' helps to illustrate this effect. Borrowed from the realm of mathematics and physics, Aarseth uses this concept to describe any form of literature where 'nontrivial effort is required to allow the reader to traverse the text' (1997: 1). The term itself combines the Greek word for 'work' (ἔργον) with that for 'path' or 'way' (ὁδός). Consequently, an ergodic text does not offer itself as a straightforward and linear experience of reception in time and space. Rather, it requires a certain amount of physical and mental struggle and agility on the part of readers to navigate their way through it. Ergodic reading is therefore performative as much as it is receptive. Aarseth initially uses this notion in order to distinguish the skills needed for the analysis of what he calls cybertexts as opposed to more conventional, plot-driven forms of reception, which he subsumes under the category of hypertext. According to Aarseth,

> the concept of hypertext focuses on the mechanical organization of the text, by positing the intricacies of the medium as an integral part of the literary exchange. However, it also centers attention on the consumer, or user, of the text, as a more integrated figure than even reader-response theorists would claim. The performance of their reader takes place all in his head, while the user of cybertext also performs in an extranoematic sense. (1)[22]

A cybertext is characterized by a process of reception where 'the user will have effectuated a semiotic sequence, and this selective movement is a work of physical construction that the various concepts of "reading" do not account for' (ibid.).[23] In other words, the hypertext already dictates the outcome of the reception process through its narrative structure. The author of a hypertext is always necessarily one step ahead of the user. In contrast to this, a cybertext does not pre-structure the reception process but only provides the framework of rules in which this process takes place. The outcome and embodiment of this process must literally be accomplished by the user of the text. One criterion for the cybertext is 'whether the user has the ability to transform the text into something that the instigator of the text could not foresee or plan for' (164). Ergodic literature, Aarseth argues, involves a movement from epistemological aporia to epiphany, and it is this very step which marks the emergence of authenticity and which makes his theory a relevant descriptive tool in the context of an aesthetics of reconstruction.

It is important to note that his differentiation between cybertext and hypertext does not concern the medium or genre of a given text. Novels as well as computer

---

[22] Kirby's description of the internet as the quintessential pseudo-modern device adopts some of Aarseth's ideas and terms. For Kirby, the internet's 'central act is that of the individual clicking on his/her mouse to move through pages in a way which cannot be duplicated, inventing a pathway through cultural products which has never existed before and never will again' (2006).

[23] Aarseth employs the term 'user' for the various manifestations of the receptive entity in a media-based encounter, from readers of books to players of games. He justifies this term by claiming that 'the political connotations of the word *user* are conveniently ambivalent, suggesting both active participation and dependency, a figure under the influence of some kind of pleasure-giving system' (1997: 174; emphasis in the original). I have decided to follow this use only in the explicit context of Aarseth's theory and otherwise stick with the term 'reader'.

games can be cybertextual or hypertextual. According to Aarseth, the difference is not 'between games and literature but rather games and narrative' (4–5). This ludic dimension of the cybertext is further highlighted by the fact that the 'ergodic work of art is one that in a material sense includes the rules for its own use, a work that has certain requirements built in that automatically distinguishes between successful and unsuccessful users' (179).

In my analysis, I narrow the focus of Aarseth's notion of ergodic reception to the particular field of narrative literature. Even Aarseth acknowledges that the traditional material constitution of a novel predestines it for the status of a cybertext, as the 'book form ... is intrinsically neither linear nor nonlinear but, more precisely, random access (to borrow from computer terminology)' (46). One of the distinctive criteria I claim for reconstructive texts can be located in its ergodic reception process. On the one hand, this refers to the playful nature of the reconstructive text, for the fact, in other words, that its metareferential indeterminacies and tangled hierarchies constitute a game to be creatively engaged with rather than a plot to be slavishly retraced. Moreover, the connotation of ergodic with 'physical construction' also can be used to describe the actual handling of reconstructive texts, which often involves non-linear, and certainly non-trivial, effort. In *The Pleasure of the Text* (1976), Roland Barthes coins the term *tmesis* for the practice of a 'reader's unconstrained skipping and skimming of the passages, a fragmentation of the linear text expression that is totally beyond the author's control' (Aarseth 1997: 78), and it is this very procedure of being able to access and approach the text in individual, random patterns which facilitates the novel's status as ergodic literature, as the case studies of Fforde's series and Eggers's novel in particular will demonstrate.

Intertextuality

So far I have used the term 'reconstructive literature' to refer to a revaluation of either the conventional role attributions in the act of literary communication or the ontological levels of mediation of which this act is constituted. There is, however, another hierarchical set of relations which lends itself to reconstruction: the connections between and among individual texts. Traditionally, this interplay among texts or bodies of texts has been theorized under the label 'intertextuality', and I will now briefly comment on such aspects of this very broad field as are pertinent for the specific argument of this book. As in the case of self-reference, intertextuality occurs in a weak and a strong form. If Derrida is right that the world as we can know it is essentially *textual*, then it follows that any reference inside this world can formally be identified as *intertextual* (cf. Sobchack 1990: 57). Any single referential expression is necessarily and inescapably tied up in a byzantine rhizomatic network of interconnections. This assumption, in turn, renders the conception of a work of art as an autonomous, monolithic and, in a Benjaminian sense, auratic entity null and void and replaces it with an inherently dialogic and interdependent model in the vein of Bakhtin. It is Julia Kristeva who first uses the term 'intertextuality' in this way, when she writes in *Revolution of Poetic Language* that 'If one grants that every signifying practice is a field of transpositions of various signifying systems (an inter-textuality), one then understands that its "place" of enunciation and its denoted "object" are never single, complete, and identical to themselves, but always plural, shattered, capable of being tabulated' (1984: 60). Ricœur pursues a similar argument:

> The semantic autonomy of the text and the poetic nature of language turned in upon itself engender a new type of relation between texts, an intertextuality which serves to cut fiction off from the world of actual action, in such a way that texts, in completing, correcting, quoting, and crossing out one another, form a closed chain, a library in the precise sense of the term. (1991: 144)

In this all-pervasive and inescapable manifestation, which I call *weak intertextuality*, the term may indeed provide an apt description of the 'textual condition' of postmodernism (see McGann 1991), but it loses much of its critical rigour for individual analyses.[24] In order to show the implications of intertextuality for metareference, a more specific understanding of the term is necessary. I will therefore use the notion of a *strong form of intertextuality* to denote instances where the metareferential element which gives rise to a metalevel inside a source text consists of a reference, implicit or explicit, to another distinct text or body of texts. Margaret Rose emphasizes the strong link between this form of intertextuality, which she rather sweepingly subsumes under the heading of parody, and metareference. She points to parody's potential to transform conventional frameworks of reference and epistemology and describes parody as an intentional confusion 'to challenge the reader to the task of interpretation' (1979: 62). In *Palimpsests*, Genette describes as *hypotext* the text that is being referenced and *hypertext* the text in which the referencing occurs (see 1997: 107–12). Although this dichotomy looks straightforward enough, it has fallen prey to a terminological obfuscation similar to that which has befallen other Genettian terms. In keeping with the terminology used in my typology, I will refer to the text that is invoked or referenced by the metareferential element as the *allo-text*, and to the text in which the reference occurs as the source text.

Again, it must be emphasized that just as not every instance of self-reference is necessarily metareferential, not all cases of intertextual reference automatically tangle the hierarchies between these textual levels. In order to account for this difference, I will redeploy a distinction which Jameson has introduced to the field of intertextuality: parody vs. pastiche. Jameson sees the difference between the two mainly in terms of reverence. While parody 'capitalizes on the uniqueness' of the allo-text to 'produce an imitation which mocks the original', it still retains 'some secret sympathy for the original' (1989: 113). In other words, parody not only upholds the hierarchical structure of original and imitation, but this logic of antecedence is a basic requirement for parody to function in the first place. While parody thus is very much an enactment of 'the anxiety of influence', as described famously by Harold Bloom,

---

[24] Since this book is not predominantly concerned with intertextuality, I can only scrape the historical development of the concept as well as its aesthetic and formal intricacies. I refer to works such as Riffaterre (1984), Hutcheon (1985), Broich and Pfister (1985) and Allen (2000) for more comprehensive accounts.

the metareferential version of intertextuality works towards effacing these very structures of prominence and ascendancy. In Jameson's notion of pastiche, this levelling and relativizing effect of intertextuality is foregrounded. If parody can be seen as an attempt to revive the allo-text, pastiche is premised on the assumptions that all allo-texts are to all intents and purposes stone-dead, that no communication between the texts is possible any more, and that in postmodernism 'all that is left is to imitate dead styles, to speak through the masks and with the voices of the styles in the imaginary museum' (115). For Jameson, pastiche is a bleak business, 'a statue with blind eyeballs', symbolic of postmodernism's all-encompassing superficiality and triviality (17).[25] Here, I would propose to revaluate the significance of pastiche. In my view, it is precisely the abolition of structures of eminence and influence implied in pastiche which mark it out as a quintessentially metareferential device. To be more specific, the metareferential moment which is engendered by pastiche can be imagined as an oscillation between the allo-textual level and the level of the source text, to an extent which abolishes the hierarchical structures between these two levels. This abrogation of hierarchy, in turn, forces the readers to reconfigure and reconstruct on their own ergodic terms the relationship between the texts. By subverting one-dimensional conceptions of originality, influence or descent, metareference literally breaks open traditional notions such as canonicity, adaptation or parody and installs in their place an aesthetics of enmeshment, of an inextricable interdependence between the texts. In its metareferential guise, intertextuality is not primarily interested in origins and adaptations any more. Rather, it is the interplay itself that is the thing, as might be punned with an apologetic nod towards Elsinore.

What unites both the structural characteristics of metareference and its various stylistic manifestations is that they all result in an augmentation of the role of the reader in the act of literary communication. There are quite a few critics who have remarked on this increased importance granted to the reader in contemporary literature and the aesthetic and ethical implications this shift in perspective might incur. Adam Kelly, for example, highlights the move towards an essential structural openness that accompanies this concession of interpretative authority from the author to the reader. He observes how 'in the spiralling search for the truth of intentions, in an era when advertising, self-promotion and irony are endemic, the endpoint to the infinite jest of consciousness can only be the reader's choice whether or not to place trust and Blind Faith' (2010a: 148). Huber similarly proposes to 'understand the new development by foregrounding the renegotiation of the communicative bond between author/narrator and reader' (2014: 40), and Kirby bases his conception of 'pseudo-modernism' on the notion that 'the culture we have now fetishizes the *recipient* of the text to the degree that they become a partial

---

[25] Hutcheon's understanding of parody highlights the essential ambiguity of the concept and can be situated halfway between the two poles described by Jameson. To parody, she argues, 'is not to destroy the past; in fact to parody is both to enshrine the past and to question it. And this, once again, is the postmodern paradox' (1988: 126). Elsewhere, Hutcheon elaborates on this paradox: 'Postmodern intertextuality is a formal manifestation of both a desire to close the gap between past and present for the reader and a desire to rewrite the past in a new context' (1996: 487).

or whole author of it' (2006; emphasis in the original). This new empowerment of the reader in reconstructive texts, which concerns readers as individual recipients of texts but also their structural role in the framework of media-based and artistic communication, can be seen as literature's answer to two fundamental cultural and social transformations of recent times. On the one hand, it reflects the current predominance of what I have previously described as a culture of virtual involvement and participation, which manifests itself most evidently in the dialogic and interactive creed of social media worlds and which redefines traditional notions of production, reception and communication. On the other hand, reconstructive texts address and mirror new forms of human self-representation and self-conception, which are virtual and digital in nature and which result from this development. There are two key aesthetic conclusions to be drawn at this point. Both developments question the stability of traditionally self-evident literary categories by blurring the boundaries of terms like authorship, reading, fictionality and mimesis. Irina Rajewski argues that any transgression of the narrative system 'makes it apparent to the reader that his or her assumptions as to the nature of established narrative situations are already based on habitualised reception patterns, established norms and boundaries which, as the texts show, could indeed just as well be constructed differently' (2009: 148). Reconstruction, as I understand it, is a formal attempt to rewire these habitualized patterns. By leaving the task of reconstructing the tangled hierarchies of epistemology and ontology to the recipient, these texts attempt 'to make something happen *off* the page, *outside* words' (Smith 2003: xx; emphases in the original). David Foster Wallace also highlights the reversal of impact aspired to in such texts: 'We're not keen on the idea of the story sharing its value with the reader. But the reader's own life "outside" the story changes the story' (quoted in McCaffery 1993: 141).

What unites these reconstructive texts in structural terms is their emphasis on epistemological and ontological ambiguity and undecidedness. The texts try to emulate this uncertainty by re-enacting and giving a form to this oscillation between fixed concepts and binary oppositions. They become permeable and invite, or even necessitate, penetration. According to Diana Piccitto, such texts come to symbolize for their recipients 'the possibility for an altered identity, one that leads to an authentic existence not founded on an authorizing essence but on multiplicity and expansion' (2012: 259). They represent a challenge to reflect upon the possibility of knowledge and representation itself by confronting the reader with an aesthetic configuration of the essential paradoxicality inherent in every act of representation. Thus they generate what J. Hillis Miller calls an 'ethical moment', which entails 'a claim made on the author writing the work, on the narrator telling the story within the fiction of the novel, on the characters in the story at decisive moments of their lives, and on the reader, teacher, or critic responding to the work' (1987: 8). Piccitto also stresses the ethical implication of this participatory aesthetics when she claims that 'participation in inspirational moments necessitates disturbing one's perception of the impenetrable authentic self in order to shift one's perception of reality from the way things are to the way things could be' (2012: 260). Adam Kelly concisely summarizes the ethical impetus of this new paradigm, which 'seeks to rehabilitate concepts such as love, communication, and responsibility by renewing the possibility of literature as an open and oscillating transaction between writer and reader, in which sincerity is an event that can never be presently established, but operates on the model of Derrida's secret beyond representation, or gift without exchange' (2010c: 328).

When I try to make a case for authenticity as an apt concept to describe these texts in terms of the relation between experience and representation, it is due to precisely this mode of oscillation between authority and participation, absence and presence, between representation and 'a secret beyond representation'. Like authenticity, these texts can be imagined as black boxes, which cannot be understood or analysed according to apparently straightforward patterns such as mimesis, alienation or parody, but rather defy the validity of such categorizations. They do so by enacting and emplotting paradoxes, in the form of tangled hierarchies, which cannot be solved within the logic of their own conventional system of description and representation. These texts encourage, even demand, the active reconstruction of these hierarchies in an act which Derrida described as 'performative interpretation, that is ... an interpretation that transforms the very thing it interprets' (1994: 51).

4

From Innocence to Ignorance: Julian Barnes's *England, England*

Julian Barnes's *England, England* displays rather than performs struggles for authenticity. It gives an account of attempts, both collective and individual, to stage and refabricate intimations of a lost feeling of innocence and direct access to the world. By occupation, Martha Cochrane, protagonist and first-person narrator of *England, England*, helps to devise elaborate constructions which aim at producing an effect of authentic experience. The novel eventually exposes the inherent futility of these schemes. Nevertheless, it takes up many *topoi* that have shaped the discourse on authenticity, such as its precarious location at an impossible juncture of personal and interpersonal experience and its connection with a unique location in time and space. It also gives evidence of the paradoxical status of authenticity between mediation and immediateness, of an abstract yearning for origins and first causes and the iterative and performative expressions in which this yearning manifests itself. To an extent, *England, England* constitutes a dystopian parable on the impossibility of authentic experience. In the structural set-up of my argument, it serves as a literary and philosophical treatise on the significance of authenticity in a contemporary context and so acts as a bridge between the theoretical deliberations of the previous chapters and their practicable application in the analyses that follow.

The difficulty of reassembling memories of the past into a consistent narrative of the present can count as a leitmotiv in the literary work of Julian Barnes. From *Flaubert's Parrot* via *Talking it Over* to *Arthur and George*, his protagonists are frequently confronted with the inadequacy and incompatibility of individual and communal recollections when it comes to forming a coherent personal, let alone collective, memory. Later on I will demonstrate how this instability and unreliability of memory is elevated to a structural principle in Barnes's latest novel, *The Sense of an Ending*.

In its very first sentence, *England, England* establishes the ethereal nature of personal memories as a key topic:

'What's your first memory?' someone would ask.
And she would reply, 'I don't remember.' (3)

Based on the conviction that 'in all her years she was never to come across a first memory which was not in her opinion a lie', Martha Cochrane, offers to the reader the reconstruction of 'her first memory, her first artfully, innocently arranged lie' (4). Central to this contrived primordial memory is a jigsaw puzzle of the Counties of England, which figures as the fundamental and ingenious metaphor for the key topic of the novel: the interlinking of personal and collective memories and their roles in the construction of individual and national identity, an example of what Wendy Joy Darby calls 'the construction of identity through recreational participation in valued and symbolic landscapes' (2001: 1). In order to further emphasize this point, Barnes has Martha conceive of the jigsaw in anthropomorphic concepts of relationship and exclusion. She imagines, for example, how 'Norfolk and Suffolk sat on top of one another like brother and sister, or clutched one another like husband and wife' or 'Kent pointing its finger or its nose out at the Continent in warning – careful, foreigners over there' (*EE*: 5). Elsewhere in the novel, Dr Max, resident historian with the England, England project, notes that most people 'remembered history in the same conceited yet evanescent fashion as they recalled their own childhood' (82). The jigsaw, for Martha, comes to symbolize the most dramatic episode of her childhood: when her father leaves wife and daughter, the significance of this event manifests itself in Martha's memory mainly because her father's departure coincides with the loss of the county of Nottinghamshire from the jigsaw. In a puerile misinterpretation of cause and effect, Martha feels guilty about her father's leaving – 'Daddy had gone off to find Nottinghamshire', which she had previously lost (14) – and disposes of the jigsaw puzzle by stuffing the counties one by one into the seats of her school bus (17). The imperfect state of family affairs is suggested earlier by the fact that Martha repeatedly cannot finish the puzzle, as one piece (usually from the Midlands section) is always missing. Only once her father found 'the missing piece in the unlikeliest of places', order is restored, and 'her jigsaw, her England, and her heart had been made whole again' (6). Years later, when her estranged father tries to get in touch with Martha, the unbridgeable distance which the lack of shared memories has created between him and his daughter is again made evident by means of the jigsaw puzzle. Martha seeks to attain a form of symbolic closure by asking her father about the whereabouts of Nottinghamshire, a request he meets with devastating ignorance:

He shook his head. 'You did jigsaws? I suppose all kids love them … '
'You don't remember?'
He looked at her.
'You really, really don't?' (25)

The subsequent events in parts two and three of the novel can be understood as Martha's attempts to symbolically reassemble this jigsaw puzzle. In a model case of Freudian *Verschiebung*, she devotes the better part of her life to symbolic reconstructions of England. In a logically apt development of the initial jigsaw motif, the tenability of these is mirrored in the stability of Martha's own emotional set-up, and the concept of authenticity serves as the yardstick for assessing the consistency of the respective constructions.[1] I will now examine the three parts of the novel according to

---

[1] *England, England* has frequently been analysed in the context of authenticity. Nick Bentley suggests

the three different versions of authenticity which characterize the respective collective imaginaries of the states of 'England', 'England, England' and 'Anglia' in which they are set. I will use the Romantic notion of the triadic nature of cultural progress to elucidate this development. Schiller writes in 'On Naive and Sentimental Poetry' that cultural history can be understood as a three-step model which locates the anxious and frenzied agitations of the here and now between an Arcadian state of a bucolic unity of humankind with nature and the prospective transcendental reunion of nature and culture in a prospective state 'which realizes that pastoral innocence even in the subjects of culture and among all conditions of the most active, most ardent life, of the most extensive thought, of the most refined art, of the highest social refinement, which, in a word, leads the man, who can now no longer return to *Arcadia*, up to *Elysium*' (Schiller 2005).

Correspondingly, Martha in *England, England* undergoes a journey from the innocent authenticity of childhood experience through the simulated inauthenticity of England, England towards a 'reflective authenticity' in the sense of Ferrara in the last part of the novel. In the following, I will try to describe this process as a movement from an Arcadian, purely aesthetic, approach to experience via the cynical subordination of materiality under form to an Elysian state of an experience beyond the constrictions of form.

For Schiller, children figure as the quintessential manifestation of mankind's Arcadian condition, as their experience of the world is undiscriminating, unconditional and absolute, 'their perfection is not their merit, because it is not the work of its choice' (ibid.). This ideal of a pointless and therefore unmediated rapport with the world, which also echoes Kant's definition of the beautiful as 'a purposiveness without a purpose' (2008: 57), would appear to present a way around authenticity's gate-keeper paradox of mediated immediacy. Childhood experience can be described as authentic, because it is not channelled through formal conventions and solidified frames of reference.

In Martha's case, these intimations from early childhood are condensed into two distinct sets of memories. One involves a happy family outing to an agricultural fair and the other is the result of the rote-learning routine of historical dates through chanting. In keeping with the novel's fundamental structural principle of aligning personal and collective identity formation, these two memories, representing the temporal and material aspect of English national identity respectively, supplement the geographical dimension symbolized by the Counties of England jigsaw puzzle. What stands out in Martha's recollection of the agricultural fair is not the actual animals and plants on show but rather the 'strange poetry' of the booklet containing the 'District Agricultural and Horticultural Society's Schedule of Prizes':

Three Carrots – long
Three Carrots – short

that the novel 'laments the belief that we cannot access an authentic place of origin, whilst it simultaneously critiques those who celebrate the fact' (2007: 494), while Christoph Henke reads Barnes's text as an expression of post-postmodern man's yearning for authentic existence (see 2001: 284). See also Vera Nünning (2001), Korte (2002), Heiler (2004) and Birte Neumann (2007).

> Three Turnips – any variety
> Five Potatoes – long
> Five Potatoes – round
> Six Broad Beans
> ...
> Jar of Pickled Onion
> Jar of Salad Cream
> Friesian Cow in milk
> Friesian Cow in calf
> Friesian Heifer in milk (*EE*: 8–9)

Even though she can hardly make sense of these words, for Martha this is 'a picture book, though it contained only words, an almanac; an apothecary's herbal; a magic kit; a prompt-book of memory' (9). A similarly formalistic approach informs Martha's history lessons in school, which are invariably started with chants such as

> 55BC (clap clap) Roman Invasion
> 1066 (clap clap) Battle of Hastings
> 1215 (clap clap) Magna Carta
> 1512 (clap clap) Henry the Eighth (clap clap)
> Defender of Faith (clap clap) (11)

What is striking here is that the immediacy of access that characterizes Martha's childhood recollections is not at all directed to the world as it is the case (beans, cows, battles, invasions) but rather occurs on a level of pure formalism, of a radical subordination of content to structure. Form, here in the shape of rhythm and rhyme, is not a secondary category which is superimposed on the contingent actuality of an outside reality. On the contrary, it figures as the enabling, in itself purposeless, aesthetic precondition for any kind of reference. In his essay 'The Paradox of Form', Luhmann writes that 'Form not only *is* the boundary [between the process of observation and that which is being observed], but also contains the two sides it separates. Form has, as it were, an open reference to the world' (1999: 17; emphasis in the original). It is only when these unrestricted and universal aesthetic capacities are forced to take into account the physical reality of the world that a paradoxical alignment of form and matter occurs. It is the factual which imposes a purpose on the formal. In this understanding, mankind's fall from Arcadian grace and innocence is constituted by the recognition of the materiality of experience rather than by its symbolic mediation (as Lacan famously suggested). It is a paradise of pure form from which the irruption of the reality principle expels us.

Just as Schiller's pre-symbolic and prelapsarian childhood is irrecoverably lost to the adult human being, so Martha cannot return to the pure, purposeless and authentic formalism of her childhood experience. The second section of the novel shows Martha involved in a decidedly purposeful experiment with various manifestations of national identity. She is employed as 'Appointed Cynic' by a company called Pitco, run by one Sir Jack Pitman. Sir Jack is a media mogul of the calibre of Robert

Maxwell, even down to his dubious Eastern European extraction, with a distinct vision of how to turn the emblems of English identity into a money-spinning tourist experience and business venture, while at the same time updating the philosophical foundations of what authentic experience can actually mean.

England, England is a theme park designed with the aim of bringing England up to scratch for the twenty-first century, or as Jerry Batson, Sir Jack's financial consultant, puts it: 'So England comes to me, and what do I say to her? I say, "Listen, baby, face facts. We're in the third millennium and your tits have dropped"' (*EE:* 37). His solution is to 'sell our past to other nations as their future' (40) by lumping together the most prominent markers of English identity into a condensed but practicable, easily manageable and consumer-friendly theme park. In his book *Fields of Vision*, Stephen Daniels calls such markers England's 'legends and landscapes' and defines them as the 'stories of golden ages, enduring traditions, heroic deeds and dramatic destinies located in ancient or promised home-lands with hallowed sites and scenery' (1993: 5). Batson's strategy with regard to these legends and landscapes is based on the assumption that 'given the option between an inconvenient "original" or a convenient replica, a high proportion of tourists would opt for the latter' (*EE:* 181). In order to guarantee the 'authenticity' of this endeavour to display 'Englishness as a series of signifiers' (Bentley 2007: 486), a survey is carried out which results in a list of 50 English 'quintessences' (*EE:* 83–5). These include abstract notions like 'Snobbery' (no. 12 on the list) and the 'Stiff Upper Lip' (no. 21), landscape or architectural features such as the White Cliffs of Dover (clocking in at no. 9) and Wembley Stadium (no. 47) and historical/mythological characters like Shakespeare, Churchill, Robin Hood and Alice in Wonderland. Sir Jack and his team then set about recreating these assembled signifiers of Englishness on the Isle of Wight, a 'location dying for makeover and upgrade' according to Project Manager Mark (76).

The entire planning stage of the theme park can be understood as an applied lesson in the postmodern irrelevance of an understanding of authenticity as grounded in notions of originality and a Benjaminian aura of singularity in time and space. In its place, a regime of 'pseudo-events' in the sense of Boorstin and historical name-dropping is implemented. Free-floating signifiers and simulacra reign supreme, as the logic of the theme-park experience is quite literally based on 'substituting the signs of the real for the real itself' (Baudrillard 1994: 2): 'Parkhurst Forest easily became Sherwood Forest, and the environs of the Cave had been arboreally upgraded by the repatriation of several hundred mature oaks from a Saudi prince's driveway. The rock-style facing to the Cave was being jack-hammered into aged authenticity' (*EE:* 147).

In order to ensure the conceptual and epistemological soundness of this approach, and also to alert even the most theoretically unfazed reader to the deep philosophical significance of the novel, Barnes even has Sir Jack invite a French intellectual, who in best Baudrillardian fashion expounds on the present-day fatigue with reality and the fact that we 'prefer the replica to the original' (53). His defence of the simulacrum takes in the architectural reconstructions of Viollet-Le-Duc, which he describes as an attempt 'to *abolish the reality* of those old edifices' (54; emphasis in the original), as well as a few direct quotations from Guy Debord's *The Society of the Spectacle* to the effect that 'all that was once directly lived ... has become mere representation' (54; cf. Debord 1999: 12). Even Dr Max, 'probably the only innocent person on the whole Island' (*EE*: 203), admits that from a historian's point of view this approach is not without merit, as it constitutes a faithful re-enactment of the process of historiography: 'there *is* no authentic moment of beginning, of purity ... What we are looking at is almost always a replica, if that is the locally fashionable term, of something earlier' (132; emphasis in the original). In an almost exact analogy to the idea of the authenticity of the fake as voiced by Doniger and Römer, the nameless French intellectual goes on to expound the benefits of simulation and augmented reality:

> Once there was only the world, directly lived. Now there is the representation – let me fracture that word, the re-presentation – of the world. It is not a substitute for that plain and primitive world, but an enhancement and enrichment, an ironisation and summation of that world. This is where we live today. A monochrome world has become Technicolor, a single croaking speaker has become wraparound sound. Is this our loss? No, it is our conquest, our victory ... We must demand the replica, since the reality, the truth, the authenticity of the replica is the one we can possess, colonise, reorder, find *jouissance* in, and, finally, if and when we decide, it is the reality which, since it is our destiny, we may meet, confront and destroy. (55)

Such embellishment of late capitalist principles of appropriation, instant availability and conspicuous consumption with trendy French philosophy not only neatly illustrates Jameson's supposition of postmodernism as the logic of late capitalism but also gives evidence of how the cultural capital of the term 'authenticity' is being utilized and exploited by the market forces of consumer capitalism. For even though Sir Jack is at pains to portray himself as a true-blue Englishman, for example by wearing fake membership braces of the MCC or the Garrick Club, there can be little doubt that it is net revenue rather than patriotic sentiment that really powers the whole enterprise. Along the way, the runaway success of England, England reveals the tenuousness of any national identity construction and the fickleness of any form of collective memory, as the quintessential identity markers of (Old) England are easily relocated, either manifestly or symbolically, across the Solent to serve as tourist attractions.[2]

It would be rash, however, to dismiss England, England as merely the big bad replica that devours the fragile innocent aura of the real and original England. It is Sir Jack of all people who points out that there is no such thing as an original to start with. When Mark, in spite of the French intellectual's allegations, doubts that the theme park is actually 'offering *the thing itself*' (59; emphasis in the original), Sir Jack graces him with the following parable:

> I stood on a hill the other day and looked down an undulating field past a copse towards a river and as I did a pheasant stirred beneath my feet. You, as a person

---

[2] One could argue that national monuments are used in a similar way in the real England as well. Heritage industry is a matter of attracting euros, dollars and yen just as England, England is, and it is certainly true that the 'link between tourism and postmodern existence is made not least through the concept of authenticity', as Barbara Korte claims (2002: 289).

passing through, would no doubt have assumed that Dame Nature was going about her natural business. I knew better, Mark. The hill was an Iron Age burial mound, the undulating field a vestige of Saxon agriculture, the copse was a copse only because a thousand other trees had been cut down, the river was a canal and the pheasant had been hand-reared by the gamekeeper. (60; emphasis in the original)

If even nature, which is traditionally taken to be real by dint of its location outside any man-made frame of reference, is always already shaped by prior levels of interpretation and, literally, cultivation, then, so Sir Jack's logic goes, it must be folly to assume the existence of untouched and pristine states, let alone original or real historical events or persons.[3] Sir Jack's business venture can be seen as a timely illustration of the fact that the aesthetic and symbolic value of national myths has become disconnected once and for all from their material rootedness in the real world. The authenticity of any national marker, be it geographical, material or historical, has itself become an anachronistic sentiment in a theme park which has 'beetle-black taxis shuttling through the London fog to Cotswold villages full of thatched cottages serving Devonshire cream teas' (142). National identity, as an individual and collective sentiment generated through the common knowledge and appreciation of such authentic markers, is being comprehensively abolished by the simulations of England, England. The empty conceptual husks that define this past, the term 'White Cliffs of Dover' for example, are free to be filled in accordance with current requirements, in this case with the Isle of Wight's very own Whitecliff Bay (see 85). This – so Barnes's novel assumes – is in consequence of a rampant consumerism which seeks to annihilate any distinct localization of the individual in time and space. In its stead, there is only the continuous present of all-inclusive simulation, which for the mere sake of profit still pretends to be all about the past.

The theme-park experience of England, England is mediated through and authenticated by two essentially and entirely formal and aesthetic registers. On the one hand, authentic experience is vouchsafed by the postmodern tenet of the authenticity of the simulacrum as a form of representation which has lost any concrete point of reference in reality. The 'quintessential' markers of English identity are not defined by any genuine physical location or historic moment but rather become free-floating signifiers, immaterial, purely aesthetic concepts to be filled or substituted with random material content. On the other hand, the validity of this assumption, and thus the authenticity of the experience of England, England, is apparently confirmed by the theme park's overwhelming commercial success, which is set out in great detail in an article for the *Wall Street Journal* titled 'A Tourist Mecca Set in a Silver Sea'. In this article, the reporter claims that the 'best of all that England was, and is, can be safely and conveniently experienced on this spectacular and well-equipped diamond of an Island' (185). Seen from a purely structural perspective, this authenticity of the simulation is not unlike the authenticity which Martha bestows on her

---

[3] Cf. in this context Darby's study on *Landscape and Identity* and in particular her analysis of the shaping of the Lake District, which strangely enough features neither in the list of 'quintessences' nor in England, England, as a national icon for a detailed example of a similar process (2000: 51).

childhood recollections. In England, England too, it is the primacy of pure form that supposedly confers and generates intimations of authenticity. The innocence of mankind's Arcadian state is irretrievably lost once the materiality of life encroaches on a prior, purely formal approach to the world. In this regard, the hermetically aesthetic experience of England, England can be read as an artificial reconstruction of this Arcadian artlessness of pure form. Quite possibly, the hordes of tourists visiting the former Isle of Wight are only superficially paying a visit to a 'fast-forward version of England' (164) but are unconsciously on a quest for the lost innocence and authenticity of childhood. The maintenance of the spotless appearance of these simulated forms also involves the removal of all aspects that might hint at the material dimension of the Island experience, for example when 'Pitco shipped the old, the longterm sick and the socially dependent off to the mainland' (183).

The fate of Sir Jack himself supports this interpretation. He eventually falls prey to his very own quest for the authenticity of childhood, which takes the form of regular visits to 'Auntie May', a high-end service facility where customers can re-enact for ready money their fantasies of childhood, including baby talk, being breastfed, changed, cleaned and rubbed dry. Martha and Paul Harrison, her lover and the project's 'Ideas Catcher', get wind of Sir Jack's compromising ventures into infancy and send in a reporter to have video cameras installed on 'Auntie May's' premises. They use the recorded evidence of how their employer 'parted and unparted his legs most authentically as ['nurse' Lucy] tucked the nappy round him' (155) and how he eventually 'let out a string of ploppy farts, came joltingly in Lucy's joined hands, and shat spectacularly in his nappy' (158) to blackmail Sir Jack into handing over control of England, England. Sir Jack's decidedly physical reconstruction of childhood experience at long last proves incompatible with his symbolic recreation of aesthetic innocence in England, England. It is, in other words, the intrusion of materiality that puts paid to the simulation of pure form for him. Adding to the irony of Sir Jack's demise is the fact that his downfall, just as the success of the theme park, is brought about by the reproduction of images – in this case by means of video cameras. Sir Jack is ultimately vulnerable to his own petard because his symbolic recreation of innocence has disregarded one central aspect of the authentic experience of innocence, that is, its purposelessness. Although he himself may have naïvely believed in the authenticity of his simulations, in the radical supremacy of form over content, by subordinating the alleged authenticity of England, England to the external objective of commercial success, Sir Jack does not allow for the aesthetic autonomy and disinterestedness authenticity necessarily entails. Consequently, he not only loses control over the simulation of innocence but becomes himself subsidiary to the cynical logic of simulation and consumption: in his role as the Island's Governor, he first 'dwindled into what he was supposed to be – a mere figurehead with no real power' (185). After his death he is himself turned into a simulacrum when he is replaced by a replica 'descending from his landau to plunge into the crowds, lecturing on the history of the Island, and showing key leisure-industry executives around his mansion' while, in the mausoleum housing the mortal remains of the real Sir Jack, 'visitors were outnumbered by gardeners' (250).

Martha, in contrast, does not suffer from Sir Jack's naïve and essentially nostalgic disposition. For her, the theme park never amounts to more than 'a plausible and well-planned means of making money' (192). After the coup d'état which ousts Sir Jack, she takes over as CEO of Pitco and is at first able to secure the smooth running of England, England in spite of the fact that 'Sir Jack Pitman vociferously believed in his product whereas Martha Cochrane privately did not' (191). I have suggested above that Martha's life can be understood as an attempt to symbolically regain the completeness of the Counties of England jigsaw puzzle of her childhood. In a chapter reviewing her sex life, she admits that most of her relationships were driven by the 'assumption that completeness was possible, desirable, essential – and attainable only in the presence and with the assistance of Another' (49). Accordingly, the disintegration of her relationship with Paul, who still believes in the authenticity of Sir Jack's vision, indicates that despite its apparent success there is something fundamentally rotten in the state of England, England. After another falling-out, Martha ponders the question why she 'could make the Project work, even though she didn't believe in it; then at the end of the day, she returned home with Paul to something she believed in, or wanted and tried to believe in, yet didn't seem able to make work at all' (193). A possible answer is provided by Dr Max who, in his role as supplier of dependable historical background data and interpreter of the links between past and present, has become surplus to requirements now that history and national identity have become disconnected from memories of the past, and is therefore about to be sacked. After starting the interview in typical business fashion with the question of whether Dr Max was happy with his present situation, Martha is treated to a concise exposition of the virtues of reflection, disinterestedness and Keatsian negative capability. Dr Max professes, 'I am not "happy" in the bus-shelter-snogging sense. I am not happy as the modern world chooses to define happiness. Indeed, I would say that I *am* happy because I deride that modern conception. I am happy, to use that unavoidable term, precisely because I do not seek happiness' (196; emphasis in the original). In a neat metaphorical précis of the theoretical approach I am trying to pursue, Martha reacts to this speech by marvelling 'that she could be made to feel gravity and simplicity by such effervescence and delighted paradox' (ibid.).

With regard to the authenticity of England, England, Martha's cynical view on the whole project derives from her inability to see the whole venture from an exclusively aesthetic perspective. Unlike Sir Jack, she has fallen from the grace of innocent formalism and cannot abstract the material from the purely aesthetic and virtual. For her, content always impinges on form. Her compulsion to reflect on her situation seems to preclude immediate happiness as well as unmediated authenticity. Consequently, under her aegis the theme park itself suffers from unwelcome intrusions of reality. Martha learns that the actors inhabiting the Island's replicated smugglers' village diorama are not merely trafficking Pitco-approved merchandise in the form of jewellery or gloves but have branched out into importing prohibited commodities such as alcohol, pornography and prostitution into the 'peaceable Kingdom' of England, England (202). They have also started a lucrative side-line of counterfeiting the official Island currency and make good money through 'pirating of Island guidebooks and forging of official Island souvenirs' (200). Neither is this a singular incident: Nell Gwynn, 'a woman who gave sex a good name' (93), who had been included in the theme park to add a sense of innocuous, because historical, sexual frisson, is being molested and abused in earnest by the King. The Royal Family, by the way, is one of the few apparently genuine items in England, England, as the King and his Queen Denise have taken up permanent residence in the theme park, because their former subjects in England 'had grown querulous, either dismayed by the Family's normality, resentful of its cost, or simply tired from bestowing millennia of love' (143). It could be argued, though, that this move, in spite of the King's physical relocation to England, England, amounts to a purely formal transfer and also merely results in a simulation of kingship. Monarchy, after all, only functions within its traditional framework of the body politic, symbolic and geographic. Without this contextualization, even the real King can never be more than an actor playing the role of King. Adding to Martha's agenda of problems, Robin Hood and his Band of Merrie Men start hunting for their own food in the Island's heritage parks, and World War II fighter pilots prefer to live in their replica Nissen huts instead of the accommodation provided for the actors. All around, Martha is confronted with an 'adhesion of personality' (197) or, in other words, with the simulacrum creating and acting out its own hyperreality. Sir Jack's dream of a serene kingdom of purely aesthetic form founders on the imponderability of the material reality of human experience. Content, as it were, always exceeds the scope of pure form.

Martha's final recognition of the incompatibility of her quest for authentic experience and the experience provided by England, England is triggered by an encounter with the actor impersonating 'Dr Johnson' in a scene which James J. Miracky calls the novel's 'only authentic moment' (2004: 170). Originally intended to provide 'examples of high-class traditional British humour' as part of the supplementary Samuel Johnson Dining Experience, the actor has been so completely absorbed in his role that guests are complaining about his moodiness and frequent xenophobic comments (*EE*: 209). In dealing with 'Dr Johnson', Martha is faced with a paradoxical corollary of simulated authenticity, a confrontation which results in a temporary suspension of the aesthetic construct of simulation and allows Martha a moment of pure, unmediated and unformalized, that is, authentic experience:

> 'When we hired Dr Johnson,' she began, and then stopped. His great bulk seemed to cast her desk into darkness. 'When we engaged you ...' No, that wasn't right either. She was no longer a CEO, or a business woman, or even a person of her time. She was alone with another human creature. She felt a strange and simple pain. (211)

Only in the epistemological absurdity of a perfect simulacrum, of the simulation actually attaining material human essence, can materiality and form be joined together in 'a creature alone with itself, wincing at naked contact with the world' (218). Driven by the force of this epiphanic moment, Martha feels an urge to return to the innocent authenticity of her Arcadian childhood experience and visits an abandoned church that has not been made part of the theme park. There, in the little individual narratives engraved on the tombstones, Martha discovers a version of aimless, and therefore authentic, history, an echo of the purely formalistic and repetitive authenticity of the chants and lists of her childhood. In stark contrast to her experience of the cynical authenticity of England, England, these intimations are elevated through Martha's reflections on history in general and her place in the world in particular. Only in and through the form of the paradox and by means of serious, rather than cynical, reflection can Martha get a glimpse of an authenticity of experience, which – in the vein of Schiller's Elysium – can ultimately unite form and content. Only when unfettered from the necessities of external motivation can the materiality of history and its aesthetic representation be reconciled in a visceral and emotional encounter: 'The seriousness', Martha realizes, 'lay in celebrating the original image: getting back there, seeing it, feeling it' (238).

For the moment, though, Martha cannot act on these insights. Back in the real world of England, England, she attempts a very different form of resolution. In order to punish Robin Hood and his Band for transgressing their role in the aesthetic rationale of the theme park, Martha stages, 'as a one-off cross-epoch extravaganza, limited to Premier Visitors on payment of a double supplement', a dramatic raid of Robin Hood's Cave by the Island's SAS unit, whose members usually feature in the re-enactment of the Iranian Embassy Siege of 1980 (227). This constitutes a desperate attempt to salvage the authority of the simulacrum. At the same time, however, it exposes the cynicism and fraudulence on which this authority is based, in so far as it sacrifices the last bit of pretence to historical accuracy or at least plausibility for the sake of maintaining control and generating extra profits. But, anyway, the simulation cannot be contained any more. The punitive expedition turns out to be a spectacular failure, as the SAS's fake grenades are no match for the material reality of the Merrie Men's pikes and arrows. Just as England, England before could easily usurp the empty husks of the signifiers of English identity, now these simulations are themselves being effortlessly rewritten by the contingency of events. What's more, the audience does not seem to bother: 'They'd loved it, that was clear. The special effects had been terrific; Mad Mike [the squad leader, who ends up with an arrow in his shoulder], in his wounded heroism, was utterly convincing; any mishaps merely confirmed the action's authenticity' (231). The cynical logic of the simulacrum, that is, the complete supremacy of form over content, has become so ingrained into the visitors' horizon of expectation that the formulaic design of the myth (good vs. bad; underdog vs. authority) overrules any factual impossibility or historical anachronism. In this context of the radical here and now, where any human transaction is motivated by business interest and executed in a strictly prescribed formal framework, there is no room for purposelessness and contingency. Any authenticity that lays claim to the national or collective imaginary therefore can never be anything but cynical. Again Martha's unease with the prevalent manifestations of English identity is aptly mirrored in her personal life, when her lover Paul eventually teams up with Sir Jack and she is banished from the Island, bringing her involvement with England, England to a close.

Martha's quest for authentic experience eventually brings her back to England. But, and again in keeping with Schiller's model, innocent and unmediated experience is not to be recovered. The country formerly known as England has been rechristened 'Anglia' and has undergone a fundamental change in terms of communal identification.[4] Travelling to and in Anglia is well-nigh impossible and there are no mass media to speak of and therefore little transpersonal communication. Due to this self-imposed confinement concerning space and information, collective identity has once again become a concrete process rather than an abstract concept. The village is now the point of reference for integration, with the symbols of identification being of local rather than global description. But this bucolic invocation of rural England in the vein of Orwell's 'old maids biking to Holy Communion through the mists of the autumn mornings' (2000: 139) is itself only a simulation and on the surface no more authentic than the theme park of England on the former Isle of Wight. Most of the inhabitants of Anglia are enacting their roles as village dwellers in just the same way that the employees of Pitco enact the myths and legends of England, England. The folklore, fables and place names generated in order to endow the village community with a common ground for identification – the Village Fête, the Dance of the May Queen or the stories invented by retired American legal expert Jack Oshinsky, now known as Jez Harris – are no more than bogus imitations and replications of traditional folklore. Similar to the streamlined and consumer-friendly version of English culture envisioned by Sir Jack, the analogy concerning names is certainly no coincidence, these simulated myths and stories are rooted neither in time nor space.

So, is there any difference as concerns the authenticity of these two simulations of Englishness at all? In both cases, the markers of identity are certainly not authentic in the sense of being the real thing, of having a natural, unbending and manifest location in the temporal and spatial memoir of the community they are supposed to delineate and celebrate. Quite the contrary, they are pure simulations, aesthetic fabrications, free-floating signifiers, which achieve meaning only through performative acts of name-giving and/or play-acting. On the other hand, both communities are authentic in so far as the exchanges which bestow and sustain collective identification occur between individual agents rather than on an abstract symbolic level. In England, England, traditional markers of Englishness are restructured and simplified in order to be consumed, that is, to be interacted with. They are being remade into marketable goods, turned into commodities. The symbolic interaction of the inhabitants/visitors of England, England with the markers of national identity adheres to the rules of consumer capitalism. In a different context, Lyotard succinctly summarizes the dynamics underlying this process when he writes that 'capitalism inherently possesses the power to derealize familiar objects, social roles, and institutions to such a degree that the so-called realistic representations can no longer evoke reality except as nostalgia or mockery' (2004: 74). With a view to the etymological link of the word 'consume' to notions of waste and destruction, which are still evident in phrases like 'consumed by fire' or the erstwhile designation of tuberculosis as 'consumption', it could be argued that the version of Englishness propagated in and through England,

---

[4] The third part of the novel, which deals with Anglia, was originally titled 'Albion' and changed to 'Anglia' with the fourth edition of the novel by explicit request of the author.

England has a damaging and caustic effect on the symbols of this identification. They are literally consumed beyond recognition and significance, displaced not only literally but also theoretically by the logic of the 'pure market state' across the Solent (*EE*: 183). In a world that aspires to be a village (either global or local), Benedict Anderson's notion of the nation as an 'imagined community' appears to have fallen into disuse. In both England, England and Anglia, communal identification is not established through the experience of a collective imaginary of national myths and markers but by either the unadulterated formalism of economic interaction, as in the former, or the disordered and formless accumulation of local and individual mythologies and re-mystified nature, as in the latter. What unites both designs is the apparent desire for a community based on the materiality of shared experience, which is based either on the exchange and consumption of simulated commodities or in the communal invention of new traditions based on individual contributions. Landscape features can serve as a useful illustration for this discrepancy in approach. As shown above, the White Cliffs of Dover are relocated to England, England by superimposing the traditional name and associated mythological connotations onto another cliff, thereby perpetuating the form of the myth while refashioning its material content. In Anglia, in contrast, new mythologies, like those invented by Jez Harris, are foisted onto existing landscape features, thus mapping out the given topography with new stories, thereby fashioning ex nihilo the traditions which enable communal identification in the first place. This recalls Eric Hobsbawm's seminal account of *The Invention of Tradition*, where tradition is defined as 'a set of practices, normally governed by overtly or tacitly accepted rules and of a ritual or symbolic nature, which seek to inculcate certain values and norms of behaviour by repetition, which automatically implies continuity with the past' (1983: 1).

The motivation behind the cynical mock-up authenticity of England, England is essentially and unashamedly commercial in purpose, with the notion of an authentic experience being exploited for the sake of revenue and convenience. Anglia, in contrast and despite its own origins in simulation and fake originality, still carries with it the promise of a new kind of authentic experience, one which is sought at the expense of material wealth, convenience and, most significantly, purpose. No violent oppression of symbolic form onto landscape and history is apparent in Anglia; the churchyard is allowed to be 'a place of informality and collapse, of time's softer damage' (*EE*: 241). Autonomy is granted to the materiality of nature, freed and independent from any formal representation and interpretation:

> Weather, long since diminished to a mere determinant of personal mood, became central again: something external, operating its system of rewards and punishments, mainly the latter. It had no rivalry or interference from industrial weather, and was self-indulgent in its dominance: secretive, immanent, capricious, ever threatening the miraculous. Fogs had character and motion, thunder regained its divinity. Rivers flooded, sea-walls burst, and sheep were found in treetops when the water subsided. (255)

This re-mystification of nature, its re-authentication as it were, eventually leads to a renewed form of communal existence: 'Common land was re-established; fields and farms grew smaller; hedgerows were replanted ... Without traffic, the village felt safer and closer; without television, the villagers talked more, even if there seemed less to talk about than before. Nobody's business went unobserved; pedlars were greeted warily' (255-6). The logic of England, England denies any but the most cynical version of authenticity, whereas the inhabitants of Anglia accept authenticity not as an end to achieving communal identification but as its enabling condition. In that, Anglia very much approximates Berman's vision of a 'politics of authenticity', which he sees enacted in 'an ideal community in which individuality will not be subsumed and sacrificed, but fully developed and expressed' (2009: xvii).[5]

Martha – after an initial adaptation period – seems to have accepted this new world order, which centres on the local village rather than on the global one, as her spiritual home. Both physically and spiritually, Anglia provides a suitable habitat for her, who in retrospect regards her own life as a failure in terms of personal and professional fulfilment. Again, this personal failure is reflected in the description of Anglia. According to England, England's very own *The Times of London* newspaper, the former home country attracts 'only those with an active love for discomfort or necrophiliac love for the antique' (*EE*: 185); it is lampooned as 'a place of yokeldom and willed antiquarianism' (254). Martha's quest for authentic experience only comes to an end once she admits to herself the futility of her former strivings. Sitting atop Gibbet Hill and looking down on her new homeland, she finally resigns herself to the contingency of life, realizing that 'you beat your wings all your life, but it was the wind that decided where you went' (242). Reneging on her former vision of completeness in and through interaction (real or symbolic), she comes to appreciate the virtue of private reflection: 'she had returned to Anglia as a migrant bird rather than a zealot. She fucked no-one; she grew older; she knew the contours of her solitude' (257). Only like this, unconstrained by the presumed obligations and compulsions of her former existence, Martha finally gets an intimation of her very own Elysium when she accepts that this 'was how the human spirit should divide itself, between the entirely local and the nearly eternal. How much of her life had been spent with all the stuff in the middle: career, money, sex, heart-trouble, appearance, anxiety, fear, yearning' (260-1). Using Ricœur's words, Martha's journey could be described as a movement 'from a prefigured world to a transfigured world through the mediation of a configured world' (1991: 151).

Martha describes the sentiment governing the community spirit in Anglia as a 'nostalgia of a truer kind: not for what you knew, or thought you had known, as a

---

[5] There is strong disagreement among critics as to how positive Barnes's final vision of Anglia is meant to be. Dominic Head senses a 'tentative investigation of a more positive construction of Englishness, rooted in humility' (2006: 17), and Ene-Reet Soovik even argues that in Anglia 'the inhabitants' personal involvement with the country bespeaks of an authentic attitude towards it that makes it emerge as a true place' (2001: 161). Korte, on the other hand, perceives how Anglia 'seems to have turned into a permanent heritage condition itself – not one enacted for tourists, however, but for oneself. In both England, England and Anglia, a tourist version of England has universalized into the thing itself' (2002: 298). Miracky presents a somewhat more balanced summary when he writes that 'just when one suspects Barnes is validating postmodern theory, he incorporates elements that reach for an authentic human experience of the real ultimately leaving the novel positioned somewhere between homage and parody of the dominance of the "hyperreal"' (2004: 165).

child, but for what you could never have known' (*EE*: 260). Both on the individual and the communal level, so the trajectory of the novel suggests, authenticity cannot result either from an innocent, immediate experience of pure form or from a functional and cynical attempt to re-enact and simulate these pure forms. Instead, authenticity can arise only where no ulterior motive or superior rationale is attached to it. It is, in the terms used in the first part of this book, necessarily emergent, purposeless and unknowing, a means rather than an end in itself. This authenticity can only result from a profound process of reflection. It is never innocent but rather wilfully oblivious and ignorant; if at all, it occurs circumspectly, arising from the impossible logic of paradox and professed disinterestedness. For Martha and for Anglia, the only authentic form of identity formation must emanate from aimless individual reflection, while attempts to achieve a sense of completeness or authenticity in symbolic or personal interaction are bound to fail. Authenticity is indeed a lonesome business. What is more, Martha finally comes to appreciate Dr Max's advice when she claims that in Anglia 'if there was stupidity then it was of the old kind, based on ignorance, rather than the new, based on knowledge' (256).

While Anglia undoubtedly presents a society more in tune with itself than England, England, it should not go unmentioned that, even though life in Anglia might in some aspects resemble a prelapsarian Garden of Eden with animals roaming freely and everybody being at ease with their own insignificant lot, *et in Arcadia* existence is not free from considerations of economy and exclusion; Martha is only allowed to become a permanent resident because she has never stopped paying taxes in Old England, and the integrity of the newly formed community is rigorously maintained in so far as Anglia has 'banned all tourism except for groups numbering two or less, and introduced a Byzantine visa system' (253). Anglia is also by no means a homogeneous structure, as 'new dialects emerged, based on the new separations' (254).

To conclude, I would like to extend Martha's praise of folly to the notion of authenticity. This, likewise, cannot be actively pursued or brought about by positivist knowledge, which could be described in this context as the 'information' of subject matter in Borgmann's sense of imposing form on something (see 1999: 9). Rather, it emerges from the reflective acceptance of the purposeless and inordinate nature of the materiality of life, from an engagement and interaction beyond formal restrictions. According to Critchley, it is only 'when we learn to shake off the delusions of meaning and achieve meaninglessness, then we might see that things merely are and we are things too' (1997: xxiv). Schiller's Elysium lies in the overcoming of form and the supremacy of sheer experience, the return of form into itself as it were. Seen in this light, the development of human experience can be described as a journey from the innocent authenticity of pure form to the reflective authenticity of pure materiality.

5

Reconstructing the Author: Dave Eggers's *A Heartbreaking Work of Staggering Genius*

A Heartbreaking Work of Staggering Genius comes with an explicit warning against any formal categorization of the book and an endorsement of an instinctive and impulsive trust in the reader's aesthetic capacities:

> Many were these people, for example, who felt that the entire story should have been told within the structure of the front matter, therefore better couched/ clothed. At the very same time, there were those who felt that the front matter was (and is) *pomo garbage*, and that as a result, the entire story is being told with a tongue in its author's cheek, a wink toward the skybox – these people saying, in essence, Good God, why couldn't he simply have left the story, as poignant as it is, be? So. This book cannot win. For some, at least. And when this book is not winning, attached to it are labels: *Post* this, *meta* that. Gosh. Where to start? These are the sort of prefixes used by those without opinions. In place of saying simply 'I liked it' or 'I did not like it' they attempt to fence its impacts by affixing to it these meaningless stickers. Oh, we should free ourselves from these terms, used only to make confusing something that we already understand. Because honestly: everyone who actually reads this book, or any book, will understand it:
>
> PEOPLE, FRIENDS, PLEASE: TRUST YOUR EYES, TRUST YOUR EARS, TRUST YOUR ART. (*MKM*: 34; emphases in the original)[1]

Simply on account of its generic form as an autobiographical text, the novel oscillates between reality and fiction. It recounts events that have actually happened in reality, in particular the death from cancer of the author's mother and father in the space of 32 days and his subsequent role as ersatz parent to his brother Toph. It also charts the development of the author's career as a writer and literary editor. The narrative of these events, however, becomes significantly fictionalized in the sense of being refracted and aesthetically modulated at the hands of a very intrusive and self-aware narrator

---

[1] The first paperback edition of *A Heartbreaking Work of Staggering Genius* includes another, formally independent, publication titled *Mistakes we Knew we were Making*. In order to limit to a minimum the inevitable confusion this entails for quotations from the book, I will indicate material from the 'original' novel with the abbreviation *HW* and quotations taken from *Mistakes we Knew we were Making* by *MKM*. See Hamilton (2010: 47–64) for an extended comment on the role of *MKM* in the media controversy that followed the initial publication of *HW*.

figure. I hope to show that the blurring of the formal demarcation line of reality and its aesthetic representation and the subsequent staging of authenticity constitutes the fundamental structural principle of *A Heartbreaking Work of Staggering Genius*.

Eggers supplements the events narrated in the text with an elaborate apparatus of paratextual material. This includes among other things a section titled 'Rules and suggestions for enjoyment of this book', which starts with the somewhat self-defeating announcement that 'there is no overwhelming need to read the preface' (*HW*: vii), an 'Incomplete guide to symbols and metaphors' (xliv) as well as a substantial body of 'Acknowledgments' (xxi–xlv).[2] In what looks at first like a classic example of what Mark Crispin Miller calls 'preemptive irony' (1988: 14), this metareferential framework could be understood as an attempt to anticipate and thereby forestall any teleological and purposefully interpretive engagement with the book, which would be in perfect agreement with the caveat mentioned above. At various points, however, Eggers fiercely rejects the notion that his metareferential ploys amount to anything merely faintly resembling irony. In *Mistakes we Knew we were Making*, he writes that 'there is almost no irony, whatsoever, within [the book's] covers', further elaborating that 'irony should be considered a very particular and recognizable thing ... and thus, to refer to everything *odd, coincidental, eerie, absurd* or *strangely funny* as *ironic* is, frankly, an abomination upon the Lord' (*MKM*: 33; emphases in the original). Liesbeth Korthals Altes acutely identifies the structural paradox inherent in this denunciation of irony. She notes how on the one hand Eggers discounts irony as 'a despicable cultural phenomenon, which destroys all authenticity and real emotion' while on the other hand it is precisely the novel's fundamental 'prudence or irony [which] can be constructed ... as a complex form of sincerity' (2008: 123, 109). It is this very question, if and how this apparent paradox of irony can be reconciled, that my investigation will be mainly concerned with. In very broad terms, the only possible way to attain such reconciliation is to accept that an excess of ironic, tongue-in-cheek self-awareness can actually result in a form of reflective sincerity, which I call authenticity.

I will return to the paratextual sections of the novel in more detail below. For the moment I want to show how Eggers sets the tone for his particular use of metareference, which aims to incessantly foreground the mediated character of what is related and to reveal the aesthetic processes involved in this mediation. As part of the Acknowledgements section, 'the author also wishes to acknowledge the major themes of this book' (*HW*: xxvii), which include among others 'the painfully, endlessly self-conscious book aspect', which, so it is claimed, derives from the fact that 'the author doesn't have the energy or, more important, skill, to fib about this being anything other than him telling you about things, and he is not a good enough liar to do it in any competently sublimated narrative way' (xxix). While this in itself does not entail the

---

[2] This page number is arrived at through a mechanical counting of pages based on the few page numbers provided in this section. The book's 'official' list of contents (*HW*: xviii–xix) gives a different page number. Whether this is due to an intentional obfuscation on behalf of the author or a somewhat shaky grasp of roman numerals on the editors' side could not be clarified. The resulting existence of both possibilities exemplifies the oscillatory pattern that runs like a thread through the entire book and forces the reader to engage in an initial, albeit inconclusive, effort of reconstruction.

epistemological undecidability which I claim to be crucial to metareference, Eggers performs another conceptual turn of the screw by conceding that the author 'will be clear and up-front about this being a self-conscious memoir, which you may come to appreciate, and which is the next theme ... the knowingness about the book's self-consciousness aspect' (xxx).

In formal terms, this proleptic self-awareness constitutes an infinitely duplicating *mise-en-abyme* and engenders a space of epistemological ambiguity. This in turn figures as the enabling condition for the authenticity of this act of literary communication, because it offers and outlines a space where the reciprocity between author and reader can be enacted. In his analysis of what he describes as 'self-depicting novels', Stonehill points out this correlation between metareference and mutuality. He claims that by 'dramatizing its own subversiveness, self-depicting fiction enters a conspiracy with the willing reader' (1988: 8). Rather than taking it as a gesture of authorial hubris and presumption, I propose to accept the author's strategic one-upmanship as an indication of humility, as an act which interpellates the trust of the reader through an enactment of epistemological indeterminacy and which eventually results in a suspension of interpretative authority and an exhortation to readers to judge for themselves the truthfulness of the experience communicated in the text. I would further propose to read this excessive self-reflectivity as a gesture of *parrhesia* in the Foucauldian sense, in so far as it reformulates the role of the author as someone who 'does not hide anything, but opens his heart and mind completely to other people through his discourse' (Foucault 2001: 12). When Foucault stresses that this discourse 'does not take place in a (mental) experience, but in a *verbal activity*' (14; emphasis in the original), he underlines the essentially performative nature of this gesture. Korthals Altes also points out the fundamental reciprocity involved in this process and, in the vein of Ihab Hassan, describes how the author 'tries to establish a pact of trust between himself/the narrator and his reader' (2008: 123). In the novel itself, Eggers explicitly advocates the benefits of such trust: 'Trust is fun. It is fun to trust strangers. It is fun to risk what you can reasonably risk – like, your car, or your reputation – on the trust of people you know only through something ephemeral shared, something like taste in books or cartoons, or having watched people suffer' (*MKM*: 12).

This communalization of the narrative act, which is based on trust and a shared aesthetic experience, is paradigmatic for an aesthetics of reconstruction. In the following I will now try to retrace how the metareferential conditions for such reconstructive efforts are established on the three levels on which – according to my typology of metareferential element – endo-reflective metareference can occur. On the paratextual level, metareference is employed to collapse the boundary between the real-life author Dave Eggers, the eponymous autobiographical narrator of as well as the character in the novel. At least since Rousseau, the genre of autobiography has been seen as a key domain for the negotiation of literary authenticity as it requires the author to formally reconcile three ontologically incommensurable roles. Philippe Lejeune defines the autobiographical novel as 'any piece of fiction for which the reader may have reason to suspect ... that there is identity between the author and the *protagonist*' (1982: 201; emphasis in the original), and Handler and Saxton assert that

'Heideggerian authenticity, writ large, is life as a readable first-person narrative, operationally read in the process of its composition, a life individuated in its authorship, integrated through its emplotment, and creative by dint of its invention' (1988: 250). The authenticity of the autobiographical 'I' is contingent on a reliable and correct fictionalization (*Vertextung*) of the real, historical person of the author through the narrating 'I' of the enunciation into the character of the narrated 'I' of the enounced. This constellation exposes autobiographical writing as such to the same fundamental paradox of mediated immediacy which Zeller takes to be constitutive for any aesthetics of the authentic. Eggers responds to this structural challenge by unremittingly undermining the stability and autonomy of each of these ontological role ascriptions. By performatively drawing attention to the incompatibility of the roles of author, narrator and character by means of metareferential paradox, he manages to keep the autobiographical 'I' in a state of continuous oscillation. This indeterminacy operates as the formal precondition for authenticity to emerge. Both the reciprocal and the ludic aspect inherent in this enactment tie in with Lejeune's famous designation of autobiography as 'a *contractual* game' (1982: 219; emphasis in the original).

The first and most obviously physical response to *A Heartbreaking Work of Staggering Genius* is triggered by the material object of the book itself, its *Gestalt*, which consists of two apparently autonomous publications, both complete with title page, author's name and copyright page, though no separate ISBN number. The first metareferential moment in the reading of *A Heartbreaking Work of Staggering Genius* coincides with the action of turning the book around its two axes to get to the appendix called *Mistakes we Knew we were Making*. This encounter with the corporeality of the book activates in the reader an awareness of the material dimension of every form of literary communication and is also a pertinent example of Aarseth's notion of 'ergodic reading' as a 'nontrivial effort … required to allow the reader to traverse the text' (1997: 1). In terms of the typology I put forward in the first part of this book, this metareferential element can be classified as implicit, interactional and focusing on the textuality of the source text. On the one hand, the supplementary body of text that is *Mistakes we Knew we were Making* serves as an ex-post commentary on how Eggers changed some of the names and settings of the original events, while also drifting off, often in irritatingly small typeface, into debates of a more general theoretical nature, such as the misuse of irony in general and its application to his novel in particular (see *MKM*: 33–5).[3] When he writes, for example, that 'I'm sitting here, in late September of 2000, and I have at this moment four days to finish whatever revisions I'd like to make' (8), the author enacts an integration of the reader into the creative process. Such performative laying bare of the author's narrative methods and practices and the challenge this entails for the reader also manifests itself in another material aspect which concerns the handling of the book's *Gestalt*. At the point where

---

[3] Eggers claims that this appendix had already been part of the original outline of the book, as it 'afforded the opportunity to be completely factual about things that in the narrative had to be compressed or altered slightly so the book could continue apace', but was scrapped in the original version because Eggers had become aware that a similar ploy is used in Mary McCarthy's *Memories of a Catholic Girlhood* (*MKM*: 6).

the two texts meet, between page 437 of *A Heartbreaking Work of Staggering Genius* and page 48 of *Mistakes we Knew we were Making*, there are seven blank pages, an empty space which implicitly invites readers to construct their own links between the two sections. The confrontation with the blankness of these pages represents another metareferential moment. It serves not only as a reminder of the material preconditions on which any act of literary interaction is premised but also provides an aesthetic correlative for the author's withdrawal from the interpretive process. By means of this indeterminate space, Eggers symbolizes the unbridgeable gap between actual events and their representation in aesthetic form, a gap which has traditionally been accepted as both the enabling condition for literature and its necessary limitation. This gap, so the novel implies, can only be filled in the reciprocal process of an author revealing the formal dimension of this representation and readers substituting the materiality of the underlying events based on their own intuitive reconstruction of these aesthetic depictions. Nicoline Timmer refers to this narrative strategy as 'meta-honesty' (2010: 237).

Metareferential elements feature prominently in the sizable paratextual apparatus with which both ends of the book are framed. Eggers appropriates the copyright pages, prefaces and acknowledgement sections ostensibly in order to poke fun at the conventional use to which these spaces are put:

> The author wishes to reserve the right to use spaces like this, and to work within them, for no other reason than it entertains him and a small coterie of readers. It does not mean that anything ironic is happening. It does not mean that someone is being *pomo* or *meta* or *cute*. It simply means that someone is writing in small type, in a space usually devoted to copyright information, because doing so is fun. (*MKM*: copyright page; emphases in the original)

Here, methinks, the author doth protest too much. I would argue that this allegedly ludic pretext actually serves a higher and much more serious function. This disclaimer is immediately followed by a statement, again shrouded in very small print, which could be read as programmatic for the aesthetic agenda of the novel itself: 'Not everything that is truthful must fall within well-known formal parameters' (ibid.). *Mutatis mutandis*, this implies that the formal challenging and renegotiation of conventional structures and parameters of literary discourse can generate an innovative configuration of truthfulness, one which I describe as an effect of authenticity.

On a structural level, paratexts function as a key link between the person of the author and the autobiographical self mediated through text. Therefore they represent an apt starting point for questioning the (onto)logical framework that connects these entities. Traditionally, the copyright page provides a space where the material reality of the author, as manifested in the author's name, is incorporated into the legal, economical and organizational framework and processes of publication, represented by the name and address of the publisher and printer, copyright notices, the CIP record or the ISBN number. In *A Heartbreaking Work of Staggering Genius*, Eggers counteracts this depersonalization of the author by providing data on the actual physical reality behind the abstract marker 'Dave Eggers'. The copyright notice, this most solemn and momentous act of legal signification, is played down first by its association with the author's nickname: 'Copyright © David ('Dave') Eggers 2000: 2001' and then supplemented by specification about his height (5'11"), weight (175), eye colour (blue), hair colour (brown) and sexual orientation (3 out of 10 'with 1 being perfectly straight, and 10 being perfectly gay'). These rather categorical markers of identification are, in turn, complemented by more particular information such as an allergy to dander and the author's hands being 'chubbier than one might expect' (*HW*: copyright page). In similar fashion, the copyright page of *Mistakes we Knew we were Making* ends with a direct allusion to the material reality beyond the covers of the book: 'Look now, outside: the kids with the bikes are riding down the hill screaming.' These metareferential elements can be classified as explicit displays on the paratextual level with a focus on the alethiology of the author figure of the source text. In contrast to the traditionally depersonalizing function of the copyright page, the author uses this space to fashion himself as a person of flesh and blood, a strategy he also employs in other parts of the paratextual apparatus. In *Mistakes we Knew we were Making*, for example, he gives an account of his struggles with editing the original text: 'The first chapter in particular will have almost no changes, because I just, a few minutes ago, tried to get in there, and after scrolling through the first half-page, I was already having trouble breathing. Now, twenty minutes later, I am still having trouble breathing. I hate being in that chapter again' (*MKM*: 8).

By using exact time indications like 'a few minutes ago' and the present continuous form, a grammatical marker which signalizes immediacy, Eggers performatively positions the reader in the simulated here and now of the editing process by laying open his aesthetic deliberations, his visceral fears and their physical repercussions. In formal terms, this use of metareference is again an explicit display on the paratextual level, this time with the focus on the textuality of the source text.

The insistence on the material reality of the events described in the novel is not restricted to the author, however, but also encompasses the experience of other characters. Again, this interlinking of reality and representation is expressed in a metareferential challenge to conventional hierarchies of form, for example when Eggers rededicates what is commonly known as the 'all persons fictitious disclaimer':

> This is a work of fiction, only in that in many cases, the author could not remember the exact words said by certain people, and exact descriptions of certain things, so had to fill in gaps as best he could. Otherwise, all characters and incidents and dialogue are real, are not products of the author's imagination ... Any resemblance to persons living or dead should be plainly apparent to them and those who know them, especially if the author has been kind enough to have provided their real names and, in some cases, their phone numbers. All events described herein actually happened, though on occasion the author has taken certain, very small liberties with chronology, because that is his right as an American. (*HW*: copyright page)

In her analysis of Eggers's 2002 novel *You Shall Know Our Velocity*, Sarah Brouillette observes how the author 'makes form and content inseparable to an unusual degree' (2003: 10). This applies in equal measure to *A Heartbreaking Work of Staggering*

Genius, where the performative insistence on the material reality behind formal representations pervades the entire paratextual apparatus. In addition to the aspects already cited, this includes a list of the material costs incurred by the publication set off against the author's royalties (*HW*: xxxix), insights into the convoluted process of arriving at the book's eventual title (xxv–xxvi), an admission that the 'book was seen by its author as a stupid risk, and an ugly thing, and a betrayal, and overall, as a mistake he would regret for the rest of his life but a mistake which nevertheless he could not refrain from making, and worse, as a mistake he would encourage everyone to make' (*MKM*: 35) and – quite incongruously – a drawing of a stapler (*HW*: xlv).[4] This self-revelation of the author and the radical disclosure of the compositional process of turning experience into narrative summons readers to participate, albeit vicariously, in this process. It calls them up to reconstruct not only the reality behind the events presented in the novel but also the process by which these events are moulded into (literary) form. Eggers even tries to embrace those readers who prefer their novels to be squarely imaginary: 'if you are bothered by the idea of this being real, you are invited to do what the author should have done, and what authors and readers have been doing since the beginning of time: PRETEND IT'S FICTION' (xxiii–xxiv). Added to this implicit activation of the reader is the occasional explicit parabasis, or direct address, for example when the author promises that the 'first 200 readers of this book who write with proof that they have read and absorbed the many lessons herein will each receive a check, from the author, for $5' followed by detailed instructions on how to prove that requirements are met and the exact address where to apply (xl–xli). For $10, readers can also purchase 'a complete digital manuscript of this work, albeit with all names and locations changed' (xxiii), which in theory enables readers to fill the formal outline of events with their own names: 'This can be about *you*! You and *your* pals!' (xxv; emphases in the original). This gesture can be read as both an enactment and a critique of a contemporary aesthetics of participation, because it outwardly includes the individual reader into the narrative and the processing of experience into narrative. This inclusion, however, is itself merely a simulation, because the narrative structure remains unchanged. The reconstructive, that is, ambiguous, potential of this gesture is only valid in its unfulfilled and inconclusive potentiality and collapses once it is actually implemented by the individual reader.[5]

This essential inconclusiveness is central to Eggers's use of metareference in general. All three dominant strategies pursued in the paratextual corpus to *A Heartbreaking Work of Staggering Genius* – the personalization of the author, the disclosure of the creative process and the activation of the reader's participation – are actually eventually pointless and self-defeating. The logic of participation and involvement must necessarily founder on the insuperableness of the gap between experience and representation. Any gesture that implies a closing of this gap can in the end never

---

[4] Benjamin Widiss reads the image of the stapler as a symbol for Eggers's attempt to create a union between reader and author, as for him it 'seems to promise that the myriad provocations of the opening pages might be collated in some productive fashion' (2010: 115).
[5] In *Mistakes we Knew we were Making*, Eggers gives the number of readers who have actually done so as four (*MKM*: 16).

amount to more than cynical pretence and premeditated posturing. On the contrary, so the author insists, any self-revelation and tactical laying bare of how fictional illusion is fabricated in fact operates as a protective shield to defend and safeguard the privacy and solipsism of the experience conveyed: 'the gimmickry is simply a device, a defence, to obscure the black, blinding, murderous rage and sorrow at the core of this whole story, which is both too black and blinding to look at: *avert ... your ... eyes*' (xxx; emphases in the original). The candid admission of this circumstance even constitutes one of the 'major themes of the book' as enumerated in the 'Acknowledgments' section (xxvii), to wit, 'I.2) The easy and unconvincing nihilistic poseurism re: full disclosure of one's secrets and pain, passing it off under a semi-high-minded guise when in fact the author is himself very private about many or most matters, though he sees the use in making certain facts and happenings public' (xxxv). Elsewhere, Eggers further underlines how the enactment of openness and transparency shrouds rather than reveals what he claims to be the concealed, incommunicable core at the heart of his story:

> What am I giving you? I am giving you nothing ... I tell you how many people I have slept with (thirty-two), or how my parents left this world, and what have I really given you? Nothing ... We feel that to reveal embarrassing or private things, like, say, masturbatory habits (for me, about once a day, usually in the shower), we have given someone something ... But it's just the opposite, *more is more is more* – more bleeding, more giving. These things, details, stories, whatever, are like the skin shed by snakes, who leave theirs for anyone to see ... Hours, days or months later, we come across a snake's long-shed skin and we know something of the snake, we know that it's of this approximate girth and that approximate length, but we know very little else. Do we know where the snake is now? What the snake is thinking now? No. (214–16; emphasis added)

Taking up Baudrillard, one could argue that this metareferential enactment of transparency generates the imaginary detachment which distinguishes the real from the hyperreal. Seen from a formal perspective and against all of Eggers's protestations, this effect would render his use of metareference genuinely ironic, in that it functions counter to its explicitly stated purpose. In Julian Barnes's *A History of the World in 10½ Chapters*, the unnamed narrator of the segment 'A Dream' realizes at some point that 'getting what you want all the time is very close to not getting what you want all the time' (1990: 306). Adapting this insight to the aesthetics of *A Heartbreaking Work of Staggering Genius*, one could conclude that revealing everything about oneself is very close to not revealing anything about oneself. In spite of every effort of self-awareness and sincerity, the blinding essence at the heart of the story confounds any attempt at participation and connectivity. It cannot be communicated or shared and evades representation as it can only ever iteratively refer to itself:

> I could be aware of the dangers of the self-consciousness, but at the same time, I'll be plowing through the fog of all these echoes, plowing through mixed metaphors, noise, and will try to show the core, which is still there, as a core, and

is valid despite the fog. *The core is the core is the core.* There is always the core, that can't be articulated.' (*HW*: 270; emphasis added)

The formal similarity of 'the core is the core is the core' and 'more is more is more' in the quotation above illustrates this correspondence of revelation and concealment. Timmer claims in this context that the formal self-reflections 'are no longer presumed to undermine or *deconstruct* the presentation of direct experience or emotion, but instead it seems that this form of narration is to *preconstruct* this "core"' (2010: 239; emphases in the original). In its utter and unqualified formlessness, this elusive 'core' is akin to the ideal state of pure and immediate materiality envisioned in the third chapter of *England, England*. In both cases it is precisely the indeterminate condition beyond any system of representation that charges experience with authenticity, an authenticity which cannot be depicted but only ever be hinted at through the aesthetic form of paradox. This then constitutes another turn of the metareferential screw. Only *because* all the ploys invoked to bridge the gap between experience and representation are actually doomed to fail, only because they are formally pointless, can they invoke intimations of the material immediacy of the very experience which they so unsuccessfully try to re-enact. Eggers's use of paratexts can be read as an attempt to short-circuit the relationship between the various facets of the autobiographical self, between fiction and reality, between experience and representation. They are a resistance strategy against what Taleb calls 'the narrative fallacy', that is, the innate human 'predilection for compact stories over raw truths' (2008: 63). At the same time, however, they function as potent markers for the insurmountable ontological gap between these entities. It is this paradoxical status – as encouraging participation *and* hermetically closed, affirmative *and* forbidding, revelation *and* concealment – which accounts for their relevance in an aesthetics of authenticity.

This dual strategy of revelation and concealment also characterizes the use of metareference when it comes to tangling the hierarchy of enunciation and enounced in *A Heartbreaking Work of Staggering Genius*. Even though it might appear to be a futile exercise, I will try to distinguish between the two levels depending on where the metareferential element originates. I will first examine one instance in which the narrator intrudes upon the narration, before reversing the direction by focusing on examples where characters from the enounced encroach on the level of the enunciation.

As shown above, it is already in the 'Acknowledgments' section that the author positions himself squarely within the interminable and paradoxical logic of the infinite *mise-en-abyme*, which, if taken to the extreme, will eventually absorb itself in the interminable regression of self-reflection: 'While the author is self-conscious about being self-referential, he is also knowing about that self-conscious self-referentiality. Further, and if you're one of those people who can tell what's going to happen before it actually happens, you've predicted the next element here: he also plans to be clearly, obviously aware of his knowingness about his self-consciousness of self-referentiality' (*HW*: xxx). This persistent and potentially aporetical foregrounding of self-awareness and self-reflection also permeates the novel's enunciation. Dave Eggers, as the narrator of the events in *A Heartbreaking Work of Staggering Genius*, constantly interrupts and intrudes into the narrative process in order to communicate and disclose the tactical and artistic deliberations behind this very process: when confronted with the question of how to relate the apparent suicide attempt of his friend John, the narrator muses:

> This will make some kind of short story or something. Or no. People have done stuff about suicides before. But I could twist it somehow, include random things, what I was thinking on the way to the hospital … But I could take it further. I should take it further. I could be aware, for instance, in the text, of it having been done before, but that I have no choice but to do it again, it having *actually happened that way*. (269; emphasis in the original)

As with the infinite regression of the self-aware author figure, the narrator as well apparently loses himself in the loops of regressive metareferential self-reflection, this time explicit in display, pan-reflective in direction and alethiological in focus, only to come up in the end against the unparalleled actuality of the events conveyed. Again, the authenticity of the narrator's stance is premised on the unsuccessful attempt to aesthetically contain the reverberations of experience by means of infinite reflection while at the same time incessantly asserting the formal impossibility of this endeavour. Experience cannot be accessed directly, without any form of mediation. Through the relentless refraction and reflection of the process of this mediation, however, experiences can be aesthetically elevated, or as the novel's narrator puts it:

> So instead of lamenting the end of unmediated experience, I will *celebrate* it, revel in the simultaneous living of an experience and its dozen or so echoes in art and media, the echoes making the experience not cheaper but *richer*, aha! being that much more layered, the depth luxurious, not soul-sucking or numbing but edifying, ramifying. (270; emphases in the original)

The invisible conceptual boundary between enunciation and enounced is not only challenged from the admittedly privileged position of the narrator. There are also frequent infringements from the other direction. Characters on the level of the enounced all of a sudden abandon their appointed position within the narrative in order to subject the narrator to an interrogation concerning their allocated roles and strategic significance on the level of enunciation, thereby tangling the hierarchies between these two levels. Eggers describes this scheme in the preface to the paperback edition as 'people break[ing] out of their narrative time-space continuum to cloyingly talk about the book itself' (ix). These ontological shifts usually happen during conversations other characters have with Dave Eggers, the protagonist on the level of the enounced, who then all at once morphs into Dave Eggers, the narrator on the level of the enunciation. So, an exceedingly colloquial and apparently inconsequential bantering between Dave and his brother Toph abruptly transforms into a metadiegetic explanation and justification of the author's handling of plot:

> 'So. Big day, huh?' I say.
> 'Yeah,' he says.

'I mean, a lot happened. A full day, this was.'
'Yeah. The half day at school, then the basketball, and then dinner, and the open house, and then ice cream, and a movie – I mean, it was almost as if it was too much to happen in one day, as if a number of days had been spliced together to quickly paint a picture of an entire period of time, to create a whole-seeming idea of how we are living, without having to stoop (or rise) to actually pacing the story out.'
'What are you getting at?'
'No, I think it's good, it's fine. Not entirely believable, but it works fine, in general. It's fine.' (114)

The ensuing discussion on narrative condensation sees Dave defend and excuse the liberty he has taken with the representation of actual events:

> This is just a caricature, this, the skeleton of experience – I mean, you know this is just a slivery, wafer-thin slice. To adequately relate even five minutes of internal thought-making would take forever – It's maddening, actually, when you sit down, as I will once I put you to bed, to try to render something like this, a time or place, and ending up with only this kind of feebleness – one, two dimensions of twenty. (115)

By entangling the ontological distinctness of the levels of mediation, this dialogue between the two brothers at the same time figures as an externalization of the narrator's struggle with the enunciation, even including an attempt to get Toph back into character with the equally unexpected remark 'You have toothpaste on your chin' (117). This constitutes an example of explicit metareference on the level of the enounced with a focus on the alethiology of the text. Such tangling of hierarchy can provoke an almost corporeal sensation of astonishment, a jolt of surprise as it were, which results from the subtle shift from one ontological level to the other, thereby conforming to the criteria Selwyn proposes for what he classifies as 'hot authenticity'. This physical reaction also links Eggers's use of metareference with Höltgen's somaticizing strategy of authenticity. With that, *A Heartbreaking Work of Staggering Genius* features all three registers of the aesthetics of authenticity as described in Höltgen's model. The *historicizing* aspect is accounted for by Eggers's attempt to locate the author in material reality, while the tangling of the levels of mediation constitutes the *ontologizing* dimension. In accordance with what I have delineated earlier, the use of metareference has two principal effects. First, by performatively disclosing the operating mode of the process by which experience is being transformed into representation, it incorporates the reader into this very process. In addition, it dissolves the boundaries between the three aspects of the autobiographical self. Dave's justification cannot be conclusively attributed to either the author, the narrator or the character; it oscillates between these positions. I would argue that this ontologically inconsistent simultaneity and concomitance of the autobiographical trinity of the self, in turn, works to authenticate the autobiographical 'I' and with it the act of literary communication as such. Toph's interrogations, for their part, could also be said to oscillate between the character who speaks them and an implied reader on the level of the enunciation.

A similar case in point for this use of metareferential confusion occurs in a scene where Dave auditions for a part in the 1994 edition of the reality TV show *The Real World*. To begin with, the interview runs its predictable course, with Laura, the casting agent, asking Dave about his family, school and formative experiences from his youth. At this point, Dave clearly positions himself on the level of the enounced, while already foreshadowing the level switch ahead. He was, he claims, 'feeling a formal change coming, one where quotation marks fall away and a simple interview turns into something else, *something entirely so much more*' (184; emphasis in the original). This shift comes in due course when Dave recounts how the father of his friend Ricky had doused himself in petrol and burned himself to death:

> We sat with Ricky, sat there for a while watching TV, and then got bored and went out into the front yard to see if there were any marks anywhere on the grass, or blood or anything. But there was nothing. The grass looked perfect, lush and green.
>
> *And why are you telling me this?*
> I don't know. These are the stories I tell. Isn't that what you're looking for? These terrible deaths tearing through this pristine community, all the more strange and tragic given the context, the incongruity –
>
> *So, tell me something: This isn't really a transcript of the interview, is it?*
> No.
>
> *It's not much like the actual interview at all, is it?*
> Not that much, no.
>
> *This is a device, this interview style. Manufactured and fake.*
> It is.
>
> *It's a good device though. Kind of catchall for a bunch of anecdotes that would be too awkward to force together otherwise.* (196–7)

Here, the oscillation of the characters not only concerns the levels of enunciation and enounced but extends to the real author Dave Eggers as well. Also as part of the interview, he makes a case for both the genuineness of the interview and its usefulness as a narrative device:

> You know, the great thing is that this format makes sense, in a way, because an interview where I opened up to a stranger with a video camera actually did take place ... and besides, squeezing all these things into the Q&A makes complete the transition from the book's first half, which is slightly less self-conscious, to the second half, which is increasingly self-devouring. (200)

It should have become clear by now that the conceptual demarcation line between enunciation and enounced is penetrated from both sides, to the point even that the demarcation itself becomes a moot exercise. As a further illustration, this is a scene following on directly from the narrator's musings about how to deal with John's suicide attempt, where the character Dave sits at John's hospital bed:

I lean my shoulders against the wall then rest my head against it and watch for a while, palm on the white cinder block ... I try for a second, something to do, to time my breaths to his, watching his chest rise and fall, the rest of his body immobile, the hands in fists, the hands tied down, as the color continues to drain I watch the stupid fucking dickhead asshole sleep.
Then he gets up. He is awake and he is standing, and pulling the tubes from his mouth, from his arms, the nodes and electrodes, barefoot. I jump.
'Jesus fucking Christ. What are you doing?'
'Fuck it.'
'What do you mean, fuck it?'
'I mean fuck it, asshole. I'm leaving.'
'*What?*'
'Screw it, I'm not going to be a fucking anecdote in your stupid book.' (272; emphasis in the original)

There ensues an argument about whether an author is entitled to use and thereby misrepresent real persons for his narrative. John, who is surprised to find out that – in congruence with the 'Incomplete guide to metaphors and symbols', which lists the item 'John = Father' (xliv) – he has been renamed after Dave's father, tells him to 'find someone else to be symbolic of, you know, youth wasted or whatever' but eventually agrees to be put into the book in a trade-off for the attention that Dave has lavished on him, 'listening to you ramble about every fucking up and down you have' (273). Towards the very end of the novel, this discussion is taken up once more: John again reproaches Dave for exploiting the materiality of his friends' lives for his own aesthetic ends:

'It's entertainment. If you back up far enough, it all becomes a sort of show. You grew up with comforts, without danger, and now you have to seek it out, manufacture it, or, worse, use the misfortunes of friends and acquaintances to add drama to your own life. But see, you cannot move real people around like this, twist their arms and legs, position them, dress them, make them talk –'
'I am allowed.'
'You're not.'
'I am owed.'
'You're not. See – You're just not. You're like a ... a cannibal or something. Don't you see how this is just flesh-eating? You're making lampshades from human sk–' (424)

Once again in these scenes, both the autobiographical subject and the character John are suspended in oscillation between the levels of enunciation and enounced. What this confusion does is again implicate the reader into the narrative process, this time by externalizing the author's aesthetic considerations into fictional dialogues between him and his creations, thereby performatively shattering the author's armour of interpretative and narrative authority and forcing the reader to retrace and reconstruct the process of mediation.

Eggers provides a fitting image for this inclusive and reconstructive interpretation of literature in the metaphor of the lattice which is repeatedly invoked throughout the book and which is described as 'connective tissue' (211). This can be read as an aesthetic response to and reflection of a multimedia environment where rhizomatic interaction has become the default mode of communication and the authoritative has given way to the dialogical. It could be argued that Eggers's imaginary lattice corresponds to the pluralistic, decentred, swarming and limitless connectedness and interactivity implied, for example, by Rotman's notion of the para-self.[6] With *A Heartbreaking Work of Staggering Genius*, Eggers formally goes through the motions of such a radically interactive epistemology and ontology. He presents the literary process as a refracted and reciprocal endeavour with no ultimate authority granted to either of the constituting factors, 'a tool for simple connectivity for its own sake' (*MKM*: 10). And yet, it should not be forgotten that this entire lattice can only function on the basis of the oblique, non-conveyable 'core' of individual experience, which emerges as both the enabling condition and irremediable structural obstacle to this communal effort. This dark and blinding experience, which in the case of *A Heartbreaking Work of Staggering Genius* has its roots in the trauma of having lost both parents in a short space of time, is the reason why – in spite of Eggers's own statement that 'SELF-AWARENESS *is* sincerity' (34; emphasis in the original) – I consider authenticity rather than sincerity to be the more appropriate paradigm in which to frame this aesthetic approach. With reference to Trilling's famous distinction, sincerity is primarily aimed at an external point of reference. Authenticity, on the other hand, is 'the downward movement through all the cultural superstructures to some place where all movement ends, and begins' (1971: 13) and is therefore essentially directed towards the within. My emphasis on authenticity foregrounds the formal paradox involved in the attempt to reconcile experience and representation and posits this paradox of the dark and blinding core as the premise for an aesthetics of reconstruction.

Let me recapitulate the three main aspects of Eggers's employment of metareference on the levels of the paratexts, the enunciation and the enounced as they bear on an aesthetics of reconstruction:

1) The autobiographical 'I' of *A Heartbreaking Work of Staggering Genius* is authenticated by the constant tangling of the hierarchy between its three constitutive components, the authoring self, the narrating self and the narrated self, all of which are inextricably amalgamated in the marker 'Dave Eggers', which therefore can be said to be oscillating between the different ontological states of the self. With Rotman, this oscillatory form of selfhood could be described as a 'quantum self', which he defines

---

[6] It is worthwhile noting that Gergen connects Rotman's assumption of the plural nature of the contemporary self with a reflective and ludic form of self-awareness as envisioned and enacted by Eggers. He claims that the postmodern condition 'is marked by a plurality of voices vying for the right to reality – to be accepted as legitimate expressions of the true and the good ... Under postmodern conditions persons exist in a state of continuous construction and reconstruction; it is a world where anything goes that can be negotiated. Each reality of self gives way to reflexive questioning, irony, and ultimately the playful probing of yet another reality. The center fails to hold' (2000: 7).

as 'a co-occurrence of virtual states, an "I" which becomes actual or "realized" and fixed as an experienced and "objective" whole precisely when it is observed, subjected to psychic measurement or social control, or otherwise called upon to act, respond, be affected, and project agency' (2008: 135). In *A Heartbreaking Work of Staggering Genius*, Eggers enacts this interactive and reciprocal ontology in formal terms *and* simultaneously disavows its propensity for giving an account of human experience, as the 'core' of selfhood rooted in unmediated, formless and material actuality. This by definition cannot be communicated, symbolized or represented.

2) Eggers uses the tangling of ontological hierarchies effected by metareference in order to externalize and disclose the creative process of rendering the materiality of real events and experience into a formal structure of representation. This exposure of the authorial function formally implicates the reader's response into this very process, thereby elevating an open and apparently transparent interaction between author, reader, event and representation into a structural principle of an aesthetics of reconstruction. This interactivity could be described by way of Alan Moore's concept of 'second-person authenticity' (see 2002: 220). Unlike Timmer, who observes that 'a sense of honesty and openness that is (unfortunately or not) constantly corrupted by that same self-consciousness' (2010: 187), I would emphasize that it is *precisely* by means of constantly foregrounding and externalizing this self-awareness that an honest, that is, authentic, literary communication is enabled.[7]

3) Both aspects can be reconciled through the paradoxical model of authenticity as proposed in the first part of this book, in so far as they reiterate and enact a radical indeterminacy and oscillation between stable and established forms and concepts, while at the same time paradoxically falling back upon a highly individualistic, not to say solipsistic, position of experience, which is characterized by its elemental autonomy and incommunicability. Accordingly, *A Heartbreaking Work of Staggering Genius* ends with a virtually orgasmic unification of the autobiographical self and the reader:

> I'm trying to get your stupid fucking attention I've been trying to show you this, just been trying to show you this – What the fuck does it take to show you motherfuckers, what does it fucking take what do you want how much do you want because I am willing and I'll stand before you and I'll raise my arms and give you my chest and throat and wait and I've been so old for so long, for you, for you, I want it fast and right through me – Oh do it, do it, you motherfuckers, do it do it you fuckers finally, finally, finally. (*HW*: 437)

Widiss uses this enactment of the physical self-abandonment of the author figure, which he describes as a 'fashioning of narrative into performative' (2010: 125), as the basis for a Christian reading of the novel, which aims to transmit 'a renewed possibility

---

[7] Elsewhere, I have defined this dialogical and mutual form of literary interaction as 'reciprocal realism' (*reziproker Realismus*), an aesthetic register that rejects the possibility of material truth in representation and aims rather at a truthful re-enactment of the formal conditions of representation based on accepting the unbridgeable gap between experience and representation (see Funk 2012).

of faith to the entire cohort of his readership' (112). He argues that 'the ending's sudden, simultaneous chopping into both the book's narrative and Eggers's body positions the book *as* his body, held in the reader's hand like a communion wafer, and already figuratively consumed on this, its last page' (128; emphasis in the original). This ultimate 'explosion of emotions' (Timmer 2010: 235) formally represents an example of explicit, interactional and alethiological metareference with a reconstructive effect. In combination with the blank pages that follow, it gives form to a desperate craving for reciprocity as well as to the radical solipsism at the heart of the novel. If at all, this formal paradox of simultaneous reciprocity and solipsism can only be overcome by insinuating the bodily, and therefore material rather than formal, fusion and congress of the entities of author, reader and text. It is only when the materiality of experiential reality becomes aesthetically re-enacted and opened to aesthetic reconstruction that an intimation of authenticity can emerge. Authenticity can therefore formally be described as a 'self-transcending construction' in the sense of Goldstein.

In order to clarify my understanding of the materiality of formlessness in this context, I will finish this chapter by briefly resorting to Heidegger's differentiation between *Sein* and *Dasein*. In *Being and Time*, Heidegger pronounces 'being' (the standard English translation of *Sein*) to be 'the most universal concept' (2010: 2), to the extent even that it transcends any formal and positivist attempt at definition: 'Being cannot be derived from higher concepts by way of definition and cannot be represented by lower ones' (3). In an argument which parallels Eggers's insistence on a 'dark and blinding core', this universality of 'being' for Heidegger renders it opaque and impenetrable: 'If one says accordingly that "being" is the most universal concept, that cannot mean that it is the clearest and that it needs no further discussion. The concept of "being" is rather *the most obscure* of all' (2; emphasis added). This dark formlessness of 'being' can only be brought to the light of human perception in the shape of its ontological manifestation, which Heidegger calls *Dasein* or *das Seiende*. Heidegger himself admits that this differentiation is of purely philosophical, that is, not practical, relevance, as *Sein* cannot but manifest itself as *Dasein*. This does not, however, invalidate the theoretical significance of its formlessness. Heidegger's *Sein* may be a hypothetical projection which cannot be described in formal parameters; it can, however, be traced in its effects. Just like authenticity, *Sein* in its fundamental formlessness and purposelessness could be described as a black box, which can generate understanding without itself being understood, or as Heidegger puts it, 'The explicit and lucid formulation of the question of the meaning of "being" requires a prior suitable explanation of a being (*Dasein*) with regard to its "being"' (7). As with *England, England* in the previous chapter, *A Heartbreaking Work of Staggering Genius* implies that the quest for authenticity can be read as a movement from the purely formal to the fundamentally material. Widiss also emphasizes this attention on the material aspect of reading the book, when he notes how 'Eggers casts the very material of his book – the paper itself – as a Eucharistic substance hovering at the cusp of reembodying its author' (2010: 111). This material objective of pure formlessness, however, cannot be actively pursued but rather emerges from the excessive and necessarily self-defeating deployment of formal structures in the shape of metareference.

6

Reconstructing Literary Influence: Jasper Fforde's Thursday-Next Series

The previous chapter investigated how Dave Eggers employs metareference to implicate the reader in the creative process involved in the transformation of experience into representation, of rendering material reality in aesthetic form. The reconstructive effort I see as essential for this innovative use of metareference is premised on the fragmentation of the author function and the subsequent challenge to the reader to reciprocally reimagine what it means to convey one particular story in and through narrative. While *A Heartbreaking Work of Staggering Genius* primarily reflects on its own textual condition, I will now focus on a very different use of metareference, one which has long been subsumed under the label 'intertextuality'. This concerns instances where the metareferential element that gives rise to the metalevel does not reflect back upon itself but invokes another text or body of texts, which I call the allo-text.

In order to demonstrate how the metareferential use of intertextual allusion can be employed to engage the reader in a process of reconstruction, this chapter investigates Jasper Fforde's Thursday-Next series (2001–present). With regard to Jakobson's model of communication, Eggers's renegotiation of literary communication can be said to start with the role and function of the (autobiographical) *author*, whereas Fforde gets to work on the *context* in which literary communication takes place. Context, in this case, very specifically refers to the web of cultural and literary allo-texts in which any given work is situated. It will become apparent that Fforde's reconstruction of the context, just like Eggers's fragmentation of the author, is effected by an entangling of traditionally hierarchical conceptions, in this case of cause and effect, original and copy, influence and derivation. The solidity and validity of these categories is performatively undone through Fforde's strategic generation of epistemological undecidability and ontological paradox, with the result that readers are called up to reconstruct the chains of influence on their own terms.

Revisitations and revisions: *The Eyre Affair*

As is often the case with the first book in a prospectively longer series, *The Eyre Affair* is heavy on exposition. It first introduces the two most significant narrative suppositions on which the entire series is founded, that is, the possibility and paradoxical consequences of time travelling and the penetrability of the boundary between reality and fiction, before embarking on a profound metareferential revision of its principal allo-text, *Jane Eyre*. At first glance, the two novels do not appear to have too much in common. Charlotte Brontë's 1847 text is one of the most revered novels in the English language, clocking in at number ten in the BBC's *The Big Read* survey (see 'The Big Read' 2004). A classical *Bildungsroman*, it very roughly follows its eponymous first-person narrator through the vicissitudes of childhood, education, working life and finding the right husband until, Reader, she marries him and becomes a proto-feminist example of female self-assertion and independence. In stark contrast to this, *The Eyre Affair* with its shoot-outs, car chases, pistols drawn from the most incongruous places, corrupt policemen and insatiable multinational companies presents a decidedly more exciting, sensational and altogether more contemporary world. Its protagonist, Thursday Next, could be described as a combination of Carrie Mathison and Bridget Jones with a bit of Buffy Summers thrown in for good measure. In spite of this apparent lack of gravity, I believe that Fforde's attempts on *Jane Eyre* still represent a highly relevant case of reconstructive literature. To substantiate this claim, a few words on the extraordinary setting of the novel are necessary. Modifying a term introduced by Mark Berninger and Katrin Thomas, who call *The Eyre Affair* a 'parallelquel' to *Jane Eyre* and define this as a 'story line which runs parallel to (and sometimes against) an established, well-known text' (2007: 181), I suggest the category 'parallelotopia' as an alternative to refer to an essentially utopian text, which is not – as most prominent utopias are – set either in the distant (Atwood's *The Handmaid's Tale*, Wells's *The Time Machine*) or not-so-distant (Orwell's *1984*, McCarthy's *The Road*) future or in some remote and inaccessible part of the universe (Swift's *Gulliver's Travels*, More's *Utopia*, Cavendish's *The Blazing-World*). Instead, it confronts readers with an apparently familiar world, which is peppered with just enough manifestations of the unfamiliar so as to trigger suspicions about the validity of those individual and collective mnemonic archives and sensory tools which construct the readers' everyday reality. Traditionally, literary utopias are based on a clear distinction between the societies depicted in the text and currently prevalent social and political parameters. This difference is instrumental for emphasizing, usually by means of satire or parody, what are considered to be the disadvantages or dangers inherent in the current state of affairs. A parallelotopia, on the other hand, explicitly collapses any all too clear-cut distinctions between the real and the fictional world by slyly introducing the unfamiliar and fictitious into a supposedly realistic setting, which in the case of *The Eyre Affair* means London, Swindon and Merthyr Tydfil in the year 1985. In doing so, the novel locates itself in an ambiguous epistemological space, a position from which it can very conveniently redraw the boundaries of prototype and adaptation.

The year 1985 in which Thursday Next operates only very superficially resembles the year 1985 we assume to know or remember. Society is regulated by economic and political considerations, the sovereignty of nation states and the mechanisms of cultural capital, while human interaction is conducted according to familiar parameters such as romantic love, bonds of kinship and friendship or hierarchical relationships in the workplace. In this apparently very recognizable framework, however, the reader soon realizes that not everything is as it might be expected in this version of England in the mid-1980s. The political agenda of the day is very much dominated by the Crimean War, which is now in its 131st year and still nowhere near any sign of a cease-fire. Airships are the main means of transport. Railways and planes are unheard of, a fate they share with the banana, which will only be 'designed completely from scratch seventy years from now ... by a brilliant engineer named Anna Bannon' (*EA*: 116). Even apart from the Crimean War, the past is also not quite as our history books suggest. Wellington was killed at Waterloo, and England is still reeling from the effects of the German Occupation after World War II.

In another rather substantial change from the world as the reader may know it, Thursday Next's father works as a so-called ChronoGuard, an occupation that involves travelling in time. In this capacity, he inhabits a parallel spatial and chronological universe, a circumstance which allows him to conduct an affair with Lady Emma Hamilton while still being happily married to Thursday's mother. On the rare occasion when he visits his daughter, time stands still in the 'real' world, a fact that more than once saves Thursday's life (see *EA*: 312–13; *LGB*, 357–60). The great significance of time travel in Fforde's parallelotopian universe is emphasized by the fact that *The Eyre Affair* opens with the words 'My father had a face that could stop a clock. I don't mean that he was ugly or anything; it was a phrase the ChronoGuard used to describe someone who had the power to reduce time to an ultra-slow trickle' (1). For Fforde, travelling in time not only constitutes a rather unoriginal plot device which enables him to rescue his heroine from the brink of death, but more importantly, he uses it to subvert the notion of time as a linear process, governed by the categorical and indispensable sequence of past, present and future. By challenging the fixity of this structure, Fforde poses fundamental questions about how notions of identity and the self are firmly anchored in the chronological arrangement of experience (past) and possibility (future) which shapes the individual existence in the here and now.

Fforde's predominant formal device to disrupt traditional conceptions about the linearity of time is his use of paradox. A case in point is the explanation he offers for one of the most persistent puzzles in literary history: Throughout the novel, there are fierce debates about the authorship of Shakespeare's plays (39–41; 216–17; 259–62), to the extent even that 'the radical wing of the "New Marlovians" fire-bombs the monthly meeting of the Baconians (41), who for their part go from door to door to dissuade infidels that 'a Warwickshire schoolboy with almost no formal education could write works that were not for an age but for all time' (40). It is Thursday's father who eventually unravels the mystery:

> I went to London in 1610 and found that Shakespeare was only an actor with a potentially embarrassing sideline as a purveyor of bagged commodities in Stratford ... no one had even *heard* of the plays, much less written them ... Time is out of joint *big time*. Obviously something had to be done. I took a copy of the complete works back with me and gave them to the actor Shakespeare in 1592 to distribute on a given timetable. (367–8; emphases in the original)

In Fforde's parallelotopia, Shakespeare's works are not merely for all time. They rather defy the logic of time itself, since they exist merely through and in a temporal and ontological impossibility. They are, as it were, authenticated through paradox. For all the vigour with which the debate about Shakespeare's authorship has been conducted in the world we call 'real', to the best of my knowledge no party has yet resorted to the use of fire-bombs. This circumstance points to another major difference between Thursday's world and the reader's reality: in Fforde's literary universe, art in general and literature in particular are essential and ubiquitous features of everyday life. Pre-Raphaelites and Neo-Surrealists are fighting it out in the streets. There are 'Will-Speak machines' on every corner which dispense quotations from the Bard for ready money, and children are swapping Henry Fielding bubble-gum cards in the streets. The significance of literature also accounts for the fact that there is a special operations division called the Literary Detectives, or SpecOps 27, who safeguard literature against all sorts of sinister machinations and for whom Thursday works as the novel begins.

One of the most poignant manifestations of this popular enthusiasm for and obsession with classic works of literature comes when Thursday and Landen Parke-Laine, her former and future love-interest, attend a performance of *Richard III*. Not only are the performers of the night randomly picked from the audience, a procedure which presupposes a certain level of familiarity with the text on behalf of the audience, but when the performance actually gets under way, it is the anticipatory audience who kick proceedings into action, thus integrating both text and actor discursively into a reciprocal game of question and answer:

> Richard opened his mouth to speak and the whole audience erupted in unison:
> '*When* is the winter of our discontent?'
> '*Now*,' replied Richard with a cruel smile, '*is the winter of our discontent* ...'
> A cheer went up to the chandeliers high in the ceiling. The play had begun. (182; emphases in the original)

This performative appropriation of the canonical text by the audience and the ensuing confusion of the functions of text, author/actor and audience can serve as a first light-hearted illustration for Fforde's reconstructive use of metareferential intertextuality.

The potential of intertextuality for a reconstructive literary paradigm is not restricted, however, to such playful and irreverent set-pieces, which may temporarily question the authority of the author/performer but which leave the authority of the text itself essentially untouched. Fforde does not shy away from actually redrawing lines of literary influence, a procedure which results in a thorough metareferential tangling of conventional hierarchies of cause and effect. This confusion is based on the second essential narrative conceit which structures the Thursday-Next universe, that is, the assumption that the boundary between reality and fiction is permeable and can be crossed either by a select handful of gifted readers who have the ability to read themselves into books or with the help of technical gadgets such as the Prose Portal invented by Thursday's genius uncle Mycroft (see 126–8).

In a world where literature is of such paramount importance and presence as described above, it is not surprising that books can quite literally save one's life. In the case of Thursday, it is the novel *Jane Eyre*, or rather its back cover, which serves in this function. She only survives a messy shoot-out with the novel's villain Acheron Hades because his bullet cannot pierce the back cover of Brontë's novel, which Thursday had put in her breast pocket shortly before (see 55). As Imke Neumann points out, this occurrence in itself is a rather conventional plot element, as bullets stopped by books, albeit usually of a religious provenance, have long been a staple feature of literature and films and – due to their undeniable potential for propaganda – part and parcel of war narratives from the American Civil War to the invasion of Iraq (see 2008: 188). It is only when Thursday regains consciousness after the shooting that the metareferential confusion really sets in. She finds on herself a handkerchief decorated with the monogram 'EFR', which – so the nurses tell her – belonged to a man who dressed her wounds and kept her alive until the medics arrived (see *EA*: 62). This textile item, which the inclined reader should have no difficulty in linking with Edward Fairfax Rochester, constitutes the first short circuit between the different levels of fictionality in *The Eyre Affair*.

Rochester's handkerchief reminds Thursday how she herself had experienced a border crossing between reality and fiction as a child, at a time when her 'mind was still young and the barrier between reality and make-believe had not yet hardened into the shell that cocoons us in adult life' (63).[1] During a family visit to Haworth House, a Japanese tourist had read to her from the original manuscript of *Jane Eyre* on display there, and Thursday was instantaneously transported into the plot of the novel, or as Thursday herself describes it, the 'barrier was soft, pliable and, for a moment, thanks to the kindness of a stranger and the power of a good storytelling voice, I made the short journey – and returned' (ibid.). Inside *Jane Eyre*, her appearance for the first time affects the plot of Brontë's novel. I will reproduce at this point the two corresponding passages from *Jane Eyre* and *The Eyre Affair* which describe this first encounter of Jane with Rochester at some length in order to demonstrate Fforde's strategy of making use of gaps in the established narrative of the original – who has ever wondered why Rochester's horse shies when it does? – and then immediately to fill them with his own version of events, thus enacting a playful interrogation of notions of causality and authorship. On the same note, this passage also exemplifies how the hierarchy between the different levels of fictionality is undermined:

> It [Rochester's horse] was very near, but not yet in sight; when, in addition to the tramp, tramp, I heard a rush under the hedge, and close down by the hazel stems glided a great dog, whose black and white colour made him a distinct object

---

[1] This remark implies that the absolute distinction between reality and fiction, between experience and representation, is not an ontological given but rather itself a convention, a formal construction which facilitates the categorization of and knowledge about the world. With regard to Schiller and Barnes, however, the strict maintenance of this boundary could also be read as a compensation strategy for the individual's expulsion from the pre-symbolic and irretrievable Arcadia of pure, formless materiality, which Fforde presents as an actual rather than imaginary immersion in the world of fiction.

against the trees. It was exactly one mask of Bessie's Gytrash – a lion-like creature with long hair and a huge head: it passed me, however, quietly enough; not staying to look up, with strange pretercanine eyes, in my face, as I half expected it would. The horse followed – a tall steed, and on its back a rider. The man, the human being, broke the spell at once. Nothing ever rode the Gytrash: it was always alone; and goblins, to my notions, though they might tenant the dumb carcasses of beasts, could scarce covet shelter in the commonplace human form. No Gytrash was this, – only a traveller taking the short cut to Millcote. *He passed, and I went on: a few steps, and I turned: a sliding sound and an exclamation of 'What the deuce is to do now?' and a clattering tumble, arrested my attention. Man and horse were down; they had slipped on the sheet of ice which glazed the causeway.* The dog came bounding back, and seeing his master in a predicament, and hearing the horse groan, barked till the evening hills echoed the sound, which was deep in proportion to his magnitude. He snuffed round the prostrate group, and then ran up to me; it was all he could do – there was no other help at hand to summon. I obeyed him, and walked down to the traveller, by this time struggling himself free of his steed. His efforts were so vigorous, I thought he could not be much hurt; but I asked him the question: – 'Are you injured, sir?' (Brontë 2001: 95–6; emphasis added)

***

I was just thinking about asking [Jane] where the museum had gone when a sound in the lane made us both turn. It was an approaching horse, and the young woman seemed startled for a moment. The lane was narrow, and I stepped back to give the horse room to pass. As I waited, a large black-and-white dog rushed along the hedge, nosing the ground for anything of interest. The dog ignored the figure on the stile but stopped dead in his tracks when he saw me ... I looked up and noticed that the horse and rider had just passed the young woman. The rider was a tall man with distinguished features and a careworn face, bent into a frown by some musings that seemed to envelop him in thoughtful detachment. *He had not seen the small form and the safe route down the lane led right through where I was standing; opposite me was a treacherous slab of ice. Within a few moments the horse was upon me, the heavy hooves thumping the hard ground, the hot breath from its velvety nose blowing on my face. Suddenly, the rider, perceiving the small girl in his path for the first time, uttered: 'What the deuce –' and reined his horse rapidly to the left, away from me but on to the slippery ice. The horse lost its footing and went crashing to the ground.* I took a step back, mortified at the accident I had caused. The horse struggled to gain a footing and the dog, hearing the commotion, returned to the scene, presented me with a stick and then barked at the fallen group excitedly, his deep growl echoing in the still evening. The young woman approached the fallen man with grave concern on her face. She was eager to be of assistance and spoke for the first time. 'Are you injured, sir?' (*EA*: 66–8; first emphasis in the original, all emphasis added)

The metareferential moment here occurs when Rochester spots Thursday in his track. First, this entails an ontologically impossible fusion of different levels of fictionality, as a character from Fforde's text significantly affects the logic of Brontë's narrative. Without Thursday having been in the way, Rochester's horse arguably would not have slipped, and had Rochester not fallen he would not have encountered Jane out there in the country lane, which, in turn, leads to her supporting him while he limps to recapture his horse. This again foreshadows Jane and Rochester's eventual married state which can only come to pass after the hierarchical structure of master and governess has collapsed together with Thornfield Hall, bringing Rochester back full circle to being in a position where he has to rely on Jane's support. Whereas the character of Jane remains largely oblivious to Thursday's manipulations throughout *The Eyre Affair*, Rochester is fully aware of the interplay between the different levels of fictionality. He shares this intertextual awareness with other characters from the novel, one example being Grace Pool. When Hobbes, Acheron's accomplice, tries to kidnap Jane from the manuscript with the words 'I want Jane Eyre', the enigmatic servant drily observes, 'So does Mr Rochester ... But he doesn't even kiss her until page one hundred and eighty-one' (294).

As with the epistemological contradictions which result from travelling in time, the tangling of hierarchies between the different levels of fictionality engenders an irresolvable confusion of cause and effect. Thursday Next paradoxically figures as both a consequence of and the enabling condition for the events in *Jane Eyre*, as it is her presence that triggers Jane and Rochester's complicated relationship. Without this relationship, however, there would not have been a manuscript of Brontë's novel for Thursday to read herself into in the first place. The effect of this ontological inconsistency could be described as a vacillation between clearly definable states of fictional existence, as both source text and allo-text are being cut loose from their allocated position in the framework of prototype and epigone, originality and adaptation. Fforde's oscillation between different levels of reality and fiction therefore constitutes an example of metalepsis, which Margarete Rubik defines, quite fittingly for the occasion, as 'the leaping and diving from one narrative level to another' (2005: 190).

Thursday is not the only person in Fforde's fictional universe with the ability to transcend the borders of their reality and fiction. With the help of the Prose Portal, her antagonist Acheron Hades and his crony Hobbes also manage to enter the original manuscript of *Jane Eyre*, where they abduct the novel's heroine in order to hold the nation to ransom.[2] This again leads to veritable epistemological confusion between the different levels of fictionality, as the following scene neatly demonstrates:

> The door closed behind her as a voice shouting 'Wake, wake!' brought Hobbes's attention back to the blazing room. Within he could see the night-robed Jane

---

[2] The logic underlying this attempt at blackmail is that by removing the first-person narrator from the original manuscript, the whole novel *Jane Eyre* will be eradicated. In a world like Fforde's parallelotopian 1985, where literature is of such national importance, the threat of the extermination of *Jane Eyre* is obviously prone to cause quite a stir; it was, in Thursday's words, 'as if a living national embodiment of England's literary heritage had been torn from the masses' (297).

throwing a jug of water over the recumbent form of Mr Rochester. Hobbes waited until the fire was out before stepping into the room, drawing his gun as he did so. They both looked up, the 'elves of Christendom' line dying on Rochester's lips.
'Who are you?' they asked, together.
'Believe me, you couldn't possibly begin to understand.'
Hobbes took Jane by the arm and dragged her back towards the corridor.
'Edward! Edward!' implored Jane, her arms outstretched to Rochester. 'I won't leave you, my love!'
'Wait a minute,' said Hobbes, still backing away, 'you guys haven't fallen in love yet!'
'In that you would be mistaken,' murmured Rochester, pulling out a percussion pistol from beneath his pillow. (*EA*: 295; cf. Brontë 2001: 127)

The attempt to recapture Jane and hunt down Acheron finally unites Jane, Rochester, Thursday and Acheron inside the manuscript of *Jane Eyre*, where they eventually bring about the very course of events known from Brontë's original text. Again, however, relationships of cause and effect are seriously being upended. For instance, it is not Bertha Mason who 'set fire first to the hangings of the room next to her own ... and made her way to the chamber that had been the governess's ... and she kindled the bed there' (Brontë 2001: 364), but Acheron Hades who 'took a spirit lamp from the sideboard and hurled it to the end of the corridor; it burst into flames and ignited some wall hangings' (*EA*: 338). In *Jane Eyre*, the mad-woman from the attic causes the blaze and represents the dangerous backlashes of the suppressed Victorian other, which has to be overcome and self-annihilated before the 'happily-ever-after'. In *The Eyre Affair*, it is only through Bertha's frenzied attack on Hades with a pair of scissors that Thursday finally understands that Hades, who so far has proved to be immune to every weapon fired or thrown at him, is vulnerable only to silver, a susceptibility which aligns him with literary villains from Eugene O'Neill's Emperor Jones to Stephen King's werewolves. At this point, Fforde not only inserts his own narrative into gaps gushed into the original, but in fact he rewrites the events of *Jane Eyre*. For, while Brontë's Bertha explicitly commits suicide by jumping from the roof – 'she yelled, and gave a spring, and the next minute she lay smashed on the pavement' (Brontë 2001: 365) – Fforde's 'Hades took two quick steps to the parapet and threw Bertha over, her yell only silenced by the dull thud as she hit the ground three storeys below' (*EA*: 340).[3] The intervention of a character from the source text in the allo-text initiates a paradoxical eternal braid of authorship and causation, with Brontë, Fforde and Hades vying for the authorial sovereignty in the case of Bertha's death.

The ontological confusion between different levels of fictionality is exacerbated by the introduction of a further metareferential element, the allusion to a fictitious hypothetical 'original' text of *Jane Eyre*. According to *The Eyre Affair*, it is Thursday who is responsible for the eventual happy ending of Brontë's novel as it is known today.

---

[3] Imke Neumann indicates in this context that by depriving Bertha of this ultimate gesture of her self-determination, Fforde objectifies her to an even greater extent than Brontë ever does (see 2008: 185).

Before her intervention, Jane had supposedly accepted St. John Rivers's proposal to join him on his mission to India and become his wife; this 'rather flawed climax of the book was a cause of considerable bitterness within Brontë circles. It was generally agreed that if Jane had returned to Thornfield Hall and married Rochester, the book might have been a lot better' (38). As Thursday still owes a favour to Rochester for saving her life after the shooting with Acheron Hades, she intervenes in Brontë's supposedly 'original' story and reinvents it as the text we have come to be familiar with. As any well-disposed reader of Brontë's novel knows, Jane's decision to come back to Ferndean and its blinded and broken resident is in consequence of hearing his voice calling out for her across the moor. Unlike Brontë, who leaves this manifestation of the supernatural unexplained, Fforde inserts Thursday into the text as the material origin of this mysterious voice. Again, these are the parallel scenes from the two novels:

> I saw nothing; but I heard a voice somewhere cry – 'Jane! Jane! Jane!' nothing more.
> 'O God! what is it?' I gasped. I might have said, 'Where is it?' for it did not seem in the room – nor in the house – nor in the garden: it did not come out of the air – nor from under the earth – nor from overhead. I had heard it – where, or whence, for ever impossible to know! And it was the voice of a human being – a known, loved, well-remembered voice – that of Edward Fairfax Rochester; and it spoke in pain and woe wildly, eerily, urgently. (Brontë 2001: 357)

***

> I made it back to Ferndean and Rochester just before Jane did. I met Rochester in the dining room and told him the news; how I had found her at the Rivers' house, gone to her window and barked: 'Jane, Jane, Jane!' in a hoarse whisper the way that Rochester did. It wasn't a good impression but it did the trick. I saw Jane start to fluster and pack almost immediately. Rochester seemed less than excited about the news. (*EA*: 346)

Through the metareferential ploy of imagining Thursday as the author of the novel's ending in its real-world version and juxtaposing this with Brontë's role as author of a fictitious original version of *Jane Eyre*, Fforde playfully questions the idea of canonicity and the anxiety of literary influence as such by subverting the linear historical and chronological framework on which such notions are based and replacing it with an epistemologically paradoxical circular model. In formal terms, this represents an example of an implicit, pan-reflective use of exo-metareference with a focus on the alethiology of its allo-text. Re-reading *Jane Eyre* through the metareferential prism of *The Eyre Affair* produces an effect of uncertainty as to the relationship between source text and allo-text by positioning both texts in a state of oscillation between these ostensibly stable demarcations and thus engages readers to reconstruct their notion of chains of literary influence.

I have claimed earlier that not every intertextual allusion must necessarily result in an ontological paradox and can thus count as metareference. In order to illustrate how this categorical difference relates to *The Eyre Affair*, I want to take up and slightly modify Fredric Jameson's distinction of parody vs. pastiche. I would classify as 'parody' all the elements in *The Eyre Affair* which parallel and mock events, constellations and characters from its allo-text *Jane Eyre* without, however, interfering with the ontological distinctiveness of the two texts. The characters of Jane and Thursday, for example, share a rather unassuming outward appearance. While Jane Eyre admits to have 'felt it a misfortune that I was so little, so pale, and had features so irregular and so marked' (Brontë 2001: 84), Thursday looks in the mirror and encounters a 'woman with somewhat ordinary features … Her hair was a plain mousey colour and of medium length, tied up rather hastily in a ponytail at her back' (*EA*: 20). In similar fashion, the love plot of Fforde's book is in many ways a rather obvious copy of that of *Jane Eyre*. Jane finds herself caught between her object of desire, the uncouth, wayward and apparently recalcitrant Rochester, and the zealous, affable but ultimately mind-numbing St. John Rivers, who asks her to become his wife almost as soon as she awakes at Moor House. Thursday, likewise, is courted by her kind-hearted if slightly dull colleague Bowden Cable, who – in lieu of India – asks her to accompany him to Ohio, while Thursday herself carries a torch for Landen, who not only shares Rochester's bodily impairment – he lost a leg in the Crimea – but also his rather curt and capricious behaviour. Like Jane, Thursday is confronted with the aspect of her heart-throb marrying another, apparently completely unsuitable, woman: Blanche Ingram's counterpart in *The Eyre Affair* is Daisy Mutlar, the unsuitable bride-to-be Fforde appropriated from George and Weedon Grossmith's 1892 novel *The Diary of a Nobody*.[4]

While such analogies do generate engaging, humorous and sometimes even startling intertextual connections between the texts, they do not interfere with the ontological distinctness of the different levels of fictionality, let alone the boundary between reality and fiction as such, and therefore do not qualify as metareferential. In the context of intertextuality, this category is reserved for the paradoxical subversion of chronological and causal relations and the impossible intermingling of ontologically

---

[4] For a more detailed study on the parallels between the plots of the novels, see Juliette Wells (2007) and Imke Neumann (2008). While *Jane Eyre* is by far the most significant allo-text for *The Eyre Affair*, others should not go unmentioned. In one subplot of the novel, Wordsworth's poem 'Daffodils' constitutes another intertextual, though not metareferential, reference point. In order to pressure Mycroft into handing over the Prose Portal, Acheron Hades imprisons his wife Polly in this poem, where she meets its creator. Wordsworth tries to share his romantic mood with Polly, an endeavour which definitely cuts no ice with her: 'Mr W over there seems to think that he's God's gift to women. He invited me to join him in a few unpublished works. A few flowery phrases and he thinks I'm his' (232). In similar fashion, Jack Schitt, representative of the behemoth corporation Goliath and Thursday's permanent nemesis, ends up locked in Edgar Allen Poe's poem 'The Raven', the first stanza of which subsequently reads:

Once upon a midnight dreary, while I pondered weak and weary,
o'er a plan to venge myself upon that cursed Thursday Next –
This Eyre affair, so surprising, gives my soul such loath despising,
Here I plot my temper rising, rising from this jail of text.
'Get me out!' I said, advising, 'Pluck me from this jail of text –
⠀⠀⠀⠀⠀⠀or I swear I'll wring your neck!' (370)

distinct levels which I have delineated above. I would suggest the term 'pastiche' to describe this metareferential form of intertextuality. Unlike Jameson, however, who rather negatively defines pastiche as 'blank parody, parody that has lost its sense of humour', and regards it as representative of a 'world in which stylistic innovation is no longer possible' (1989: 114, 115), I would propose to revaluate the term by stressing the liberating and inclusive effect produced by Fforde's challenges to the idea of the literary canon. Parody, with its carnivalesque, satirical, occasionally derisive, yet generally confirmatory attitude towards its allo-texts, actually works towards the conservation and continuation of literary traditions and advocates the sacrosanctity of the canon by emphasizing its own derivative and secondary nature. In doing so, it reinforces rather than questions the ontological barrier between source text and allo-text. It is therefore an essentially imitative and reactionary form. According to Waugh it has been often 'regarded as a sign of generic exhaustion' (1984: 69) and thus expresses almost by definition the anxiety of intertextual influence. Pastiche, on the other hand, does not accept, let alone sympathize with, the authority of tradition and convention. It does not deferentially look up to and cheekily wink at its allo-text. Instead, pastiche in my understanding constitutes an effort to cancel out the hierarchies between source text and allo-text. It presents a profound structural challenge to the sovereignty of the allo-text by implicating it in an incongruous and contradictory exchange which eventually obliterates any clear-cut ascriptions of precedence and appropriation and replaces them with a potentially interminable play of mutual interdependence. By playfully excoriating both the individual allo-texts and the idea of one-dimensional, linear cultural and literary influence, pastiche in this sense forces the reader to actively engage in an effort of reconstruction. This effort relates both to the ontological disentangling of the individual textual levels of fictionality and to a fundamental reflection on the epistemological and chronological framework in which literary interaction is traditionally situated and expressed. I find myself in agreement with Rubik here, who observes in *The Eyre Affair* a celebration of the 'idea that all literature is pastiche' (2005: 197).

Let me recapitulate how Fforde's use of metareference intertwines three major relationships/hierarchies that are usually employed to describe the context in which literature exists. First, Fforde challenges the notion of a one-directional and teleological timeline. It is this convention of chronologically sequencing and arraying events which enables traditional conceptions of intertextuality in terms of cause and effect, original and parody/copy, innovation and adaptation. Furthermore, Fforde undermines the traditional hierarchy of pre-eminence and adaptation between the allo-text and the source text, when he not only uses *Jane Eyre* as a given intertextual context for his own story but also inserts his narrative into gaps of the allo-text and even reimagines a rival version of it. Finally, Fforde subverts the convention of the authority of authors over their work. In traditional conceptions of art, the authenticity of an artwork derives from its explicit and immediate origin in the author's imagination. When Fforde infringes on the aesthetic autonomy of *Jane Eyre* by writing his own characters into the literary imaginary of the allo-text, he performatively lays to rest this monolithic understanding of authenticity based on the idea of authority. In its stead, he offers a form of authentic literary communication which is grounded in an aesthetics of mutuality. In this form, literary communication is authenticated by its constant oscillation between stable categories and clear lines of influence. The canon and the canonical works are not forever set in stone but rather amount to a free-for-all assembly set, from which authors and readers alike can reconstruct their individual reading experiences.

It may seem easy to dismiss Fforde's metareferential ploys as mere tomfoolery, as elaborate and erudite but essentially solipsistic pranks by an admittedly clever and enviably well-read author, which can, however, never really compromise the autonomy and indeed inviolability of Brontë's original text. There can be no doubt that in a very real sense the principal hierarchy between the author and the reader of *The Eyre Affair* remains untouched, so that any tangling of epistemological hierarchies or ontological levels is safely confined inside this one particular novel, which, in turn, would mean that the traditional model of agency in literary communication remains firmly in place. In purely formal terms, this represents a logically coherent and unassailable argument. On a more material level, however, this line of argument indicates a profound misconception of the cognitive process of reading in general and the specific aesthetics of intertextuality in particular.[5] It grants to *Jane Eyre*, and implicitly to any canonical text, a status of objective and unchangeable materiality beyond its formal manifestation as text. If one accepts that this view is outmoded and that, in order to signify, every text, even the most revered and canonical, must necessarily be confronted, studied or experienced by the individual reader, then one must also acknowledge that reading *The Eyre Affair* indeed transforms the reading experience of *Jane Eyre*. In other words, even though the reader might be convinced that Rochester's horse has merely slipped because of the icy road and that the cry across the moors is indeed a mysterious and unsolved supernatural occurrence, they will be hard pushed not to think of Thursday scaring the horse or whispering underneath the window of Moor House. It is this effect on the actuality of the individual reading experience, an effect which affects the visceral and corporeal rather than the theoretical and rational dimension, which justifies the inclusion of Fforde's apparently inconsequential literary pranks in an aesthetics of reconstruction.

Inside literature: Reconstructing Thursday Next

The subsequent books in the Thursday-Next series can to some extent be seen as mere variations on the subject introduced in its first instalment. I will nevertheless argue for the significance of the novel sequence as a whole, as the very format of a series provides Fforde with additional structural conditions and operational areas for

---

[5] For a specific application of theories of cognition to *The Eyre Affair*, see Rubik (2007). For more detailed analyses of the cognitive approach to narratology and reading in general, see Fludernik (2010: in particular 10–14).

metareference. Two major strands of development stand out. *The Eyre Affair* primarily focuses on the allo-textual dimension of exo-reflective metareference by playing fast and loose with one specific allo-text (*Jane Eyre*), with pan-reflective considerations of general literary conventions and canonicity arising more or less as a side-effect. With books two to four of the series, the pan-reflective dimension becomes more and more foregrounded, until *First among Sequels*, the fifth book in the series, strikes a spectacular new path by systematically historicizing the series itself, thereby tangling the chronological and causal hierarchies between the individual books in the series so far. I will now first introduce in an exemplary and rather condensed fashion some of the pan-reflective instances of metareference that are dominant in *Lost in a Good Book* (2002), *The Well of Lost Plots* (2003) and *Something Rotten* (2004), before examining in more detail the implications of the self-historicization of the series in *First among Sequels* (2007), *One of Our Thursdays is Missing* (2011) and *The Woman who Died a Lot* (2012).

To set the tone, let me begin with a preliminary and prototypical example of the metareferential interconnections which Fforde establishes between the different books in his series, a strategy I will refer to as *cross-sequential referencing*. On the journey north towards Haworth House from where the manuscript of *Jane Eyre* was stolen in *The Eyre Affair*, Thursday and her partner Bowden experience a spontaneous rupture in the time-space continuum which propels them three years into the future to end up at a nondescript motorway service area:

> Suddenly, the doors to the cafeteria burst open and a woman pushed her way out ... We peered cautiously out and saw that the woman had unwelcome company; several men had appeared seemingly from nowhere and all of them were armed. 'What the – ?' I whispered, suddenly realising what was happening. 'That's me!'
> ...
> We watched as one of the three men told the other me to drop her gun. I-me-she said something we couldn't hear and then put her gun down, releasing her hold on the man, who was then grabbed roughly by one of the other men.
> ...
> 'I can't leave her – me – in this predicament!'
> ...
> I struggled free, pulled out my automatic and hid it behind one wheel of the nearest car, then ran after Bowden and leaped into the back of the Speedster. (*EA*: 280)

Merely seen in the context of *The Eyre Affair*, this excursion into the future is inconsequential and remains a narratological non sequitur. It is only in *Something Rotten*, the fourth book in the series, that this episode is taken up again. The motorway service station turns out to be a kind of purgatory where dead souls await their final transfer to the Eternal Beyond – symbolized by crossing over to the other side of the motorway. Thursday, who has come to the service area on a dangerous SpecOps mission, finds herself heavily outnumbered and in a very tight corner, when suddenly she experiences a certain 'sense of déjà vu':

> I *had* been here before, during a leap through time nearly three years ago. I witnessed the jeopardy I was in and left a gun for myself. I looked around. Behind me a man and a woman – Bowden and myself, in point of fact – were jumping into a Speedster – *my* Speedster. I smiled and dropped to my knees, feeling under the car tyre for my weapon. My hands closed around the automatic and I flicked off the safety catch and moved from the car, firing as I went. (*SR*: 256; emphases in the original)

The effect of this cross-sequential use of metareference is twofold. First, and in keeping with Fforde's paradoxical employment of time travel, it subverts the linear succession of the series and its narrative. By recurrently short-circuiting the plot lines of his novels, Fforde generates a paradoxical simultaneity of the non-simultaneous. At the same time he undermines the chronological structure of past, present and future as well as the logical sequence of cause and effect that derives from it. A second consequence logically follows from this and concerns the series' narrative perspective. As a result of the chronological anomaly, the sovereignty of Thursday as the first-person narrator is challenged, which manifests itself in her indecisive use of personal pronouns: her self-reference as 'I-me-she' reveals an uncertainty as to the stability of her own identity as a character on the level of the enounced (I ⇔ she). Simultaneously, it contests her authority as a narrator on the level of the enunciation by obscuring her point of view in relation to the narrated events (I ⇔ me). Again, the aesthetic effect of these metareferential elements can be described by way of an oscillation, both between chronologically distinct and incommensurate ontological states and between epistemologically conflicting perspectives with regard to the narrative. All the examples that will be outlined here give evidence of the comprehensive sense of indecision and uncertainty which pervades Fforde's textual cosmos and which the reader is called up to acknowledge and accommodate in the very process of reading. Moreover, in scenes like the one just described, Fforde already prefigures a radical fragmentation of narrative perspective, an aspect which will become his predominant focus in the second part of the series.

The main novelty in the remaining three books of the first Thursday-Next tetralogy is that, while *The Eyre Affair* only contains occasional visits to the world of fiction, the subsequent books are to a greater extent set inside the literary universe, or BookWorld as it is called in the novels. The plot of *Lost in a Good Book* is rather incidental and suffers from a perceptible lack of structure and coherence. In the book, however, Fforde introduces a subject that will pervade all subsequent novels, that is, the fragility and vulnerability of individual memory. In order to coerce Thursday into releasing Jack Schitt from 'The Raven', the Goliath corporation have her husband Landen eradicated from the official timeline – but not from her private memories. This provides the motivation for Thursday to enter the BookWorld in the first place. *Lost in a Good Book* also introduces Aornis Hades, Acheron's little sister and one of Thursday's main adversaries during the rest of the series. As a so-called 'mnemonomorph', Aornis can invade and manipulate people's memories without being detected.

Inside the BookWorld, Thursday is employed by Jurisfiction, the policing agency responsible for the smooth operation of literature from within. Jurisfiction is staffed by a wide range of real, fictional and fictitious characters from Percy Shelley to the Red Queen, from Falstaff to one Commander Bradshaw, the hero of a fictitious succession of ripping yarns set in Britain's colonial past.[6] Thursday is apprenticed to Mrs Havisham from *Great Expectations*. Although *Lost in a Good Book* lacks much of its predecessor's ingeniousness, effortless irreverence and indeed metareferential significance, it exhibits a number of idiosyncratic features which revisit or develop some of the strategies introduced in *The Eyre Affair*. Not only does Fforde play his gambit of time travel for all its worth, but he also uses it to introduce a further twist in the relationship of reality and fiction. At the end of the book, her father offers Thursday a chance to be transferred to another parallel reality. This world now appears to have much in common with the real world as the readers might know it. World War II, for example, ended in 1945 with the defeat of Nazi Germany, jetliners are the principal means of long-distance travelling and 'Carravaggggio will be there too, although his name will be spelt more sensibly' (*LGB*: 368).

Also in *Lost in a Good Book*, Fforde builds on the metareferential dimension that concerns the material reality of the book by blurring the boundaries between the textual and the paratextual domain. A common form of communication in the BookWorld is the Footnoterphone, by means of which communication between individual books and indeed even between the BookWorld and the Outland is possible. As its name indicates, this form of communication uses footnotes as part of a conversation on the diegetic level, thereby entangling the paratextual level with the enunciation. This, in turn, necessitates a somewhat erratic and non-linear reading effort in the vein of Aarseth's ergodic reading.

All in all, *Lost in a Good Book* is the least convincing novel in the entire series. Neither the plot in the Outland nor the scenes in the BookWorld add up to a consistent and compelling storyline. The novel haphazardly veers between the two worlds and remains no more than an assemblage of individual anecdotes and set-pieces, interspersed with a good measure of more or less witty intertextual allusions. At best, it can be described as a transitional book, which prepares the ground for some of the more substantial issues and aspects negotiated as the series progresses. With the embellishment of the BookWorld and the introduction of Jurisfiction, Fforde lays the foundations for the two major innovations that characterize the subsequent novels. First, he reconceptualizes the abstract and cognitive realm of literature as a definite, reified and material cosmos, as 'a tangible universe which can be entered, explored and physically altered' (Berninger and Thomas 2007: 189). Second, in the novels that follow, Fforde employs this allegorical cosmos to describe by way of a number of extended metaphors the cognitive and epistemological particularities of how literature and its reception operate.

The next book in the series, *The Well of Lost Plots*, is almost entirely set within the

---

[6] I am using the term 'fictional' for works and characters that are part of our actual literary imaginary, like Falstaff or the Cheshire Cat, who acts as Chief Librarian in the Great Library of the BookWorld, and 'fictitious' for works and characters invented by Fforde, like Commander Bradshaw, Emperor Zhark, the 'tyrannical ruler of the known galaxy' (*WLP*: 57), or the immensely prolific and immensely repetitive writer Daphne Farquitt.

BookWorld. So as to be safe from Goliath's continuing intimidations and in order to concentrate on her pregnancy, Thursday participates in the so-called Character Exchange Programme, 'a scheme to allow characters a change of scenery' by swapping place with a character from another book (*WLP*: 2). This programme takes Thursday into the Well of Lost Plots, the under-construction area of the BookWorld, 'where books are constructed, honed and polished in readiness for a place in the library above' (1). This library, called the Great Library, is the principal organizational structure in the BookWorld. It represents a space where every book, and every edition of every book, ever published is stored and where it can be accessed by readers from the Outland. It covers 26 floors, one for every letter in the alphabet. There is a separate library for every language.[7] In the Well of Lost Plots, Thursday takes up residence in a half-baked and 'dreary crime thriller set in Reading entitled *Caversham Heights*' (2). With this rather incongruous setting, Fforde extends his game of self-reference beyond the confines of the Thursday-Next series, as Thursday swaps places with one Detective Sergeant Mary Jones, the partner of Inspector Jack Spratt, protagonists of Fforde's second, marginally less successful outfit, the Nursery-Crime series, which so far comprises *The Big Over Easy* (2005) and *The Fourth Bear* (2006).

There are two major and interrelated themes that shape the plot of the novel. One is Thursday's, and with her the reader's, initiation into the intricacies of the BookWorld. She accompanies Miss Havisham on a number of missions to all parts of the literary universe, from the lofty heights of the Great Library's 26th floor, where the Council of Genres resides, to the deepest abyss where the Library opens up to the Text Sea below. In doing so, she acquaints herself with the laws, arrangements and mechanisms that govern the place.[8] She learns, for example, about the administrative structures of the literary cosmos: the ultimate legislative power in BookWorld is the Council of Genres, a quarrelsome and rarely consentaneous body not unlike the United Nations. The everyday running of the BookWorld and its smooth transaction with the Outland, in other words its executive branch, is in the hands of an obscure entity named Text Grand Central, to which Jurisfiction is also assigned. The judiciary is independent, as law is administered in various courts throughout the BookWorld, from Kafka's *The Trial* to *Alice in Wonderland* to King Solomon's Court.

Thursday also learns about the processes involved in the gestation and destruction of an individual literary work, from the protracted training of generics into 'real' characters to the demolition of manuscripts deemed non-publishable, which are broken down into their letters and cast back into the vast Text Sea (see *FS*: 90). The epigraph to Chapter 9 explains in detail how a story is actually constructed:

> ImaginoTransference Recording Device: A machine used to write books in the Well, the ITRD resembles a large horn (typically eight foot across and made of

---

[7] The Great Library can be seen as an allo-textual reference to Borges's famous story 'The Library of Babel' which images the universe as an infinite library containing all the books that have been or could ever be written (see 1964: 51–9).

[8] In order not to disrupt the narrative too much, Fforde moves some of the more detailed explanations of how the BookWorld works into the epigraphs which introduce each chapter.

brass) attached to a polished mahogany mixing board a little like a church organ but with many more stops and levers. As the story is enacted in front of the *collecting horn*, the actions, dialogue, humour, pathos, etc., are collected, mixed and transmitted as raw data to Text Grand Central where the wordsmith hammers it into readable story code. Once done it is beamed direct to the author's pen or typewriter, and from there through a live footnoterphone link back to the Well as plain text. The page is read and if all is well, it is added to the manuscript and the characters move on. (*WLP*: 91; emphasis in the original)

This rather mechanistic take on the process of literary creation can again be seen as playfully undermining conventional notions of cause and effect. It demotes the author's imagination to yet another step in the mechanical process of assembling a story in so far as it assumes a prior existence of the formal constituents of a story before their imaginative compilation by the author. While Fforde's elaborate and meticulous description of the BookWorld and its organizational structures and inter-relations significantly contributes to the plausibility of the setting of his novel, his interest is not restricted to the inner workings of literature but rather extends to issues of mediation and interaction, in other words, to the question of how the reading of a literary text works for the individual reader.

The main conflict in the novel is concerned with two rival operating systems for how the transfer from text on page to the reader's imagination is brought about: the currently used standard version BOOK V8.3 versus the all-modern and apparently vastly superior new UltraWord. With their version numbering, capitalizations and abstract names, both are evidently taken from the language of computing. At first glance, this would seem to suggest that the process of reading, traditionally thought of as a highly original and radically unconstrained act of the individual imagination, can be fully explained by being broken down to the purely formalistic and schematic representation of binary code. In an adaptation of Schiller's triadic model of human development, this could be read to imply that form always precedes or underlies the physical actuality of any imaginative act. This, in turn, would mean the ultimate confession of failure of any free creative force of imagination in the face of the positivistic regime of digital binary code. Fforde, however, uses this apparently rather defeatist metaphor to stick up for the material autonomy and sovereignty of the individual imagination, which he sees in need of protection against the joint forces of pragmatism and commercialization.

Fforde's allegorically hedged but nevertheless intense and harsh condemnation of this unholy alliance makes *The Well of Lost Plots* the most political and – in spite of its playful irreverence and its countless little intertextual larks – the most serious book in the series. When Xavier Libris, the technocrat representative of Text Grand Central, extols the virtues of UltraWord to the assembled staff at Jurisfiction, he does it in an all too familiar jargon of user-friendliness, marketability and consumer economics. The new system, he explains, comes brim-full of 'Enhanced Features' with colourful but essentially meaningless names like PlotPotPlus, ReadZip, PageGlow and WordClot. The demarcation of all these features with the trademark symbol already suggests the ultimately commercial nature of the whole enterprise, a suspicion that is confirmed by the vocabulary Libris uses to expound additional advantages of UltraWord: 'At present levels the fastest throughput we can manage is about six words per second. With UltraWord we will have the technology to quadruple the uptake – something that will be very attractive to new readers' (*WLP*: 115).[9]

The climax of *The Well of Lost Plots* is set at the annual BookAwards, a long-standing institution which features categories such as 'Most Impossible Premise in an SF Novel' or 'Best Chapter Opening in the English Language' and which traditionally culminates in the accolade for 'Most Troubled Romantic Lead (Male)', an accolade which has been won by Heathcliff for 77 years running. This time round, the event provides the festive backdrop for the constitutionally required vote on the launch of UltraWord. In the eventual showdown, Thursday can only rescue herself and the traditional format of reading by invoking the God of literature itself. At the last moment she presses an emergency button in her Jurisfiction manual, upon which the Great Panjandrum appears, the undisputed deity of the BookWorld. Under the aegis of this quintessential goddess from the machine, the vote goes ahead without manipulation and UltraWord is unanimously defeated.

Literature in its traditional form has been saved by two of the oldest clichés in its (text)book: the last-minute emergency rescue and the *dea ex machina*. Without straining the Great Panjandrum's metaphorical capacity too far, there are two conclusions I want to draw. With regard to Fforde's own agenda, one could imply that he sees literature at present as beset by pernicious forces of commercial exploitation and enhanced usability. These forces invade and threaten the traditional relationship of human beings (the Outland) to literature (the BookWorld), whose aesthetic autonomy is under threat of being superseded by commercial and pragmatic deliberations. Since this book is not primarily political or media-oriented, I cannot comment any further on this. I am much more interested in the aesthetic implications. Thursday describes the appearance of the Great Panjandrum as shocking to all those present, as she 'had been so long a figure of speech that seeing her in the flesh was startling' (353). In other words, what saves the literary cosmos is a literal incarnation ('seeing her in the flesh'), a materialization of pure form ('figure of speech'). Consequently and in retrospect, one could understand Fforde's literalized version of the world of fiction as an applied attempt to make physical, tangible and accessible the abstract formal term 'literature', to flesh it out in the actual sense of the word.

In summary, Thursday's explorations in the BookWorld allow Fforde to set up one grand allegory to describe in materialistic terms the abstract processes involved in the creation and reception of literature. The BookWorld is a metaphorical device which amalgamates the figurative with the literal, the concrete with the abstract. As Berninger and Thomas have correctly asserted, Fforde's investigations of the BookWorld result in a reification and concretization of the abstract realm of literature. With recourse to

---

[9] It seems hard not to compare UltraWord and the exuberant marketing campaign spun by Libris to the hyperbole surrounding every new version of every new product by the Apple Corporation. This comparison is not restricted to Fforde's almost clairvoyant prediction of literary apps but also includes a user interface which is 'read sensitive', meaning that words 'know when they are being read' and react accordingly (*WLP*: 115).

the terms employed to approach authenticity in the previous chapters, I would claim that the authenticity of Fforde's intertextual pranks can again be understood as arising from the interplay between form and materiality. By having Thursday travel inside this literary cosmos, Fforde literally makes accessible and tangible the abstract notions that inform any understanding of what literature actually is or how it works. In other words, what happens is that the formal criteria that are commonly used to approach literature (authorship, genre, plot, reception) are endowed with an imaginary material existence. Fforde's extended allegory of literature tries to imagine pure form in a decidedly material, reified shape. All these elaborate metaphors for how the world of literature is structured can be described as pan-reflective self-reference with a focus on the textuality of the allo-textual universe. They cannot, however, be classified as metareferential, because on the whole they lack the element of ontological and/or epistemological paradox which characterizes metareference.

The same largely holds true for the fourth book of the series, *Something Rotten*. Therefore, I will only briefly touch on its most significant features and plot developments, before putting my focus on the second tetralogy, which again takes up the metareferential attitude displayed in *The Eyre Affair*. In many ways, *Something Rotten* suffers from similar structural deficits as *Lost in a Good Book*, as it also veers somewhat undecidedly between the Outland and the BookWorld and presents a string of loosely related incidents rather than a tightly constructed plot. As the novel's title indicates, one of the protagonists of the book is a well-known prince of Danish origins, who joins Thursday on her trip back to the Outland 'concerned over reports that he was being misrepresented as something of a "ditherer"' (*SR*: 21).

Hamlet's presence in the 'real world' threatens to cause major disruptions to the original manuscript he sprang from. After consultations with a conflict management specialist, who points out to the prince his unresolved Oedipal fixation, Hamlet decides to actively work against his negative image: 'It's the end of Hamlet the ditherer and the beginning of Hamlet, the man of action. There's something rotten in the state of Denmark and Hamlet says … it's payback time!' (321). In the meantime, his absence engenders some remarkable alterations to his original play. Not only has Ophelia tried to usurp the title role of the play, which as a result briefly ran under the title of '*The Tragedy of Fair Ophelia, driven mad by the callous Hamlet, Prince of Denmark*' (112). There has also occurred a hostile takeover from another of the bard's plays. Thursday learns from Emperor Zhark, her former colleague at Jurisfiction, that the play is 'now called *The Merry Wives of Elsinore*, and features Gertrude being chased around the castle by Falstaff while being outwitted by Mistress Page, Ford and Ophelia. Laertes is the king of the fairies and Hamlet is relegated to a sixteen-line sub-plot where he is convinced Dr Caius and Fenton have conspired to kill his father for seven hundred pounds' (162). Answering Thursday's question as to the dramatic quality of these changes, Zhark delivers one of the more hilarious lines in the book: 'It takes a long time to get funny and when it does everyone dies' (ibid.).

The only real narratological novelty in the book is Fforde's first experimentation with the narrative perspective. When Thursday is in a coma following a run-in with a Minotaur on the loose, Landen takes over as first-person narrator for the length of one chapter (see 359–64). In contrast to the subsequent books of the series, however, this change in narrative perspective is explained and clearly established by the chapter heading 'Second First Person' and owes its existence to narrative pragmatism rather than a serious metareferential meddling with hierarchies. The novel also reveals that Thursday herself exists in a constant temporal anomaly. It turns out that her Granny, who has repeatedly helped her make the right decisions, is actually herself in a different time-space configuration. In what could amount to a mission statement for the entire series of novels, Thursday is advised by her older self to abandon any linear conception of time or causality, before being treated to the rare opportunity to be present at her own death (see 391–2).

In effect, Thursday's second-hand experience of her own death in many ways presents an obvious and adequate conclusion to the *Bildungsroman* which is the first part of the series. Commenting on the finale of *Something Rotten*, Juliette Wells claims that by 'narrating the eventual end of his heroine's life, at the advanced age of 110, Fforde both achieves closure for his tetralogy and leaves Thursday available for new adventures' (2007: 207). She accepts the essentially unfathomable structure of time and her paradoxical role within it as a given and leaves behind the allegorical cosmos of the BookWorld to dedicate herself fully to her 'real-life' role as a Literary Detective, mother and wife. Had Fforde abandoned his heroine at this point, it would be all too easy to discount the series as a disappointment, as a learned and admittedly very successful joke, which, in spite of the abundance of intertextual bons mots, ingenious allegories and the occasional flash of metareferential activity, fails to measure up to the expectations promised by the irreverent and substantially metareferential seriousness of *The Eyre Affair*. This view is exposed by some of the critics of the successors of *The Eyre Affair*. In his review of *The Well of Lost Plots*, John Sutherland complains about Fforde's use of 'excruciating puns and heavy-handed allusion' (2003). Likewise, Elizabeth Hand's review of *Something Rotten* in the *Washington Post* notes that the novel is 'too long and ramshackle to sustain its overly elaborated narrative' (2004).

It seems as if Fforde was experiencing a similar feeling of having reached a narrative cul-de-sac after the end of *Something Rotten*. Not unlike Thursday, who takes a respite from her real world inside *Caversham Heights*, Fforde leaves the Thursday-Next universe in order to write the first two episodes of the Nursery-Crimes series. When he returns to his heroine with *First among Sequels*, set some 14 years after the events in *Something Rotten*, he takes up familiar subjects and ideas but also introduces a few major alterations to the set-up of the series as such.

While the first tetralogy is shaped to a great extent by challenges to notions of causality and intertextual influence, with the second tetralogy Fforde takes a sharp turn towards an avowedly narratological focus, which places an emphasis on the instability of the narrator figure and the series' status as a literary work itself. The shift could in very broad terms be described thus: books one to four are anchored by the steadiness and reliability of Thursday as the first-person narrator. Fforde uses this firm narrative perspective to subvert, suspend and reconstruct in short order a number of conventional regulations and ascriptions that structure traditional conceptions of literary communication. Starting with *First among Sequels*, Fforde reverses this supposition. He gradually closes down the narrative propositions which facilitate this reconstruction of the series' context, so as to prepare a level playing field on which to reconstruct some of the key narratological assumptions behind the series itself. Along the way, he installs a radically new allegorical framework for the metaphorization of literature. The first tetralogy presented the workings of literature as a highly technical, almost mechanistic and automated, in any case profoundly inanimate, procedure, lacking as Thursday puts it 'the rich texture that nature's randomness brings to the real world' (*FS*: 49). The second tetralogy, in contrast, takes a fundamentally different route, as it aims its focus on the imaginative and cognitive processes involved in the reception of a literary text; on the question, in other words, of how literature is imaginatively 'brought to life' in the act of reading.

Large parts of *First among Sequels* are concerned with Fforde's narrative abolition of the notion of time travel. The world is once again threatened by annihilation, this time, however, of a more philosophical nature. It is revealed that in order to power the machines that make time travelling possible, the ChronoGuards have been using up contemporary time supplies. This results in the so-called 'Short Now', a dramatic decrease in attention spans and long-term planning abilities and an increase in 'uncaring self-interest and short term instant gratification', which would in due course cause the world to plunge 'into a dark age of eternal indifference' (287). Fforde's pessimistic reflections on the contemporary abuses and disfigurations of time may sound tendentious but they exhibit distinct parallels with Jameson's observation on the 'End of Temporality' or Bauman's description of the liquidity of current life. Echoing Fforde, Bauman observes in *Liquid Times* how

> the collapse of long-term thinking, planning and acting, and the disappearance or weakening of social structures in which thinking, planning and acting could be inscribed for a long time to come, lead to a splicing of both political history and individual lives into a series of short-term projects and episodes which are in principle infinite, and do not combine into the kinds of sequences to which concepts such as 'development', 'maturation', 'career' or 'progress' (all suggesting a preordained order of succession) could be meaningfully applied. (2007: 3)

The only way to prevent this collapsing of time into a singularity is to abolish the possibility of time travel in the first place, which as it turns out is premised on a fundamental (chrono)logical paradox anyway. As one ChronoGuard explains to Thursday, time travel technology only functions on the basis of 'Retro-deficit-engineering': 'We use the technology *now*, safe in the assumption that it will be invented in the *future*' (*FS*: 130; emphases in the original).[10] Thursday's son Friday eventually travels back in time to destroy this formula, thereby eliminating the possibility of time travel once and for all (see 378–81).

[10] Again, it might be tempting to discount this plot device as preposterous and outrageous. It was a very similar principle, however, which, under the only marginally more convincing title 'mark-to-market accounting', caused the infamous collapse of the US energy company Enron in 2001. For more detailed and knowledgeable accounts of this scheme and the entire scandal, see Fox (2003) and Lucy Prebble's dramatization of these events in her play *Enron* (2009).

The most crucial narratological innovation in *First among Sequels* is Fforde's fragmentation of the narrative perspective. In order to be able to evaluate the full implications of this device, it is necessary to retrace this fragmentation in some detail. For most of the novel, the first-person narrative voice belongs to the Thursday Next the reader knows from the previous books of the series. Fforde's stunning narrative innovation now consists in Thursday's claim that – in her capacity as narrator of *First among Sequels* – she is not fully congruent with the Thursday known from the series so far, that she actually has a life, or a level of reality of her own, which is independent of that of her character in the series. At the beginning of *First among Sequels*, a parcel arrives 'that contained a copy of the third book in my series: *The Well of Lost Plots*' asking Thursday for an autograph (6). Her explanation to Landen as to why she refuses to sign this book illustrates the intricate play with different versions of Thursday that will dominate the rest of the series:

> The first four Thursday Next books were about as true to real life as a donkey is to a turnip, and my signature somehow gave a credibility that I didn't want to encourage. The only book I *would* sign was the fifth in the series, *The Great Samuel Pepys Fiasco*, which unlike the first four had my seal of approval. The Thursday Next in *The Great Samuel Pepys Fiasco* was much more of a caring and diplomatic heroine – unlike the Thursday of the previous four, who blasted away at everything in sight, drank, swore, slept around and generally kicked butt all over the BookWorld. I wanted the series to be a thought-provoking romp around literature; books for people who like stories or stories for people who like books. It wasn't to be. The first four in the series had been less light-hearted chroniclings of my adventures and more 'Dirty Harry meets Fanny Hill', but with a good deal more sex and violence. The publishers not only managed to be factually inaccurate but dangerously slanderous as well. By the time I had regained control of the series for *The Great Samuel Pepys Fiasco*, the damage to my reputation had been done. (7; emphases in the original)

Fforde challenges the reader to imagine not only three simultaneous but different manifestations of his heroine but also a fictitious fifth book to the series. In an instance of metareference on the paratextual level, this fictitious novel even makes an appearance in the front matter of *First among Sequels*, where it is listed in the 'Also by Jasper Fforde' section as '~~The Great Samuel Pepys Fiasco~~ (No longer available)' (*FS*: front matter). The fact that this original fifth instalment of the series is no longer available is explained by the lack of appeal of its protagonist, who was written to be 'sensitive, caring, compassionate, kind, thoughtful – and unreadable' (39). As a consequence of all this, there are now three Thursdays involved in the story of *First among Sequels*: the 'real' Thursday known from the first tetralogy; Thursday1–4 (the protagonist of the fictitious first four, very successful, books in the series), who according to the real Thursday is 'mostly action with very little thought' and who becomes the real Thursday's main antagonist in the book; and Thursday5 (the heroine of the hapless and equally fictitious fifth novel), who is 'mostly thought with very little action' (189). I do not want to relay the events that result from the various interactions of these three

Thursdays in their entirety but focus on one exemplary scene where Fforde employs an unmarked change in the narrative voice to great effect in the climactic fight between the real Thursday and Thursday1–4, who turns out to be in cahoots with the Council of Genres. Fforde forces the reader to experience and participate in the resulting confusion over identities by imperceptibly shifting the first-person narrative during the fight:

> After we had grappled and rolled around on the carpet for about five minutes ... we both switched tactics and went for each other's throats. The most this achieved was that Landen's birthday locket was torn off, something that drove *me* [the real Thursday] to a rage that I never knew I had.
>
> *I* [Thursday1–4] knocked her hand away, rolled on top of her and punched her hard in the face. She went limp and I climbed off, breathing hard, picked up my bag and locket and turned to Jobsworth and the rest of the Security Council, who had come into the corridor to watch. (355; emphases added)

For the remainder of the chapter, the narration is taken over by Thursday1–4, a deception which is only made explicit with the beginning of the next. The realization of this change in perspective results in an almost visceral sensation of astonishment in the reader and thereby contributes to the aesthetic propensities of authenticity as proposed by Höltgen.

There are two crucial aspects to this manipulation of the narrative perspective. First, it compromises the reliability of the first-person narrative position by fragmenting it into different, in this case even antagonistic, perspectives. This constitutes a metareferential element, since it generates a moment of epistemological uncertainty and indecision in the reader. This moment can be described as an oscillation of the first-person narrative authority between two characters. As a result, the reader is forced to retroactively reconstruct the narrative perspective in a process of ergodic reading, which, in turn, would render the entire series a cybertext as described by Aarseth.

The new direction taken by *First among Sequels* rests on one principal narrative supposition: the metareferential opening up of a space between the characters and events of the first tetralogy and those that come after. Fforde uses this imaginary space not only to question the narrative integrity of his heroine but also to submit the entire series to a metareferential reconstruction not unlike the performative rewriting of *Jane Eyre* which started off the series. As inclined readers soon realize when reading *First among Sequels*, there is large-scale incompatibility between the novels as they exist in their world and the novels as they appear in the book. For example, when the real Thursday bemoans the slanderous inaccuracy of books one to four, she explains how

> the series had sacrificed characterisation over plot, and humour over action and pace. All atmosphere had evaporated, and the books were a parade of violent set-pieces interspersed with romantic interludes, and when I say 'romantic', I'm stretching the term. Most famous was her [Thursday1–4's] torrid affair with Edward Rochester and the stand-up cat fight with Jane Eyre. I had thought it

couldn't get any worse until Mrs Fairfax turned out to be a ninja assassin and Bertha Rochester was abducted by aliens. (189)

Fforde's narrative suggests that it is only in consequence of the events in *First among Sequels* and the erasure of Thursday1–4 that the first four books end up the way they actually do.

There are again two crucial aspects to this literal reconstruction of the series: it obviously constitutes a metareferential element, since it generates an ontological and chronological paradox of cause and effect between the individual episodes of the series. Similar to the tangling of original and adaptation between *Jane Eyre* and *The Eyre Affair* in the first book of the series, *First among Sequels* involves itself in an irresolvable (chrono)logical contradiction with the first part of the series. In other words, Fforde uses and reimagines his own previous texts as allo-textual references and compels the reader to deploy a reconstructive approach in reading the series. As with Eggers's use of metareference, the cross-sequential referencing which necessitates the reconstructive approach in Fforde embraces all textual levels, from the reimagination of plot lines and characters on the level of the enounced to the fragmentation of the narrative perspective in the enunciation and the use of paratexts to reinforce the fictitious self-historicization of the series. It even includes references to the material actuality of the book as print on paper, so for example when Thursday asks Jurisfiction for a substitution for Felix8: 'I've lost a C-3 generic, Felix8, from page two hundred and seventy-eight of *The Eyre Affair* ISBN-0-340-820470. I'm going to need an emergency replacement asap' (392).

First among Sequels also prepares the ground for the subsequent novels in the series by employing a new conceptual framework for the pan-reflective allegorization of literature. While the first part of the series used technological and political metaphors to symbolize the creation of stories and the influences between literary works, *First among Sequels* begins to reconceptualize literature in terms of dramatic re-enactment, a development which intensifies with the next book. It appears that Fforde felt that the design of the BookWorld was no more in keeping with the conceptual direction the series had taken with the second tetralogy. Consequently, the next instalment in the series, *One of Our Thursdays is Missing*, starts with a spectacular relaunch of the entire BookWorld. This relaunch abolishes the Great Library and supplants it with a geographical arrangement where every genre consists of a separate island, all of which are floating on the inside of a vast sphere. Fforde's new BookWorld goes one step further in replacing the abstract with the concrete, as it substitutes the technocratic and formalistic organization of the Great Library with the physical actuality of landscapes and neighbourhoods. The pre-eminent consequence of this new configuration of the BookWorld is the end of book-jumping, which is superseded by more conventional forms of transport like buses, paddle-steamers or, for inter-insular journeys, the TransGenreTaxis. After putting an end to time travelling in *First among Sequels*, Fforde abolishes the second main imaginary premise which structured the first tetralogy. Taking up the key ideas from *First among Sequels*, four dominant strategies can be identified for *One of Our Thursdays is Missing*: a further deconstruction of the narrative identity of Thursday; the continuation of cross-sequential self-referencing; the revision of the reading experience of the series so far; and, as an enabling condition, a focus on re-enactment as the guiding metaphor for the creation and reception of literature.

In the book, Fforde develops a new allegorical framework for the process of reading. The basic narrative device in this context is the assumption that every time a book is read in the Outland, each individual scene has to be performed in the scenery and by the protagonists of the book in question. With this supposition, Fforde further increases the imagined distance between the two tetralogies, as an explicit level of mediation and enactment is interposed between them. Now, it is no longer only Thursday's identity which is suspended between two or more rival versions; all the major characters in the series double as characters from the previous books and their impersonators on the diegetic level of *One of Our Thursdays is Missing*. Arch villain Acheron Hades, for instance, is impersonated by a rather reticent man collecting stamps and writing 'really bad poetry' (109), and even the role of Thursday's infamously clumsy pet dodo Pickwick is performed by a 'bespectacled know-all' named Lorina Peabody III, who, dodos being somewhat scarce in the world of literature, is on loan from *Alice's Adventures in Wonderland* (see 22).

On the basis of this gambit of imagining literature as incessant performance, Fforde resumes his challenge to the stability and narrative coherence of the series' protagonist, to the extent even that the 'real' Thursday, that is, the (predominant) first-person narrator of books one to five, only appears in one scene at the very end of the book, where her speaking part comprises a mere eight words (see 377). The first-person narration in *One of Our Thursdays is Missing* is taken over by Thursday5, who now calls herself 'the written Thursday'. Unlike in *First among Sequels*, the confusion about the identity of the first-person narrator is not the result of surreptitious manipulations in the enunciation, as the narration stays with the written Thursday all the way through. On her mission to find the real Thursday, who has gone missing while on a mission, however, a sneaking suspicion grows in the written Thursday that she might be the real one after all. She finds herself inexplicably in possession of Thursday's real Jurisfiction shield (see 85) and she is able to see and talk to Jenny, the real Thursday's imagined daughter, who is actually a mind-worm planted in her memories by Aornis Hades (see 218–25). Throughout large sections of the novel, the narration is left undecided as to the distinctness of the real and the written Thursday. Before this ambiguity about Thursday's relative degree of reality can be solved, the first-person narrator – and with her the reader – must run the whole gamut of possible narrative explanations. When the written Thursday finally discovers the whereabouts of the real Thursday in a lunatic asylum in the out-of-the-way genre of Psychological Thriller, she is accosted by synthetic versions of Jenny and her own faithful butler Sprockett, who between them proffer a wide choice of possible resolutions to the convoluted storyline:

'Hello, Jenny,' I said.
'Did anyone figure you out?' she asked. 'Hiding in plain sight as the written

version of you. How did the written Thursday feel about taking a back seat for a while? And where is she, by the way?'
'I'm really Thursday?' I asked.

...

'Did you try her on the *You really are Thursday* twist ending?' asked Sprockett.
'She didn't buy it. I tried the *It's all in your last moment before dying* gambit, too.' Ersatz Sprockett thought for a moment.
'What about the *You're actually a patient in a mental hospital and we've been enacting all of this to try to find out if you killed Thursday*? That usually works.'
'Goodness,' said faux-Jenny, 'I'd clean forgotten about that one.' (374–5)

Further adding to the confusion of Thursday's identity, in a subplot in the Outland the Goliath corporation start using so-called 'day-players', synthetically produced doppelgangers of other characters.

Just as the transformed BookWorld in *One of Our Thursdays is Missing* adds a further twist to the uncertainties about the series' heroine, and based on the recurring device of suggesting an alternative prior textual existence of the earlier books, Fforde also continues to retroactively rewrite the history of the series so far. This includes details of the content of the fictitious fifth novel, *The Great Samuel Pepys Fiasco*, as well as significant alterations like the fact that the purported previous version did not include Landen or the children. It turns out that explicit references to the BookWorld and its inner workings, including Jurisfiction and the Well of Lost Plots, also do not feature in the 'original' version of the series, lest the knowledge about the mechanistic processes behind the creation of literature might threaten the reader's confidence in its creative and imaginative potential. In formal terms, this use of auto-reflective metareference reimagines events from the first tetralogy on a metalevel in the second tetralogy. It is explicitly displayed, with a focus on the alethiology of the text and reconstructive in effect.

At the end of *One of Our Thursdays is Missing*, Fforde eventually threads together the two principal metareferential routes pursued in the second tetralogy: the narrative fragmentation of Thursday and the self-historicization of the series. In a penultimate plot twist, the novel claims that the undecidability it has performed and displayed throughout is in actual fact intrinsic to the nature of fiction itself. After successfully filling in for the real Thursday, saving Fiction Island from a potentially devastating inter-genre war and securing the future supply of vital metaphors, the written Thursday is being offered her job at Jurisfiction by Commander Bradshaw. This move would reunite the different levels of fictionality and reality concerning the identity of Thursday Next. The ensuing conversation neatly recapitulates the prevailing ontological confusion and is therefore quoted at length:

'Are you sure you're not her?'
'It's a tricky one,' I replied after giving the matter some thought, 'and there's evidence to suggest that I am. I can do things only she can do, I can see things only she can see. Landen thought I was her, and although he now thinks I'm the written one, that might all be part of a fevered delusion. His or mine, I'm not sure.'

...

'Carmine might actually be the Thursday I think I am,' I added. 'It's even possible I'm suffering the hallucinatory aftershock of a recent rewriting. And while we're pushing the plausibility envelope, the BookWorld might not be real at all, and I'm simply a carpet-fitter at Acme with a vibrant imagination.'
I shuddered at the possibility that none of this might be happening at all.
'This is Fiction,' said Bradshaw in a calm voice, 'and truth is whatever you make it. You can interpret the situation in any way you want, and all of the scenarios could be real – and what's more, depending on how you act now, any one of them could *become* real.'
I frowned.
'I can be Thursday just by thinking I am?'
'More or less. We may require you to undergo a short narrative procedure known as a "Bobby Ewing" where you wake up next chapter and it's all been a dream, but it's pretty painless so long as you don't mind potential readers throwing up their hands in disgust.' (365–6; emphasis in the original)

Unifying the real and the written Thursday would also retroactively eliminate the fundamental assumption on which the second tetralogy rests, so the written Thursday has to reject this tempting offer. Instead, she insists on her duty to 'depict the real Thursday doing everything she *really* did' (366; emphasis added). This, in turn, necessitates a comprehensive reconstruction of the entire series so as to include Landen and the children, the BookWorld as it once was – including Thursday's adventures with Jurisfiction – as well as occasional references to toast.[11] Fforde's use of metareference yet again challenges conventional notions of cause and effect, as it is only in consequence of chronologically posterior events in book six that earlier books are purportedly modified so as to assume the shape familiar to the reader.

In a sense, this scene represents the culmination of Fforde's continued metareferential entangling of various levels of reality and fictionality. It boils down to the rather simple claim that fiction is not a product of reality but that, on the contrary, there is always another level of fiction underlying any construction of reality. This, in turn, suggests an essential precedence of form over matter. Material experience as well as creative imagination can only ever be the result of formal processes. What is more, mirroring Schiller's triadic model, Fforde diagnoses an apparent longing for the abstract formalism inherent in any act of literary communication.

The next, and so far latest, book in the series, *The Woman who Died a Lot*, hinges on one principal idea: the technology that enables Goliath to synthetically produce day-player versions of other characters has become so refined that they can, for the length of 24 hours, pass off as decent impersonations of their 'originals'.[12] The novel

---

[11] In one more example of Fforde's use of cross-sequential connections, there are a number of these apparently inconsequential references to toast throughout the series (see *EA*: 191; *LGB*: 10; *WLP*: 153; *OTM*: 20) as well as advertisements for toast in the back matter of *The Eyre Affair* and *Something Rotten*. As it turns out, these are in consequence of the written Thursday having been bribed by the Toast Marketing Board into this form of literary product placement (see *OTM*: 222).

[12] As of September 2014, there is no information as to when *Dark Reading Matter*, the concluding novel to the second tetralogy, will be published. The title and a few scattered intimations in *The*

chronicles the real Thursday's new job as Chief Librarian for Wessex, to which she is side-lined in order to recover from the events in *One of Our Thursdays is Missing*. It also includes a number of very entertaining cross-sequential links, such as Daisy Mutlar's return as the revengeful Mother Superior of the Blessed Ladies of the Lobster. Its plot, however, is not on a par with its predecessors. It lacks a convincing arc of suspense and offers only one striking new feature: based on the supposition of the enhanced day-players, Fforde reverts to a narrative ploy he had introduced in *First among Sequels*, that is, the imperceptible shift of the first-person narrative between different versions of the protagonist. This time the narration oscillates between the real Thursday and a sequence of synthetically recreated player versions of her. As in *First among Sequels*, these shifts in perspective are not indicated in the narrative and thus catch the reader unawares. When this shift occurs for the first time, it takes four pages until the reader, and Thursday herself, realizes the transformation. As a precaution against the day-players, Thursday and Landen always agree on a password, and so upon returning home, the following sequence unfolds:

'No. I can't remember.'
'And why do you think that might be?'
...
'Shit,' I muttered, 'I've been replaced', and I looked stupidly around to see whether the real me might be somewhere close by. I wasn't, so I looked back at Landen, who raised an eyebrow.
'This is a novel approach,' he said, 'a synthetic aware that it *is* a synthetic?'
'Wait, wait,' I said, knowing only too well what we did with synthetics, 'this is different. I'm me. I'm conscious, I have some of the real me's memories. Maybe not all of them, but some, and enough.' (116; emphasis in the original)

Although these shifts in perspective are employed much more regularly in this novel than in any of its predecessors, the underlying concept and objective of disrupting the reliability of the first-person narrator is already well-established and does not offer a new theoretical perspective on Fforde's use of metareference.

To conclude, let me sum up the issue of metareference and reconstruction in Fforde's increasingly complex and escalating literary universes. First, it must be said that not all novels in the series are equally successful and significant in the context of this study and that even the most daring imaginative novelty is in danger of losing its effectiveness through habituation. Admittedly, Fforde's idiosyncratic reconceptualization of literature in general and his performative rewriting of *Jane Eyre* and his own series in particular may occasionally come across as merely playful, frivolous or even quaint. I would nevertheless argue that some of the novels – in particular *The Eyre Affair*, *The Well of Lost Plots*, *First among Sequels* and *One of Our Thursdays is Missing*, on which this analysis has therefore focused – offer a significant contribution

Woman who Died a Lot suggest that Fforde once again returns to the BookWorld to explore – apparently from a scientific point of view – the phenomenon of Dark Reading Matter, which makes up around 80 per cent of the BookWorld and consists of 'the unobservable remnants of long-lost books, forgotten oral tradition and ideas locked in writers' heads when they died' (*WDL*: 61).

to an aesthetics of reconstruction. In spite of its apparent and undisputed playfulness, Fforde's work is to be taken seriously, as it envisions and displays novel ways of imagining the relationships, hierarchies and interconnections that structure every instance of literary communication. Let me recapitulate the most significant of Fforde's metareferential strategies:

1) Through tangling conventional hierarchies of linear chronology, literary influence and the primacy of original over adaptation, Fforde's series challenges the reader to reimagine relationships of cause and effect. This happens in two ways primarily. Based on the narrative supposition of time travel, Fforde creates a number of chronological paradoxes, which subverts the idea of a linear progressive historical timeline and confronts the reader with an irresolvable epistemological contradiction.

2) In the more specific context of literary history, Fforde performatively undermines the notions of canonicity and authority by entangling directions of influence and adaptation, in a technique that I want to describe as pastiche. While the first part of the series uses canonical literary works, and in particular *Jane Eyre* as the allo-textual basis for its metareferential reflections, with the second tetralogy Fforde begins to rewrite his own earlier books. These processes of rewriting also produce epistemological and ontological paradoxes which cannot be resolved on the level of the texts themselves.

3) Based on the second substantial narrative supposition underlying his series, that is, the permeability of the boundary between fiction and reality, Fforde instigates a complex system of interlinking levels of reality and fictionality which deprives the reader of a dependable basis from which to assess the relative plausibility and stability of narration and narrator alike.

4) Beginning in earnest with the second tetralogy, Fforde employs various narrative strategies to challenge and undermine the stability and reliability of the first-person narrator. This again results in a sensation of epistemological uncertainty in the readers, who are compelled to continually reconstruct their conception of the series' protagonist and with it her narrative perspective in relation to the events she narrates.

7

Reconstructing Narration: Jennifer Egan's *A Visit from the Goon Squad* and Julian Barnes's *The Sense of an Ending*

In my concluding pair of literary case studies I want to take up an issue which already features prominently in the second of Jasper Fforde's Thursday-Next tetralogies. I have tried to show how one of the key effects of Fforde's use of metareference is the destabilization of the first-person narrator. In doing so, he stages a challenge to the reliability of this crucial intratextual authority. The two novels I want to examine in this chapter attempt to do a similar thing. Both Jennifer Egan's Pulitzer Prize-winning *A Visit from the Goon Squad* (2010) and Julian Barnes's *The Sense of an Ending*, which won the Man Booker Prize in 2011, are primarily concerned with the question of how experiences and memories can be conveyed in and as narrative. Both novels are fictional narratives in their own right as well as theoretical reflections on the terms and conditions of fictional narration. For this aim, however, they employ two very different metareferential approaches. Egan explicitly fragments both the chronology of events and the narrative perspective in her novel in order to draw attention to the underlying structural principle of *plotting* as a communal and reconstructive effort which requires active participation on the part of the reader. Barnes, on the other hand, presents a narrator who overtly appears to be very much in control of the events he narrates. In the case of Tony Webster, the challenge to the reliability of the first-person singular is indirect and transcends the textual framework of the novel in which it originates, because it results from reconstructions of the events narrated which are triggered by a narrative device I will describe as *implicit narrative*.

Narrative assemblage: Jennifer Egan's *A Visit from the Goon Squad*

In his review of *A Visit from the Goon Squad* for the *New York Times Sunday Book Review*, Will Blythe concedes that plot summaries have long been considered of inferior significance when it comes to analysing fiction, a necessary evil at best on the road towards profound narratological, contextual or intertextual discernments (see 2010). In universities, students of literature are regularly exhorted *only* to recapitulate plot elements if they are actually relevant for a multifaceted interpretation which usually expects them to connect aspects of content, form and context.

In literary criticism a novel's plot has traditionally been understood as the organizational principle and logic behind the author's presentation of the events that make up the story. In this capacity, it represents an interface of the three aspects context, content and (narrative) form. It describes a procedure which transforms the 'raw material' of the story into narrative by subjecting it to authorial considerations concerning chronology, causality, direct characterizations or commentaries. I will now investigate *A Visit from the Goon Squad* with a special focus on this relation between the events on the story level and their representation as narrative. I will argue that the authenticity of Egan's approach emerges from the implicit foregrounding and enactment of *the process of plotting* itself. By performatively withdrawing from this process, the author formally forfeits her authority to structure the representation of the story. In its stead, she provides an explicit stimulus for readers to reconstruct the story and the plotting themselves from the sheer textual material that represents the *Gestalt* level of the novel. This strategy could be described as an attempt at formalized formlessness, a paradox well in line with the notion of authenticity as proposed in this book so far, which likewise insists on the aesthetic challenge of mediated immediacy.

One cannot preach the reinstated significance of plot and plotting, of course, without practising the long-disregarded form of the plot summary. Egan's novel is made up of 13 chapters which depict in a chronologically random order events ranging from the late 1970s to the 2020s. The individual episodes are loosely held together by the explicit or implicit significance of the events narrated for the lives of music producer Bennie Salazar and a woman called Sasha. This is a short summary of the chapters in the order in which they appear in the novel:

1. 'Found Objects' describes Sasha's one-night stand with a guy called Alex and reveals her affliction with kleptomania.
2. 'The Gold Cure' introduces Bennie as a successful music producer trying to fire up his sagging libido. Sasha, who works as his assistant at this point, successfully diverts her employer's sexual advances.
3. 'Ask me if I Care' shows Bennie with his high-school friends Rhea, Jocelyn, Alice and Scotty in the heyday of punk in the 1970s. At a concert they meet Lou, a successful producer, who seduces Jocelyn and later becomes Bennie's mentor in the music business.
4. 'Safari' recounts Lou's trip to Africa with his children Rolph and Charlene and his student girlfriend Mindy.
5. 'You (Plural)' visits Lou on his deathbed, where he is called on by Rhea and Jocelyn.
6. 'X's and O's' describes a meeting between Bennie and Scotty, who has fallen on hard times as a musician.
7. 'A to B' depicts Bennie's family life in Crandale and introduces his wife Stephanie and her brother, the journalist Jules Jones.
8. 'Selling the General' follows Dolly, Stephanie's boss, on a trip to save the

reputation of a genocidal dictator. She is accompanied by her daughter Lulu and fading film-star Kitty Jackson.
9   'Forty-Minute Lunch' consists of a newspaper article written by Jules Jones, in which he recapitulates his failed rape of Kitty Jackson during an interview.
10 'Out of Body' relates how Rob, Sasha's university pretend boyfriend, drowns while swimming with Sasha's real boyfriend Drew.
11 'Good-bye, my Love' recounts a meeting of Sasha with her uncle Ted in Naples, where she had ended up after running away from home.
12 'Great Rock and Roll Pauses by Alison Blake' portrays in the form of a slide show the family life of Sasha, who is by now married to Drew and has two children, Lincoln and Alison.
13 'Pure Language' describes how Bennie, Alex and Lulu, who is Bennie's current assistant, manage a concert Scotty gives at the site of the World Trade Center. After the show, Alex and Bennie try to locate Sasha's old flat.

Throughout these chapters, Egan places hints as to the chronological sequence of these events, such as the recurring references to 9/11, and to the interconnections between the various characters. It is from these hints that the reader must piece together the actual temporal and causal chain of events and the stories of the individual characters. Very crudely and with no claim to accuracy or completeness, this story level of the book might be reconstructed like this. I am using imprecise temporal markers in this summary on purpose, because Egan provides no clear and definite indication for the exact sequence of the individual incidents and episodes:

After an unsuccessful stint with a punk band in high school, *Bennie Salazar* meets Lou (Chapter 3), a successful producer and philanderer without much empathy towards his own children (4, 5). After seducing Bennie's friend Jocelyn, Lou acts as his mentor and sets up Bennie to become a successful producer himself (2). Bennie is married to and later divorced from Stephanie (7, 2). Stephanie's brother Jules, a journalist, had once tried to rape the actress Kitty Jackson during an interview (9). Some time later, Kitty travels with Dolly, Stephanie's former boss, and her daughter Lulu to rescue the reputation of General B, the autocratic ruler of an unnamed country (8). At some point, Bennie re-encounters his former high-school friend and band mate Scotty (6). Together with Alex and Lulu, he organizes a concert for Scotty at the site of the former World Trade Center (13).

Sasha runs away from home and her divorced parents to Naples at the age of 17, where her uncle Ted finally tracks her down (11). Back home again she studies at NYU, where Rob, who acts as her pretend boyfriend, drowns while taking a swim with Drew, her real boyfriend (10). Some time later Sasha is employed as Bennie's assistant. While in this position she embarks on a one-night sexual affair with Alex (1). After re-encountering Drew on Facebook years later, they get married, start a family, and she becomes an artist (12).

In conventional literary theory, the plot of a work of narrative fiction is commonly described as the author's premeditated arrangement of the events that make up the story, the movements in time and space of the central characters, their relationships and confrontations, their petty dramas and great aspirations, their loves, affairs, divorces and deaths. Usually, the reader is required to (re)construct the storyline, that is, the chronological and causal succession of events, from the plot, that is, the arrangement of these events by the author, on the basis of the actual material reality of the text on paper (cf. Forster 2005: 85–100). In the case of *A Visit from the Goon Squad*, however, this relationship is performatively inverted. The narratological focus of Egan's book is not first and foremost on the reconstruction of the story. What it does instead is compel readers to retrace the process of plotting in the very act of reading itself. Before they have a chance to establish the chronology of events or the relations between characters on the level of the enounced, readers first have to determine the temporal and causal connections between the 13 chapters which constitute the novel's enunciation. In an act of ergodic reading, this textual arrangement of narrated events has to be renegotiated in the very process of reading. I suggest that this process of reconstruction can be seen as an aesthetic re-enactment on a metalevel of the process of plotting done by the author and therefore as a structural parallel to Eggers's metareferential refraction of the author figure.

Egan's fragmentation of chronology and causality constitutes an implicit, autoreflective metareferential element with a focus on the textuality of its source text. It generates a necessity of reconstruction, which transfers the responsibility of establishing consistency to the readers. Redolent of Levinasian notions of constitutive alterity and the 'age of responsibilization', as invoked by Charles Taylor (1993: 77), Egan, as the author, emphasizes the need for a significant and signifying other, the reader, in order to induce order into her narrative. Formally, this reconstructive effort is premised on the tangling of hierarchies between the constituents of the act of literary communication, because the author relinquishes her authority and endows the reader with the authority and obligation to create coherence. Faced with the materiality of the text without the guidance usually derived from a persistent narrative perspective and form, the epistemological uncertainty generated by the novel's fragmented and random narrative set-up throws readers back onto themselves, challenging them to use, as Bauman calls it, 'their own subjectivity as the ultimate ethic authority' (1992: xxii). It is this individual obligation, which *A Visit from the Goon Squad* both demands and enacts, that makes Egan's book a significant contribution to an aesthetics of reconstruction. It should not be ignored, however, that the withdrawal of the author is itself an aesthetic effect and a potentially manipulative gesture. It could equally be interpreted as an act of self-limitation *and* of self-aggrandizement. As the previous analyses have demonstrated, engaging with authenticity always requires a minimum of cooperation, a leap of imaginary faith as demanded by Hassan's 'aesthetic of trust'. In other words, an authentic literary exchange cannot be formally and categorically inscribed in a text or prescribed by an author to the reader but depends on their joint and reciprocal interplay and emerges in a state of oscillation in between them.

Egan's arrangement of the different episodes is remarkable not only in view of its chronological indeterminacy but also with regard to the individual narrative forms she employs. She offers a variety of different points of view – from rather traditional authorial narrator figures (Chapters 2, 4, 7) to first-person narrations (3, 5, 6), from personal reflection (1, 8, 11, 13) to the rather less common form of second-person narration (10).[1] She also includes presumably non-literary genres like a newspaper report (9) and a slide show (12). These variations of form again work towards a fragmentation of a monolithic and authorial perspective. The reader is thus faced with the bare *materiality* of the events depicted and is unable to rely on the epistemological guidance usually provided by the distinctive and defining characteristics adhering to the respective narrative *forms*. The variety and equivocality of narrative perspectives also correspond to Egan's understanding of how literature as an art form can convey experience. She symbolizes the contingency of human experience as a heap of broken stories without an ordering, authorial narrative instance to guide the reader through the incongruity of this mortal coil.

At various points in the novel, Egan draws on metaphors which echo this strategy of reconstructing stories from ostensibly accidental episodes and random objects. These can be classified as an implicit, auto-reflective self-referential element with a focus on the alethiology of the text and an illustrating effect. The character Sasha, for example, is subject to frequent bouts of kleptomania and even displays the stolen items openly in her apartment. Although these things are superficially no more than just 'a heap of objects that was illegible yet clearly not random', they still 'contained years of her life compressed' and thus represent for Sasha 'the raw, warped core of her life' (*VGS*: 15). I would argue that this idea, that is, that if there is an essence to experience at all, it can only be accessed or approximated obliquely, through the assemblage of indiscriminate events and random encounters, epitomizes *en miniature* the narratological agenda of Egan's book. Sasha's display of stolen goods mirrors metaleptically Egan's display of stories. By the end of her own story, Sasha has managed to channel her compulsion to appropriate objects into a form of artistic creativity. In the slide-show diary which makes up Chapter 12, Sasha's daughter Alison reports that her mother makes collages from everyday objects 'from our house and our lives' which she glues 'onto boards and shellacs'. These objects include a shopping list, flight tickets and memos reminding someone to pick up shoes or call grandma. According to Sasha, these objects are 'precious because they're casual and meaningless' yet 'they tell the whole story if you really look' (265). Retaining the analogy of Sasha's collages to Egan's narratological agenda, this could be read as an implicit exhortation to the reader, as Sasha's progress from compulsive kleptomaniac to careful and reflective collagist can be seen to mirror the reader's envisioned progress from bewildered and passive reception of loose plot elements to thoughtful and active reconstruction of (life) stories.

It is not only through Sasha's objects, however, that life stories are to be (re)constructed in the novel. Characters in *A Visit from the Goon Squad* more often than not exist as fragments rather than clearly defined personalities. They are either distorted by the obscurity of individual memories or disintegrate into a number of

---

[1] All terms, except for second-person narration, are taken from Stanzel's dusty but still useful model of narrative situations (1995: 240–300). For an extensive bibliography on the phenomenon of second-person narration, see Fludernik (1994).

rival perspectives. Egan seems to imply that it is only by relinquishing any pretence to a consistency of personal identity that anyone can actually have an effect on the experience of other human beings. For instance, in the run-up to her sexual tryst with Alex in Chapter 1, Sasha experiences an almost epiphanic moment of metaleptic self-awareness: 'It jarred Sasha to think of herself as a glint in the hazy memories that Alex would struggle to organize a year or two from now: *Where was that place with the bathtub? Who was that girl?*' (14; emphasis in the original). In the very last scene of the book, set sometime in the 2020s, Alex and Bennie prowl the streets trying to remember the exact location of Sasha's flat and their respective feelings towards her. While Alex struggles to remember Sasha as a person, the one thing that has stuck in his memory is the bathtub, which has superimposed itself on any other features of Sasha's personality he is able to recall: 'A bathtub in the kitchen – she'd had one of those! It was the only one he'd ever seen' (339). In Alex's recollection, the objectivity and thingness of the bathtub has replaced Sasha's subjectivity and personality. Alex cannot even call to mind the sex that presumably occurred that evening, which would imply that the pure materiality of objects even trumps the physicality of human beings when it comes to the reliability of individual memories.

In Chapter 11, which recounts Sasha's time in Naples, we find another powerful image for how memories can be absorbed by innocuous and apparently inconsequential objects. Her uncle Ted has at long last managed to descry her whereabouts and finds himself in her flat wondering about 'a crude circle made from a bent coat hanger' which adorns a window (232). Even 20 years on, while paying a visit to Sasha and her family, he still remembers 'the jolt of surprise and delight he'd felt when the sun finally dropped into the center of her window and was captured inside her circle of wire' (233). The memory of his trip to Naples is retained and encapsulated in the material reality of this apparent piece of junk. In such moments of spontaneous reminiscence, the purposeless contingency and material actuality of an object, its sheer and pointless existence, intrudes upon the apparent consistency and discipline of the narrated identity of the self. This epiphanic and formless mode of recollection, which could be called *existential memory*, is contrasted with the conscious and deliberate arrangement of personal recollections, which could be called *constructed memory*. I would argue that such moments of unstructured revelation, where the formless abyss of experience and memory encroaches on the fabricated narrative of the self, present instances of an intrusion of the authentic. The formless materiality of incidental objects can function as a mediator for immediacy. Seen in this light, the apparently incidental and unstructured episodes of *A Visit from the Goon Squad* can be seen as an aesthetic echo of this objective immediacy. As a heap of broken stories the novel itself becomes a conduit of authenticity.

The significance of *A Visit from the Goon Squad* for an aesthetics of literary authenticity not only derives from the narrative enactment of authenticity as analysed above. Some passages of the novel offer profound theoretical reflections on the subject as well. By way of Sasha's uncle Ted, Egan supplies an exquisite metaphorical illustration for how human interaction and communication is enabled by the codification and systematization of essentially uncoded, unstructured and contingent emotions, relationships or circumstances. Referring back to the semiotic investigation of authenticity in the first part of this book, it could be argued that everyday experience is only possible when the directness and immediacy which account for its authentic dimension are transferred into symbolic code. In a neat illustration of the process Taleb describes as 'platonicity', Ted emblematizes his diminishing desire for his wife Beth as being folded in half every couple of years, until it 'was so small in the end that Ted could slip it inside his desk or a pocket and forget about it, and this gave him a feeling of safety and accomplishment, of having dismantled a perilous apparatus that might have crushed them both' (210). By systematizing and rationalizing what before appeared as 'a drowning, helpless feeling', Ted finds a way to make sense of his emotion. By imagining his attitude in economical and 'realistic' terms, he manages to take the edge off the bottomless authenticity of 'an edgy terror of never being satisfied' (ibid.).

In his retrospective account of the interview-turned-rape with Kitty Jackson (Chapter 9), Jules Jones also sheds theoretical light on the issue of authenticity. He explores how every human being exists in the form of fragmented identity constructions, which can be reproduced as befits the particular occasion. He recalls a scene from the restaurant where the interview takes places:

> The waiter's treatment of Kitty is actually a kind of sandwich, with the bottom bread being the bored and slightly effete way he normally acts with customers, the middle being the crazed and abnormal way he feels around this famous nineteen-year-old girl, and the top bread being his attempt to contain and conceal this alien middle layer with some mode of behavior that at least approximates the bottom layer of boredom and effeteness that is the norm. In the same way, Kitty Jackson has some sort of bottom bread that is, presumably, 'her,' or the way Kitty Jackson once behaved in suburban Des Moines where she grew up, rode a bike, attended proms, earned decent grades and, most intriguingly, jumped horses, thereby winning a substantial number of ribbons and trophies and, at least briefly, entertaining thoughts of becoming a jockey. On top of that is her extraordinary and possibly slightly psychotic reaction to her new-found fame – the middle of the sandwich – and on top of that is her own attempt to approximate layer number one with a simulation of her normal, or former, self. (170–1)

Jules's article very much resembles an 'anatomy of authenticity' in which he investigates his own personality sandwich by laying open, dissecting and examining the constructed layers of his own identity as a male, celebrity journalist. With the benefit of hindsight, Jules construes the dramatic failure of his attempt to force himself on Kitty, which ends with him being teargassed and stabbed in the calf with a Swiss Army knife (see 183), as an applied lesson in the difficulty of matching authentic expression with the norms and regulations of real life. He describes the event in terms of immediacy and epiphany which are well known from the history of authenticity. He experiences touching Kitty as 'revelatory, urgent, as if, in bridging the crevasse between myself and this young actress, I am lifted above the encroaching darkness' (181), and his sexual harassment of the girl is retrospectively explained as a quest for the inalienable core of her existence: 'What I have no interest in doing is killing her and *then* fucking her, because it's her life – the inner life of Kitty Jackson – that I so desperately long to reach' (182; emphasis in the original). The fact that Jules's attempt at rape misfires so spectacularly demonstrates that authenticity is not something that can be willed into being. Neither self-revelation nor the inner life of other people can be accessed by means of force. As in the anecdote of Apelles and his sponge, authenticity only reveals itself in a serendipitous and random act of creation.

Jules, however, does not give up on his quest for authenticity. Once released from prison he dedicates himself to chronicling the last tour of Bosco, a former punk guitarist who has more or less reached the end of his tether and for whom Jules's sister Stephanie does the occasional PR job. Touted by Bosco himself as his 'Suicide Tour', this final creative outburst patently and purposefully features every insalubrious cliché of rock 'n' roll life on the road, leading up to and including a celebrated death: 'I don't want to fade away,' Bosco explains to an increasingly captivated Jules, who senses a rare instance of authentic performance, 'I want to *flame* away – I want my death to be an attraction, a spectacle, a mystery. A work of art' (129; emphasis in the original). Egan again strikes a familiar chord in the repertoire of authenticity: Heidegger, Levinas and Baudrillard have variously argued that authentic existence can ultimately only be inspired by the conscious integration of one's own eventual non-existence. Consequently, the staging and meticulous chronicling of one's own end appears to be an appropriate form of authentic self-expression, because only death can collapse the crevasse between experience and its aesthetic representation. Again, however, this *deliberate* attempt to generate and set down authentic expression is thwarted. Much later in the book the reader learns that though Jules wrote a book on Bosco's 'Suicide Tour', the expressed aim of the project did not materialize as planned. In Chapter 12, Sasha's daughter Alison relates in her slide show that her mother owns a book with the title *Conduit: A Rock-and-Roll Suicide*, which is 'about a fat rock star who wants to die onstage, but ends up recovering and owning a dairy farm' (257).

It is no coincidence that Egan's narrative vehicle to illustrate this perspective on authenticity is a washed-up musician, whose former band was ominously called The Conduits. Throughout the book she uses music as a yardstick to gauge the authenticity of human expression. For example, Alison's slide show tells how her brother Lincoln's principal interest in music is confined to songs which include long pauses, such as 'Bernadette' by the Four Tops or 'Foxy Lady' by Jimi Hendrix (see 244). Since he is after all Sasha's son, Lincoln interprets these songs as miniatures of real life, which through absence or non-utterance can actual touch on the material reality of experience: 'The pause makes you think the song will end. And then the song isn't really over, so you're relieved. But then the song *does* actually end, because every song ends, obviously, and THAT. TIME. THE. END. IS. FOR. REAL' (281; emphasis in the original).

Another character besides Jules and Lincoln who is obsessed with the notion of authenticity is Bennie Salazar. In Chapter 2 he bemoans the culture of inauthenticity which dominates the music business nowadays, where markers of authenticity are simulated to cater for current tastes: 'He listened for muddiness, the sense of *actual* musicians playing *actual* instruments in an *actual* room. Nowadays this quality (if it existed at all) was usually an effect of analogue signalling rather than bona fide tape

– *everything was an effect* in the bloodless constructions Bennie and his peers were churning out' (22; emphases added). Bennie's resentment towards the inauthentic is not restricted to theoretical lamentation, however. He is fired from his record label 'after serving his corporate controllers a boardroom lunch of cow pies' in an attempt to visually and olfactorily illustrate his assessment of the company's products (312). In its unquestionable physicality and materiality, this gesture could be interpreted as an attempt to reclaim the authentic by deploying the materiality of the cow pats against the formalism of simulated authenticity.

The last chapter of *A Visit from the Goon Squad* takes this formalistic approach to representation to its extreme. It is set in the early 2020s and presents a dystopian vision of the near future which Egan envisions as the consequence of a way of life which has lost the ideal of self-reflection and authenticity as a guiding metaphor. In their stead, the insensitive and unconsidered adoption of a gadget-oriented form of hyperconsumerism reigns supreme. Egan offers an uncomfortably plausible development of current trends which Bauman describes as follows: 'In a world filled with consumers and the objects of their consumption, life is hovering uneasily between the joys of consumption and the horrors of the rubbish heap' (2005: 9). In her critical assessment of the 'Novel in the Age of Technology', Madalena Gonzales provides an even more detailed description of the

> contemporary technoverse, where human beings are imprisoned within, as much as liberated by, a mobile network of cell phones, iPods, and laptops, the battery of technology which is now part and parcel of everyday life and contrives to furnish our twenty-first century bodies with an array of artificial limbs, allowing us to experience nostalgically the occasional twitches and tremors of real feeling. (2008: 114–15)

According to thinkers like Schiller and Rousseau, childhood is the archetypal embodiment of an authentic rapport with one's being-in-the-world. In Egan's novel, it is this state of presumed innocence and authenticity that is primarily targeted and invaded by a variety of electronic implements. Most notably among those is a mysterious device called Starfish, which not only comes with a GPS system to help kids learn to walk but enables them to make consumer decisions as soon as they can point their fingers at the screen. Accordingly, the advertising industry disparagingly refers to this preverbal target group as 'the pointers' (*VGS*: 313). By depicting how the pointing of the finger, the quintessential deictic and pre-symbolic gesture of direct reference, is incorporated into the system of consumer capitalism, Egan's narrative implicitly challenges the idea of reference as such as being literally pointless.

Egan further accentuates the dangers inherent in the impending demise of conventional forms of reference by satirizing two prevalent forms of communication. Lulu, Bennie's current assistant, is described as 'a living embodiment of the new "handset employee": paperless, deskless, commuteless, and theoretically omnipresent' (317). She is fluent in a marketing and business idiom which primarily functions by translating complex concepts into two- or three-letter acronyms. It represents a crude attempt to annihilate the potential ambiguity of language by subordinating it to a heavily formalized system of apparently unambiguous allocation. Examples for this novel system of reference are the abbreviation EA for 'ethical ambivalence' or DM for 'disingenuous metaphor'. The latter abbreviation neatly exemplifies the Newspeak-like ratio behind this new vernacular: Lulu explains that the acronym DM refers to terms which 'look like descriptions, but they are really judgments', such as 'selling out' or 'being bought' (319). Personal value judgements are, of course, regarded with a fair amount of suspicion in a world based on the uncritical acceptance of marketing ploys. By being marked as DMs, these terms are branded as ambiguous and therefore insignificant. They are dismissed as 'part of a system we call atavistic purism. AP implies the existence of an ethically perfect state, which not only doesn't exist and never existed, but it's usually used to shore up the prejudices of whoever's making the judgments' (ibid.).

The first victim of this extremely formalized and thus inauthentic form of reference is the infinite capacity of language as a tool to make sense of and induce sense into the world. To illustrate this further, Egan's vision of the future also includes 'T'ing', a version of the abbreviated SMS jargon known as *textese* or *txtspk* today. This form of interaction has become so ubiquitous in the novel that it is not only used in handset communication but has also crept into people's thinking, an occurrence Alex refers to as 'brain-T' (330). Seeing how many young people are making their way to Scotty's concert, Alex muses that '*if thr r children, thr mst b a fUtr, rt?*' (331). A gadget-centred consumerism, in the form of T'ing, has, so it would seem, even infiltrated and disabled utopian thinking itself. Egan here mirrors Turkle's gloomy assessment of the effects technology may have on human interaction. Turkle complains that 'we communicate in a new language of abbreviation in which letters stand for words and emoticons for feelings' (2011: 19).

Other major casualties in this brave new world of digitalized referencing are those concepts and sentiments which Egan's book itself has previously connected to the idea of authentic experience. Rebecca, Alex's wife, has gained considerable academic reputation for her research on the phenomenon of 'word casings, a term she'd invented for words that no longer had meaning outside quotation marks' (*VGS*: 323). It is significant to note that these empty signifiers, 'drained of life by their Web usage', include words – and therefore necessarily concepts – like 'friend', 'real', 'story', 'search' and 'change', all of which have been erased by a simulated corporeality or corporate reality that has apparently transformed reasoning human beings into consuming cyborgs (324). In Egan's dystopian vision of the future, humankind is deploying technology to systematically disinvest itself of the tools to make sense of the world and thus also of its own being-in-the-world. What remains is a society trapped in endless, solipsistic and inauthentic self-reference, without the means to imagine and appeal to an authentic other and therefore bereft of the ability to know itself.

It is again through music that the authentic stages its ultimate confrontation with the forces of simulation, inauthenticity and consumer capitalism which are rampant in the dystopian world of Egan's final chapter. After many a struggle and deliberation, Scotty Hausmann gives a concert at the site of the former World Trade Center, an apt location for the staging of authentic expression, as it consists of reflecting pools called 'the Footprint' which evoke the memory of 9/11 in the form of incommensurable absence rather than concrete presence: 'The weight of what had happened here more than twenty years ago was still faintly present for Alex, as it always was when he came to the Footprint. He perceived it as a sound just out of earshot, the vibration of an old disturbance' (331). Scotty performs

> ballads of paranoia and disconnection ripped from the chest of a man you knew just by looking had never had a page or a profile or a handle or a handset, who was part of no one's data, a guy who had lived in the cracks all these years, forgotten and full of rage, in a way that now registered as pure. Untouched. But of course, it's hard to know anymore who was really *at* that first Scotty Hausmann concert – more people claim it than could possibly have fit into the space, capacious and mobbed though it was. Now that Scotty has entered the realm of myth, everyone wants to own him. And maybe they should. Doesn't a myth belong to everyone? (336; emphasis in the original)

On the one hand, Scotty's concert evidently epitomizes a deep-seated longing for authentic expression by an authentic character. At the same time, however, it provides evidence for authenticity's inevitable inability to signify in and by itself. Scotty can only come to incorporate and transmit authenticity because he is not part of the symbolic structures that shape this society. He is 'pure' because he has evaded interpellation and is therefore 'part of no one's data'. As soon as the authenticity he symbolizes and communicates is being enacted and performed, however, it immediately becomes entangled with regimes of symbolic representation and is thus open to appropriation and exploitation. Authenticity presents an aspiration and a promise of fulfilment which can itself never be fulfilled. Like Rumpelstiltskin's name, it loses its magic power once it is spelled out. It is a gift in the Derridean sense in that it has no exchange value and can only function if it is not reciprocated. Authenticity is both irreducible and non-reproducible. Its power is purely imaginary and abstract. Itself necessarily evading signification, it can only indirectly allude but never directly designate or demarcate. It thus refers to a realm of pure, unmediated and formless presence, described – or rather circumscribed – variously as *jouissance* or *sinthome* by Lacan, the sémiotique by Kristeva or *khôra* by Derrida. In keeping with its intangible and paradoxical nature, authenticity likewise does not come to light directly but can only be obliquely enacted by formal and aesthetic means. It appears only in reflections and refractions but can never denote directly or signify immediately.

The tone and subject matter of the last chapter of *A Visit from the Goon Squad* is considerably bleaker than in the rest of the novel. It is through the gravity of the final vision, which laments what Bukatman describes as a 'lost relationship to the real' (1993: 30), that these potentially ludic shenanigans attain the status of serious meditations on the significance of life and literature. Authenticity, in *A Visit from the Goon Squad*, is no cypher for a misty nostalgia for pre-postmodern times. It is not an indicator for those prelapsarian days when experience and representation, signifier and signified, were supposedly reconcilable. Rather, the version of authenticity expressed in and through Egan's narrative very much starts out from decidedly postmodern positions: it can only be experienced as an aesthetic effect. It is not essentialist but always necessarily the result of a process of reconstruction. It emerges from the creative collapse of materiality and form. Egan's novel is emblematic, even celebratory, of the irremediable fragmentation of everyday experience and reality, which it narrates and enacts at the same time. Its significance in the context of an aesthetics of reconstruction and authenticity is twofold. On the level of the enounced, it explicitly discusses various aspects pertaining to contemporary discourses on authenticity. It makes a case for its enduring relevance while at the same time highlighting its essential paradoxicality and evasiveness. It implies that authentic experience can never be actively pursued but only emerges serendipitously, as a result of an inadvertent and accidental course of events or conjunction of circumstances. On a narratological level, *A Visit from the Goon Squad* represents an attempt to formally recreate such an unplanned and non-teleological assemblage of random events, objects and circumstances, which need to be reconstructed into a coherent narrative in the very act of reading.

Implicit narrative: Julian Barnes's *The Sense of an Ending*

Jennifer Egan obliterates the narrative authority in *A Visit from the Goon Squad* by dispersing it to several viewpoints and presenting it as a collage of different formal configurations. The question of the reliability of the narrator does not come into the equation as there is no consistent narrative voice to which the criterion of reliability could be applied in any meaningful way. In *The Sense of an Ending*, Julian Barnes takes the opposite path to arrive at a very similar conclusion. His novel features a clearly defined and even meticulously self-reflective narrator, Tony Webster, who is conscious of the fundamental problems and difficulties that accompany his attempts to reconstruct the story of his life from disordered and potentially fallacious fragments of memory. The reliability of the narrator in this case is very much foregrounded and discussed by the narrator himself. In the following I will first demonstrate how Barnes innovatively employs the first-person narrative perspective in an attempt to force the reader to re-enact the uncertainty and changeability of Tony's recollections in the very process of reading the novel. In a second step I will then apply these findings to a reconceptualization of unreliable narration by introducing the term *implicit narrative* to account for Barnes's strategy of suspending any final decision as to the reliability of his narrator and deferring the ultimate judgement to the reader.

Prefixing his narrative with a disclaimer, Tony Webster presents himself in the opening lines of the novel as being aware of the fact that (his) individual memories are not to be trusted in all details. He knows full well that there is always a gap between actual events and their reconstructions as and into memories and (life) stories:

> I remember, in no particular order:
> – a shiny inner wrist;
> – steam rising from the wet sink as a hot frying pan is laughingly tossed into it;

- gouts of sperm circling a plughole, before being sluiced down the full length of a tall house;
- a river rushing nonsensically upstream, its wave and wash lit by half a dozen chasing torchbeams;
- another river, broad and grey, the direction of its flow disguised by a stiff wind exciting the surface;
- bathwater long gone cold behind a locked door.
This isn't something I actually saw, but what you end up remembering isn't always the same as what you have witnessed. (*SE*: 3)

Tony is duly cognizant of the philosophical implications of this fickleness of memory, for example when he contemplates how changing attitudes and sensitivities that accumulate over the course of one's life occasionally occlude an unbiased view on self and others: 'It strikes me that this may be one of the differences between youth and age: when we are young, we invent different futures of ourselves; when we are old, we invent different pasts for others' (80). All in all, Tony promotes the view that it is impossible to develop and believe in *one* coherent and seamless narrative of oneself. This height of self-awareness and ontological reflectivity at first glance increases Tony's reliability as a narrator.

When he is suddenly forced to shine a light on one particular episode from his past, that is, the suicide of his erstwhile friend Adrian, he asseverates his intention to recall the events and circumstances leading up to this death to the very best of his knowledge and ability:

But school is where it all began, so I need to return briefly to a few incidents that have grown into anecdotes, to some approximate memories which time has deformed into certainty. If I can't be sure of the actual events any more, I can at least be true to the impressions those facts left. That's the best I can manage. (4)

The following is a short summary of these circumstances as related by Tony. After forming a friendship at school, Tony and Adrian part ways. While studying History at Bristol, Tony meets a girl called Veronica and they embark on a relationship. This liaison, however, is conducted in an atmosphere of mutual emotional and sexual indifference. Spending a weekend with Veronica's family, Tony deems himself treated condescendingly by her father and her brother. Only Sarah, Veronica's mother, approaches him with kindness and sympathy. Shortly after, Tony's relationship with Veronica ends. Some time later a letter from Adrian arrives, asking Tony for his permission to start dating Veronica. As far as Tony remembers, his answer to this entreaty is that he 'told him pretty much what I thought of their joint moral scruples. I also advised him to be prudent, because in my opinion Veronica had suffered damage a long way back. Then I wished him good luck, burnt his letter in the grate ... and decided that the two of them were now out of my life for ever' (42–3). With this answer, he considers the business of Adrian and Veronica settled as far as he is concerned. He goes on to marry Margaret, has a daughter and a mortgage, commutes to work every day and generally leads a life of quiet desperation.

In the second part of the novel, it slowly transpires that in spite of his scrupulous reflections and admissions of insufficiency, the unreliability of Tony's memory could be of an altogether more fundamental nature. Following Sarah's death, Tony is sent a page torn from Adrian's diary which includes a sequence of puzzling algebraic formulas and ends with the enigmatic and ominous sentence 'So, for instance, if Tony …' (86). The rest of the diary in question is in Veronica's possession and in order to clarify the meaning behind Adrian's cryptic allusions and formulas, Tony decides to contact his former girlfriend. Starting with their subsequent meeting, Tony's original version of the story gradually unravels and proves to be incomplete if not downright fictitious. Veronica confronts him with a first major revision of his recollections. She reminds him of the actual phrasing of his reply to Adrian's letter. Among a litany of other taunts and vituperations, this apparently contained the statement that 'part of me hopes you'll have a child, because I'm a great believer in time's revenge, yea unto the next generation and the next' (95) as well as Tony's recommendation to Adrian that even Veronica's 'own mother warned me against her. If I were you, I'd check things out with Mum – ask her about damage a long way back' (96). At this point the reliability of Tony's memories and with it the reliability of the narratorial authority suffers a first major blow. After rereading the letter several times, he must concede 'that I had been its author then, but was not its author now. Indeed, I didn't recognise that part of myself from which the letter came' (97). After an initial bout of guilt and bewilderment, Tony regains his composure and proceeds to integrate the information into a consistent new narrative of his role in the events. He defuses any urge to face up to the awfulness of the allegations implied in the letter by reverting to pseudo-moral reflections and a profound sense of self-pity. He uses a philosophical meditation on the changeability of the self in order to distance himself from his earlier misdeeds: 'My younger self had come back to shock my older self with what that self had been, or was, or was sometimes capable of being' (98). The only regret he is capable of pertains to his own wasted life:

> I began to feel a more general remorse – a feeling somewhere between self-pity and self-hatred – about my whole life. All of it. I had lost the friends of my youth. I had lost the love of my wife. I had abandoned the ambitions I had entertained. I had wanted life not to bother me too much, and had succeeded – and how pitiful that was. (99–100)

Tony's capacity for self-reflection still appears to be intact. His memories might have betrayed him in this one instance, but his supreme intellectual endowments allow him to generate a new consistent narrative. Or so it would seem.

To corroborate the new version of events and in order to fill in the details, Tony commences an email exchange with Veronica which, in turn, leads to a meeting between the former lovers. But instead of tackling the question of his responsibility for Adrian's death head-on, Tony allows himself to uncover another set of apparently well-hidden memories. On the train back from the meeting, he indulges in reminiscences of how 'attracted to one another we had been; how light she had felt on my lap; how exciting it all had been' (117). He might, so the reader is inclined to deduce, not even be above recommencing the relationship. The happy memories and the hopes he attaches to them, however, turn out to be utterly self-delusional. During their next meeting Veronica encounters a group of mentally disabled people, one of whom shows a particular attachment to her and calls her by her middle name, Mary. Tony evidently fails to realize the significance of this, even despite Veronica's desperate declaration 'You just don't get it, do you? You never did, and you never will' (126). Instead, he takes refuge in fond recollections of a romantic night they once had looking at the Severn bore. Throughout the novel, Tony uses the image of the bore, a tidal wave which travels against the current of the river Severn in Gloucestershire, to embellish his meditations on the nature of time and to explain away the inconsistency of his memory. On the train journey to meet Veronica, he reminisces about a romantic outing they had to see the bore, which prompts him to muse

> that there is objective time, but also subjective time, the kind you wear on the inside of your wrist, next to where the pulse lies. And this personal time, which is the true time, is measured in your relationship with memory. So when this strange thing happened – when these new memories suddenly came upon me – it was as if, for that moment, time had been placed in reverse. As if, for that moment, the river ran upstream. (122)

When he finally asks Veronica 'Why did that goofy chap call you Mary?', she throws him out of the car, leaving him to his own narrative devices (129). The first thing he does, however, is to bemoan the dashing of his own idle hopes, again with full cerebral and self-reflective flourish: 'The main reason I felt foolish and humiliated was because of – what had I called it to myself, only a few days previously? – "the eternal hopefulness of the human heart"' (130). After a stint of self-searching, he finally comes up with a rational explanation of her obverse reaction, an explanation which is again decorated with metaphors, self-serving philosophical niceties and literary allusions:

> I thought I could overcome contempt and turn remorse back into guilt, then be forgiven. I had been tempted, somehow, by the notion that we could excise most of our separate existences, could cut and splice the magnetic tape on which our lives are recorded, go back to that fork in the path and take the road less travelled, or rather not travelled at all. Instead, I had just left common sense behind. Old fool, I said to myself. (130-1)

The one aspect that so far resists integration into any consistent narrative is the encounter with the young disabled man. Consequently, Tony starts his own investigations and begins to frequent a pub the young man apparently patronizes.

Some time later he does actually meet him, and this confrontation requires Tony once more to rethink his role in the story. Tony accosts the young man with the information that he is a friend of Veronica, whereupon the man 'first began to smile, then panic. He turned away, gave a muted whine' (136). Finally, the truth reveals itself to Tony, and again the revelation comes muffled in sophistry and fake self-analysis:

> Now I knew … I saw it in his face. It's not often that's true, is it? At least, not for me. We listen to what people say, we read what they write – that's our evidence,

that's our corroboration. But if the face contradicts the speaker's words, we interrogate the face. A shifty look in the eye, a rising blush, the uncontrollable twitch of a face muscle – and then we know. We recognise the hypocrisy or the false claim, and the truth stands evident before us. (137)

The truth which so evidently stands before Tony is that the disabled man is Adrian's son by Veronica: 'I didn't need a birth certificate or DNA test – I saw it and felt it' (ibid.). Tony responds to this new revelation with his standard reaction of guilt and rationalization. He again manages to integrate this latest information into a consistent and reasonable narrative. Veronica's son is disabled because 'the trauma of [Adrian's] suicide had affected the child in the womb' (139). It is not lost on Tony that in view of this circumstance his careless remarks in answer to Adrian's letter take on a new and very acute significance. Revenge, it seems, was indeed meted out 'unto the next generation' as he had envisioned. Tony shows himself duly conscious of his guilt and expresses this in an email to Veronica: 'I was a man against whom backs should be turned. If life did merit reward, then I deserved shunning' (ibid.). Throughout the letter, however, his pricks of conscience are displayed with an air of equanimity and reflective aloofness, which suggests that even these new insights cannot eventually shake the foundations of his rationality and detached self-composure. He even embellishes his concessions of contriteness with linguistic casuistry: 'Remorse, etymologically, is the action of biting again: that's what the feeling does to you. Imagine the strength of the bite when I reread my words' (138).

Yet, even Tony's latest account does not fully concur with the facts of the matter and he will be required to reconstruct his memories once again. This comes as a result of a conversation he has with the carer of the disabled man, whose name turns out to be Adrian Jr. After an exchange riddled with misunderstandings, Tony at last understands that Veronica is not Adrian Jr.'s *mother* but his *sister*. In other words, the disabled man is Sarah's child (see 148). Tony again manages to incorporate this new twist into a coherent narrative. Following his advice in the letter to 'check things out with Mum', he concludes, Adrian must indeed have taken Sarah into his confidence. A sexual affair ensued, the issue of which is Adrian Jr. The reason for his disability Tony finds in the 'dangerously late age' of the boy's mother (149). The novel ends with Tony once more wringing his hands and beating his breast about his apparent role in this unhappy malaise, not failing for one last time to embellish his reflections with high-flying rhetoric about responsibility and the strange vicissitudes of fate in general:

> You get towards the end of life – no, not life itself, but of something else: the end of any likelihood of change in that life. You are allowed a long moment of pause, time enough to ask the question: what else have I done wrong? ... There is accumulation. There is responsibility. And beyond these, there is unrest. There is great unrest. (149–50)

The reader who finishes and closes the book re-enacts Tony's gesture of finally closing the chapter on his involvement with Adrian, Veronica, Sarah and Adrian Jr. But the story is not yet finished. The unrest which Tony invokes in the very last words of the book does indeed extend beyond accumulation and responsibility. It transcends the boundaries of the written text and challenges the reliability of the narrator from outside the text itself. For, without apparently intending to do so, Tony has peppered his recollections with just enough insinuations to suggest another possible scenario: Adrian Jr. is actually Tony's own son, the result of a sexual escapade with Veronica's mother Sarah during his weekend stay with the family. The hints pointing in this direction are never made explicit. They are merely indiscriminate and licentious shreds of memory, which could or could not be explained by a process Freud called displacement. There is, for instance, this surprisingly vivid recollection of Sarah preparing an egg for Tony's breakfast:

> She eased another egg on to my plate, despite my not asking for it or wanting it. The remnants of the broken one were still in the pan; she flipped them casually into the swing-bin, then half-threw the hot frying pan into the wet sink. Water fizzed and steam rose at the impact, and she laughed, as if she had enjoyed causing this small havoc. (29)

Moreover, Tony remembers a strange gesture made by Sarah when he took his leave after the weekend, a gesture which could have been incidental but which might just as well have implied a plea for secrecy: 'I waved goodbye, and she responded, though not the way people normally do, with a raised palm, but with a sort of horizontal gesture at waist level. I rather wished I'd talked to her more' (30). On a more straightforward register, there is also his recollection of 'gouts of sperm circling a plughole, before being sluiced down the full length of a tall house' (3).

That Tony could indeed be the father of the child is nowhere overtly offered as an option. It is structurally impossible to opt for one particular version of events solely based on the evidence presented in the book. In a literary version of Schrödinger's poor radioactively contaminated cat, (at least) four rival storylines – two explicit and two implicit – exist at the same time without the authority of a reliable narrator or indeed a reliable author to prefer one over the other. Which of those versions readers accept to be true depends on the importance they attribute to the ambiguities and omissions in Tony's own reconstructions. I therefore propose the term 'implicit narrative' for this kind of *storyline which is never overtly mentioned in the text but which must be reconstructed by the reader from apparent contradictions and omissions or insinuations 'unintentionally' dropped by the narrator*, in this case Tony Webster. Barnes's technique of implicit narrative can be classified as an implicit, interactional metareferential element with a focus on the alethiology of the source text and a reconstructive effect.

Of course, a novel that offers the reader two or more possible storylines is no invention of Barnes's. Among the more famous examples are John Fowles's *The French Lieutenant's Woman* (1969) and Yann Martel's *Life of Pi* (2002). What distinguishes *The Sense of an Ending* from those earlier cases is precisely the circumstance of its implicit narrative. The narrative authority in Barnes's novel does not explicitly present all the options that are available so that readers can choose the one they prefer. Tony Webster is not merely unreliable as a narrator because he beautifies, falsifies or symbolically elevates an otherwise cruel sequence of events, as Pi Patel in *Life of Pi* does. Quite the contrary; by constantly conceding the potential inadequacy and selectiveness of his memories he creates the impression that he is actually doing his level best to provide the most reliable and thorough source of information to the reader. Barnes also does not offer external corrections or alternatives to the story, as does the intrusive third-person narrator in *The French Lieutenant's Woman*. The verdict on Tony's reliability is deferred entirely to the readers. Through his unique use of first-person narrative perspective, Barnes forces them to enact Tony's attempts to adjust the stability of his self-narrative to every new development. This again can be described as a process of ergodic reading, in so far as every new turn of events requires the reader to literally page back and revaluate the importance of the narrator's allusions or omissions.

The device of implicit narrative might open up a new perspective on the narratological phenomenon of the unreliable narrator. Although this term has been a staple feature in literary criticism since its introduction by Wayne C. Booth in *The Rhetoric of Fiction* (1961), its use has often been marked by a measure of trepidation and unease. This discomfort is a result of the dubious and uncertain ontological status of the concept of unreliable narration as such. Although any number of highly metaphysical aspects can be attached to this issue, the fundamental problem boils down to the question: unreliable with regard to what or whom? Is there any valid frame of reference by which the unreliability of a narrator can actually be determined? Which criteria can serve as the basis for this judgement: historical facts or moral principles, contemporary standards or past convictions? Must the reliability of a narrator be assessed against the background of the facts and norms presented in the text itself or with regard to extratextual conventions and opinions?[2] Essentially, the disagreement about what defines an unreliable narrator is a matter of reference. Ansgar Nünning shows how, beginning with Booth, this basic conundrum has been 'resolved' by aligning it with an even more indistinct narrative category, the implied reader (see 1998: 9).

Nünning claims that the traditional lowest common denominator for analysing unreliable narration has been that it resulted from a discrepancy between the norms valid for the reader and those valid for the narrator (see 11). The concept of the implied reader, which, according to Wolfgang Iser, implies 'both the prestructuring of the potential meaning by the text, and the reader's actualization of this potential through the reading process' (1978: xii), is just as effective as it is deceptive. It creates the impression of a critical consensus of how the text in question should be understood by interposing an artificial paradigm of idealized reception between the actual reader and the text. The implied reader can be seen as an attempt to streamline the reception of a text. As a first step towards a more precise understanding of unreliable narration, the notion of the implied reader must therefore be abandoned. Nünning has thankfully taken this task upon himself. In his attempt to rethink unreliable narration in the context of frame theory, he makes clear that it is only ever the actual reader who can determine such unreliability. He further assumes that as a result of this, no

---

[2] For more in-depth investigations of the device of unreliable narration, see Yacobi (1981, 2001), Olsen (2003), Nünning (2005), Phelan (2005) and Hansen (2007).

narrator can be unreliable per se and that perceptions of reliability are subject to socio-political and cultural developments (see 1998: 25).

Nünning's reconceptualization of unreliable narration as not instigated by the author and mediated through an untrustworthy narrator figure but rather to be inferred by discerning readers in accordance with their own individual ethical and epistemological categories is undoubtedly significant. I would nevertheless argue that it does not go far enough. When Nünning proposes to apprehend unreliable narration as a strategy to dissolve intratextual contradiction, he imagines the literary text as a stable, monolithic and authoritatively given object. Any inconsistency which may give rise to suspicions of unreliability can only occur in the interface between this apparently fixed fictional universe and the empirical reality of the individual reader. With this claim, he sets up two ontologically incommensurable categories as the parameters by which unreliable narration can be ascertained. In a manner of speaking, he compares apples and oranges. If the world created in a literary text and by its narrator is understood to be unchanging and hermetic, no individual reader can have valid access to this world. Any judgement as to the consistency and reliability of the mediation would thus be mere conjecture, because there are no formal criteria according to which these inconsistencies can be formally attributed. The fictional world and the real world just do not connect.

I would claim that narrative unreliability can function as a valid and useable narratological category, if and only if it is considered to be a textually self-contained phenomenon. The unreliability of narration can only be formally appreciated and analysed when it is inconsistent with itself, that is, in the context of the fictional discourse of which it is part, and not with external, erratic and inconsistent norms and principles. Shlomith Rimmon-Kennan provides a terminological framework for describing the correlation of Barnes's use of implicit narrative with the narrator's assumed reliability. She claims that 'when the narrator's language contains internal contradictions, double-edged images, and the like, it may have a boomerang effect, undermining the reliability of its user' (2002: 104). Let me illustrate this with an example taken from Fforde. The unreliability of Thursday Next as a narrator is not due to the fact that she claims to be able to read herself into any work of fiction, although this evidently presents a case where the textual universe is at odds with the reality of most readers. Her unreliability as a narrator in the second part of the series is rather the consequence of the fragmentation of her character and the concomitant challenges to the stability of the diegetic world, which are both emphatically and exclusively intratextual phenomena. This is not to say that it is not the reader who ultimately decides on the inconsistency. It means, however, that the discrepancy which gives rise to unreliable narration must be a result of phenomena which can be situated squarely within the textual universe. My suggestion would be to describe this intra-textual inconsistency as an oscillation between rival and formally equivalent narrative versions of the same underlying set of events and circumstances. The narratological device of implicit narrative, as employed by Barnes in *The Sense of an Ending*, warrants that the ambiguity of the narrative perspective cannot be resolved conclusively within the logic of the text itself.

In doing so, the novel runs counter to Frank Kermode's influential study, with which it shares its title. Kermode argues that one of the main objectives of literature has always been to inspire an idea of order and temporality in a reality which is experienced as contingent and devoid of purpose, in other words to impose narrative form onto the sheer materiality of life. Barnes, on the other hand, emphasizes the structural indeterminacy of his protagonist's narration, both in the sense of its oscillation between different accounts of reality and in its reach beyond the materiality of the book's pages. Within the context of an aesthetics of reconstruction, both Egan's strategy of narrative assemblage and Barnes's new take on unreliable narration cannot be resolved but can only be re-enacted by the reader. Metareferential devices lead to a structural undecidability concerning the reliability of the narrative in both cases. This, in turn, generates epistemological uncertainty and confusion in the readers and compels them to reconstruct their very own, authentic, version of events. At the same time, both novels are centrally concerned with questions of (narrative) time and memory, which links them implicitly with a modernist, rather than postmodern, literary tradition. This again might be taken as an indication for the conceptual proximity of the reconstructive approach I have tried to delineate in this study to modernism's renegotiation of the parameters of literary expression. Both involve a rethinking of the relationship between experience and representation and both can be attributed to momentous changes in the way the human self conceives of itself in relation to a (potential) world outside of it. The main difference is that while modernist and postmodernist aesthetics signified the final call for a realist tradition which assumed a direct rapport between the world and its representation in art, an aesthetics of reconstruction suggests that this gap or *différance* can be used as a starting point for a new conception of authentic literary communication.

8

Remainder

In Tom McCarthy's novel *Remainder*, the nameless first-person protagonist relentlessly pursues the perfect authentic moment. In consequence of a freak accident, when a nondescript heavy object hit him literally out of thin air, he is plagued by an inability to experience life directly. He has not only lost his memory but must relearn even the simplest movements and motions. This circumstance forces him to imagine every physical movement and process before he can actually carry it out: 'Every action is a complex operation, a system, and I had to learn them all. I'd understand them, then I'd emulate them' (McCarthy 2007: 22). He deplores this state of compulsive self-reflection as deeply inauthentic. Comparing himself to Robert de Niro in *Mean Streets*, he observes how de Niro 'flows into his movements, even the most basic ones. Opening fridge doors, lighting cigarettes … He doesn't have to think about them because he and they are one. Perfect. Real. My movements are all fake. Second-hand' (23). He leads an existence, as it were, one remove from actual experience. With recourse to the interplay of form and materiality, one could say that the compulsory formality of his self-reflection bars the way to the pure material reality of authentic experience. Then all of a sudden, while looking at himself in the mirror while at a party, authenticity hits him squarely in the face. He experiences a feeling of déjà vu and recalls in vivid detail how

> inside this remembered building … all my movements had been fluent and unforced … I'd merged with them, run through them and let them run through me until there'd been no space between us. They'd been *real*; I'd been real – *been* without first understanding how to try to be: cut out the detour. I remember this with all the force of an epiphany, a revelation. (62; emphases in the original)

From this moment onwards he dedicates his entire life to the re-enactment of this one apparently authentic moment of unmediated experience. Apparently cognizant of Baudrillard's contention that to 'gain exit from the crisis of representation, the real must be sealed off in a pure repetition' (1993: 72) and in utter denial of any Benjaminian notion of aura, he devotes every waking hour and a not insubstantial amount of money to recreating this instant when experience and representation had apparently become one. The explicit aim of the re-enactment is 'to allow me to be fluent, natural, to merge with actions and with objects until there was nothing separating us – and nothing separating me from the experience that I was having: no understanding, no learning first and emulating second-hand, no self-reflection, nothing: no detour. I'd gone to these extraordinary lengths in order to be real' (222–3). Once he attains such a moment of first-hand experience, he becomes addicted to the authenticity of the perfect simulation and goes on to restage ever more intricate set pieces, including a street shooting and culminating in the re-enactment of a bank robbery.

I do not want to analyse the novel in all its complexity. Instead I suggest using the narrator's attempt to '*accede* to … a kind of authenticity through this strange pointless residual' (240; emphasis in the original) to mirror the approach to authentic experience which I have outlined in this book. In both cases, authenticity is seen as a paradoxical ontological singularity where experience and representation, life and art, supposedly merge into one another. Both describe attempts to aesthetically recreate and re-enact such singular instances. Moreover, this study and McCarthy's novel likewise situate this paradoxical re-enactment of immediacy within the dialectic of form and matter, as in both cases an excess of form provides access to the pure materiality of experience.[1] Yet, here the similarities end. The authentic moment as pursued in *Remainder* is one of pure form. It can occur only at the point where 'matter is distilled into aesthetic form' (Huber and Seita 2012: 269). It is the authenticity of the perfect simulation, where the resistance of the materiality of experience is completely absorbed in its symbolic representation and where signs cease to refer to anything but themselves. This version of authenticity is ultimately solipsistic and self-contained. It reduces interaction to a perfectly choreographed sequence of movements, utterances and stage directions. It is an escape from reality by way of its complete aesthetic recreation. Consequently, it can function merely in the realm of the abstract and must collapse once it is brought out into the open of material reality. Once the simulation is released from the strict confines of formal enactment, the cocooning effect of its self-referential repetitiveness vanishes. Outside the formal context, a perfect simulation of reality is indistinguishable from reality and thus *becomes* material reality. In the novel the narrator crosses this boundary between the pure formalism of simulation and material reality with a re-enactment of a bank robbery in a real bank. He describes this endeavour as an attempt at lifting

> the re-enactment out of its demarcated zone and slotting it back into the world, into an actual bank whose staff didn't know it was a re-enactment: that would return my motions and my gestures to ground zero and hour zero, to the point at which the re-enactment merged with the real. It would let me penetrate and live inside the core, be seamless, perfect, real. (244–5)

The concrete reality of matter hits home in the shape of a bullet which kills one of the performers who help him 'enact' the bank heist. Inevitably, the path of the perfectly simulated authentic experience leads but to the grave. The final scene of the novel sees the narrator enter an aeroplane and end up drawing an endless figure-of-eight in the indifferent sky. It is only in death that this perfect simulation can be reunited with its

---

[1] Cf. here Pieter Vermeulen, who situates *Remainder* in the context of 'McCarthy's larger aim to retrieve the world in its materiality and to record the material remainder of things that resists every attempt at abstraction or spiritualization' (2011: 260).

abject physicality. Experience and representation of the self only merge in its annihilation. His attempts at re-enactment cannot eventually bridge the gap between form and matter, because they subordinate material reality to a quest for perfect representation. Taking Schiller's triadic model into account again, the narrator's understanding of authenticity is Arcadian in nature, because it is informed by a naïve confidence in the innocence of pure form. It therefore necessarily founders on the concreteness of manifest reality.

My book suggests an alternative path to authentic representation. Like the protagonist of *Remainder*, I acknowledge that authenticity can only be experienced as an effect of aesthetic re-enactment and performance. In order to break through the confines of formal abstraction, however, any such performance must also at the same time reflect and enact its own paradoxical condition. It must, in other words, simultaneously perform the authenticity of immediate experience *and* its formal impossibility. I consider metareference as the aesthetic correlative of this paradox of authenticity, because it can mirror authenticity's transcendental, oscillatory and paradoxical disposition on a structural level. The literary case studies I have presented all demonstrate in different ways how the use of metareferential elements challenges the formal integrity of the individual act of literary communication. In each case this attack on formal congruity generates intimations of ontological uncertainty and/or epistemological ambiguity which cannot be resolved within the texts themselves. Only a metareferential fragmentation and refraction of form can eventually reunite form and matter and transform authenticity from a hermetic aesthetic exercise into an interactional process. The formal authenticity envisioned in *Remainder* can never transcend its status as mere formal and deliberate *re-enactment*. It is forever enclosed within the irredeemable inescapability and formal closure of the figure-of-eight. An authenticity based on metareference, in contrast, can only emerge in a communal and unpremeditated act of *reconstruction*. Its symbol is not the figure-of-eight but the paradoxical openness and transcendental iterability of the Moebius band or of Hofstadter's 'eternal golden braid'. In his capacity as General Secretary of the International Necronautical Society, Tom McCarthy himself summarizes these two options when he declares that 'all art and literature is divided between these two temptations: either to extinguish matter and elevate it into form or to let matter matter by making form as formless as possible' (International Necronautical Society 2009: 4). I understand metareference as a tool for the latter. It can prepare the ground for an Elysian version of aesthetic authenticity which, by returning the innocence of form into itself, renders literature in this new millennium open to an encounter with the immediacy of experience.

Bibliography

Aarseth, Espen J. *Cybertext: Perspectives on Ergodic Literature*. Baltimore, MD: Johns Hopkins University Press, 1997.
Adorno, Theodor. 'On the Use of Foreign Words'. 1961. In *Notes to Literature*, VI, edited by Rolf Tiedemann, translated by Shierry Weber Nicholson, 286–91. New York: Columbia University Press, 1992.
Adorno, Theodor. *Jargon of Authenticity*. 1964. Translated by Trent Schroyer. London: Routledge, 2003.
Adorno, Theodor. *Aesthetic Theory*. 1970. Translated by Robert Hullot-Kentor. London: Bloomsbury, 2013.
Allen, Graham. *Intertextuality*. London: Routledge, 2000.
Alphen, Ernst van and Mieke Bal. 'Introduction'. In *The Rhetoric of Sincerity*, edited by Ernst van Alphen, Mieke Bal and Carel Smith, 1–16. Stanford, CA: Stanford University Press, 2009.
Alter, Robert. *Partial Magic: The Novel as a Self-Conscious Genre*. Berkeley: University of California Press, 1975.
Améry, Jean. *On Suicide: A Discourse on Voluntary Death*. 1976. Translated by John Barlow. Bloomington: Indiana University Press, 1999.
Amrein, Ursula. 'Einleitung'. In *Das Authentische: Referenzen und Repräsentationen*, edited by Ursula Amrein, 9–24. Zurich: Chronos, 2009.
Anderson, Benedict. *Imagined Communities: Reflections on the Origin and Spread of Nationalism*. London: Verso, 1983.
Anton, Corey. *Selfhood and Authenticity*. Albany: State University of New York Press, 2001.
Aristotle. Poetics *with Tractatus Coislinianus, Reconstruction of* Poetics II *and the Fragments of* On the Poets. Translated by Richard Janko. Indianapolis, IN: Hackett, 1987.
Aristotle. *Nicomachean Ethics*. Translated by Terence Irwin. Indianapolis, IN: Hackett, 2000.
Arnheim, Rudolf. 'The Two Authenticities of the Photographic Media'. *Journal of Aesthetics and Art Criticism* 51 (4): 537–40, 1993.
Assmann, Aleida. 'Authenticity: The Signature of Western Exceptionalism?' In *Paradoxes of Authenticity: Studies on a Critical Concept*, edited by Julia Straub, 33–50. Bielefeld: transcript, 2012.
Attridge, Derek. *The Singularity of Literature*. London: Routledge, 2004.
Auerbach, Erich. *Mimesis: Dargestellte Wirklichkeit in der abendländischen Literatur*. Berne: Francke, 1946.
Badiou, Alain. *The Century*. Translated by Alberto Toscano. Cambridge: Polity Press, 2007.
Baecker, Dirk. *Postheroisches Management: Ein Vademecum*. Berlin: Merve, 1994.
Baker, Timothy C. 'The (Neuro)-Aesthetics of Caricature: Representations of Reality in Bret Easton Ellis's *Lunar Park*'. *Poetics Today* 30 (3): 471–515, 2009.

Bantleon, Katharina. 'From Readymade to "Meta²": Metareference in Appropriation Art'. In *The Metareferential Turn in Contemporary Arts and Media: Form, Functions, Attempts at Explanation*, edited by Werner Wolf, 305-37. Amsterdam: Rodopi.
Barnes, Julian. *Flaubert's Parrot*. London: Jonathan Cape, 1984.
Barnes, Julian. *A History of the World in 10½ Chapters*. New York: Vintage, 1990.
Barnes, Julian. *England, England*. London: Picador, 1998.
Barnes, Julian. *The Sense of an Ending*. London: Jonathan Cape, 2011.
Barth, John. 'The Literature of Exhaustion'. In *The Novel Today: Contemporary Writers on Modern Fiction*, edited by Malcolm Bradbury, 70-83. Glasgow: Fontana/Collins, 1972.
Barth, John. 'Tales within Tales within Tales'. *Antaeus* 43: 45-63, 1981.
Barth, John. 'Very like an Elephant: Reality versus Realism'. In *Further Fridays: Essays, Lectures, and other Nonfiction*, 136-43. Boston, MA: Little, Brown, 1995.
Barthes, Roland. *S/Z*. Translated by Richard Miller. New York: Hill and Wang, 1974.
Barthes, Roland. *The Pleasure of the Text*. Translated by Richard Miller. London: Jonathan Cape, 1976.
Barthes, Roland. 'The Death of the Author'. 1967. In *Image, Text, Music*, edited and translated by Stephan Heath, 142-8. New York: Hill and Wang, 1978.
Barthes, Roland. *The Rustle of Language*. Translated by Richard Howard. Berkeley: University of California Press, 1989.
Baudrillard, Jean. *Symbolic Exchange and Death*. 1976. Translated by Iain Hamilton Grant. London: Sage, 1993.
Baudrillard, Jean. *Simulacra and Simulation*. 1981. Translated by Sheila Faria Glaser. Ann Arbor: University of Michigan Press, 1994.
Baugh, Bruce. 'Authenticity Revisited'. *The Journal of Aesthetics and Art Criticism* 46 (4): 477-87, 1988.
Bauman, Zygmunt. *Intimations of Postmodernity*. London: Routledge, 1992.
Bauman, Zygmunt. *Liquid Modernity*. Cambridge: Polity Press, 2000.
Bauman, Zygmunt. *Liquid Times: Living in an Age of Uncertainty*. Cambridge: Polity Press, 2007.
Bauman, Zygmunt. *The Art of Life*. Cambridge: Polity Press, 2008.
Beck Ulrich, Anthony Giddens and Lash Scott. *Reflexive Modernization: Politics, Tradition and Aesthetics in the Modern Social Order*. Cambridge: Polity Press, 1994.
Beck Ulrich and Edgar Grande. 'Varieties of Second Modernity: The Cosmopolitan Turn in Social and Political Theory and Research'. *British Journal of Sociology* 61 (3): 409-43, 2010.
Benjamin, Walter. *The Work of Art in the Age of Mechanical Reproduction*. 1936. Translated by J. A. Underwood. London: Penguin, 2008.
Bennett, Lance, Regina W. Lawrence and Steven Livingston, eds. *When the Press Fails: Political Power and the News Media from Iraq to Katrina*. Chicago, IL: University of Chicago Press, 2007.
Bennington, Geoffrey. *Interrupting Derrida*. London: Routledge, 2000.
Bentley, Nick. 'Re-Writing Englishness: Imagining the Nation in Julian Barnes's *England, England* and Zadie Smith's *White Teeth*'. *Textual Practice* 21: 483-504, 2007.
Benveniste, Émile. *Problems in General Linguistics*. Translated by Mary Elizabeth Meek. Coral Gables, FL: University of Miami Press, 1971.
Berger, Peter L. 'Sincerity and Authenticity in Modern Society'. *The Public Interest* 31: 81-90, 1973.

Berger, Peter L. and Thomas Luckmann. *The Social Construction of Reality: A Treatise in the Sociology of Knowledge*. New York: Anchor Books, 1966.
Berman, Marshall. *The Politics of Authenticity: Radical Individualism and the Emergence of Modern Society*. 1970. London: Verso, 2009.
Berninger, Mark and Katrin Thomas. 'A Parallelquel of a Classic Text and Reification of the Fictional: The Playful Parody of *Jane Eyre* in Jasper Fforde's *The Eyre Affair*'. In *A Breath of Fresh Eyre: Intertextual and Intermedial Reworkings of Jane Eyre*, edited by Margarete Rubik and Elke Mettinger-Schartmann, 181–96. Amsterdam: Rodopi, 2007.
Bertens, Hans. *The Idea of the Postmodern: A History*. London: Routledge, 1995.
Bewes, Timothy. *Cynicism and Postmodernity*. London: Verso, 1997.
'black box, n.'. OED Online. September 2014. Oxford University Press. http://oed.com/view/Entry/282116?redirectedFrom=black%20box (accessed 16 September 2014).
Blitz, David. *Emergent Evolution: Qualitative Novelty and the Levels of Reality*. Dordrecht: Kluwer, 1992.
Bloom, Harold. *The Anxiety of Influence: A Study of Poetry*. New York: Oxford University Press, 1973.
Blythe, Will. 'To Their Own Beat'. *New York Times Sunday Book Review*, 11 July. http://www.nytimes.com/2010/07/11/books/review/Blythe-t.html (accessed 16 September 2014), 2010.
Bohrer, Karl Heinz. *Der romantische Brief: Die Entstehung ästhetischer Subjektivität*. Frankfurt am Main: Suhrkamp, 1989.
Bolz, Norbert. *Blindflug mit Zuschauer*. Munich: Fink, 2004.
Boorstin, Daniel. *The Image: A Guide to Pseudo-Events in America 1961*. New York: Atheneum, 1985.
Booth, Wayne C. *The Rhetoric of Fiction*. Chicago, IL: University of Chicago Press, 1961.
Borges, Jorge Luis. *Labyrinths: Selected Stories and other Writing by Jorge Luis Borges*. Edited by Donald A. Yates and James E. Irby. New York: New Directions, 1964.
Borges, Jorge Luis. 'On Exactitude in Science'. 1946. In *Collected Fictions*, edited and translated by Andrew Hurley, 325. New York: Penguin, 1999.
Borgmann, Albert. *Holding on to Reality: The Nature of Information at the Turn of the Millennium*. Chicago, IL: University of Chicago Press, 1999.
Bourriaud, Nicolas. 'Altermodern'. In *Altermodern: Tate Triennial 2009*, edited by Nicolas Bourriaud, 11–24. London: Tate Publishing, 2009.
Bousquet, David. 'Poets and the Roots: Authenticity in the Works of Linton Kwesi Johnson and Benjamin Zephaniah'. In *The Aesthetics of Authenticity: Medial Constructions of the Real*, edited by Wolfgang Funk, Irmtraud Huber and Florian Groß, 189–208. Bielefeld: transcript, 2012.
Bowie, A. M. 'The Parabasis in Aristophanes: Prolegomena, Acharnians'. *The Classical Quarterly* 32 (1): 27–40, 1982.
Boyd, Michael. *The Reflexive Novel: Fiction as Critique*. Lewisburg, PA: Bucknell University Press, 1983.
Bradbury, Malcolm. 'Writing Fiction in the 90s'. In *Neo-Realism in Contemporary American Fiction*, edited by Kristiaan Versluys, 13–25. Amsterdam: Rodopi, 1992.
Broad, William J. *The Oracle: The Lost Secrets and Hidden Messages of Ancient Delphi*. New York: Penguin, 2006.
Broich, Ulrich and Manfred Pfister, eds. *Intertextualität: Formen, Funktionen, anglistische Fallstudien*. Tübingen: Niemeyer, 1985.
Brontë, Charlotte. *Jane Eyre*. 1847. Edited by Richard Dunn. New York: Norton, 2001.

Brooks, Neil and Josh Toth, eds. *The Mourning After: Attending the Wake of Postmodernism*. Amsterdam: Rodopi, 2007.

Brouillette, Sarah. 'Paratextuality and Economic Disavowal in Dave Eggers's *You Shall Know Our Velocity*'. *Reconstruction: Studies in Contemporary Culture* 3 (2). http://reconstruction.eserver.org/Issues/032/brouillette.htm (accessed 16 September 2014), 2003.

Bruner, Jerome. 'The Narrative Construction of Reality'. *Critical Inquiry* 18: 1–18, 1991.

Bruns, Axel. *Blogs, Wikipedia, Second Life, and Beyond: From Production to Produsage*. New York: Peter Lang, 2008.

Buber, Martin. *I and Thou*. 1923. Translated by Ronald Gregor Smith. London: Continuum, 2008.

Bühler, Karl. *Sprachtheorie: Die Darstellungsfunktion der Sprache*. 1934. Stuttgart: UTB, 1999.

Bukatman, Scott. *Terminal Identity: The Virtual Subject in Post-Modern Science-Fiction*. Durham, NC: Duke University Press, 1993.

Burn, Stephen J. *Jonathan Franzen at the End of Postmodernism*. London: Continuum, 2008.

Butler, Judith. *Giving an Account of Oneself*. New York: Fordham University Press, 2005.

Carr, Nicholas G. 'Is Google Making us Stupid? What the Internet is Doing to Our Brains'. *The Atlantic* (July/August). http://www.theatlantic.com/magazine/archive/2008/07/is-google-making-us-stupid/6868/ (accessed 16 September 2014), 2008.

Cazzato, Luigi. *Metafiction of Anxiety: Modes and Meanings of the Postmodern Self-Conscious Novel*. Fasano: Schena, 2000.

Chen, Fanfan. 'From Hypotyposis to Metalepsis: Narrative Devices in Contemporary Fantastic Fiction'. *Forum for Modern Language Studies* 44: 394–411, 2008.

Chidester, David. *Authentic Fakes: Religion and American Popular Culture*. Berkeley: University of California Press, 2005.

Christensen, Inger. *The Meaning of Metafiction*. Bergen: Universitetsforlaget, 1981.

Cohen, Erik. 'Authenticity and Commoditization in Tourism'. *Annals of Tourism Research* 15 (1): 371–86, 1988.

Colapietro, Vincent. 'Distortion, Fabrication, and Disclosure in a Self-Referential Culture: The Irresistible Force of Reality'. In *Self-Reference in the Media*, edited by Winfried Nöth and Nina Bishara, 31–43. Berlin: De Gruyter, 2007.

Cornford, Francis MacDonald. *The Origin of Attic Comedy*. 1934. Cambridge: Cambridge University Press, 2011.

Corning, Peter A. 'The Re-Emergence of "Emergence": A Venerable Concept in Search of a Theory'. *Complexity* 7 (6): 18–30, 2002.

Cortázar, Julio. 'The Continuity of Parks'. In *End of the Game and Other Stories*, edited by Paul Blackburn, 63–5. New York: Harper Colophon, 1978.

Critchley, Simon. *The Ethics of Deconstruction: Derrida and Levinas*. Oxford: Blackwell, 1992.

Critchley, Simon. *Very Little … Almost Nothing: Death, Philosophy, Literature*. London: Routledge, 1997.

Culler, Jonathan D. *Framing the Sign: Criticism and its Institutions*. Oxford: Blackwell, 1988.

Currie, Mark. *Postmodern Narrative Theory*. Basingstoke: Macmillan, 1998.

Dällenbach, Lucien. *The Mirror in the Text*. 1977. Translated by Jeremy Whiteley with Emma Hughes. Cambridge: Polity Press, 1989.

Daniels, Stephan. *Fields of Vision: Landscape Imagery and National Identity in England and the United States*. Princeton, NJ: Princeton University Press, 1993.
Danner, Mark. 'Words in a Time of War: On Rhetoric, Truth, and Power'. In *What Orwell Didn't Know: Propaganda and the New Face of American Politics*, edited by András Szántó, 16–36. New York: Public Affairs, 2007.
Darby, Wendy Joy. *Landscape and Identity: Geographies of Nation and Class in England*. Oxford: Berg, 2000.
Davis, Todd F. and Kenneth Womack, eds. *Mapping the Ethical Turn: A Reader in Ethics, Culture, and Literary Theory*. Charlottesville: University Press of Virginia, 2001.
Debord, Guy. *The Society of the Spectacle*. 1967. Translated by Donald Nicholson-Smith. New York: Zone Books, 1999.
Derrida, Jacques. *Speech and Phenomena and Other Essays on Husserl's Theory of Signs*. Translated by David B. Allison. Evanston, IL: Northwestern University Press, 1973.
Derrida, Jacques. *Of Grammatology*. Translated by Gayatri Chakravorty Spivak. Baltimore, MD: Johns Hopkins University Press, 1976.
Derrida, Jacques. *Writing and Difference*. Translated by Alan Bass. Chicago, IL: University of Chicago Press, 1978.
Derrida, Jacques. *Margins of Philosophy*. Translated by Alan Bass. Chicago, IL: University of Chicago Press, 1982.
Derrida, Jacques. *Limited Inc.* Evanston, IL: Northwestern University Press, 1988.
Derrida, Jacques. 'Force of Law: The "Mythical Foundation of Authority"'. In *Deconstruction and the Possibility of Justice*, edited by Drucilla Cornell, Michel Rosenfeld and David Gray Carlson, 3–67. New York: Routledge, 1992.
Derrida, Jacques. *Spectres of Marx: The State of the Debt, the Work of Mourning, and the New International*. Translated by Peggy Kamuf. New York: Routledge, 1994.
Derrida, Jacques. *The Gift of Death*. Translated by David Wills. Chicago, IL: University of Chicago Press, 1995.
Doležel, Lubomir. 'Truth and Authenticity in Narrative'. *Poetics Today* 1 (3): 7–25, 1980.
Doležel, Lubomir. *Heterocosmica: Fiction and Possible Worlds*. Baltimore, MD: Johns Hopkins University Press, 1998.
Domínguez, César. 'Literary Emergence as a Case Study of Theory in Comparative Literature'. *CLCWeb: Comparative Literature and Culture* 8 (2). http://docs.lib.purdue.edu/clcweb/vol8/iss2/1 (accessed 16 September 2014), 2006.
Doniger, Wendy. *The Woman who Pretended to Be who she Was*. Oxford: Oxford University Press, 2005.
Dubus, Pascale. 'Screen, Support, and Trompe-L'œil: Parrhasius' Painted Fabric'. Translated by Lindsay Holowach. *Octopus* 4: 67–72, 2008.
Dupuy, Jean-Pierre. 'Tangled Hierarchy: Self-Reference in Philosophy, Anthropology, and Critical Theory'. *Comparative Criticism* 12: 105–23, 1990.
Dutton, Denis. 'Authenticity in Art'. In *The Oxford Handbook of Aesthetics*, edited by Jerrold Levinson, 258–74. New York: Oxford University Press, 2003.
Duvenage, Pieter. 'Alessandro Ferrara's *Reflective Authenticity*: Rethinking the Project of Modernity'. *Philosophy & Social Criticism* 30: 127–34, 2004.
Eco, Umberto. *Faith in Fakes: Travels in Hyperreality*. London: Vintage, 1995.
Egan, Jennifer. *A Visit from the Goon Squad*. New York: Anchor Books, 2010.
Eggers, Dave. *A Heartbreaking Work of Staggering Genius*. 2000. London: Picador, 2001.
'ethic, n. and adj.'. OED Online. September 2014. Oxford University Press. http://www.oed.com/view/Entry/64755?redirectedFrom=ethic (accessed 16 September 2014).

Federman, Raymond. 'Surfiction: Four Propositions in Form of an Introduction'. In *Surfiction: Fiction Now ... and Tomorrow*, 5–15. Chicago, IL: The Swallow Press, 1975.

Feldmann, Doris. 'Beyond Difference? Recent Developments in Postcolonial and Gender Studies'. In *English Studies Today: Recent Developments and New Directions*, edited by Ansgar Nünning and Jürgen Schlaeger, 117–37. Trier: WVT, 2007.

Ferrara, Alessandro. *Modernity and Authenticity: A Study of the Social and Ethical Thought of Jean-Jacques Rousseau*. Albany: State University of New York Press, 1993.

Ferrara, Alessandro. *Reflective Authenticity: Rethinking the Project of Modernity*. New York: Routledge, 1998.

Ferrara, Alessandro. *The Force of the Example: Explorations in the Paradigm of Judgment*. New York: Columbia University Press, 2008.

Ferrara, Alessandro. 'Authenticity without a True Self'. In *Authenticity in Culture, Self, and Society*, edited by Phillip Vannini and J. Patrick Williams, 21–35. Farnham: Ashgate, 2009.

Fforde, Jasper. *The Eyre Affair*. London: Hodder & Stoughton, 2001.

Fforde, Jasper. *Lost in a Good Book*. London: Hodder & Stoughton, 2002.

Fforde, Jasper. *The Well of Lost Plots*. London: Hodder & Stoughton, 2003.

Fforde, Jasper. *Something Rotten*. London: Hodder & Stoughton, 2004.

Fforde, Jasper. *First among Sequels*. London: Hodder & Stoughton, 2007.

Fforde, Jasper. *One of our Thursdays is Missing*. London: Hodder & Stoughton, 2011.

Fforde, Jasper. *The Woman who Died a Lot*. London: Hodder & Stoughton, 2012.

Fischer, Gerhard and Bernhard Greiner, eds. *The Play within the Play: The Performance of Meta-Theatre and Self-Reflection*. Amsterdam: Rodopi, 2007.

Fletcher, John and Malcolm Bradbury. 'The Introverted Novel'. In *Modernism: A Guide to European Literature 1890–1930*, edited by Malcolm Bradbury and James MacFarlane, 394–415. Harmondsworth: Penguin, 1978.

Fluck, Winfried. 'Surface Knowledge and "Deep" Knowledge: The New Realism in American Fiction'. In *Neo-Realism in Contemporary American Fiction*, edited by Kristiaan Versluys, 65–85. Amsterdam: Rodopi, 1992.

Fludernik, Monika. 'Second-Person Narrative: A Bibliography'. *Style* 25: 525–48, 1994.

Fludernik, Monika. 'Metanarrative and Metafictional Commentary: From Metadiscursivity to Metanarration and Metafiction'. *Poetica* 35: 1–39, 2003.

Fludernik, Monika. *Towards a 'Natural' Narratology*. London: Routledge, 2010.

Fornäs, Johan. *Cultural Theory and Late Modernity*. London: Sage, 1995.

Forster, E. M. *Aspects of the Novel*. 1927. London: Penguin, 2005.

Foster, Hal. *The Return of the Real: The Avant-Garde at the End of the Century*. Cambridge, MA: MIT Press, 1996.

Foucault, Michel. 'What is an Author?' In *Language, Counter-Memory, Practice*, edited by Donald F. Bouchard, translated by Donald F. Bouchard and Sherry Simon, 124–7. Ithaca, NY: Cornell University Press, 1977.

Foucault, Michel. *This is not a Pipe*. Translated by James Harkness. Berkeley: University of California Press, 1983.

Foucault, Michel. *Fearless Speech*. Edited by Joseph Pearson. Los Angeles, CA: Semiotext(e), 2001.

Foucault, Michel. *The Archaeology of Knowledge*. Translated by Alan Sheridan. London: Routledge, 2002.

Fox, Loren. *The Rise and Fall of Enron*. Hoboken, NJ: John Wiley and Sons, 2003.

Friedenberg, Jay and Gordon Silverman. *Cognitive Science: An Introduction to the Study of Mind*. Los Angeles, CA: Sage, 2012.
Funk, Wolfgang. 'The Quest for Authenticity: Dave Eggers's *A Heartbreaking Work of Staggering Genius* between Fiction and Reality'. In *The Metareferential Turn in Contemporary Arts and Media: Form, Functions, Attempts at Explanation*, edited by Werner Wolf, 125–44. Amsterdam: Rodopi, 2011a.
Funk, Wolfgang. 'Seltsame Schleifen und wahrhaftiges Erzählen: Authentizität im zeitgenössischen englischsprachigen Roman'. In *Fiktionen von Wirklichkeit: Authentizität zwischen Materialität und Konstruktion*, edited by Wolfgang Funk and Lucia Krämer, 225–44. Bielefeld: transcript, 2011b.
Funk, Wolfgang. 'Reziproker Realismus: Versuch einer Ästhetik der Authentizität'. In *Authentisches Erzählen. Produktion, Narration, Rezeption*, edited by Antonius Weixler, 121–43. Berlin: De Gruyter, 2012.
Funk, Wolfgang and Lucia Krämer. 'Vorwort'. In *Fiktionen von Wirklichkeit: Authentizität zwischen Materialität und Konstruktion*, edited by Wolfgang Funk and Lucia Krämer, 7–23. Bielefeld: transcript, 2011.
Gaillard, Francoise. 'The Great Illusion of Reality, or the Real as Representation'. *Poetics Today* 5: 753–66, 1984.
Gass, William H. *Fiction and the Figures of Life*. New York: Knopf, 1970.
Genette, Gérard. *Narrative Discourse Revisited*. Translated by Jane E. Lewin. Ithaca, NY: Cornell University Press, 1988.
Genette, Gérard. 'Introduction to the Paratext'. *New Literary History* 22 (2): 261–72, 1991.
Genette, Gérard. *Palimpsests: Literature in the Second Degree*. Translated by Channa Newman and Claude Doubinsky. Lincoln: University of Nebraska Press, 1997.
Gergen, Kenneth J. *The Saturated Self: Dilemmas of Identity in Contemporary Life*. New York: Basic Books, 1991.
Gibson, John. 'Reality and the Language of Fiction'. In *Writing the Austrian Traditions: Relations between Philosophy and Literature*, edited by Wolfgang Huemer and Marc-Oliver Schuster, 49–65. Edmonton: Wirth-Institute for Austrian and Central European Studies, 2003.
Gide, André. *The Immoralist*. 1930. Translated by David Watson. London: Penguin, 2000.
Gilmore, Joseph H. and B. Joseph Pine II. *Authenticity: What Consumers Really Want*. Boston, MA: Harvard Business School Publishing, 2007.
Glenn, Joshua. 'Fake Authenticity'. *Hilobrow*. http://hilobrow.com/2010/06/01/fake-authenticity/ (accessed 16 September 2014), 2010.
Goffman, Erving. *The Presentation of Self in Everyday Life*. New York: Doubleday, 1959.
Goldstein, Jeffrey. 'Emergence as a Construct: History and Issues'. *Emergence* 1 (1): 49–72, 1999.
Goldstein, Jeffrey. 'Emergence, Creative Process, and Self-Transcending Constructions'. In *Managing Organizational Complexity: Philosophy, Theory, and Application*, edited by Kurt A. Richardson, 63–78. Greenwich, CT: Information Age Publishing, 2005.
Golomb, Jacob. 'Kierkegaard's Ironic Ladder to Authentic Faith'. *Philosophy of Religion* 32: 65–81, 1991.
Golomb, Jacob. *In Search of Authenticity: From Kierkegaard to Camus*. London: Routledge, 1995.
Gombrich, Ernst H. *Art and Illusion: A Study in the Psychology of Pictorial Representation*. 1960. London: Phaidon, 2002.

Gonzales, Madalena. 'The Aesthetics of Post-Realism and the Obscenification of Everyday Life: The Novel in the Age of Technology'. *Journal of Narrative Theory* 38 (1): 111–33, 2008.

Gracia, Jorge J. E. 'Borges's "Pierre Menard": Philosophy or Literature?' *Journal of Aesthetics and Art Criticism* 59 (1): 45–57, 2001.

Groß, Florian. '"Brooklyn Zack is Real": Irony and Sincere Authenticity in *30 Rock*'. In *The Aesthetics of Authenticity: Medial Constructions of the Real*, edited by Wolfgang Funk, Irmtraud Huber and Florian Groß, 239–60. Bielefeld: transcript, 2012.

Grossberg, Lawrence. *We Gotta Get Out of this Place: Popular Conservatism and Postmodern Culture*. New York: Routledge, 1992.

Guignon, Charles. *On Being Authentic*. London: Routledge, 2004.

Haddorff, David. 'The Postmodern Realism of Barth's Ethics'. *Scottish Journal of Theology* 57 (3): 269–86, 2004.

Hale, Dorothy. 'Aesthetics and the New Ethics: Theorizing the Novel in the Twenty-First Century'. *PMLA* 124 (3): 896–905, 2009.

Hamilton, Caroline D. *One Man Zeitgeist: Dave Eggers, Publishing and Publicity*. New York: Continuum, 2010.

Hand, Elizabeth. 'Wit's End'. *Washington Post*, 15 August. http://www.washingtonpost.com/wp-dyn/articles/A60174-2004Aug12.html (accessed 16 September 2014), 2004.

Handler, Richard and William Saxton. 'Dyssimulation: Reflexivity, Narrative, and the Quest for Authenticity in "Living History"'. *Cultural Anthropology* 3: 242–60, 1988.

Hanlon, Nick. 'Death, Subjectivity, Temporality in Baudrillard and Heidegger'. *French Studies* 58 (4): 513–25, 2004.

Hansen, Per Krogh. 'Reconsidering the Unreliable Narrator'. *Semiotica* 165: 227–46, 2007.

Haraway, Donna. 'A Cyborg Manifesto: Science, Technology, and Socialist-Feminism in the Late Twentieth Century'. In *Simians, Cyborgs and Women: The Reinvention of Nature*, 149–81. New York: Routledge, 1991.

Harpham, Geoffrey Galt. *Getting it Right: Language, Literature, and Ethics*. Chicago, IL: University of Chicago Press, 1992.

Harrison, Bernard. *Inconvenient Fictions: Literature and the Limits of Theory*. New Haven, CT: Yale University Press, 1991.

Hartman, Geoffrey. *Scars of the Spirit: The Struggle against Inauthenticity*. New York: Palgrave Macmillan, 2002.

Hartmann, Nicolai. *Der Aufbau der realen Welt*. Berlin: De Gruyter, 1964.

Haselstein, Ulla, Andrew Gross and MaryAnn Snyder-Körber. 'Introduction: Returns of the Real'. In *The Pathos of Authenticity: American Passions of the Real*, edited by Ulla Haselstein, Andrew Gross and MaryAnn Snyder-Körber, 9–31. Heidelberg: Winter, 2010.

Hassan, Ihab. 'Beyond Postmodernism: Toward an Aesthetic of Trust'. *Angelaki: Journal of the Theoretical Humanities* 8 (1): 3–11, 2003.

Hateley, Erica. 'The End of *The Eyre Affair*: Jane Eyre, Parody, and Popular Culture'. *Journal of Popular Culture* 38: 1022–36, 2005.

Hauthal, Janine, Julijana Nadj, Ansgar Nünning and Henning Peters, eds. *Metaisierung in Literatur und anderen Medien: Theoretische Grundlagen - Historische Perspektiven - Metagattungen - Funktionen*. Berlin: De Gruyter, 2007.

Head, Dominic. 'Julian Barnes and a Case of English Identity'. In *British Fiction Today*, edited by Philip Tew and Rod Mengham, 15–27. London: Continuum, 2006.

Head, Dominic. *The State of the Novel: Britain and Beyond*. Malden, MA: Wiley-Blackwell, 2008.
Heidegger, Martin. 'The Origin of the Work of Art'. 1936. In *Basic Writings*, edited and translated by David Farrell Krell, 139–212. Melbourne: HarperCollins, 1998.
Heidegger, Martin. *Being and Time*. 1927. Edited by Dennis J. Schmidt, translated by Joan Stambaugh. Albany: State University of New York Press, 2010.
Heiler, Lars. 'Transformations of the Pastoral: Modernization and Regression in Jim Crace's *Arcadia* and Julian Barnes's *England, England*'. In *Beyond Extremes: Repräsentation von Modernisierungsprozessen im zeitgenössischen britischen Roman*, edited by Stefan Glomb and Stefan Horlacher, 331–49. Tübingen: Narr, 2004.
Hempfer, Klaus. 'Die potentielle Autoreflexivität des narrativen Diskurses und Ariosts *Orlando Furioso*'. In *Erzählforschung: Ein Symposion*, edited by Eberhard Lämmert, 130–56. Stuttgart: Metzler, 1982.
Henke, Christoph. *Vergangenheitsobsessionen: Geschichte und Gedächtnis im Erzählwerk von Julian Barnes*. Trier: WVT, 2001.
Hobsbawm, Eric. 'Introduction: Inventing Traditions'. In *The Invention of Tradition*, edited by Eric Hobsbawm and Terence Ranger, 1–14. Cambridge: Cambridge University Press, 1983.
Hofstadter, Douglas. *Gödel, Escher, Bach: An Eternal Golden Braid*. New York: Basic Books, 1979.
Hofstadter, Douglas. *I am a Strange Loop*. New York: Basic Books, 2007.
Hölscher, Ludger. *The Reality of the Mind: St. Augustine's Philosophical Arguments for the Human Soul as a Spiritual Substance*. London: Routledge & Kegan Paul, 1986.
Höltgen, Stefan. *Schnittstellen: Serienmord im Film*. Marburg: Schüren, 2010.
Hubbard, Thomas K. *The Mask of Comedy: Aristophanes and the Intertextual Parabasis*. Ithaca, NY: Cornell University Press, 1991.
Huber, Irmtraud. 'A Quest for Authenticity: Jonathan Safran Foer's *Everything Is Illuminated*'. In *Paradoxes of Authenticity: Studies on a Critical Concept*, edited by Julia Straub, 115–33. Bielefeld: transcript, 2012.
Huber, Irmtraud. *Literature after Postmodernism: Reconstructive Fantasies*. Houndmills: Palgrave Macmillan, 2014.
Huber, Irmtraud and Sophie Seita. 'Authentic Simulacra or the Aura of Repetition: Experiencing Authenticity in Tom McCarthy's *Remainder*'. In *The Aesthetics of Authenticity: Medial Constructions of the Real*, edited by Wolfgang Funk, Irmtraud Huber and Florian Groß, 261–80. Bielefeld: transcript, 2012.
Hutcheon, Linda. *Narcissistic Narrative: The Metafictional Paradox*. New York: Methuen, 1984.
Hutcheon, Linda. *A Theory of Parody: The Teachings of Twentieth-Century Art Forms*. New York: Methuen, 1985.
Hutcheon, Linda. *A Poetics of Postmodernism: History, Theory, Fiction*. New York: Routledge, 1988.
Hutcheon, Linda. '"The Pastime of Past Time": Fiction, History, Historiographical Metafiction'. In *Essentials of the Theory of Fiction*, edited by Michael J. Hoffman and Patrick Murphy, 472–95. Durham, NC: Duke University Press, 1996.
Hutcheon, Linda. *The Politics of Postmodernism*. New York: Routledge, 2002.
Hutcheon, Linda. 'Gone Forever, but Here to Stay: The Legacy of the Postmodern'. In *Postmodernism: What Moment?*, edited by Pelagia Goulimari, 16–18. Manchester: Manchester University Press, 2007.

Ickstadt, Heinz. *Der amerikanische Roman im 20. Jahrhundert: Transformation des Mimetischen*. Darmstadt: Wissenschaftliche Buchgesellschaft, 1998.
International Necronautical Society, The. 'Tate Declaration of Inauthenticity'. In *Altermodern*, edited by Nicolas Bourriaud, 171–81. London: Tate Publishing, 2009.
'irony, n'.. OED Online. September 2014. Oxford University Press. http://www.oed.com/view/Entry/99565?rskey=FszeCd&result=1&isAdvanced=false (accessed 16 September 2014).
Iser, Wolfgang. *The Implied Reader: Patterns of Communication in Prose Fiction from Bunyan to Beckett*. Baltimore, MD: Johns Hopkins University Press, 1978.
Jacobs, Timothy. 'American Touchstone: The Idea of Order in Gerard Manley Hopkins and David Foster Wallace'. *Comparative Literature Studies* 38 (3): 215–31, 2001.
Jakobson, Roman. 'Closing Statement: Linguistics and Poetics'. In *Style in Language*, edited by Thomas Sebeok, 350–77. Cambridge, MA: MIT Press, 1960.
Jameson, Fredric. 'Postmodernism and Consumer Society'. In *The Anti-Aesthetic: Essays on Post-Modern Culture*, edited by Hal Foster, 111–25. Seattle, WA: Bay Press, 1989.
Jameson, Fredric. *Postmodernism, or, the Cultural Logic of Late Capitalism*. Durham, NC: Duke University Press, 1991.
Jameson, Fredric. 'The End of Temporality'. *Critical Inquiry* 29 (4): 695–718, 2003.
Jameson, Fredric. *Archaeologies of the Future: The Desire Called Utopia and other Science Fictions*. London: Verso, 2005.
Jameson, Fredric. *The Antinomies of Realism*. London: Verso, 2013.
Jenkins, Henry. *Fans, Bloggers, and Gamers: Exploring Participatory Culture*. New York: New York University Press, 2006.
Johnson, Steven. *Emergence: The Connected Lives of Ants, Brains, Cities, and Software*. New York: Touchstone, 2002.
Kaminsky, Alice R. 'On Literary Realism'. In *The Theory of the Novel: New Essays*, edited by John Halperin, 213–32. New York: Oxford University Press, 1974.
Kant, Immanuel. 'Beantwortung der Frage: Was ist Aufklärung?' *Berlinische Monatsschrift* 4 (12): 481–94, 1784.
Kant, Immanuel. *Critique of Judgment*. 1790. Edited by Nicholas Walker, translated by James Creed Meredith. Oxford: Oxford University Press, 2008.
Keen, Andrew. *The Cult of the Amateur: How Today's Internet is Killing our Culture*. New York: Doubleday, 2007.
Keller, Rudi. *On Language Change: The Invisible Hand in Language*. London: Routledge, 1994.
Kellman, Steven. *The Self-Begetting Novel*. London: Macmillan, 1980.
Kelly, Adam. 'David Foster Wallace and the New Sincerity in American Fiction'. In *Consider David Foster Wallace: Critical Essays*, edited by David Hering, 131–46. Universal City, CA: SSMG Press, 2010a.
Kelly, Adam. 'David Foster Wallace: The Death of the Author and the Birth of a Discipline'. *Irish Journal of American Studies* 2 (Summer). http://www.ijasonline.com/Adam-Kelly.html (accessed 16 September 2014), 2010b.
Kelly, Adam. 'Moments of Decision in Contemporary American Fiction: Roth, Auster, Eugenides'. *Critique: Studies in Contemporary Fiction* 51 (4): 313–32, 2010c.
Kelly, Kevin. 'Scan this Book!' *New York Times*, 14 May. http://www.nytimes.com/2006/05/14/magazine/14publishing.html (accessed 16 September 2014), 2006.

Kemal, Salim and Ivan Gaskell. 'Performance and Authenticity'. In *Performance and Authenticity in the Arts*, edited by Salim Kemal and Ivan Gaskell, 1–12. Cambridge: Cambridge University Press, 1999.

Kermode, Frank. *The Sense of an Ending: Studies in the Theory of Fiction with a New Epilogue*. 1967. Oxford: Oxford University Press, 2000.

Kirby, Alan. 'The Death of Postmodernism and Beyond'. *Philosophy Now* 58. http://www.philosophynow.org/issues/58/The_Death_of_Postmodernism_And_Beyond (accessed 16 September 2014), 2006.

Kirby, Alan. *Digimodernism: How New Technologies Dismantle the Postmodern and Reconfigure Our Culture*. London: Continuum, 2009.

Kirk, G. S., J. E. Raven and M. Schofield. *The Presocratic Philosophers*. 1957. Cambridge: Cambridge University Press, 2002.

Klepper, Martin. *Pynchon, Auster, DeLillo: Die amerikanische Postmoderne zwischen Spiel und Rekonstruktion*. Frankfurt am Main: Campus, 1996.

Klimek, Sonja. 'Metalepsis and its (Anti-)Illusionist Effects in the Arts, Media and Role-Playing Games'. In *Metareference across Media: Theory and Case Studies*, edited by Werner Wolf, 169–87. Amsterdam: Rodopi, 2009.

Knaller, Susanne. 'Genealogie des ästhetischen Authentizitätsbegriffs'. In *Authentizität: Diskussion eines Ästhetischen Begriffs*, edited by Susanne Knaller and Harro Müller, 17–35. Munich: Fink, 2006.

Knaller, Susanne. *Ein Wort aus der Fremde: Geschichte und Theorie des Begriffs Authentizität*. Heidelberg: Winter, 2007.

Knaller, Susanne. 'Authenticity as an Aesthetic Notion: Normative and Non-Normative Concepts in Modern and Contemporary Poetics'. In *The Aesthetics of Authenticity: Medial Constructions of the Real*, edited by Wolfgang Funk, Irmtraud Huber and Florian Groß, 25–39. Bielefeld: transcript, 2012.

Knaller, Susanne and Harro Müller. 'Einleitung'. In *Authentizität: Diskussion eines Ästhetischen Begriffs*, edited by Susanne Knaller and Harro Müller, 7–16. Munich: Fink, 2006.

Kohns, Oliver. 'Romantische Ironie und die Möglichkeit von Metaliteratur'. In *Metaisierung in Literatur und anderen Medien: Theoretische Grundlagen – Historische Perspektiven – Metagattungen – Funktionen*, edited by Janine Hauthal, et al. 194–205. Berlin: De Gruyter, 2007.

Korte, Barbara. 'Julian Barnes's, *England, England*: Tourism as a Critique of Postmodernism'. In *The Making of Modern Tourism: The Cultural History of the British Experience, 1600–2000*, edited by Hartmut Berghoff, Barbara Korte and Ralf Schneider, 285–303. Basingstoke: Palgrave, 2002.

Korthals Altes, Liesbeth. 'Sincerity, Reliability and Other Ironies: Notes on Dave Eggers's *A Heartbreaking Work of Staggering Genius*'. In *Narrative Reliability in the Twentieth-Century First-Person Novel*, edited by Elke D'hoker and Gunther Martens, 107–28. Berlin: De Gruyter, 2008.

Kristeva, Julia. *Revolution in Poetic Language*. New York: Columbia University Press, 1984.

Kuhn, Bernhard. *Autobiography and Natural Science in the Age of Romanticism: Rousseau, Goethe, Thoreau*. Farnham: Ashgate, 2009.

Lamla, Jörn. 'Authentizität im kulturellen Kapitalismus: Gedanken zur "konsumistischen" Subjektformation der Gegenwart'. In *Das Authentische: Referenzen und Repräsentationen*, edited by Ursula Amrein, 321–36. Zurich: Chronos, 2009.

Lanier, Jaron. *You Are Not a Gadget: A Manifesto*. New York: Knopf, 2010.
Larmore, Charles. 'Alessandro Ferrara's Theory of Authenticity'. *Philosophy and Social Criticism* 30: 5–9, 2004.
Latour, Bruno. *We have Never been Modern*. 1991. Translated by Catherine Porter. Cambridge, MA: Harvard University Press, 1993.
Laughlin, Robert B. *A Different Universe: Reinventing Physics from the Bottom Down*. New York: Basic Books, 2005.
Lauzen, Sarah E. 'Notes on Metafiction: Every Essay has a Title'. In *Postmodern Fiction: A Bio-Bibliographical Guide*, edited by Larry McCaffery, 93–116. Westport, CT: Greenwood Press, 1986.
Lee, Alison. *Realism and Power: Postmodern British Fiction*. London: Routledge, 1990.
Lehmann, Hans-Thies. *Postdramatisches Theater*. Frankfurt am Main: Verlag der Autoren, 1999.
Lejeune, Philippe. 'The Autobiographical Contract'. In *French Literary Theory Today: A Reader*, edited by Tzvetan Todorov, 192–222. Cambridge: Cambridge University Press, 1982.
Lenk, Hans. *Grasping Reality: An Interpretation-Realistic Epistemology*. Hackensack, NJ: World Scientific Publishing, 2003.
Lethem, Jonathan. 'Postmodernism as Liberty Valance: Notes on an Execution'. *Believer* 9 (8): 3–6, 2011.
Levinas, Emmanuel. *Otherwise than Being or Beyond Essence*. Translated by Alphonso Lingis. The Hague: Martinus Nijhoff, 1981.
Levinas, Emmanuel. 'Reality and its Shadow'. In *Emmanuel Levinas: Collected Philosophical Papers*, edited and translated by Alphonso Lingis, 1–13. Dordrecht: Martinus Nijhoff, 1987.
Levinas, Emmanuel. 'Wholly Otherwise'. In *Re-Reading Levinas*, edited by Robert Bernasconi and Simon Critchley, translated by Simon Critchley, 3–10. Bloomington: Indiana University Press, 1991.
Levinas, Emmanuel. *Entre Nous: On Thinking-of-the-Other*. Translated by Michael B. Smith and Barbara Harshav. New York: Columbia University Press, 1998.
Levinas, Emmanuel. *Alterity and Transcendence*. Translated by Michael B. Smith. London: Athlone, 1999.
Lewes, G. H. *Problems of Life and Mind: The Foundations of a Creed*. Ann Arbor: University of Michigan Library, 2005.
Lie, Nadia. 'Who is the Reader of Pierre Menard? Borges on Cervantes Revisited'. In *International Don Quixote*, edited by Theo D'Haen and Reindert Dhondt, 89–108. Amsterdam: Rodopi, 2009.
Lindholm, Charles. *Culture and Authenticity*. Malden, MA: Blackwell, 2008.
Lingis, Alphonso. 'Translator's Introduction'. In *Emmanuel Levinas: Collected Philosophical Papers*, edited by Alphonso Lingis, vii–xxxi. Dordrecht: Martinus Nijhoff, 1987.
Lipovetsky, Gilles. *Hypermodern Times*. Cambridge: Polity Press, 2005.
Lodge, David. 'Mimesis and Diegesis in Modern Fiction'. In *Essentials of the Theory of Fiction*, edited by Michael J. Hoffman and Patrick Murphy, 348–71. Durham, NC: Duke University Press, 1996.
Luhmann, Niklas. 'Deconstruction as Second-Order Observing'. *New Literary History* 24: 763–82, 1993.
Luhmann, Niklas. 'The Paradox of Form'. In *Problems of Form*, edited by Dirk Baecker, 15–26. Stanford, CA: Stanford University Press, 1999.

Lyotard, Jean-François. *The Postmodern Condition: A Report on Knowledge*. 1979. Translated by Geoff Bennington and Brian Massumi. Manchester: Manchester University Press, 2004.
MacCannell, Dean. 'Staged Authenticity: Arrangements of Social Space in Tourist Settings'. *American Journal of Sociology* 79 (3): 589–603, 1973.
Mair, Judith and Silke Becker. *Fake For Real: Über die private und politische Taktik des So-tun-als-ob*. Frankfurt am Main: Campus, 2005.
Major, Wilfred E. 'Aristophanes and "Alazoneia": Laughing at the Parabasis of the *Clouds*'. *The Classical World* 99 (2): 131–44, 2006.
Mann, Charles Riborg and George Ransom Twiss. *Physics*. Glenview, IL: Scott, Foresman and Co, 1910.
Martinez, Matias and Michael Scheffel. *Einführung in die Erzähltheorie*. Munich: Beck, 2000.
Mayer, Ruth. 'A Rage for Authenticity: Richard Powers's *The Time of Our Singing*, Jonathan Lethem's *The Fortress of Solitude*, and the Quest for Pure Hybridity'. In *The Pathos of Authenticity: American Passions of the Real*, edited by Ulla Haselstein, Andrew Gross and MaryAnn Snyder-Körber, 163–78. Heidelberg: Winter, 2010.
McCaffery, Larry. 'An Interview with David Foster Wallace'. *Review of Contemporary Fiction* 13 (2): 127–50, 1993.
McGann, Jerome. *The Textual Condition*. Princeton, NJ: Princeton University Press, 1991.
McGirk, James. 'The Q&A: Tom McCarthy, Author'. *Intelligent Life*. http://moreintelligentlife.com/blog/james-mcgirk/qa-tom-mccarthy-author (accessed 16 September 2014), 2010.
McGraw, Philip. *Self Matters: Creating Your Life from the Inside Out*. New York: Simon and Schuster Source, 2001.
McHale, Brian. *Postmodernist Fiction*. New York: Routledge, 1987.
Mecke, Jochen. 'Der Prozess der Authentizität: Strukturen, Paradoxien und Funktion einer zentralen Kategorie moderner Literatur'. In *Authentizität: Diskussion eines Ästhetischen Begriffs*, edited by Susanne Knaller and Harro Müller, 82–114. Munich: Fink, 2006.
Miller, Joseph Hillis. *The Linguistic Moment: From Wordsworth to Stevens*. Princeton, NJ: Princeton University Press, 1985.
Miller, Joseph Hillis. *The Ethics of Reading: Kant, de Man, Eliot, Trollope, James, and Benjamin*. New York: Columbia University Press, 1987.
Miller, Mark Crispin. *Boxed In: The Culture of TV*. Evanston, IL: Northwestern University Press, 1988.
Miracky, James J. 'Replicating a Dinosaur: Authenticity Run Amok in the "Theme Parking" of Michael Crichton's *Jurassic Park* and Julian Barnes's *England, England*'. *Critique: Studies in Contemporary Fiction* 45: 163–71, 2004.
Moore, Allan. 'Authenticity as Authentification'. *Popular Music* 21 (2): 209–23, 2002.
Mukařovský, Jan. 'Art as a Semiotic Fact'. 1936. In *Structure, Sign, and Function: Selected Essays by Jan Mukařovský*, edited by John Burbank and Peter Steiner, translated by Wendy Steiner, 82–8. New Haven, CT: Yale University Press, 1978a.
Mukařovský, Janb. 'Intentionality and Unintentionality in Art'. 1966. In *Structure, Sign, and Function: Selected Essays by Jan Mukařovský*, edited and translated by John Burbank and Peter Steiner, 89–128. New Haven, CT: Yale University Press, 1978.

Mukařovský, Jan. 'The Aesthetic Norm'. In *Structure, Sign, and Function: Selected Essays by Jan Mukařovský*, edited and translated by John Burbank and Peter Steiner, 49–56. New Haven, CT: Yale University Press, 1978c.

Müller, Harro. 'Theodor W. Adornos Theorie des authentischen Kunstwerks: Rekonstruktion und Diskussion des Authentizitätsbegriffs'. In *Authentizität: Diskussion eines Ästhetischen Begriffs*, edited by Susanne Knaller and Harro Müller, 55–67. Munich: Fink, 2006.

Müller-Zettelmann, Eva. *Lyrik und Metalyrik: Theorie einer Gattung und ihrer Selbstbespiegelung anhand von Beispielen aus der englisch- und deutschsprachigen Dichtkunst*. Heidelberg: Winter, 2000.

Neumann, Birte. 'Kollektives Gedächtnis und *Englishness*'. In *Der zeitgenössische englische Roman: Genres – Entwicklungen – Modellinterpretationen*, edited by Vera Nünning, 227–42. Trier: WVT, 2007.

Neumann, Imke. *'The Past is no Foreign Country': Der neo-viktorianische Roman in Großbritannien und Irland*. Trier: WVT, 2008.

Newton, Adam Z. *Narrative Ethics*. Cambridge, MA: Harvard University Press, 1995.

Niermeyer, Rainer. *Mythos Authentizität: Die Kunst, die richtigen Führungsrollen zu spielen*. Frankfurt am Main: Campus, 2008.

Nordhjem, Bent. 'Reality and the Novel; or, The Meaning of Fiction'. *Orbis Litterarum: International Review of Literary Studies* 42: 178–87, 1987.

Nöth, Winfried. 'Self-Reference in the Media: The Semiotic Framework'. In *Self-Reference in the Media*, edited by Winfried Nöth and Nina Bishara, 3–30. Berlin: De Gruyter, 2007.

Nöth, Winfried and Nina Bishara, eds. *Self-Reference in the Media*. Berlin: De Gruyter, 2007.

Nübel, Birgit. '"Alles sagen": Autobiographie zwischen Authentizität und Fiktionalisierung'. In *Fiktionen von Wirklichkeit: Authentizität zwischen Materialität und Konstruktion*, edited by Wolfgang Funk and Lucia Krämer, 263–88. Bielefeld: transcript, 2011.

Nunius, Sabine. 'Performative Authenticity: Identity Construction among Second-Generation Youths in Great Britain'. In *Paradoxes of Authenticity: Studies on a Critical Concept*, edited by Julia Straub, 201–22. Bielefeld: transcript, 2012.

Nünning, Ansgar. 'Unreliable Narration zur Einführung: Grundzüge einer kognitiv-narratologischen Theorie und Analyse unglaubwürdigen Erzählens'. In *Unreliable Narration: Studien zur Theorie und Praxis unglaubwürdigen Erzählens in der englischsprachigen Erzählliteratur*, edited by Ansgar Nünning, 3–39. Trier: WVT, 1998.

Nünning, Ansgar. 'On Metanarrative: Towards a Definition, a Typology and an Outline of the Functions of Metanarrative Commentary'. In *The Dynamics of Narrative Form*, edited by John Pier, 11–59. Berlin: De Gruyter, 2004.

Nünning, Ansgar. 'Reconceptualizing Unreliable Narration: Synthesizing Cognitive and Rhetorical Approaches'. In *A Companion to Narrative Theory*, edited by James Phelan and P. J. Rabinowitz, 89–107. Oxford: Blackwell, 2005.

Nünning, Vera. 'The Invention of Cultural Traditions: The Construction and Destruction of Englishness and Authenticity in Julian Barnes' *England, England*'. *Anglia* 119: 58–76, 2001.

Olson, Greta. 'Reconsidering Unreliability: Fallible and Untrustworthy Narrators'. *Narrative* 11: 93–109, 2003.

Ommundsen, Wenche. *Metafictions?* Charlton: Melbourne University Press, 1993.
Orwell, George. *Essays*. Edited by Bernard Crick. London: Penguin, 2000.
Outka, Elizabeth. *Consuming Traditions: Modernity, Modernism, and the Commodified Authentic*. Oxford: Oxford University Press, 2009.
Pausanias. *Guide to Greece 1: Central Greece*. Translated by Peter Levi. London: Penguin, 1979.
Phelan, James. *Living to Tell about It*. Ithaca, NY: Cornell University Press, 2005.
Piccitto, Diana. 'Reclaiming "The Grandeur of Inspiration": Authenticity, Repetition and Parody in William Blake's *Milton*'. In *Paradoxes of Authenticity: Studies on a Critical Concept*, edited by Julia Straub, 243–62. Bielefeld: transcript, 2012.
Pickering, Michael. 'The Dogma of Authenticity in the Experience of Popular Music'. In *The Art of Listening*, edited by Graham McGregor and R. S. White, 201–20. London: Croom Helm, 1986.
Plato. *The Republic*. Translated by H. D. P. Lee. London: Penguin, 2003.
Poe, Edgar Allan. *Marginalia*. 1848. Charlottesville: University Press of Virginia, 1981.
Poole, Steven. *Unspeak*. London: Little, Brown, 2006.
Port, Mattijs van de. 'Registers of Incontestability'. *Etnofoor* 17 (1/2): 7–22, 2004.
Potter, Andrew. *The Authenticity Hoax: How we Get Lost Finding Ourselves*. Toronto: McClelland & Stewart, 2010.
Prendergast, Christopher. *The Order of Mimesis*. New York: Cambridge University Press, 1986.
Putnam, Hilary. *The Many Faces of Realism*. LaSalle, IL: Open Court, 1987.
Radnóti, Sándor. *The Fake: Forgery and its Place in Art*. Lanham, MD: Rowman & Littlefield, 1999.
Rajewsky, Irina. 'Beyond "Metanarration": Form-Based Metareference as a Transgeneric and Transmedial Phenomenon'. In *Metareference across Media: Theory and Case Studies*, edited by Werner Wolf, translated by Katharina Bantleon, 135–68. Amsterdam: Rodopi, 2009.
Reulecke, Anne-Kathrin, ed. *Fälschungen: Zu Autorschaft und Beweis in Wissenschaften und Künsten*. Frankfurt am Main: Suhrkamp, 2006.
Rich, Frank. *The Greatest Story Ever Sold: The Decline and Fall of Truth from 9/11 to Katrina*. New York: Penguin, 2006.
Richter, Virginia. 'Authenticity: Why we Still Need it Although it Doesn't Exist'. In *Transcultural English Studies: Theories, Fictions, Realities*, edited by Frank Schulze-Engler and Sissy Helff, 59–74. Amsterdam: Rodopi, 2009.
Ricœur, Paul. 'Mimesis and Representation'. In *A Ricœur Reader: Reflection and Imagination*, edited by Mario Valdés, 137–55. Toronto: University of Toronto Press, 1991.
Riffaterre, Michael. 'Intertextual Representation: On Mimesis as Interpretive Discourse'. *Critical Inquiry* 11: 141–62, 1984.
Rimmon-Kenan, Shlomith. *Narrative Fiction*. London: Routledge, 2002.
Roberts, David. 'Self-Reference in Literature'. In *Problems of Form*, edited by Dirk Baecker, 27–45. Stanford, CA: Stanford University Press, 1999.
Römer, Stefan. *Künstlerische Strategien des Fake: Kritik von Original und Fälschung*. Köln: DuMont, 2001.
Rorty, Richard. 'Is there a Problem about Fictional Discourse?' In *Consequences of Pragmatism*, 110–38. Minneapolis: University of Minnesota Press, 1982.
Rose, Margaret. *Parody/Meta-Fiction: An Analysis of Parody as a Critical Mirror to the Writing and Reception of Fiction*. London: Croom Helm, 1979.

Rosenblatt, Roger. 'The Age Of Irony Comes To An End'. *TIME*, 24 September. http://www.time.com/time/magazine/article/0,9171,1000893,00.html (accessed 16 September 2014), 2001.

Rotman, Brian. *Becoming Besides Ourselves: The Alphabet, Ghosts, and Distributed Human Being*. Durham, NC: Duke University Press, 2008.

Rubik, Margarete. 'Navigating through Fantasy Worlds: Cognition and the Intricacies of Reading Jasper Fforde's *The Eyre Affair*'. In *Cognition and Literary Interpretation in Practice*, edited by Harri Veivo, Bo Pettersson and Merja Polvinen, 183–200. Helsinki: Helsinki University Press, 2005.

Rubik, Margarete. 'Invasions into Literary Texts, Re-Plotting and Transfictional Migration in Jasper Fforde's *The Eyre Affair*'. In *A Breath of Fresh Eyre: Intertextual and Intermedial Reworkings of Jane Eyre*, edited by Margarete Rubik and Elke Mettinger-Schartmann, 167–80. Amsterdam: Rodopi, 2007.

Russett, Margaret. *Fictions and Fakes: Forging Romantic Authenticity, 1760–1845*. Cambridge: Cambridge University Press, 2006.

Saler, Michael. *As If: Modern Enchantment and the Literary Pre-History of Virtual Reality*. New York: Oxford University Press, 2012.

Saltz, Jerry. 'Irony and Sincerity Hug it Out'. *The New Yorker*, 27 May. http://nymag.com/arts/art/reviews/66277/ (accessed 16 September 2014), 2010.

Sandywell, Barry. *Presocratic Reflexivity: The Constructions of Philosophical Discourse c. 600–450 BC*. London: Routledge, 1996.

Schiller, Friedrich. *On Naive and Sentimental Poetry*. 1795. Translated by William F. Wertz Jr. Washington, DC: The Schiller Institute, 2005.

Schindler, Sabine. *Authentizität und Inszenierung: Die Vermittlung von Geschichte in amerikanischen historic sites*. Heidelberg: Winter, 2003.

Schlegel, Friedrich. *'Athenäums'-Fragmente und andere Schriften*. Edited by Andreas Huyssen. Stuttgart: Reclam, 1986.

Schönfelder, Christa. '"I Want my Past Back": The Quest for Memory and Authenticity in Helen Dunmore's *Talking to the Dead*'. In *Paradoxes of Authenticity: Studies on a Critical Concept*, edited by Julia Straub, 135–55. Bielefeld: transcript, 2012.

Schrödinger, Erwin. *Nature and the Greeks*. 1954. Cambridge: Cambridge University Press, 1996.

Schulze, Rainer. 'Die Aktualität der Authentizität: Von der Attraktivität des Nicht-Hier und Nicht-Jetzt in der modernen Sprachwissenschaft'. In *Fiktionen von Wirklichkeit: Authentizität zwischen Materialität und Konstruktion*, edited by Wolfgang Funk and Lucia Krämer, 25–49. Bielefeld: transcript, 2011.

Schwartz, Hillel. *The Culture of the Copy: Striking Likenesses, Unreasonable Facsimiles*. New York: Zone Books, 1996.

Sconce, Jeffrey. *Haunted Media: Electronic Presence from Telegraphy to Television*. Durham, NC: Duke University Press, 2000.

Scorzin, Pamela C. 'Metascenography: On the Metareferential Turn in Scenography'. In *The Metareferential Turn in Contemporary Arts and Media: Form, Functions, Attempts at Explanation*, edited by Werner Wolf, 259–78. Amsterdam: Rodopi, 2011.

'self, pron., adj., and n'.. OED Online. September 2014. Oxford University Press. http://www.oed.com/view/Entry/175090?rskey=OM3e1j&result=3&isAdvanced=false (accessed 16 September 2014).

Selwyn, Tom. 'Introduction'. In *The Tourist Image: Myth and Myth Making in Tourism*, edited by Tom Selwyn, 1–32. Hoboken, NJ: John Wiley and Sons, 1996.

Sextus Empiricus. *Outlines of Scepticism*. Translated by Julia Annas and Jonathan Barnes. Cambridge: Cambridge University Press, 1994.
Shakespeare, William. *Hamlet*. Edited by Harold Jenkins. The Arden Shakespeare. London: Thomson Learning, 2001.
Sinanan, Kerry and Tim Milnes. 'Introduction'. In *Romanticism, Sincerity and Authenticity*, edited by Kerry Sinanan and Tim Milnes, 1–28. Houndmills: Palgrave Macmillan, 2010.
Smith, Zadie. 'Introduction'. In *The Burned Children of America: The Best Young Writers from the USA*, edited by Marco Cassini and Martina Testa, xi–xxii. London: Hamish Hamilton, 2003.
Smith, Zadie. 'Fail Better'. *The Guardian*, 27 January. http://faculty.sunydutchess.edu/oneill/failbetter.htm (accessed 16 September 2014), 2007.
Smith, Zadie. 'Two Paths for the Novel'. *New York Review of Books*, 20 November. http://www.nybooks.com/articles/archives/2008/nov/20/two-paths-for-the novel/ (accessed 16 September 2014), 2008.
Sobchack, Vivian. 'Toward a Phenomenology of Cinematic and Electronic Presence: The Scene of the Screen'. *Post Script: Essays in Film and the Humanities* 10 (1): 50–9, 1990.
Soovik, Ene-Reet. 'Re-Creation on an Island: J. Barnes's Production of Place'. In *British Studies in the New Millennium: The Challenge of the Grassroots*, edited by Pilvi Rajamäe and Krista Vogelberg, 153–61. Tartu: University of Tartu, 2001.
Sperber, Dan. 'Metarepresentations in an Evolutionary Perspective'. In *Metarepresentations: A Multidisciplinary Perspective*, edited by Dan Sperber, 117–38. Oxford: Oxford University Press, 2000.
'spin, n.1'. OED Online. September 2014. Oxford University Press. http://www.oed.com/view/Entry/186658?rskey=exEO3Y&result=1&isAdvanced=false (accessed 16 September 2014).
Stam, Robert. *Reflexivity in Film and Literature: From Don Quixote to Jean-Luc Godard*. Ann Arbor: University of Michigan Research Press, 1985.
Stanzel, Franz K. *Theorie des Erzählens*. 1979. Göttingen: Vandenhoeck & Ruprecht, 1995.
Steiner, Peter. 'Jan Mukařovský's Structural Aesthetics'. In *Structure, Sign, and Function: Selected Essays by Jan Mukařovský*, edited by John Burbank and Peter Steiner, ix–xxxiv. New Haven, CT: Yale University Press, 1978.
Stiersdorfer, Klaus, ed. *Beyond Postmodernism: Reassessments in Literature, Theory, and Culture*. Berlin: De Gruyter, 2003.
Stonehill, Brian. *The Self-Conscious Novel: Artifice in Fiction from Joyce to Pynchon*. Philadelphia: University of Pennsylvania Press, 1988.
Striker, Gisela. 'Ataraxia: Happiness and Tranquility'. *The Monist* 73: 97–110, 1990.
Sukenick, Ronald. *The Death of the Novel and Other Stories*. Tuscaloosa: University of Alabama Press, 2003.
Susanka, Thomas. 'The Rhetorics of Authenticity: Photographic Representations of War'. In *Paradoxes of Authenticity: Studies on a Critical Concept*, edited by Julia Straub, 95–113. Bielefeld: transcript, 2012.
Suskind, Ron. 'Without a Doubt'. *New York Times*, 17 May. http://query.nytimes.com/gst/fullpage.html?res=9C05EFD8113BF934A25753C1A9629C8B63 (accessed 16 September 2014), 2004.
Sutherland, John. 'If it's Thursday it Must be the Valley of Death'. *Guardian*, 26 July. http://www.theguardian.com/books/2003/jul/26/featuresreviews.guardianreview15 (accessed 16 September 2014), 2003.

Taleb, Nassim Nicholas. *The Black Swan: The Impact of the Highly Improbable*. London: Penguin, 2008.
Tapscott, Don and Anthony D. Williams. *Wikinomics: How Mass Collaboration Changes Everything*. New York: Portfolio, 2006.
Taylor, Charles. *The Ethics of Authenticity*. Cambridge, MA: Harvard University Press, 1991.
Taylor, Charles. *A Secular Age*. Cambridge, MA: Belknap Press, 2007.
Taylor, Jane. '"Why do you tear me from Myself?" Torture, Truth, and the Arts of the Counter-Reformation'. In *The Rhetorics of Sincerity*, edited by Ernst van Alphen, Mieke Bal and Carel Smith, 19–43. Stanford, CA: Stanford University Press, 2009.
Thom, René. *Mathematical Models of Morphogenesis*. Translated by W. M. Brookes and D. Rand. Chichester: Ellis Horwood, 1983.
Timmer, Nicoline. *Do you Feel it Too? The Post-Postmodern Syndrome in American Fiction at the Turn of the Millennium*. Amsterdam: Rodopi, 2010.
Tipler, Frank J. *The Physics of Immortality: Modern Cosmology, God and the Resurrection of the Dead*. New York: Anchor Books, 1995.
Toffler, Alvin. *The Third Wave*. London: Pan Books, 1980.
Toffler, Alvin and Heidi Toffler. *Revolutionary Wealth: How it Will Be Created and How it Will Change Our Lives*. New York: Knopf, 2006.
Tränkle, Hermann. 'Gnothi seauton: Zu Ursprung und Deutungsgeschichte des delphischen Spruchs'. *Würzburger Jahrbücher für die Altertumswissenschaft* 11: 19–31, 1985.
Trilling, Lionel. *Sincerity and Authenticity*. New York: Harcourt Brace Jovanovich, 1971.
Turkle, Sherry. *Alone Together: Why we Expect More from Technology and Less from Each Other*. New York: Basic Books, 2011.
Vannini, Phillip and J. Patrick Williams. 'Authenticity in Culture, Self, and Society'. In *Authenticity in Culture, Self, and Society*, edited by Phillip Vannini and J. Patrick Williams, 1–18. Burlington, VT: Ashgate, 2009.
Varela, Francisco J. *Principles of Biological Autonomy*. New York: North Holland, 1979.
Vermeulen, Pieter. 'The Novel after Melancholia'. In *The Literature of Melancholia: Early Modern to Postmodern*, edited by Martin Middeke and Christina Wald, 254–67. Basingstoke: Palgrave Macmillan, 2011.
Vermeulen, Timotheus and Robin van den Akker. 'Notes on Metamodernism'. *Journal of Aesthetics and Culture* 2. http://www.aestheticsandculture.net/index.php/jac/article/view/5677/6304 (accessed 16 September 2014), 2010.
Wallace, David Foster. 'Fictional Futures and the Conspicuously Young'. *Review of Contemporary Fiction* 8 (3): 36–53, 1988.
Wallace, David Foster. 'E Unibus Pluram: Television and U.S. Fiction'. *Review of Contemporary Fiction* 13 (2): 151–94, 1993.
Wang, Ning. 'Rethinking Authenticity in Tourism Experience'. *Annals of Tourism Research* 26 (2): 349–70, 1999.
Waugh, Patricia. *Metafiction: The Theory and Practice of Self-Conscious Fiction*. London: Routledge, 1984.
Weinstock, Michael. *The Architecture of Emergence: The Evolution of Form in Nature and Civilisation*. Hoboken, NJ: John Wiley and Sons, 2010.
Wells, Juliette. 'An Eyre-Less Affair? Jasper Fforde's Seeming Elision of Jane'. In *A Breath of Fresh Eyre: Intertextual and Intermedial Reworkings of Jane Eyre*, edited by Margarete Rubik and Elke Mettinger-Schartmann, 197–208. Amsterdam: Rodopi, 2007.

Wells, Lynn. *Allegories of Telling: Self-Referential Narrative in Contemporary British Fiction*. New York: Rodopi, 2003.
White, Hayden. 'The Value of Narrativity in the Representation of Reality'. *Critical Inquiry* 7 (1): 5–27, 1980.
Widiss, Benjamin. *Obscure Invitations: The Persistence of the Author in Twentieth-Century American Literature*. Stanford, CA: Stanford University Press, 2011.
Wiener, Norbert. *Cybernetics: Or the Control and Communication in the Animal and the Machine*. Cambridge, MA: MIT Press, 1965.
Wilde, Alan. *Horizons of Assent: Modernism, Postmodernism, and the Ironic Imagination*. Baltimore, MD: Johns Hopkins University Press, 1981.
Williams, Huntington. *Rousseau and Romantic Autobiography*. Oxford: Oxford University Press, 1983.
Williams, Jeffrey. *Theory and the Novel: Narrative Reflexivity in the British Tradition*. Cambridge: Cambridge University Press, 1998.
Williams, Zoe. 'The Final Irony'. *The Guardian*, 28 March. http://www.guardian.co.uk/theguardian/2003/jun/28/weekend7.weekend2 (accessed 16 September 2014), 2003.
Wittgenstein, Ludwig. *Tractatus Logico-Philosophicus: The German Text with an English Translation*. 1921. Translated by C. K. Ogden. London: Routledge, 1999.
Wolf, Werner. *Ästhetische Illusion und Illusionsdurchbrechung in der Erzählkunst*. Tübingen: Niemeyer, 1993.
Wolf, Werner. 'Metaisierung als transgenerisches und transmediales Phänomen: Ein Systematisierungsversuch metareferentieller Formen und Begriffe in Literatur und anderen Medien'. In *Metaisierung in Literatur und anderen Medien: Theoretische Grundlagen – Historische Perspektiven – Metagattungen – Funktionen*, edited by Janine Hauthal et al., 25–64. Berlin: De Gruyter, 2007.
Wolf, Werner. 'Metareference across Media: The Concept, its Transmedial Potentials and Problems, Main Forms and Functions'. In *Metareference across Media: Theory and Case Studies*, edited by Werner Wolf, 1–86. Amsterdam: Rodopi, 2009.
Wolf, Werner. 'Is There a Metareferential Turn, and if so, How Can It Be Explained?' In *The Metareferential Turn in Contemporary Arts and Media: Form, Functions, Attempts at Explanation*, edited by Werner Wolf, 1–47. Amsterdam: Rodopi, 2011.
Wood, James. 'Human, all too Inhuman'. *The New Republic Online*, 30 August. http://www.powells.com/review/2001_08_30.html (accessed 16 September 2014), 2001a.
Wood, James. 'Tell me how Does it Feel?' *Guardian Online*, 6 October. http://www.guardian.co.uk/books/2001/oct/06/fiction (accessed 16 September 2014), 2001b.
Yacobi, Tamar. 'Fictional Reliability as a Communicative Problem'. *Poetics Today* 2 (2): 113–26, 1981.
Yacobi, Tamar. 'Package Deals in Fictional Narrative: The Case of the Narrator's (Un)Reliability'. *Narrative* 9: 223–9, 2001.
Yurchak, Alexei. 'Post-Post-Communist Sincerity: Pioneers, Cosmonauts, and Other Society Heroes Born Today'. In *What is Soviet Now? Identities, Legacies, Memories*, edited by Thomas Lahusen and Peter H. Solomon, 257–76. Berlin: LIT Verlag, 2008.
Zeller, Christoph. *Ästhetik des Authentischen: Literatur und Kunst um 1970*. Berlin: De Gruyter, 2010.

Index

Page references in bold denote passages where a term or concept is introduced, defined or constitutes the central focus of a chapter or sub-chapter.

Aarseth, Espen 101–2, 126, 153, 161
adaptation 104, 140, 145, 149, 162, 167
Adorno, Theodor W. 7, 17, 30, 33, 40–1, 99
aesthetics 61–3, 70, 188
　see under authenticity; metareference; participation; trust
aletheia 67
alethiology **88–9**, 128, 133, 147, 164, 173, 185
allo-text 89, 94, **103–4**, 139–40, 145–9, 167
Alphen, Ernst van 25
Alter, Robert 68, 80–2
alterity 7, 33–5, 42, 77, 172
altermodern, the 3
Améry, Jean 14, 41
Anderson, Benedict 119
Apelles 51–2, 176
Aristotle 53, 60, 63, 68–72, 98
Assmann, Aleida 24, 84
ataraxia 52 n.17
Attridge, Derek 78–80
aura 6, **27–8**, 41–3, 57, 63, 102, 111–12, 189
authenticity
　as an aesthetic effect 2, 6, 9–10 n.5, 13, 17, 51–2, 59, 108, 127, 180, 191
　aesthetics of 8, 21–2, 29, 70, 93, 131–3
　and authority 15 n.1, 17–18, 46, 48–51
　as a black box 8, 20, **55–63**
　and childhood 109–10, 114–17, 177
　as a commodity 7, **42–3**
　and death 35–6, 41–2, 176, 190–1
　as an emergent phenomenon 7, 20, 33, 41, **51–5**, 64, 101, 121, 138, 172, 180, 191
　etymology of 15
　history of 6–7, **22–8**
　and metareference 6–8, **64–6**, 67
　and paradox 3–4, 7–8, 13–14, 41, 59, 63–4, 107–9, 117, 131, 136–9, 170, 179–80
　and postmodernism 7, 28–9, **36–43**
　as a quest 1, **15–16**, 31, 43, 58, 114–20, 138
　reflective 9, 19, 32, 109, 121
　as resistance to unambiguity 6, 16, 22, 32, 43, 64
　and the self 7, 23–7, **29–36**, 41, 46–8
　as a self-transcending construction 53–4
　vs. sincerity 24–5, 76–7, 136
　typologies of 18–22
　as unmediated experience 13, 16, 109, 117, 137, 189
authenticity hoax 57
authorship 60–3, 73, 105, 126–8, 136, 157
　see also authenticity and authority
autobiography 26, 123–7, 131–9

Badiou, Alain 71
Bal, Mieke 25
Barnes, Julian 99, 130
　England, England 9, **107–21**
　Sense of an Ending, The 10, 169, **180–8**
Barthes, Roland 37, 49, 69, 71, 102
Baudrillard, Jean 5, 7, 28, 37–42, 60, 111, 130, 189
Bauman, Zygmunt 41–3, 47, 159, 172, 177
Beltracchi, Wolfgang 18
Benjamin, Walter 6, **27–8**, 41, 57, 102, 111, 189
Bennington, Geoffrey 61

Benveniste, Émile 89 n.10, 94–5
Berger, Peter L. 24, 31
    and Thomas Luckmann 75
Berman, Marshall 14, 120
Bertens, Hans 2
Bewes, Timothy 37–8, 41–3, 48, 61
black box 106, 138 *see also* authenticity as a black box
Boorstin, Daniel 38–9, 111
Booth, Wayne C. 186
Borges, Jose Luis 47 n.15, 97–8, 154 n.7
Borgmann, Albert 44–7, 50, 121
Bourriaud, Nicholas 3
Buber, Martin 34
Bukatman, Scott 38, 44, 46–8, 179

capitalism 4, 9, 30, 33, 50, 112, 118, 172, 178 *see also* authenticity as a commodity
catatonic realism 73
causality 36, 54, 74, 170, 172
    in the Thursday-Next series 142–6, 149, 152, 155, 158, 162, 165–7
chronology 72, 101–2, 141, 147–9, 151–3, 158, 162, 167–72 *see also* time travel
Cohen, Eric 54
consumerism 112–13, 155, 177–8 *see also* capitalism
Critchley, Simon 29, 34–5, 42, 61, 121,
cross-sequential referencing **151–2**, 162–3, 165–6
cyberspace *see* virtual reality
cybertext 101–2, 161
cyborg 47–8, 178

Dällenbach, Lucien 97–8
Debord, Guy 111–12
deconstruction 1–2, 5, 54, 61, 80, 131
Delphic oracle 22–3
Derrida, Jacques 5, 14, 28, 37, 56, 75, 77, 99, 102, 106, 179
différance 2–5, 28, 37, 56, 70–1, 99, 188
digimodernism 3, 46
digital narcissism 49, 51
Doležel, Lubomir 9–10 n.5, 47, 68
Doniger, Wendy 58, 112
Dutton, Dennis 64
dystopia 107, 177–8

Egan, Jennifer: *A Visit from the Goon Squad* 10, 72, 94–5, **169–80**
Eggers, Dave: *A Heartbreaking Work of Staggering Genius* 9, 11, 67 94–6, **123–38**, 139, 162, 172
emergence *see* authenticity as an emergent phenomenon
enunciation/enounced 88–9, 94–7, 103, 126, 131–6, 152–3, 162–3, 172, 180
ergodic reading **100–2**, 104, 126, 153, 161, 172, 186
ethics 8, 19, 29, 31, 34–6, 57, 61–3, 78, 104–6, 187
    ethical moment 105
    ethical turn 61
experience and representation 1, 4–5, 8–9, 17, 37, 42, 45–7, 54, 60, 71–83, 106–11, 121, 129–37, 176, 179, 188

fake 56–9, 97, 112, 119
Federman, Raymond 81–2
Ferrara, Alessandro 19–20, 28, 32, 62, 117
Fforde, Jasper 10, 94, 102, **139–67**, 187
    Eyre Affair, The 10, **139–50**, 151–3, 162, 165 n.11, 166
    First among Sequels 151, **158–62**, 166
    Lost in a Good Book 151, **152–3**
    One of Our Thursdays is Missing 151, **162–5**, 166
    Something Rotten 151–2, **157–8**, 165 n.11
    Well of Lost Plots, The 151, **153–7**, 158, 166
    Woman who Died a Lot, The 151, **165–6**
Fichte, Johann Gottlieb 26, 98
Fluck, Winfried 75–6, 83
Fludernik, Monika 86
form *see under* materiality vs. form
Foster, Hal 72–3
Foucault, Michel 8, 32–3, 49, 71, 78–9, 125

Gass, William H. 81
Genette, Gérard 89, 94–5, 103
Gergen, Kenneth J. 24, 47, 136 n.6
Gestalt 94–5, 126, 170

Index

gift 56, 77, 179
Glenn, Joshua 21, 58, 91
Goffman, Erving 18
Goldstein, Jeffrey 53–5, 138
Golomb, Jacob 14, 24–5, 31, 100
Groß, Florian 21, 25, 100
Guignon, Charles 7, 18, 25–6, 29, 31, 41

Haraway, Donna 48
Harpham, Geoffrey Galt 63
Hassan, Ihab 5, 54, 125, 172
Hegel, G. W. F. 26
Heidegger, Martin 7, 30, 33, 35, 42, 67, 138, 176
history 110, 114–19, 141
    triadic model of 9, 72, 109, 155, 165, 191
    see also authenticity, history of
Hofstadter, Douglas 8–9, 31–2, 84, 91–3, 191
Höltgen, Stefan 21–2, 93, 133, 161
Huber, Irmtraud 15–16, 42, 73, 104
Humanism 23–5
Hutcheon, Linda 81–2, 86–8, 99, 104
hypermodernity 3
hyperreality 7, 37–9, 42, 58–60, 116, 120 n.5, 130
hypertext 101–3
hysterical realism 72–3

identity 7, 26, 33–5, 38, 47–8, 77, 121, 141, 171–2, 174–5 *see also* national identity
illusion 41, 69, 82–3, 86, 90, 94 n.15, 130
imagined community 119
implicit narrative 10, 169, 180, **185–7**
implied reader 133, 186–7
inauthenticity 29–30, 39, 99–100, 176–8, 189
indeterminacy 3, 5, 125–6, 137, 172, 188
    see also undecidability
influence, literary 10, 103–4, 139, 142, 147–50, 158, 162, 167
information 38–40, 44–9, 60–1, 121
interaction 7, 20, 25–7, 33, 44–6, 50, 60–1, 85, 105, 127, 136–8
    interactional metareference 88–91, 126, 185

interauthenticity 20
intermediality 80 n.7
intertextuality 9–11, 94, **102–6**, 139, 142, 147–50, 157–8
    weak vs. strong form of 103
irony 9, **98–100**, 124–6 *see also* preemptive irony; Romantic irony
Iser, Wolfgang 186

Jacobs, Timothy 49
Jakobson, Roman 78, 93–4, 139
Jameson, Fredric 5, 7, 10, 28, 37, 42, 44, 50, 68, 103–4, 112, 148–9, 159
Jane Eyre 10, 96, 140, **143–51**, 161–2, 166–7
Jenkins, Henry 49

Kant, Immanuel 25, 80, 109
Keen, Andrew 49–50
Kelly, Adam 3, 25, 76–7, 99, 104–6
Kermode, Frank 188
Kierkegaard, Søren 18
Kirby, Alan 3, 46, 51, 101 n.22, 104
Knaller, Susanne 18–21, 33, 41
Kristeva, Julia 102–3, 179

Lacan, Jacques 37, 73, 110, 179
language 13–17, 68–71, 74–9, 82, 99, 177–8
    functions 77–9
Latour, Bruno 4
Lauzen, Sarah 86
Lejeune, Philippe 125–6
Lewes, G. H. 52–3
Lindholm, Charles 1, 16, 43, 58
linguistic model of communication 93–6, 139
Lipovetsky, Gilles 3
literature as communication 5–6, 9–11, 65, 87, 125–6, 150, 158, 165–7, 172, 191 *see also* linguistic model of communication
Luhmann, Niklas 2 n.1, 91, 110
Lyotard, Jean-François 69, 118

McCarthy, Tom 29
    Remainder 11, **189–91**
McGraw, Philip 18, 30–1

Mandiberg, Michael 97
Martel, Yann: *Life of Pi* 185
materiality 11, 15, 27, 70, 95, 97, 127, 131, 135–8, 150, 188
   vs. form 9–10, 74, 109–10, 114–21, 157, 172–4, 180, 189–90
   see also *Gestalt*
Mecke, Jochen 17
media 3, 7, 27–8, 38, 44–51, 105
mediated immediacy 17, 59, 109, 126, 170
   see also authenticity as unmediated experience
memory 107–12, 152, 180–5, 188
   existential vs. constructed 174
metafiction 8, 75, 79–84, 86
meta-honesty 127
metalepsis 9, 21, 32, **95–8**, 145, 173–4
metamodernism 3, 100
metareference 2, 8–11, 22, 46, 51, 53–5, 64, 124–38, 142–4, 147–53, 157–67, 191
   definition of 84
   metareferential element 86–7, 90, 93, 95–6, 103, 125–31, 139, 146, 152, 161–2, 172, 185
   metareferential moment 87–9, 95–6, 104, 126–7, 145
   metareferential turn 8, 79, 84–5
   and paradox 2–4, 6, 11, 17, 87, 90, 95–100
   as tangled hierarchy 91–5
   typology of 86, **88–91**
   see also authenticity and metareference; self-reference vs. metareference
metaxis 3
Miller, J. Hillis 5, 63, 87 n.9, 105
Miller, Mark Crispin 124
mimesis 51, 60, 70–3, 76, 83, 105–6
mise-en-abyme 87, 96–8, 125, 131
model of communication see linguistic model of communication
modernism 6, 23, 28, 75
   and postmodernism 3–4, 83, 188
Moore, Alan 20–1
Mukařovský, Jan 77–8, 82, 94
multiphrenia 47
mutuality 7, 125, 149–50

Narcissus 22
narrative assemblage 169, 173, 180, 188
narrative authority 10, 48–9, 135, 161, 180, 185–8
narrative form 95, 170, 172–3, 188
narrative perspective 10, 152, 157–62, 167, 172–3, 180, 186–8
national identity 108–13, 115, 117–18
New Sincerity 25, 99–100
Newton, Adam Z. 61, 63
nostalgia 179
Nünning, Ansgar 86, 186–7

Omega Point 45–6
originality 8, 29, 31–2, 36–7, 54, **56–9**, 71, 103–4, 111–13, 119, 139, 145–50, 167
oscillation 3, 8, 15, 20, 34–5, 55–6, 60–1, 64, 87–9, 104–6, 126, 133–7, 145–7, 150, 161, 166, 172, 187–8, 191
other, the see alterity

parabasis 93–6, 129
paradigm change/shift 7–8, 23–5, 28, 48, 57, 61–4, 83–4
paradox 17, 51, 53–6, 67, 76–7, 91–2, 106, 124–6, 141–2, 146–8, 162, 167, 190–1 see also authenticity and paradox; metareference and paradox
parallelotopia 140–2
parallelquel 140
para-self 46–7, 136
paratexts 89, 93, 124–31, 136, 153, 160–2
Parmenides 67–8
parody 5, 103, 106, 140
   vs. pastiche 103–4, 148–9
Parrhasius 51
parrhesia 7, 30, 32–3, 125, 161, 169
participation 89, 105–6, 129–31
   aesthetics of 7, 49, 60, 77, 105
   participatory culture 49–51
pastiche 10, 167 see also parody vs. pastiche
performativity 5, 9–10 n.5, 17, 59, 76–7, 90–1, 101, 125–9, 142, 170
photography 27, 52
phronesis 19 n.5

Plato 3, 63, 67–71
platonicity 69, 175
playfulness 10, 51, 55, 85, 92–3 n.13, 102, 126–7, 136 n.6, 143, 147, 149, 166–7
plot 74, 101–2, 132, 143, 157, 162, **169–73**
Port, Mattjis van de 16, 59
postmodernism 1–8, 14–15, 23, 28–9, 33, 36–44, 47–52, 54, 57–64, 69–72, 75, 99, 112–13, 179 *see also* modernism and postmodernism
post-postmodernism 3, 7, 13, 15, 23, 99
poststructuralism 30, 52, 64, 75
Potter, Andrew 43, 57
preemptive irony 124
presence 13–14, 56, 106, 179
produsage 50 n.16
prolepsis 125
prosumerism 50–1, 61
pseudo-event 38–40, 111
pseudo-modernism 3, 101 n.22, 104
purposelessness 110, 114, 117, 121, 138, 174

realism 8, 60, **67–77**, 80–3 *see also* catatonic realism; hysterical realism; reciprocal realism; traumatic realism
reality *see* experience and representation
reception (theory) 4–8, 17, **60–1**, 65, 74–5, 79, 87, 94, 101–2, 105, 153, 156–9, 163, 173, 186
reciprocal realism 137 n.7
reciprocity 9–10 n.5, 36, 42, 53, 125–7, 136–42, 172
reconstruction 53, 66, 79, 90–1, 94, 101–2, 105–6, 136–9, 149–50, 161–2, 169, 172–3, 191
 aesthetics of 3, 13, 125, 166–7, 172, 180, 188
 vs. deconstruction 1–11
re-enactment 1–2, 8, 10, 40, 55, 72–4, 105, 112, 121, 138, 162–3, 172, 180, 188–91
reflective authenticity *see under* authenticity
resemblance vs. similarity 71

resistance to unambiguity *see under* authenticity
responsibility 6, 10, 29, 31, 34–6, 46, 51, 56, 70, 76, 91, 106, 172
Richter, Virginia 28, 57,
Ricœur, Paul 70–2, 76, 103, 120
Rimmon-Kennan, Shlomith 187
Roberts, David 98
Romantic irony 31, 98
Romanticism 6, 23, 25–8, 48, 71, 109
Römer, Stefan 57, 112
Rosenblatt, Roger 2, 99
Rotman, Brian 46–7, 136–7
Rousseau, Jean-Jacques 6, 18–19, **25–7**, 28, 31, 62–5, 125, 177

satire 140, 149
Schiller, Friedrich 9, 72, 109–10, 117–18, 121, 155, 165, 177, 191
Schwartz, Hillel 38, 41
Sconce, Jeffrey 46–9
second-order observing 2 n.1
self, the *see* authenticity and the self; alterity
self-reference/self-referentiality 6, 31–2, 37, 40, 51, 64–5, 75–82, 84–6, 90–8, 102, 178
 vs. metareference 8, 79–80, 84, 103, 157
 weak vs. strong form of 79
Selwyn, Tom 20–1, 133
Shakespeare, William 23, 111, 141–2
 Hamlet 6, **23–5**, 77, 157
simulation/simulacrum 2, 7–10, 16–17, 27–8, **36–43**, 44–8, 54–60, 70, 90, 111–19, 177–8, 190–1
sincerity 1, 124, 130 *see also* authenticity vs. sincerity; New Sincerity
Smith, Zadie 69–71, 105
social media 38, 44–5, 105
solipsism 5, 11, 22, 37, 50, 62, 99, 130, 137–8, 150, 178, 190
 solipsistic authenticity 20
spin 38–40
Stonehill, Brian 94 n.15, 125
strange loop 84 *see also* tangled hierarchy
structuralism 4, 37, 52, 64, 68, 77

subjectivity 13, 19, 23, 27, 31, 47–9, 70, 75–6, 174
surfiction 81
Suskind, Ron 39–40

Taleb, Nassim Nicholas 69, 131, 175
tangled hierarchy 8–9, 54, 64, 90, **91–5**, 102, 105–6
Taylor, Charles 62, 172
textuality 88–9, 94, 126, 128, 157, 172
time travel 140–1, 152–3, 159, 162, 167
Timmer, Nicoline 127, 131, 137–8
Tipler, Frank J. 45–6
tmesis 102
Toffler, Alvin 50–1, 61
tourism 54, 111–14, 120 n.5
transcendence 7–8, 15, 37, 42–3, 53–5, 64–5, 109, 191
trauma 16, 73
traumatic realism 72–3
Trilling, Lionel 24–5, 136
trust 123, 125, 187
  aesthetics of 5, 125, 172
truth 10 n.5, 14–15, 24–6, 31–5, 40, 49, 67–77, 89
truthiness 40
Turkle, Sherry 45, 178

uncertainty *see* oscillation
undecidability 5–8, 17, 36, 56, 59, 67, 91, 125, 139, 164, 188
unreliability/unreliable narrator 75, 107, 180, 182, 185, **186–7**, 188
unrepresentability 42, 48
utopia 10, 140, 178

Varela, Francisco J. 49
Vermeulen, Timotheus/Robin van den Akker 3, 100
virtual reality 44–50

Wallace, David Foster 66, 73, 76, 83, 93, 99, 105
Wang, Ning 30–1
Waugh, Patricia 81–2, 149
Web 2.0 49–50
Weber, Max 41
Wittgenstein, Ludwig 45, 63
Wolf, Werner 8, 79, 84–90, 95–6
Wood, James 72

Yurchak, Alexei 100

Zeller, Christoph 17, 43, 59, 126